AF473778

The Art of
DORIS & ANNA ZINKEISEN

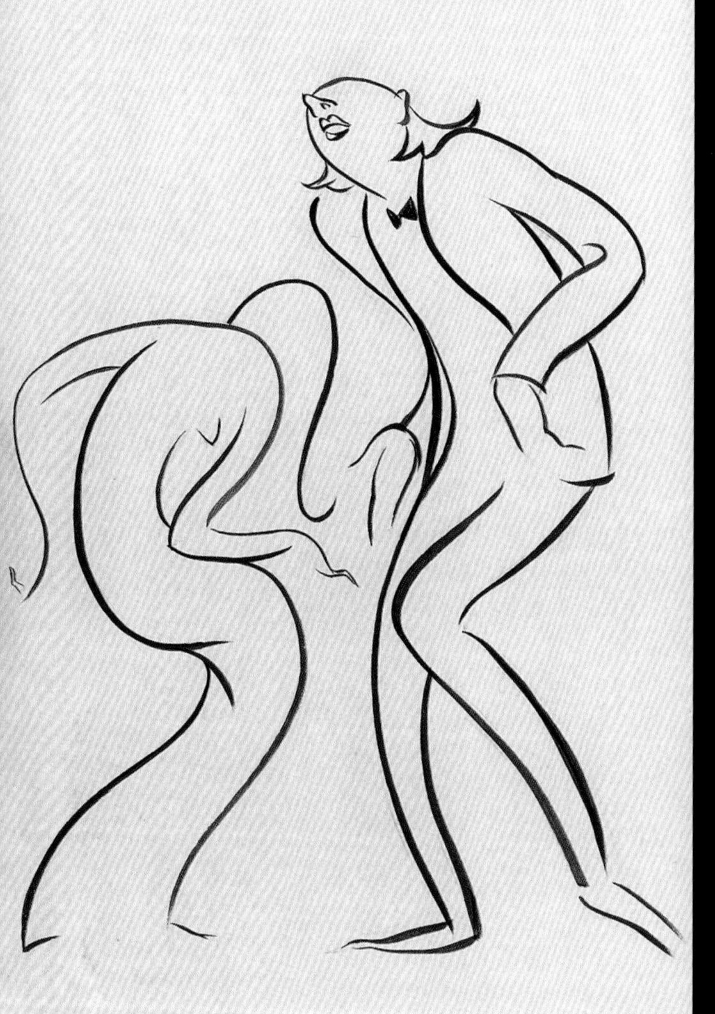

The Art of DORIS & ANNA ZINKEISEN

PHILIP KELLEWAY
EMMA ROODHOUSE
NICOLA EVANS

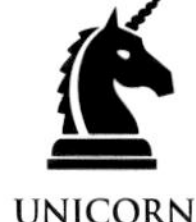

UNICORN

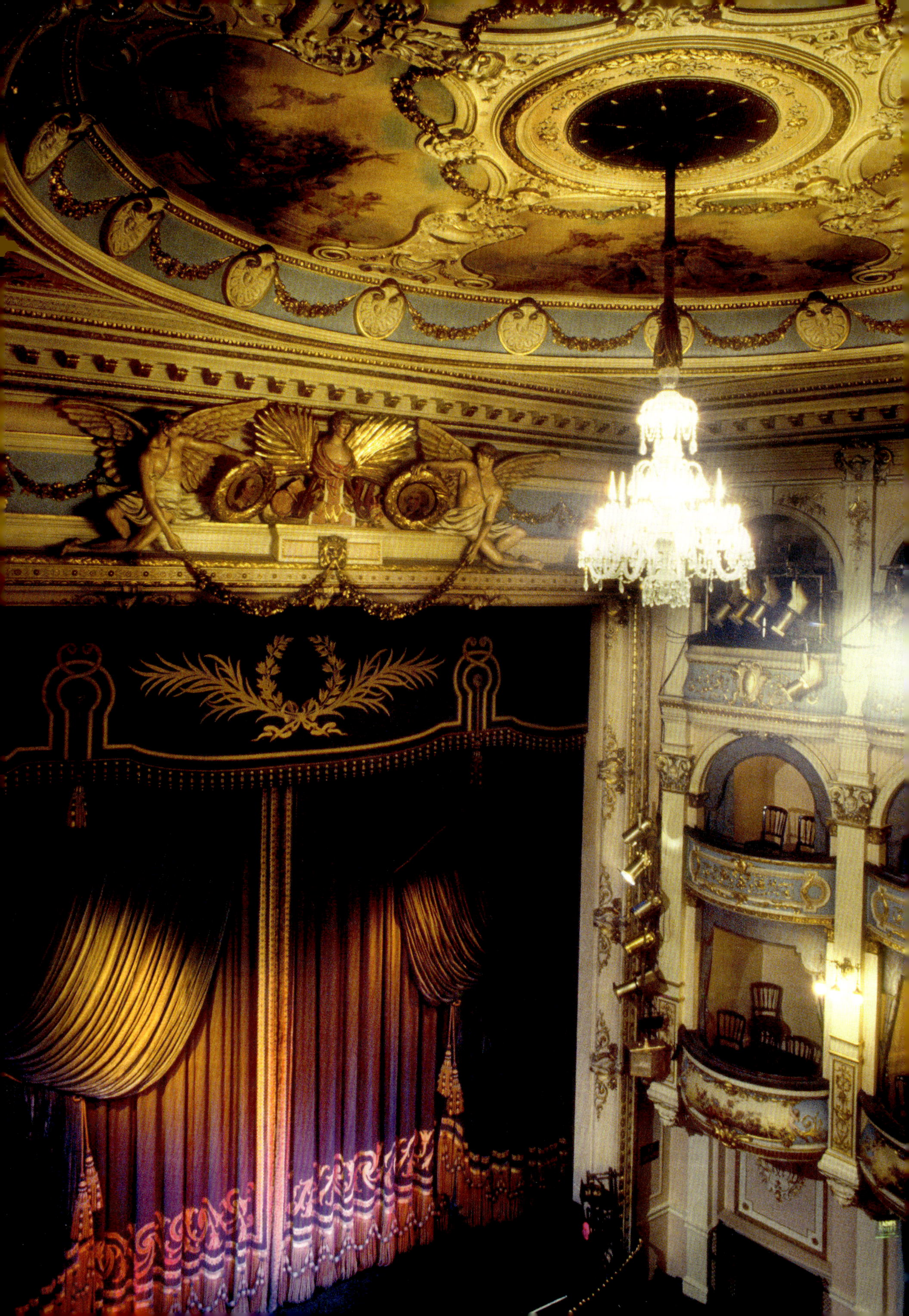

Setting the Scene

"I must confess that I have a strong leaning towards the old-fashioned theatre – the auditorium overloaded with rather swirling ornate decoration, the boxes a welter of garlands, cupids and red plush drapery. The proscenium is generally terrific in its glitter of gold and ornamentation mounting up to a glory of more cupids and almost invariably crowned with a pair of flying ladies blowing coach horns on either side of a more dignified seated lady, with rather richer curves, who is entrusted with the important duty of holding the masks of Tragedy and Comedy.

This kind of decoration seems a far truer atmosphere for a theatre than the cold unyielding interior of some modern playhouses. Architects and interior decorators today seem, when entrusted with designing a theatre, to disregard completely the fact that it is a house of entertainment and that the moment an audience enter a theatre they should be made conscious of feelings of suppressed excitement and anticipation before the curtain goes up."
Doris Zinkeisen, *Designing for the Stage*, London, 1938, p.9

Left: Fig.1.00b
Interior of Wyndhams Theatre, London. This represents the type of opulence and ambience Doris Zinkeisen found appealing and tried to capture in much of her art.

Previous page: Fig.1.00a
Anna Zinkeisen, *Dancing Figures*, *circa* 1950s, pencil and ink on paper.

First published in the UK in 2021
by Unicorn Publishing Group
This edition published 2023

Unicorn Publishing Group
Charleston Studio
Meadow Business Centre
Lewes BN8 5RW

www.unicornpublishing.org

ISBN 9781913491819

10 9 8 7 6 5 4 3 2 1

Printed by Fine Tone Ltd
Design: Jonathan Christie

Supported using public funding by

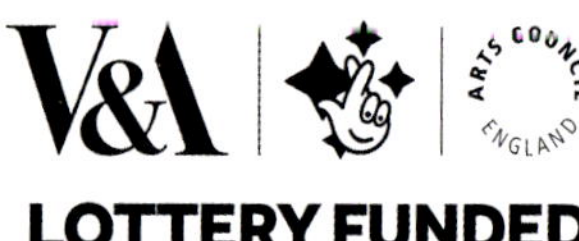

LOTTERY FUNDED

Art Fund_

Colchester+Ipswich
Museums

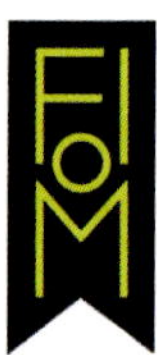

Contents

9 **Foreword** *by Julia Heseltine*

11 **Acknowledgements**

15 **Part I**
The Art of Doris & Anna Zinkeisen

Philip Kelleway

61 **Part II**
A Conversation Piece by Doris Zinkeisen

Emma Roodhouse & Nicola Evans

75 **Part III**
Gallery of Pictures

177 Suggestions for Further Reading & Websites
181 Appendices
187 Index
192 Notes on the Contributors

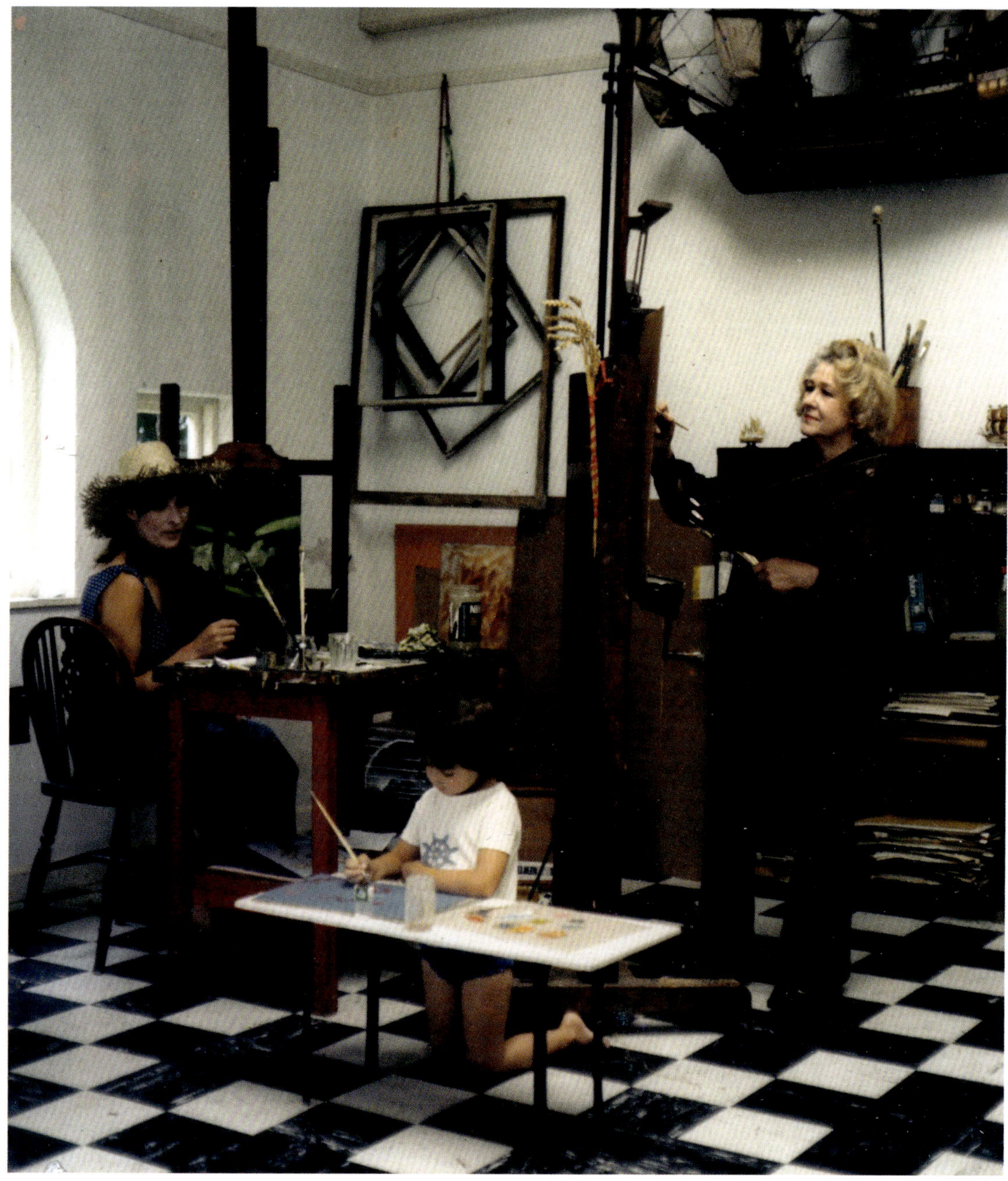

Fig.1.00c
Three generations working together: Julia Heseltine (left), her son Tristan Sam Weller (centre), and Anna Zinkeisen (right) painting together in the studio at Looms Cottage, Suffolk, *circa* mid-1970s.

Foreword

Julia Heseltine

My mother Anna Zinkeisen and I were very close. We shared a sense of humour and our deeper response to life.

As a child I had assumed that all women became painters and all men soldiers or sailors, because that was how it was in my family. It wasn't until I moved to London for art school and into my mother's life aged thirteen, that the real passion to express myself through painting truly hit and it was Anna – the way she talked about her work and the look in her eyes as she did so – that lit the fire!

I was allowed to paint with her in her studio (in spite of all the teenage angst) and just being with her while she worked taught me far more than any art school ever could. Soon I was put to work laying in backgrounds for her and by degrees even a bit more, while she painted on my early commissions, bailing me out of many a tight spot.

So sharing a studio became the norm and mutually helpful in the end, since a fresh eye is often what is needed. We had a lovely studio in Suffolk and they were happy days.

It gives me such delight to realize, that my mother's work and that of her sister, my Aunty Dee (aka Doris Zinkeisen), is so much appreciated by a considerable number of people. This has been augmented and enhanced by Philip Kelleway, who has done a great deal to raise awareness of their work, in particular through his meticulously researched book *Highly Desirable: The Zinkeisen Sisters & Their Legacy.* I hope that this publication by Philip Kelleway, Emma Roodhouse, and Nicola Evans will similarly be regarded as an accessible, enjoyable, and useful resource to those interested in the Zinkeisen sisters.

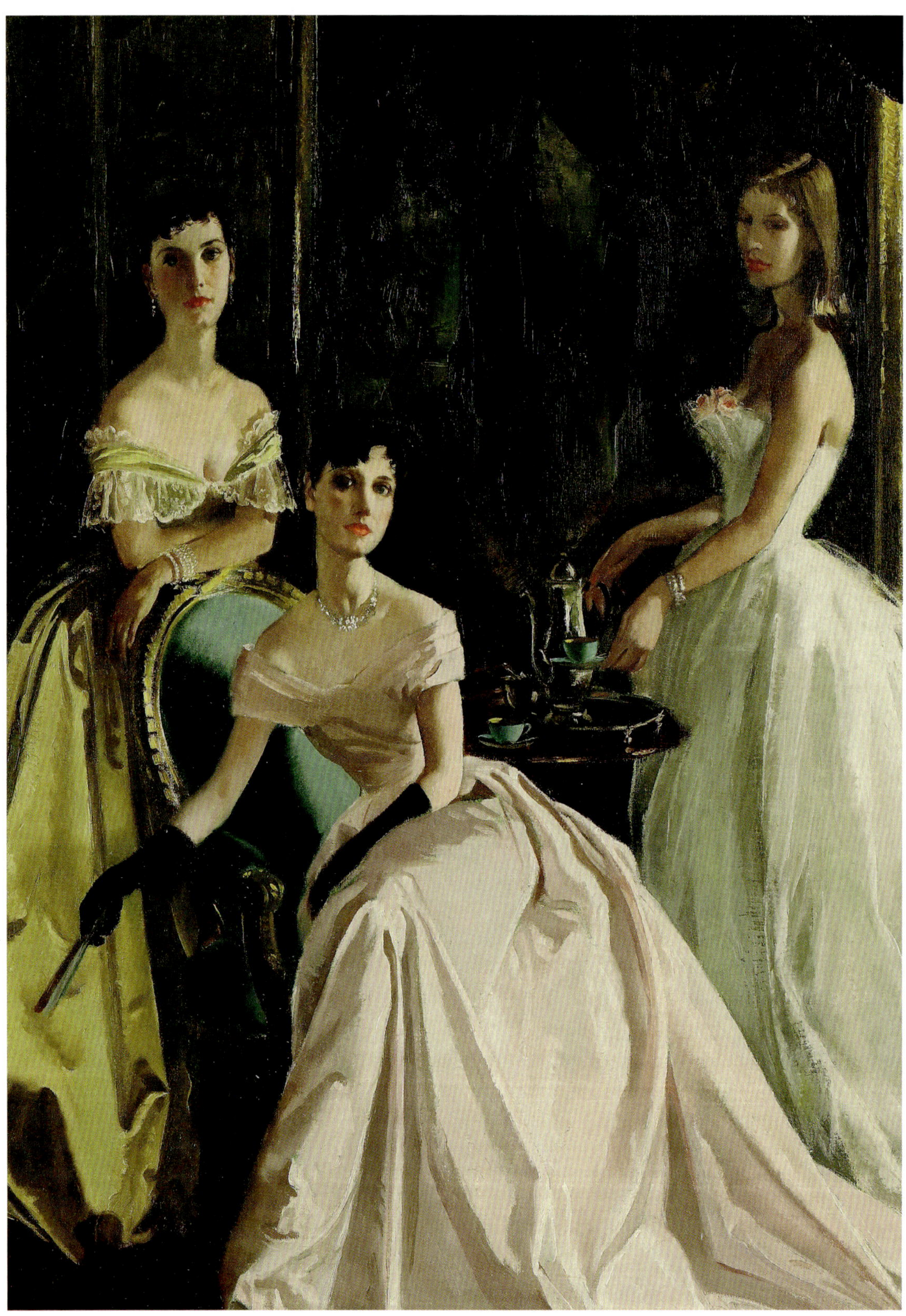

Acknowledgements

Individual paintings by both of the Zinkeisen sisters have found their way into several landmark exhibitions. Zinkeisen paintings were included in, for example, *Mirror Mirror: Self-portraits by Women Artists* (October 2001 – February 2002) at the National Portrait Gallery in London; *Women War Artists* (April 2011 – January 2012) at the Imperial War Museum; two exhibitions held at the Scottish National Gallery of Modern Art in Edinburgh, *Modern Scottish Women: Painters and Sculptors 1885-1965* (November 2015 – June 2016) and *A New Era: Scottish Modern Art 1900-1950* (December 2017 – June 2018); the groundbreaking *Ocean Liners: Speed and Style* exhibition at the Victoria and Albert Museum in London and Dundee and the Peabody Essex Museum (Massachusetts) during 2017 to 2019; in addition to *In Air and Fire: War Artists, the Battle of Britain and the Blitz* at the Royal Air Force Museum London (September 2020 – September 2021). The titles of these exhibitions give some indication as to how the reputation of the Zinkeisen sisters is being shaped and perceived through repeated emphases on key concepts including *modern*, *women*, *war artists*, and *Scottish*, together with a dash of *style* thrown in to this mix.

A few select commercial galleries have also been quick on their feet and seized on the opportunity to acquaint collectors with the work of these most unjustly neglected artists. Art dealers are the unsung heroes of art history, as they often play a crucial role in the dissemination of knowledge about individual artists and art more generally. If the truth be known it takes years to build up the expertise good dealers possess, a fact which is overlooked. Some art dealers do, of course, publish their findings in books and these studies often make for interesting reading, as the approach to the works discussed is often quite different from art history in a strictly academic sense and can provide new ideas and avenues to explore and interpret. Notable galleries, which have had good examples of Zinkeisen paintings in stock over recent years, include August Interiors, Sarah Colegrave Fine Art, Darnley Fine Art, Liss Llewellyn, and Reepham Antiques to name but a few. Also noteworthy is the Zinkeisen exhibition held by Paul Mayhew Fine Art in London back in 2009 and the same gallery's subsequent sell-out display of Zinkeisen paintings at the Winter Art and Antiques Fair at Olympia back in 2016.

In light of the fact that the Colchester and

Left: Detail of Fig.2.1

Ipswich Museums Service have purchased a painting by Doris Zinkeisen during 2020 to add to the Ipswich Borough collections, now seemed like an opportune moment to look afresh at the work of both of the Zinkeisen sisters and to assess the existing scholarship on them. The Friends of the Ipswich Museums (FOIM), the Art Fund, Arts Council England, the National Lottery, and the V&A Purchase Grant Fund all contributed towards the purchase of the triple portrait by Doris Zinkeisen and we would like to express our thanks to them all for their financial assistance, without which the acquisition and the painting's subsequent conservation by Kiffy Stainer-Hutchins and Nicola Evans of KSH Conservation Limited could not have happened. In relation to this purchase Emma Roodhouse and Nicola Evans provide an examination of the process by which the museum set about acquiring the painting and its ensuing repair and conservation, which is all too often glossed over in the literature; whilst Philip Kelleway's essay is a summary of the lives and work of the Zinkeisen sisters containing divers new insights and includes family snapshots from a private family archive. This book is not intended to be the last word on the Zinkeisen sisters. Even at the last minute paintings we were unfamiliar with were brought to our attention. Many Zinkeisen paintings remain lost and are only known through photographs in the family archives. Some of these missing paintings are included here in the hope they might be unearthed and maybe act as a springboard for research in the future. There is still much to be done, not least of all determining the identity of some of the sitters in portraits and ascertaining how commissions came about. We hope new paperwork will come to light in the future to illuminate and add to our current understanding of the work of the Zinkeisen sisters. Specifically in relation to this publication, however, there are many other people we need to thank for their encouragement, help, and information of various kinds.

Much of the work on this book was carried out during the Covid-19 pandemic period, which did rather hinder progress. Nevertheless the task was completed and many thanks are due to our publisher and their designers for such a stellar end result. Others who assisted us in our endeavours in numerous ways include in alphabetical order: Julia Beaumont-Jones (Curator of Fine Art: RAF Museum London); Nigel Castell (Reepham Antiques); Sarah Colegrave (Sarah Colegrave Fine Art); Abigail Cornick (Curator and Volunteer Coordinator: Museum of the Order of St John); James Curtis (Film Historian and Author); Sophie Fisher (Media Sales and Licensing Executive: Imperial War Museums); Lucinda Gosling (Mary Evans Picture Library); Mary Haegert (Houghton Library: Harvard University); Professor Ludmilla Jordanova (Emeritus Professor of History and Visual Culture: Durham University); Christine Kemp (Accounts Assistant: RAF Museum Enterprises); Elizabeth Kerr (Camera Press London); Lars Larsson (Chisholm Larsson

Gallery, New York: possibly the world's best vintage poster gallery); Stephen Lash (Vice Chairman and Chairman Emeritus Christie's Americas); Karen Lawson (Picture Library Manager: Royal Collection Trust); Paul Liss and Sacha Llewellyn (Liss Llewellyn Fine Art); Rupert Maas (The Maas Gallery London); Paul and Anne Mayhew (Paul Mayhew Fine Art); Geoffrey Munn OBE, MVO, FSA, FLS (Jewellery Expert, Broadcaster and Author); Emma Nichols (Picture Library Assistant: Sotheby's Picture Library); Daniel Partridge (Digital Imager: Royal Collection Trust); Professor Bruce Peter (Glasgow School of Art); Adrian Pett (Darnley Fine Art); Sian Phillips (Account Manager: Bridgeman Art Library); Andrew Renwick (Curator of Photographs: RAF Museum London); Barry Smith (Director of Visitor and Commercial Development: RAF Museum London); Kiffy Stainer-Hutchins (Director and Chief Conservator: KSH Conservation Limited); Alice Strang (Senior Curator: Scottish National Gallery of Modern Art); Nicholas Wells (Nicholas Wells Antiques); Dean Warner (August Interiors); Professor Richard Wilson; Richard Wilson (Chairman: The Friends of the Ipswich Museums); Dr Matthew Wittmann (Curator of the Harvard Theatre Collection: Houghton Library); in addition to numerous private collectors. A great deal of effort has been made to trace the copyright holders of pictures illustrated in this book. We thank all those who assisted with these permissions and the publisher will be pleased to hear from any inadvertently omitted party for redress and amendment to future editions. We would also like to thank our families for bearing the brunt of the unavoidable state of preoccupation associated with bringing this book project to fruition.

Our largest debt of gratitude is, however, reserved for the families of Doris and Anna Zinkeisen. Without their patient cooperation there would be no book. Most of the information about the Zinkeisen sisters comes from conversations with family members and Philip Kelleway was fortunate enough to have met Doris on numerous occasions, as she was a neighbour of his parents in Suffolk. Philip Kelleway was also able to peruse papers, scrapbooks, magazine and newspaper clippings held by the descendants of the Zinkeisen sisters. These sources were extensively used and helped to form the foundation of *Highly Desirable: The Zinkeisen Sisters & Their Legacy*. So many thanks to Jemima Dawson; Andrew Johnstone; Charlotte Johnstone; Elisabeth Johnstone; and Sam Weller. Our heartfelt thanks go to Julia Heseltine for agreeing to pen the foreword: we cannot imagine a better endorsement. It is a great sadness on our part that Doris Zinkeisen's son, Captain Murray Johnstone RN, passed away in 2017 before this book saw the light of day. He was a mine of information regarding his Zinkeisen roots and a joy to listen to. He is missed by all who knew him and it is to him, that this book is dedicated.

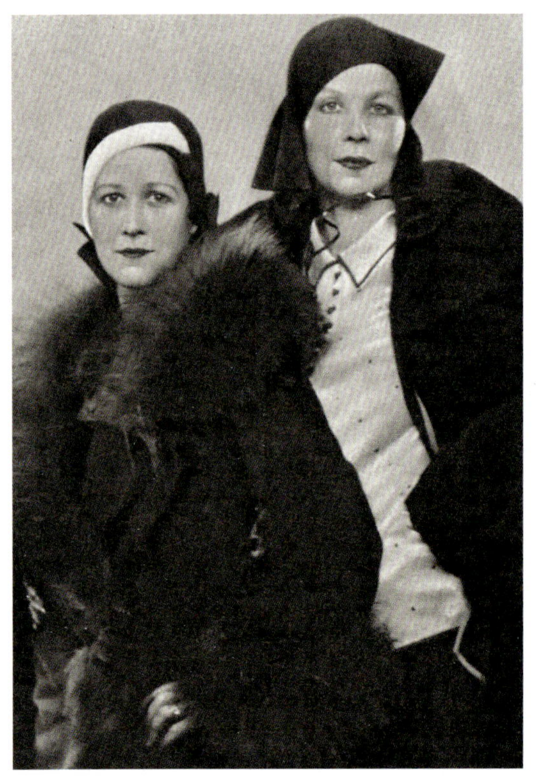

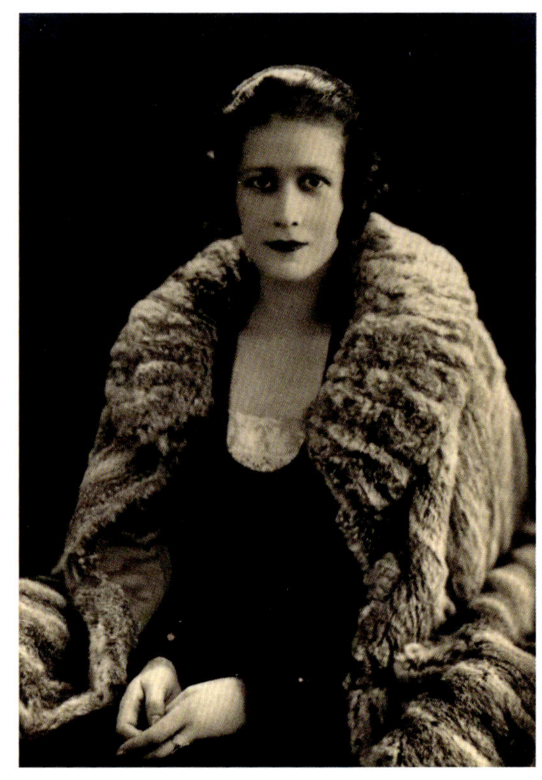

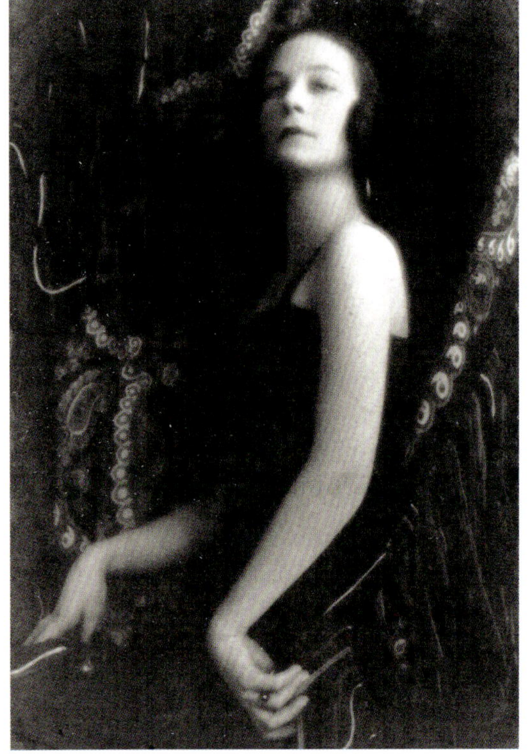

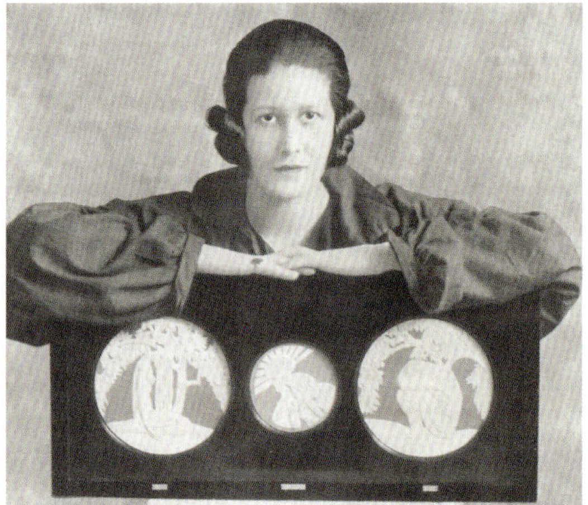

Part I
The Art of Doris & Anna Zinkeisen

Philip Kelleway

Introduction

In life the talented, beautiful, and stylish artist sisters Doris Clare Zinkeisen (1897-1991) and Anna Katrina Zinkeisen (1901-1976) were not the sort of people easily overlooked [Fig.1.1 – Fig.1.3]. During their heyday of the 1920s through to the 1950s the Zinkeisen sisters were amongst the most prominent artists in Britain and attracted attention overseas too. In the middle of that interwar, golden age of the 'Roaring Twenties' Anna successfully cut her teeth on the fickle world of art with some designs for Wedgwood. Her three jasper bas-reliefs won a silver medal at the 1925 Paris Exposition des Arts Décoratifs et Industriels Modernes [Fig.1.4]. This Parisian exhibition's title was subsequently abbreviated to coin the term 'Art Deco' and it was at this seminal event for cutting-edge design, that Anna earned a place amongst the vanguard of British art.

Both Zinkeisen sisters hung their paintings to critical acclaim at the Royal Academy in London and the Paris Salon de la Société des Artistes Français. Doris's exhibits at the Paris Salon won bronze, silver, and gold medals in 1929, 1930, and 1934 respectively, underscoring how the art cognoscenti of Paris esteemed the work of the Zinkeisens and is evidence of the duo's ambitiously pan-European outlook for their art. The popular press adored them and their work. Doris's prominent role as a designer of costumes and sets for stage and film also aroused considerable curiosity.

Looking at early pictures of Doris and her younger sister Anna, you could easily mistake the pair of them for the femmes fatales featured in film adaptations of those popular detective novels by Dame Agatha Christie (1890-1976) [Fig.1.5 – Fig.1.7]. Indeed, the Zinkeisen sisters were the epitome of that sleek sophisticated vogue with a twist of cheekiness, which typifies the foot-tapping liveliness of the legendary jazz era. Glamorous and impeccably dressed, the Zinkeisen sisters turned heads wherever they went. Indeed, Doris and Anna Zinkeisen were arbiters of taste, not merely slavish followers of fashion. Their opinions mattered and the press dedicated considerable

Top left: Fig.1.1
Anna Zinkeisen (left) and Doris Zinkeisen (right) in 1930.
© Photograph courtesy of the estate of Doris Zinkeisen.

Below left: Fig.1.3
Doris Zinkeisen *circa* 1925.
© Photograph courtesy of James Curtis.

Top right: Fig.1.2
Anna Zinkeisen in a publicity photograph from 1927.
© Photograph courtesy of Julia Heseltine.

Below right: Fig.1.4
Anna Zinkeisen in a publicity photograph together with her Wedgwood plaques, which won a silver medal at the Exposition des Arts Décoratifs in Paris during 1925.
© Photograph courtesy of Julia Heseltine.

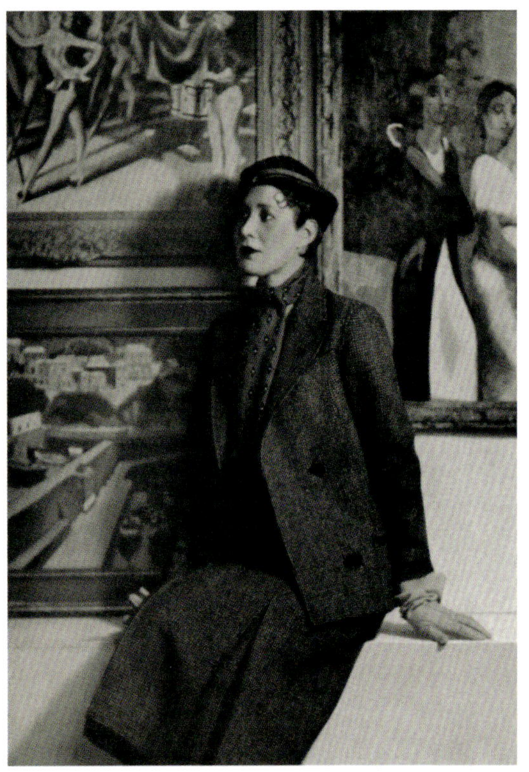

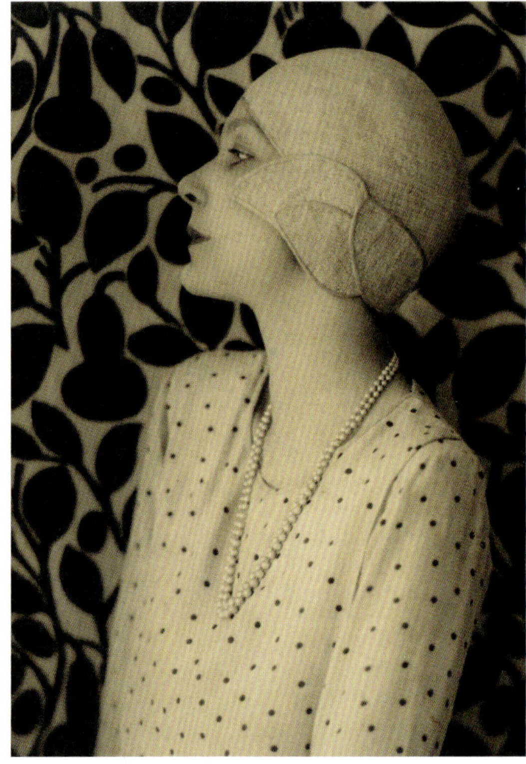

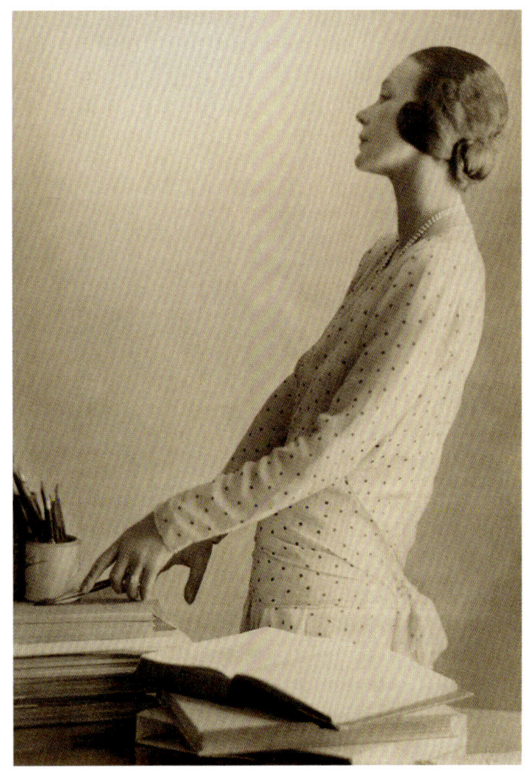

Top left: Fig.1.5

Anna seated before some paintings at an exhibition *circa* 1930. See also Fig.3.15.

Top right: Fig.1.6

Harold Pierce Cazneaux, *Doris Zinkeisen: New Idea Portrait with Leaf Background*, 1929, gelatine silver photograph.

Left: Fig.1.7

Harold Pierce Cazneaux, *Doris Zinkeisen with her Brushes*, 1929, gelatine silver photograph.

column inches to what they were up to.

Although in later years each of the sisters sought a more quiet existence in rural Suffolk, a lifelong aura of drama continued to surround both of them right to the end of their lives. Anna died following a brief illness in her mid-seventies and following her cremation at Ipswich was interred in her husband's grave at the small church of St Botolph in Burgh in Suffolk. Doris, despite making it to be a nonagenarian, kept much of her sparkle and painted at her easel right up until just a few days before she passed away [Fig.1.77]. Undeniably, Doris's burial itself was like a well-crafted piece of theatre with perfectly groomed horses pulling her elaborate hearse. It was a no expense spared farewell and the church was full to bursting. As it was January the leafless trees mirrored anthropomorphically the solemnity of the proceedings. This was Doris's final curtain call and her burial appropriately resembled the backdrop to one of the numerous plays and films she had created designs for.

Living with her daughters in The White House in Badingham, with its strong Regency flavour, added an atmosphere of mystery to Doris, along the lines of a popular work of fiction – something resembling those romantic sagas by Dame Daphne du Maurier (1907-1989) [Fig.1.8]. From time to time Doris played with this feeling and captured its mood in some of her later paintings, which were often akin to flights of fancy and can be, in fact, considered the pictorial equivalent of those enormously popular historical Regency romances by Georgette Heyer (1902-1974). In keeping with this spirit her interment was her last wave to the world and fittingly went a long way towards capturing her own sense of theatre.

In point of fact both Zinkeisen sisters possessed a certain mystique and presence. A tiny part of them always remained enigmatic, even to some close to them. There were always layers of carefully crafted, self-fashioning concealing them. So who were these artistic sisters?

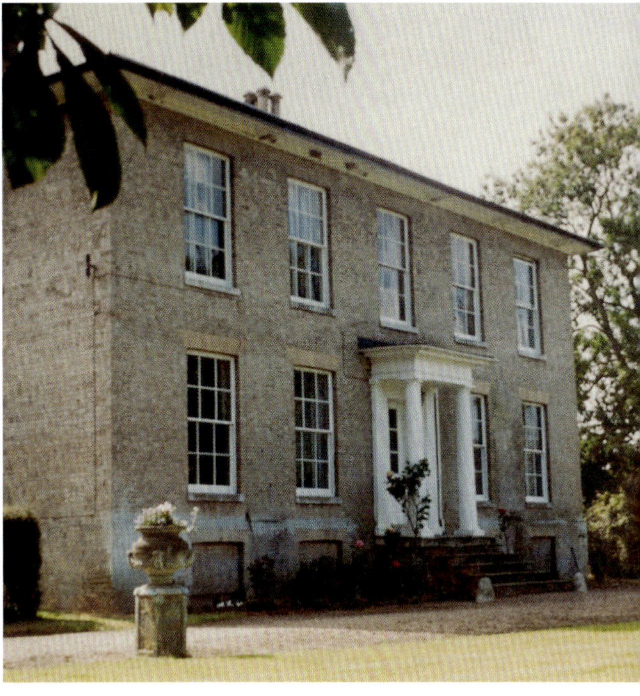

Above: Fig.1.8
The White House in Badingham, Suffolk, when Doris Zinkeisen lived there *circa* late 1970s to early 1980s.
© Photograph courtesy of the estate of Doris Zinkeisen.

Early Life

There can be little doubt that, to a certain extent, the Zinkeisen sisters edited the story of their backgrounds. This is particularly apparent in the dates given for Doris. Her very own tombstone can be found next to that of her twin daughters in the hauntingly beautiful graveyard of the Norman church of St John the Baptist in Badingham, Suffolk, and engraved into the gravestone her year of birth is set at 1898. Doris herself had engineered the confusion over her date of birth through disinformation and, in all likelihood, over time she might well have forgotten the truth.

Many printed and online sources give Doris's year of birth as 1898, including the newspaper obituaries about her from January 1991. The *Dictionary of British Equestrian Artists* [Woodbridge, 1985] lays claim to 1918, whilst a surviving passport from around the late 1950s gives her date of birth as 31st July 1909 [Fig.1.9]. Doris Zinkeisen herself would have found this fuss over her age mildly exasperating. After all, it is simply inappropriate to ask a woman her age and definitely a trifle 'non-U'. Art historians, however, must run the risk of being a tad vulgar to challenge received wisdom and establish the truth.

Delving into the original documents, the official Register of Births reveals that Doris Zinkeisen was actually born on 31st July 1897 at Clynder House, Roseneath, Dunbartonshire, Scotland. This is considerably earlier than her passport declares. The Birth Certificate

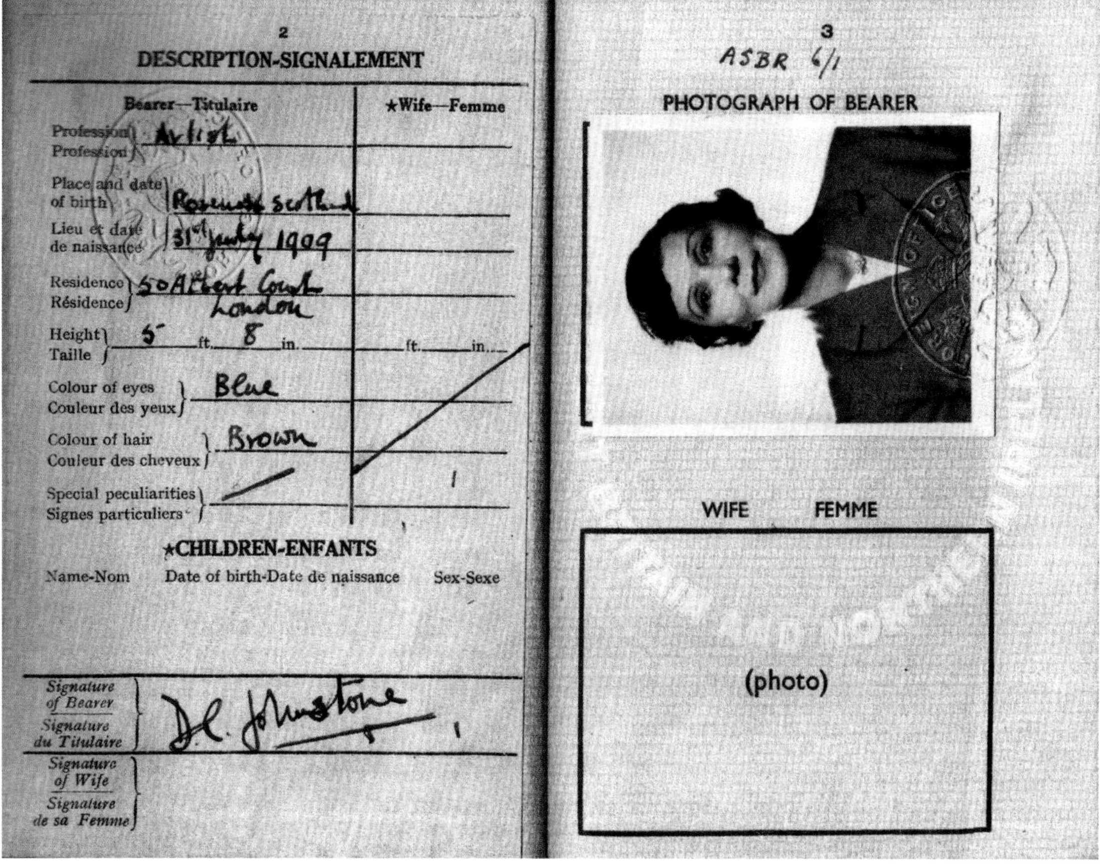

2

DESCRIPTION-SIGNALEMENT

Bearer—Titulaire | ★Wife—Femme

Profession / Profession: Artist

Place and date of birth / Lieu et date de naissance: Roseneath Scotland / 31st July 1909

Residence / Résidence: 50 Albert Court / London

Height / Taille: 5 ft. 8 in. | ft. in.

Colour of eyes / Couleur des yeux: Blue

Colour of hair / Couleur des cheveux: Brown

Special peculiarities / Signes particuliers

★CHILDREN-ENFANTS

Name-Nom | Date of birth-Date de naissance | Sex-Sexe

Signature of Bearer / Signature du Titulaire: D.C. Johnstone

Signature of Wife / Signature de sa Femme

3

ASBR 6/1

PHOTOGRAPH OF BEARER

WIFE FEMME

(photo)

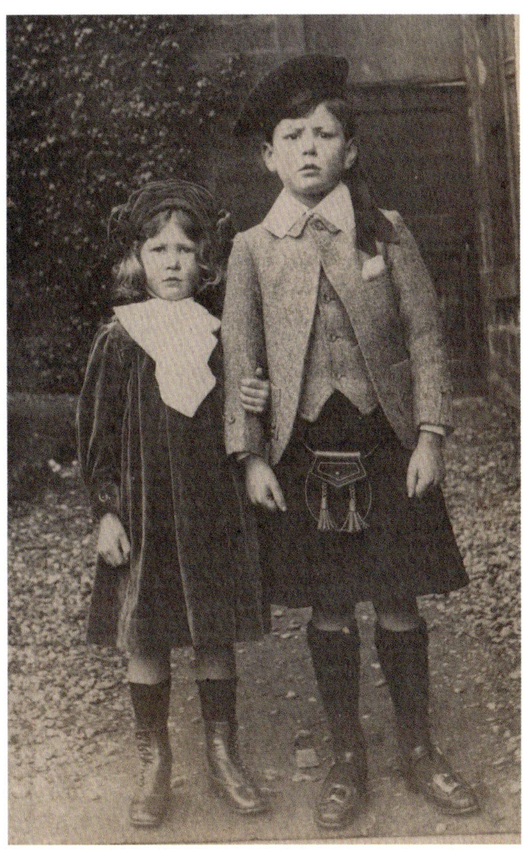

of Anna Zinkeisen also reveals an anomaly. Usually it is stated that Anna was born on 28th August 1901, but her Certificate of Birth says she was born on the 29th August at Woodburn, Kilcreggan, Dunbartonshire (today in Argyll and Bute). The sisters also had a brother, Ian Victor Zinkeisen, also named Ivan and Jack, or referred to with the fanciful sobriquet Zog, who was born on the 17th June 1900, similarly at Woodburn in Scotland. How many birthdays must have been celebrated on the wrong day? Anna made herself one day older, or was made so by her family. This can possibly be explained as a genuine error, but the mystery around Doris's date of birth is most certainly deliberate and tells us quite a lot about her, at times, audacious character.

Doris's place of birth was just a stone's throw down the road from where her two siblings were born on the peninsula overlooking Loch Long, Gare Loch, and the Firth of Clyde situated north-west of Glasgow. The area the Zinkeisen sisters hailed from lies close to some of Scotland's most diverse and magnificent scenery, namely the romantic Loch Lomond and the Trossachs National Park and Argyll Forest Park. In a couple of early photographs there are visual indications, that the Zinkeisen family were keen to emphasize their Scottish identity. Anna stands next to her brother, who wears a kilt [Fig.1.10]. In a further photograph we see their father in his Highland Light Infantry uniform [Fig.1.11]. What is more, according to Julia Heseltine (Anna Zinkeisen's daughter) her mother occasionally said that the family ought to adopt 'MacZinkeisen' as their surname, in order to emphasize their ancestral ties to Scotland.

The artists' mother, Clara Bolton Charles (1871-1952), was indeed British and had links to the Welsh nonconformist clergyman Thomas Charles of Bala (1755-1814), who provided Welsh-language Bibles to the poor. It is believed the Bolton name originated

Left: Fig.1.9
Doris Zinkeisen's passport from the late 1950s or early 1960s gives her date of birth as 1909. She was actually born in 1897.

Above: Fig.1.10
Anna Zinkeisen (left) and Ian Victor Zinkeisen *circa* 1906.

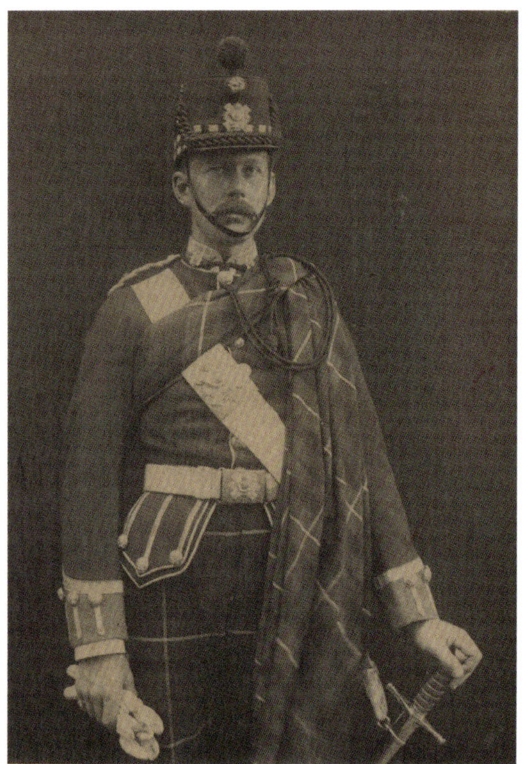

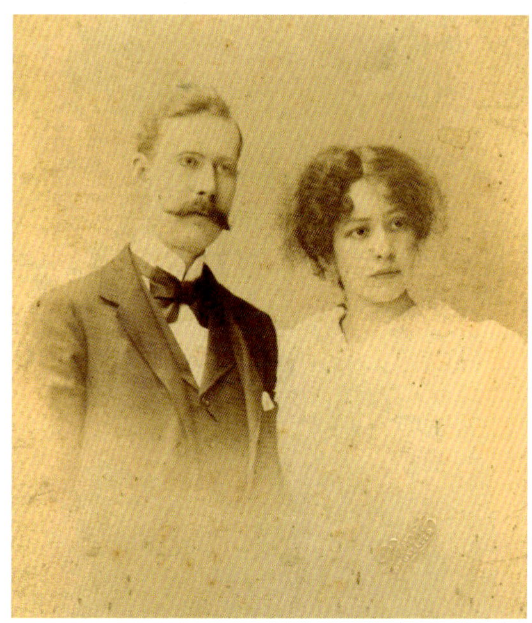

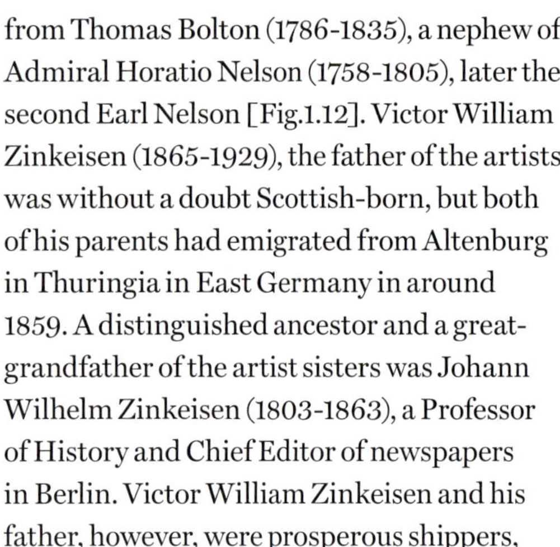

from Thomas Bolton (1786-1835), a nephew of Admiral Horatio Nelson (1758-1805), later the second Earl Nelson [Fig.1.12]. Victor William Zinkeisen (1865-1929), the father of the artists, was without a doubt Scottish-born, but both of his parents had emigrated from Altenburg in Thuringia in East Germany in around 1859. A distinguished ancestor and a great-grandfather of the artist sisters was Johann Wilhelm Zinkeisen (1803-1863), a Professor of History and Chief Editor of newspapers in Berlin. Victor William Zinkeisen and his father, however, were prosperous shippers, manufacturers, and yarn merchants. In point of fact the brother of the artists chose to distance himself from his Germanic ethnic origins, by changing his family name to that of their mother, becoming Ian Victor Charles in 1939. This was probably a wise move considering that the surname Zinkeisen could arouse unnecessary suspicion. Quite possibly at around the time Ian was changing his name, it appears that Anna was once questioned by the authorities as to whether she was some kind of fifth columnist. In part this happened because of her foreign name,

Above: Fig.1.11
Victor William Zinkeisen, father of Doris and Anna Zinkeisen, dressed in the uniform of the Highland Light Infantry (date uncertain).
© Photograph courtesy of Julia Heseltine.

Above: Fig.1.12
Late Victorian photograph of Victor William Zinkeisen and Clara Bolton Charles, the parents of Anna and Doris Zinkeisen.
© Photograph courtesy of Julia Heseltine.

but possibly also due to the fact that by chance she happened to be introduced to Joachim von Ribbentrop (1893-1946), a leading Nazi, when he was ambassador in London between 1936 and 1938. Anna was greatly shocked and dismayed at being thought of as a potential Nazi sympathizer.

The artist sisters did not, however, follow the example of their brother, but kept their surname. Instead, in order to avoid the hostility towards anything German-sounding following World War I and in the run up to the subsequent war, the Zinkeisen sisters deliberately shrouded their ancestry in mystery. During their lifetimes and beyond they have variously been reported in papers and books as being of Flemish, Austrian, French, or Bohemian extraction. The Zinkeisen name certainly helped the sisters to stand out from the crowd, especially back in early twentieth-century Britain. What is more, the vague rumour of their supposedly Bohemian origins played right into their hands. It associated the pair with the more sophisticated and exotic attributes of interwar émigré culture, in addition to a particular region of central Europe, remembering here, that the term Bohemian could also conjure up notions of free-spirited people of artistic character, or eccentric mores. This very ambiguity perfectly suited the flamboyant Zinkeisen sisters, who, at times, used it to their advantage.

In 1909 the sisters left the beauties of Scotland's hills and lochs behind them, because job opportunities for Victor meant that the Zinkeisen family had to move down to the area around Pinner and Harrow. Later they would move briefly to Onslow Gardens (Kensington and Chelsea) before settling just off Regent's Park along St Andrew's Place and closer to the heart of London. The move south occurred just as Doris was on the cusp of becoming a teenager. Family snapshots from this period show tennis parties and holidays at the seaside, some from Cooden Beach, Bexhill-on-Sea in East Sussex [Fig.1.13 – Fig.1.14]. A holiday snapshot from the coastal town of Blankenberge in Belgium from the early 1900s shows the young Zinkeisen girls dressed up for a 'Corso Fleuri', in this instance the flower

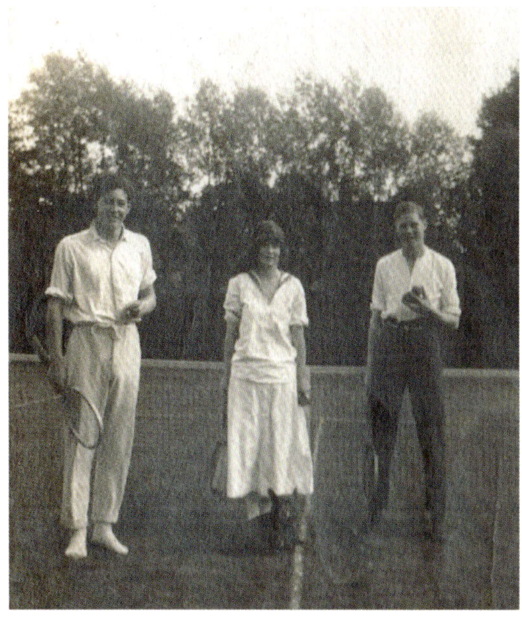

Above: Fig.1.13
Tennis party with Doris centre.
© Photograph courtesy of Julia Heseltine.

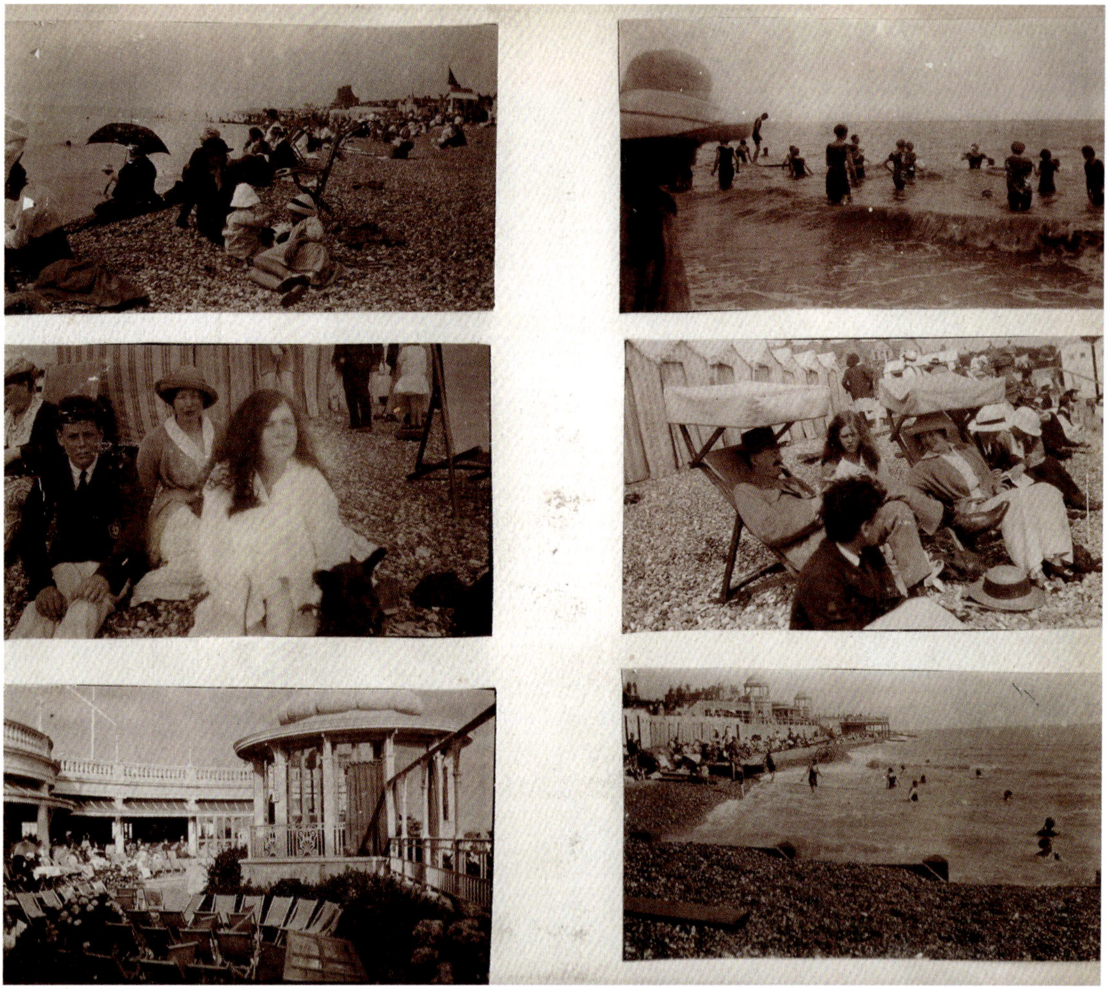

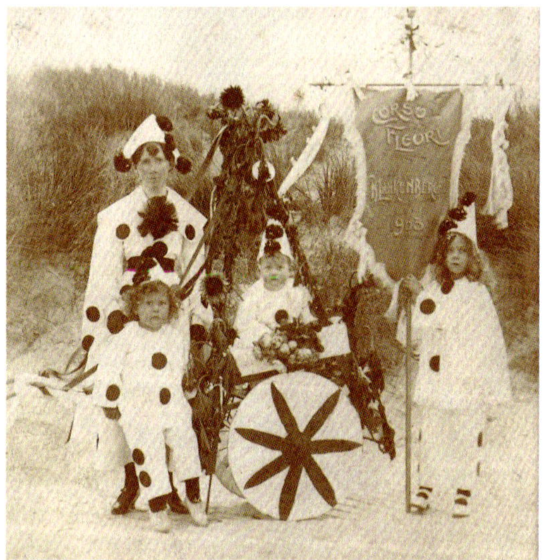

Above: Fig.1.14

Page from a family photograph album here with scenes from a holiday at Cooden Beach in *circa* 1912. Middle left are Ian and Anna with their mother; whilst middle right Ian and Anna are together with both parents.

© Photograph courtesy of Julia Heseltine.

Left: Fig.1.15

Corso Fleuri in Blankenberge, Belgium with Anna (left) and Doris (right), early 1900s.

© Photograph courtesy of Julia Heseltine.

Opposite top left: Fig.1.16

Anna Zinkeisen (centre) with hat as a V.A.D. during WWI with convalescing soldiers.

© Photograph courtesy of Julia Heseltine.

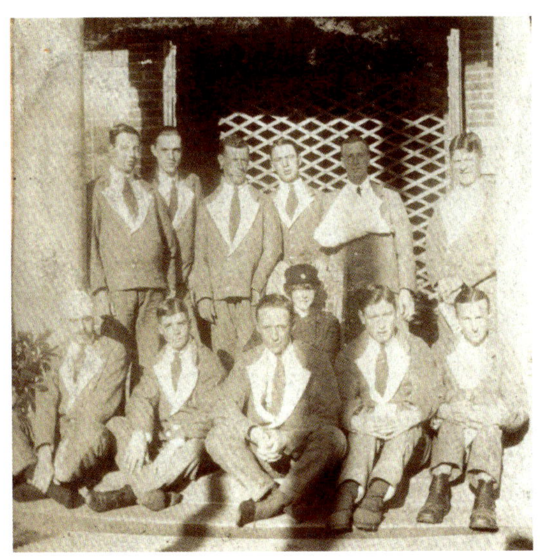

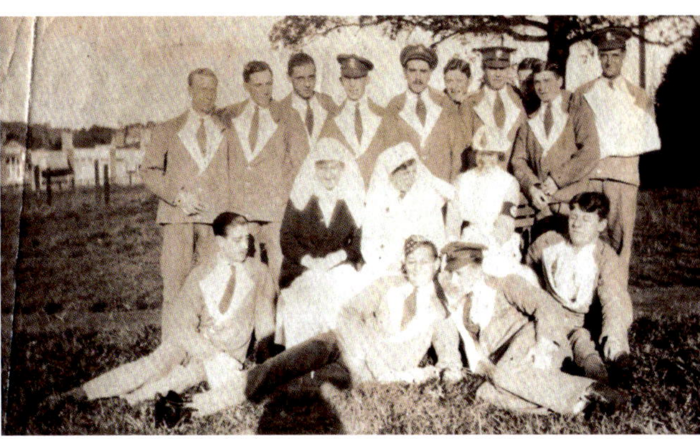

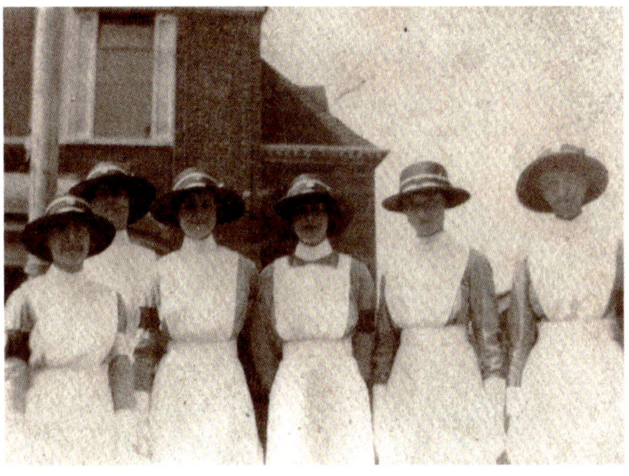

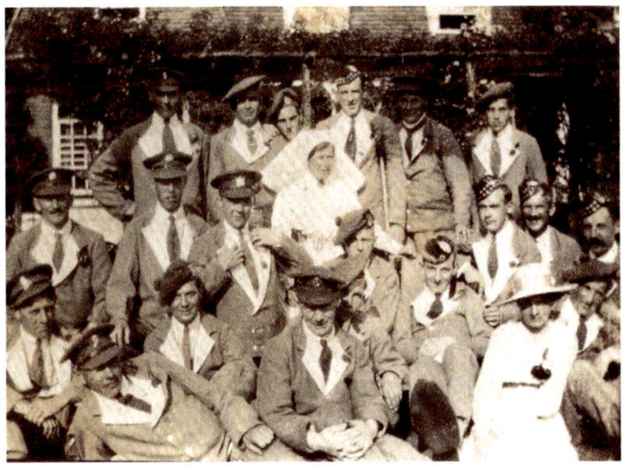

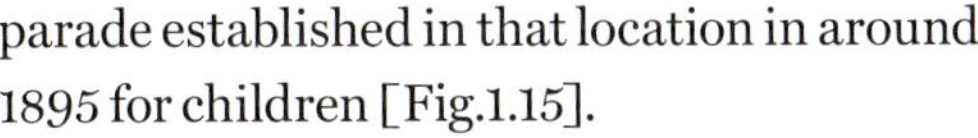

parade established in that location in around 1895 for children [Fig.1.15].

Other photographs testify to them helping out during the First World War with care duties [Fig.1.16 – Fig.1.18]. The two sisters are shown dressed as V.A.D.s and these pictures were pasted in an album alongside further photographs of convalescing soldiers, whose names are unfortunately not recorded [Fig.1.16 – Fig.1.19]. A V.A.D. (Voluntary Aid Detachment) was a non-mandatory unit of civilians providing nursing care for military personnel. These were founded by the British Red Cross and the Order of St John and both Doris and Anna became volunteers at a V.A.D. based at a hospital in Northwood, Middlesex. As an aside it is relevant to point out that this prefigures their later

Above top right: Fig.1.17
Anna Zinkeisen (middle row, first from right) as a V.A.D. during WWI with convalescing soldiers.
© Photograph courtesy of Julia Heseltine.

Above middle right: Fig.1.18
Doris Zinkeisen (fourth from left) as a V.A.D. together with other auxiliary nurses during WWI.
© Photograph courtesy of Julia Heseltine.

Above bottom right: Fig.1.19
Unnamed convalescing soldiers from a snapshot in a Zinkeisen family scrapbook. This may be Lea Croft, a small house next to the main Northwood V.A.D. Hospital established in the Lecture Hall of St John's Presbyterian Church in Hallowell Road, which was leased to accommodate extra beds during WWI.
© Photograph courtesy of Julia Heseltine.

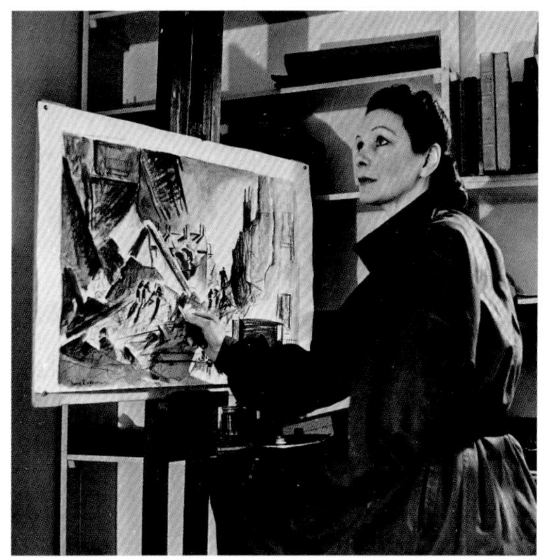

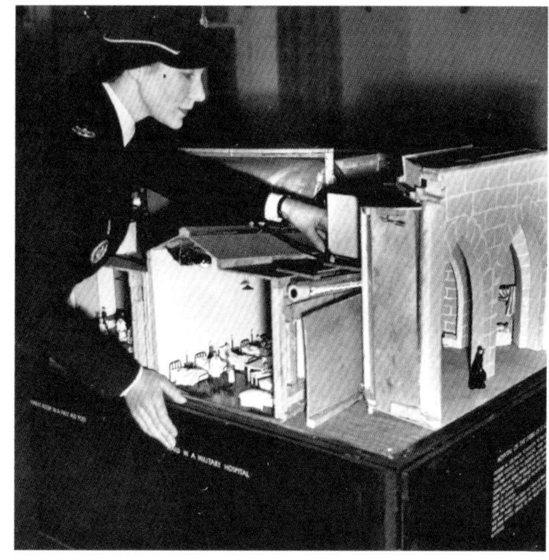

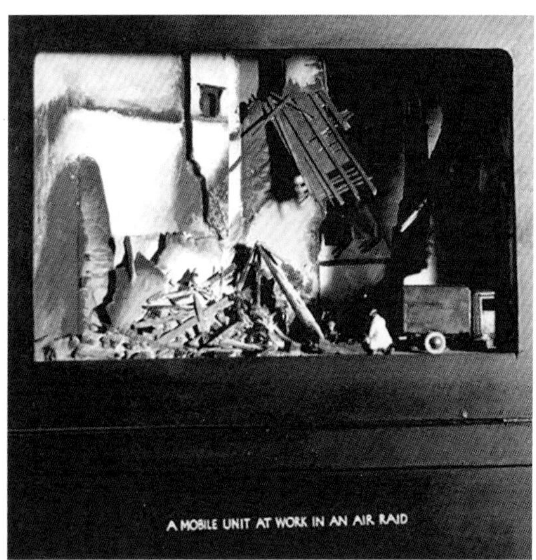

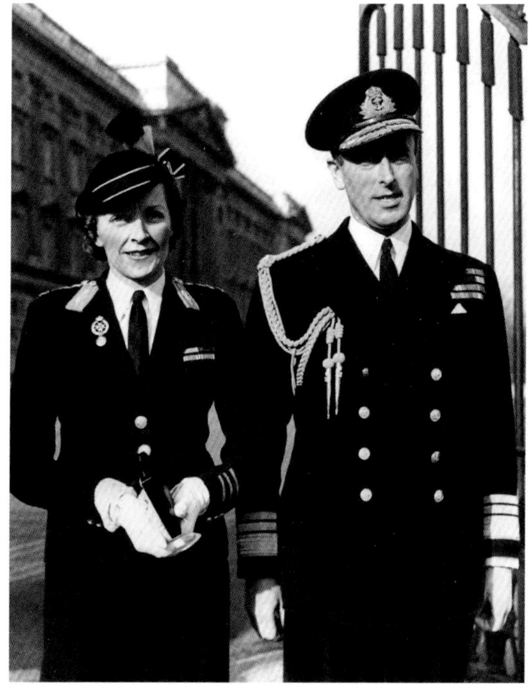

Above top left: Fig.1.20
Doris designing a diorama for St John Ambulance fundraising during WWII. See also Fig.1.22 and Fig.3.54.
© Photograph courtesy of the estate of Doris Zinkeisen.

Above top right: Fig.1.21
Doris Zinkeisen setting up one of the dioramas. See also Fig.3.53.
©Photograph courtesy of the estate of Doris Zinkeisen.

Above below left: Fig.1.22
One of the completed dioramas, which went on a three-year fundraising tour of Britain starting in 1942 and raised over £8000 in voluntary donations for the Joint War Organisation (J.W.O.), an amalgamation of the British Red Cross and the Order of St John. See also Fig.1.20 and Fig.3.54.
© Photograph courtesy of the estate of Doris Zinkeisen.

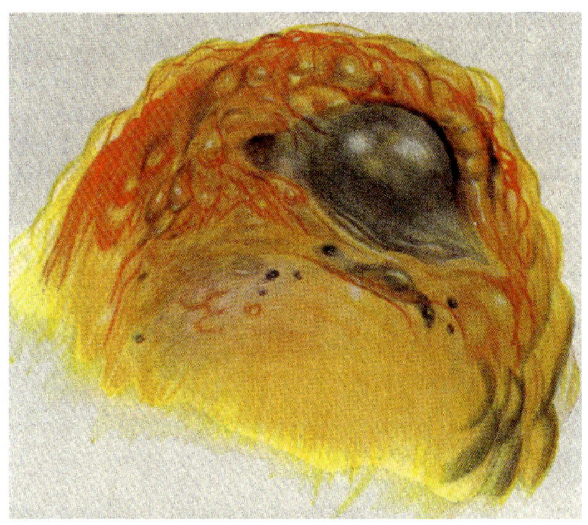

involvement as auxiliary nurses at St Mary's Hospital in Paddington after joining the St John Ambulance Brigade during the Second World War – a time when both participated in fundraising war-relief work too [Fig.1.20 – Fig.1.22]. Their association with the St John Ambulance Brigade brought them into contact with Countess Edwina Mountbatten (1901-1960), the wife of Louis, Earl Mountbatten of Burma (1900-1979), who also rendered distinguished service to the Red Cross and St John Ambulance [Fig.1.23]. Doris knew the Countess well enough to loan her dresses, most probably during the time that clothing was rationed. It is during the Second World War that the sisters would produce some of their most significant work, Anna with medical drawings and paintings, Doris with harrowing paintings of Belsen, where she was an eyewitness to the atrocities [Fig.1.24; Fig.3.50 – Fig.3.65]. Who could possibly have foreseen their careers would become so embroiled in recording the horrific consequences of warfare whilst carefree youngsters?

Neither of the sisters attended formal school and it is reported that throughout their childhoods they dedicated their time mainly to drawing and painting. Their blossoming talents as artists were quickly spotted. Amongst the many family photographs there are pictures of a sketching and painting trip and the interior of an art school [Fig.1.25 – Fig.1.29]. Then in 1917, following a stint at Harrow School of Art, the sisters won scholarships to the prestigious Royal Academy Schools in London, where they are likely to have received training from Sir George Clausen (1852-1944), Sir William Orpen (1878-1931), and Charles Sims (1873-1928). Already as art students the Zinkeisen sisters were attracting media attention for their skills as painters, but this was hard won.

Opposite below right: Fig.1.23
Countess Edwina Mountbatten and Admiral Louis, Earl Mountbatten of Burma before Buckingham Palace, London, 1943. The Countess Edwina wears her uniform of the St John Ambulance Brigade.

Above: Fig.1.24
Anna Zinkeisen started to produce medical drawings and paintings during WWII and continued thereafter. This image illustrates fibrocystic disease in a woman aged 48 and was used in *The Breast: Structure: Function: Disease* (1950) by F.D. Saner. The original is in the archives of the Royal College of Surgeons of England along with many of Anna's other medical works.

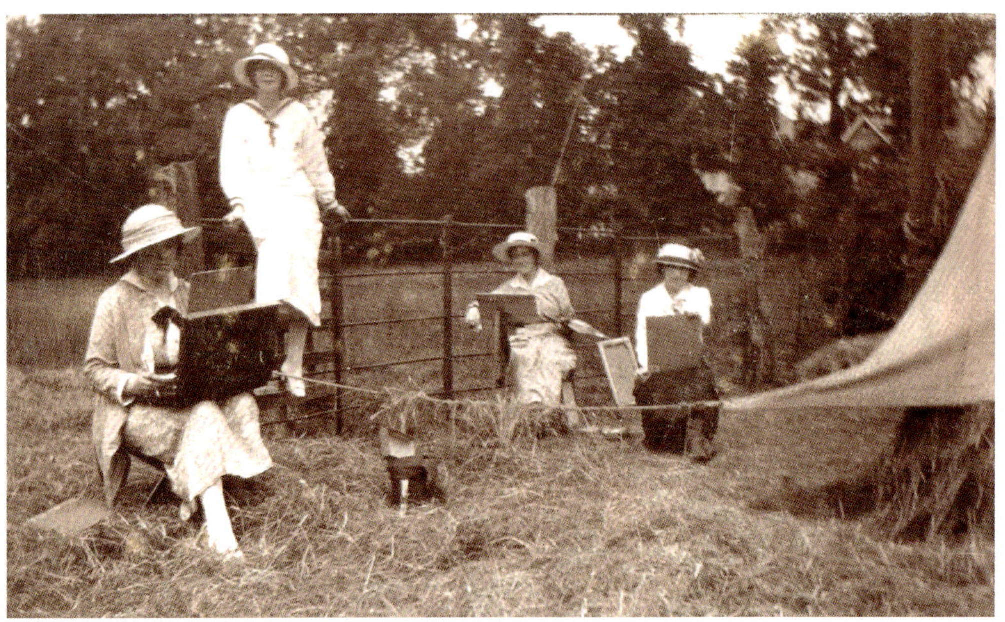

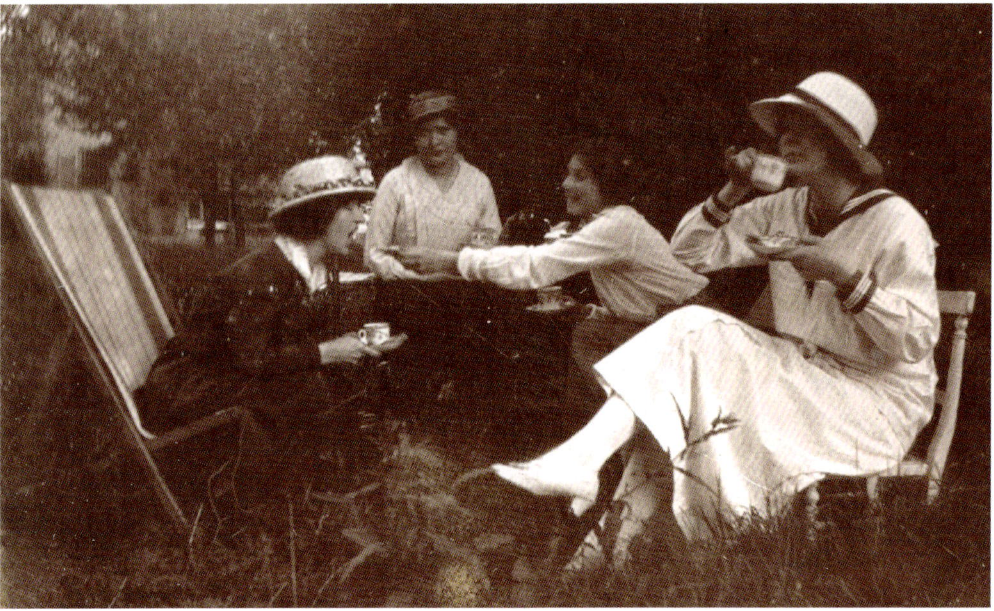

Top: Fig.1.25
Doris Zinkeisen (seated on fence) on a sketching trip whilst a student.
© Photograph courtesy of Julia Heseltine.

Above: Fig.1.26
Doris Zinkeisen (right) in a distinctive outfit horsing about with fellow art students on a sketching trip.
© Photograph courtesy of Julia Heseltine.

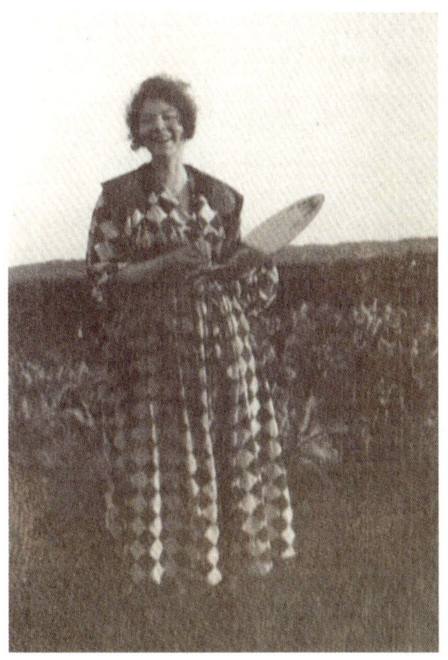

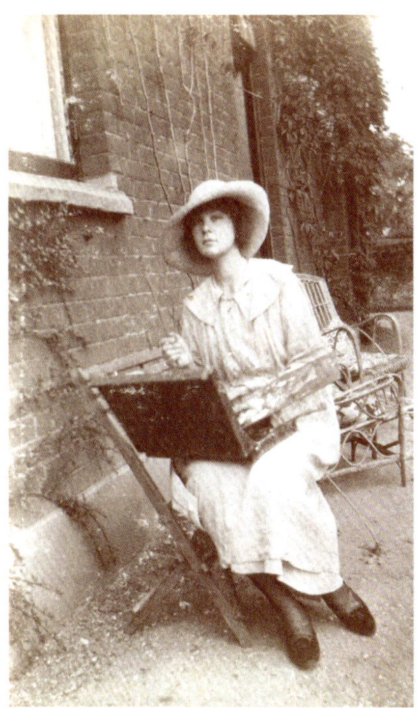

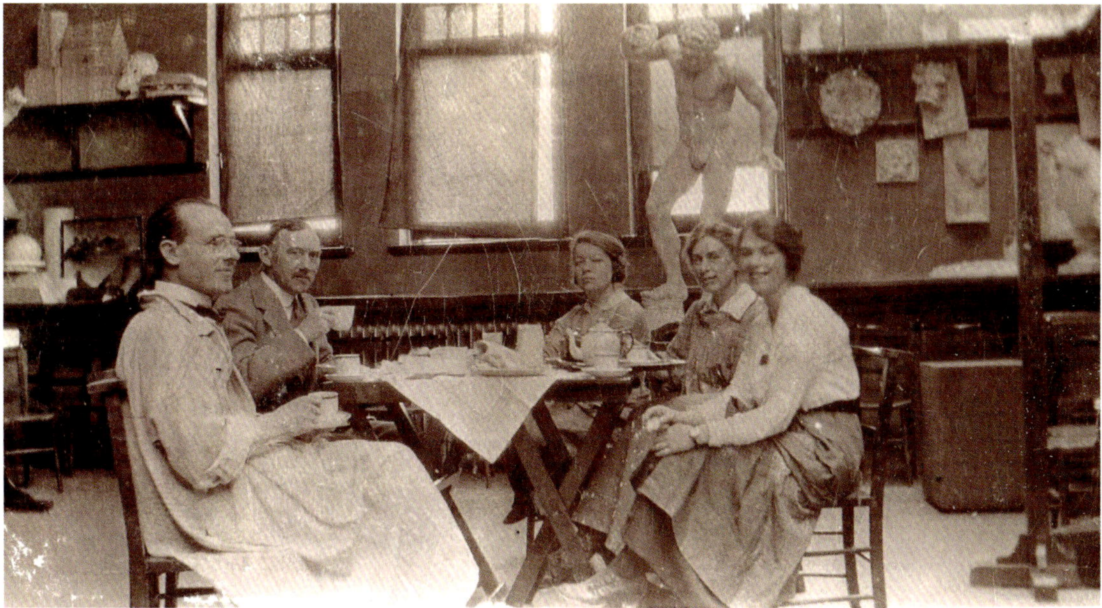

Top left: Fig.1.27
Anna Zinkeisen painting plein air in her harlequin-patterned smock wielding a palette.
© Photograph courtesy of Julia Heseltine.

Top right: Fig.1.28
Doris Zinkeisen painting plein air.
© Photograph courtesy of Julia Heseltine.

Above: Fig.1.29
Interior of an art school from a Zinkeisen family scrapbook, possibly Harrow School of Art, with unnamed teachers and students.
© Photograph courtesy of Julia Heseltine.

Flappers

As already established earlier above the Zinkeisen sisters would leave art school to become prize-winning artists and designers. Outwardly the Zinkeisen sisters could give the impression of being lively, fun-loving flappers [Fig.1.30 – Fig.1.32]. The term flapper was used in the 1920s to refer to young women, who were perhaps a little more unconventional than the norm, especially in their conduct and dress.

Looking at early photographs of the sisters it is clear they enjoyed dressing up. This almost certainly derived from their parents, who, if photographs are to be believed, were both quite extrovert and relished opportunities to put on their glad rags, or masquerade costumes [Fig.1.33 – Fig.1.35]. Anna was incontrovertibly the more demure of the two sisters and by no means a natural extrovert, whilst even early photographs of Doris expose her flamboyant personality through her showy poses and choice of garments, which are never run-of-the-mill for the period. Being a flapper, however, should in no way be confused with being superficial. If anything their appearance as flappers should be seen as a ruse to mask their steely ambition to make their mark on the world of art. It must not be overlooked that the world the Zinkeisen sisters grew up in was rapidly changing, especially for women.

Choices for women were quite limited in the early 1900s. The campaign for votes for women was beginning to bear fruit whilst the sisters were still young and impressionable. In 1914 women's right to work was accepted and few years later the Parliamentary Reform Bill was amended, which gave women over thirty years of age the right to vote – whilst simultaneously giving the vote to all men of twenty-one years and over. It would take a further decade for voting equality for men and women to be granted. In relation to employment and political power the period of the First World War and its aftermath can be seen here as an era of emancipation for British women. These

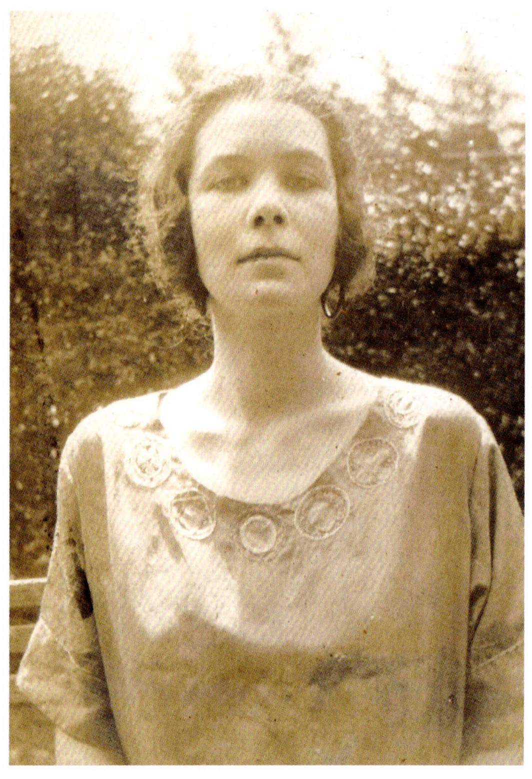

Above: Fig.1.30
Doris Zinkeisen clearly loved clothes from early on.
© Photograph courtesy of Julia Heseltine.

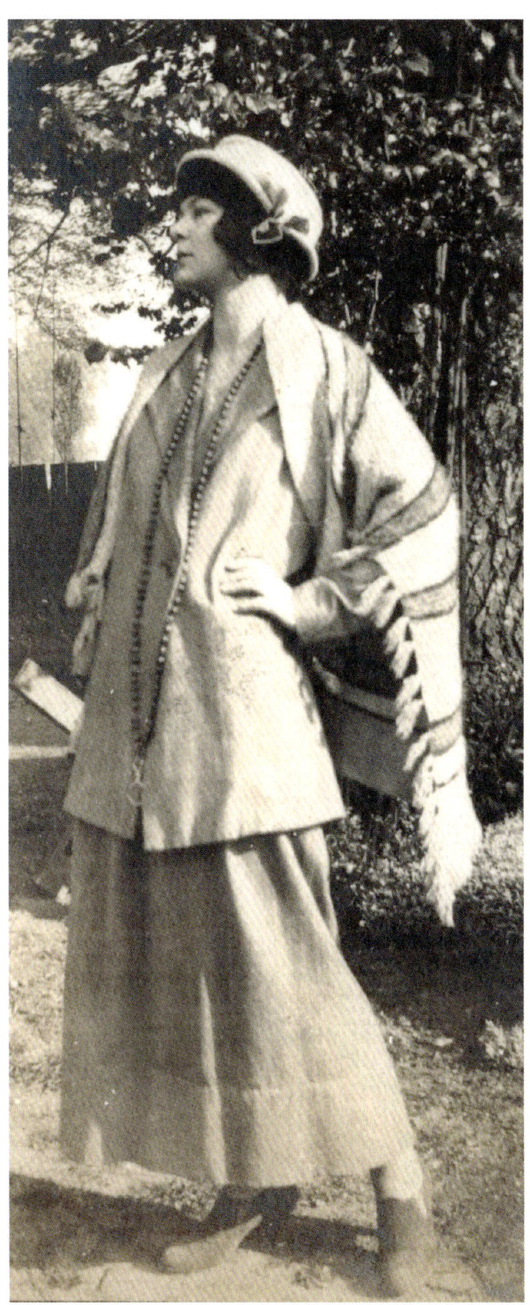

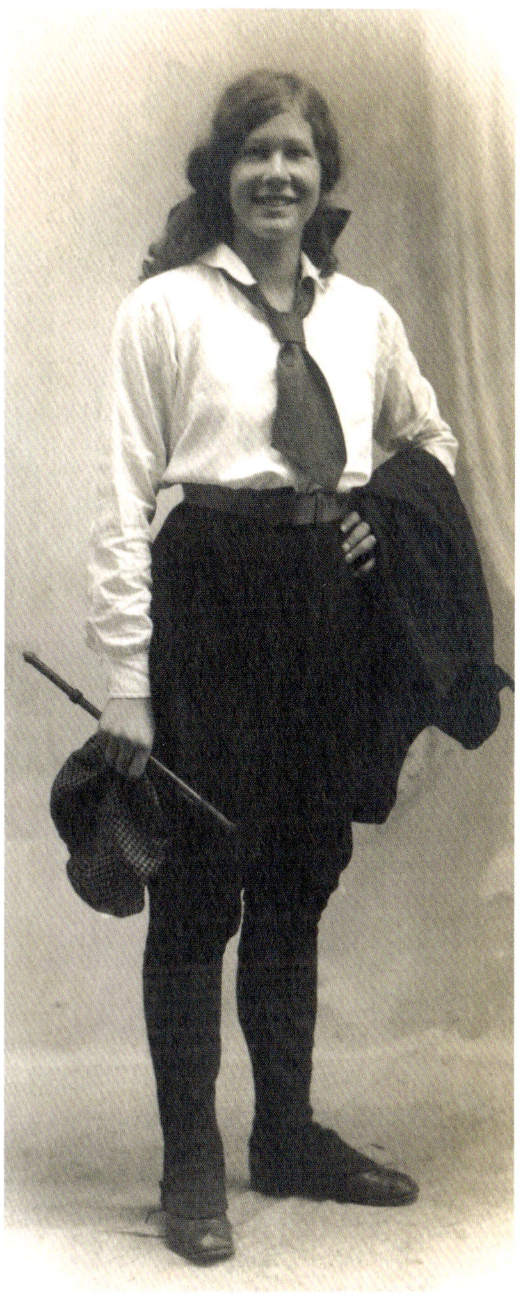

Above: Fig.1.31
Doris Zinkeisen demonstrating that already as a young art student she loved to strike a pose.
© Photograph courtesy of Julia Heseltine.

Above: Fig.1.32
Anna Zinkeisen always dressed in an appropriate sartorial style for the occasion, here in her riding attire.
© Photograph courtesy of Julia Heseltine.

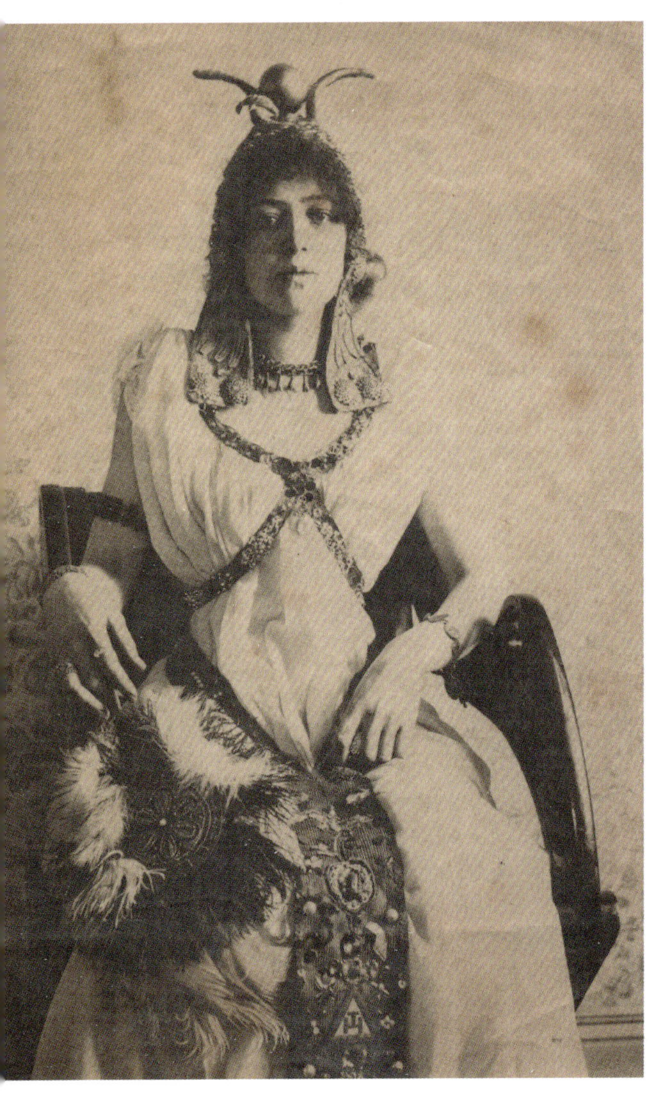

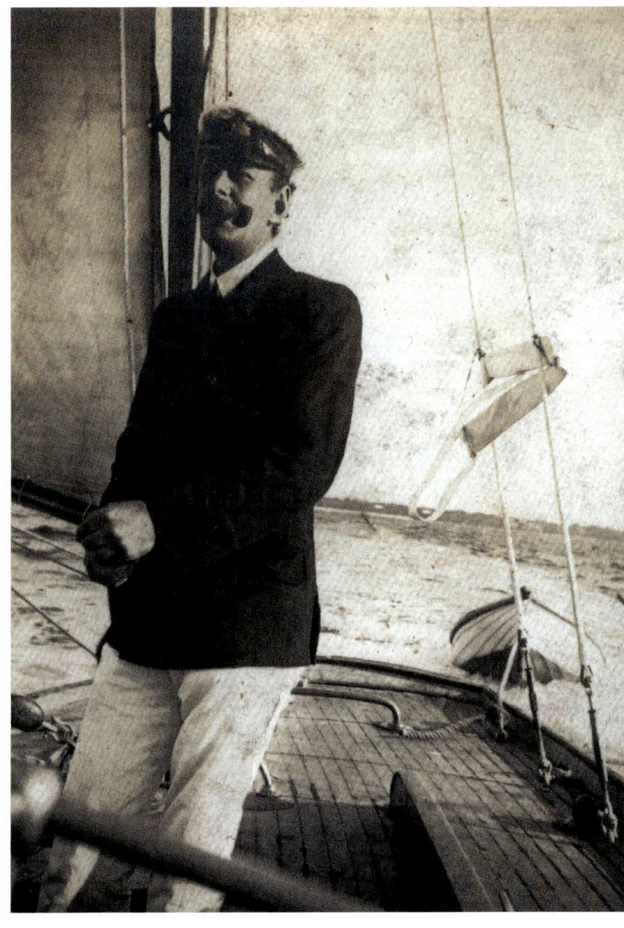

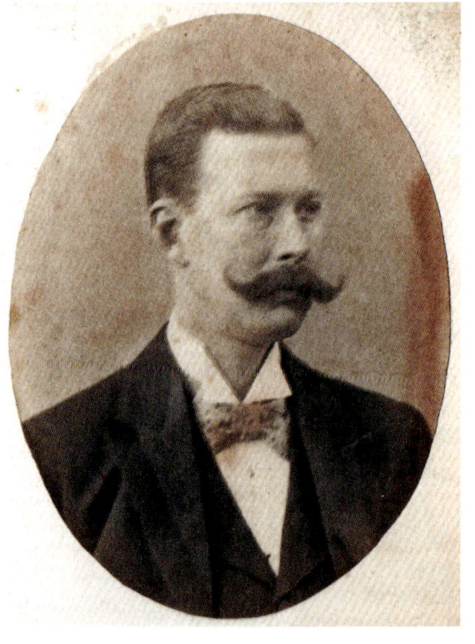

Above: Fig.1.33

Clara Bolton Charles, mother of the Zinkeisen sisters, ready for a fancy-dress ball, here possibly in the guise of Cleopatra.

Above right: Fig.1.34

Victor William Zinkeisen dressed for sailing his yacht.

Right: Fig.1.35

Victor William Zinkeisen superbly moustachioed.

changes in the status of women would have exerted a powerful influence on Doris and Anna, although it still could at times remain difficult for women to enjoy the new freedoms.

The Zinkeisen sisters were able to receive training at art schools, but women were certainly in the minority and encountered problems. For example, during the first decade of the twentieth century there remained tensions around women gaining access to life classes, in particular the male nude, which in itself limited opportunities for young women artists, as it remained a cornerstone for the proper education of artists. Women were permitted to participate, but not necessarily as equals and seldom gained prominence in either the applied or fine arts. There are a few exceptions: Clarice Cliff (1899-1972) and Susie Cooper (1902-1995) produced exciting ceramic designs, whilst Dame Barbara Hepworth (1903-1975) made it to become a famous pioneering non-figurative sculptor, although such women remained in the minority. It was Dame Laura Knight (1877-1970), an artist twenty years older than Doris Zinkeisen, so from a slightly earlier generation, who finally made it to become a Royal Academician in 1936. Today this may seem inconsequential, but in fact Laura Knight was the first woman to achieve such an important position since Angelica Kauffmann (1741-1807) and Mary Moser (1744-1819), who were both founding members of the Royal Academy in 1768. So the two Zinkeisen sisters were training and becoming professional artists right at the heart of the period when attitudes towards women were perceptibly shifting.

Profound social changes bring with them particular strains and the Zinkeisen sisters were not alone in being in the firing line of criticism. In 1921, whilst still students at the Royal Academy Schools, the sisters were amongst fifteen women students, who had one or more of their works hung on the line at the Royal Academy. There was opposition to this decision on the part of the hanging committee. The respected artists on the hanging committee for paintings in 1921 were Sir John Arnesby Brown (1866-1955), Sir David Young Cameron (1865-1945), Samuel Melton Fisher (1859-1939), Charles Sims, and Adrian Stokes (1854-1935). These committees tended to be exclusively the preserve of men, especially in the 1920s and 1930s. As a matter of fact it was Laura Knight who broke this mould when making it onto the hanging committee in 1937 and again in 1946.

The hanging committee's bold decision in 1921 to include the work of the women students was by no means universally well received. The *Sunday Herald* [May 8th 1921] reported how some in artistic circles felt the young women artists had, "taken the place of matured painters." The artist Frank O. Salisbury (1874-1962) had his opinions on the matter published in *The Times* newspaper [3rd May 1921], arguing that by accepting the paintings of the young women artists more

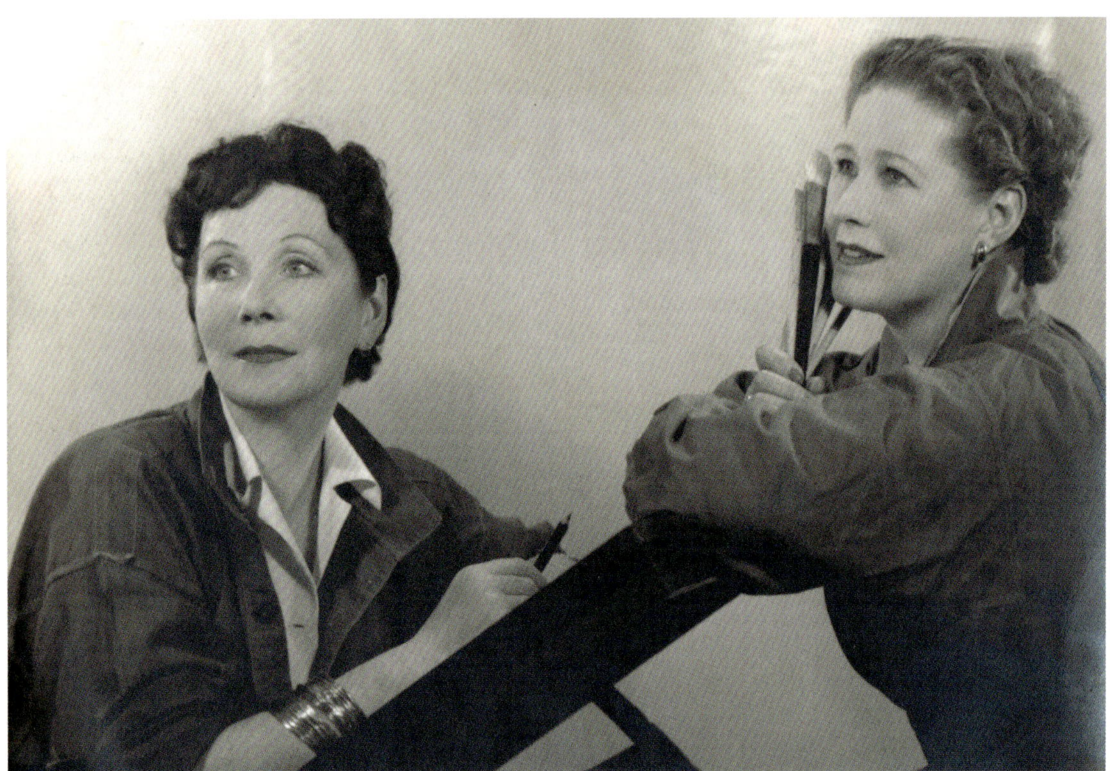

distinguished painters had been deprived of a vital opportunity to display and sell their work. This was amongst the earliest media exposure for the sisters and a baptism of fire.

Both sisters certainly had to overcome, or turn a blind eye to the generally held stereotype of women artists being little more than enthusiastic amateurs. Art produced in the early twentieth century by women like the Zinkeisen sisters was all too often treated as something apart from the mainstream and discussed in gendered terms as feminine, a word we can understand at that time and context to mean delicate and pretty, but simultaneously implying somewhat weak and insubstantial. To support this it can be noted how one critic in the magazine *Apollo* [No.5, 1927] describes Anna Zinkeisen's exhibit entitled *Olympians* [Fig.3.10] at The Society of Women Artists at the Royal Institute Galleries as, "a delightful piece of feminine inconsequence." In this quotation it is the turn of phrase "feminine inconsequence", with its overtones of triviality, the incidental and insignificant, which leaves a slightly bitter aftertaste, as it seems to overshadow the

Above: Fig.1.36
Doris (left) and Anna (right) Zinkeisen *circa* 1950.

Right: Fig.1.37
Doris Zinkeisen *circa* 1950s.

adjective "delightful" and suggests the painting may be considered to lack conceptual difficulty and imagination.

Elsewhere the critic Hermon Ould (1886-1951) in his column 'A Critic of the Arts at Large' [*Westminster Gazette*, 18th February 1927] writes on the same exhibition just mentioned above in a blatantly misogynistic manner, that women artists band themselves together because their work lacks originality of outlook and technique. Ould comments: "When the work is good – and there is much competent work this year – it is good in an ordinary sexless sense. [...] When the work is bad, it is feminine only in the uncomplimentary sense that it is weak, formless, and derivative." He goes on to state that: "It may be that in competition with men their work would fail to attract attention." This comment is not directed specifically at Anna Zinkeisen, but to all of the women exhibitors and is precisely the type of widespread, blatant sexism, which all women artists had to contend with at that particular point in time. Fortunately, later press coverage of the Zinkeisen sisters was far more positive. They also found strategies to harness and reconcile being simultaneously feminine and feminists.

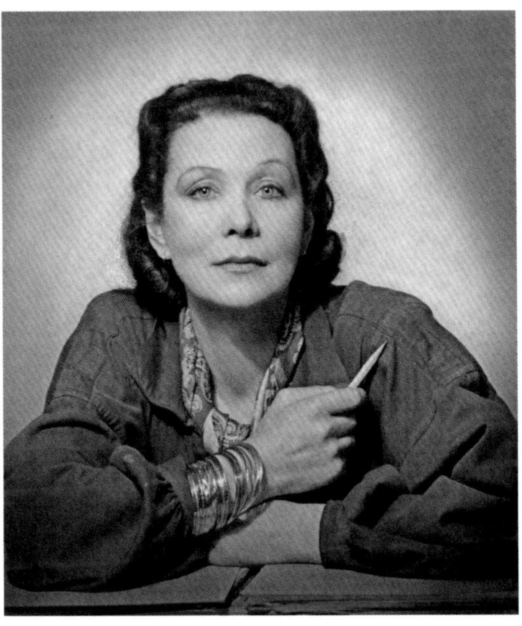

The Zinkeisen sisters became proficient at cultivating both the press and their own public image. They were not above exploiting their good looks as a means to an end to attract media attention and in this way found a useful formula to help market their work. They abandoned any vestiges of youthful gaucheness and made their début as artists in the guise of femmes fatales. Hand in hand with the increasing freedoms for women between the World Wars the Zinkeisen sisters participated in pioneering a new racy look: red nail varnish mimicking bloody talons; mascara to draw attention to the eyes; and vibrant lipstick, all beautifying cosmetics earlier generations would by and large have disapproved of. As a matter of fact interest in the sisters grew rapidly once they had completed their art-school training. It was as though nothing could hold them back, least of all small-minded and bigoted pigeonholing as women artists. Looking at photographs and paintings of Doris and Anna Zinkeisen from this late 1920s period it appears almost as if the sisters were completely transformed, as they refashioned and adapted themselves to life as confident, modern women in a challenging, competitive, fast-paced and rapidly changing world. Their self-assurance remained with them throughout their lives [Fig.1.36 – Fig.1.37].

The Interwar Period and Exploring New Opportunities: Posters, Illustrations and Costume Design

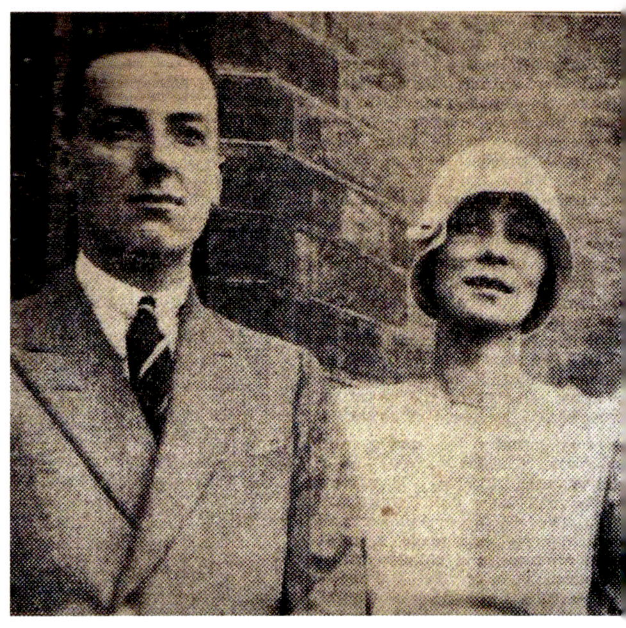

Both Doris and Anna possessed a keen eye for spotting toeholds to assist them in making further progress. Being a hobby artist is easy, but to make a good living as an artist is far trickier and can involve certain sacrifices, including to a "normal" family life. The Zinkeisen sisters were happy to take on almost any offer of work, provided it paid, and this kept them busy and in demand. In a feature on the Zinkeisen sisters from the magazine *Eve* [June 30th 1926] it reports that: "posters pay – but, according to Miss Doris Zinkeisen, no one should despise the smaller jobs: you never know where they may lead." This positive outlook on life and work almost certainly assisted the Zinkeisen sisters in securing commissions... and much more besides.

In fact, it appears to be the case that in 1927 whilst engaged in designing posters for the whisky distillers, John Walker & Sons, Doris met her future husband Captain Edward Grahame Johnstone D.S.C., R.N.V.R. (1899-1946), who was then a director at that distillery [Fig.1.38]. Anna married a year later to Colonel Guy Robert Nelson Heseltine M.C. (1897-1967) and had a daughter, Julia Heseltine (b.1933), who grew up to become a much respected portraitist and landscape artist in her own right [Fig.1.39]. In addition to the twin daughters Anne Grahame

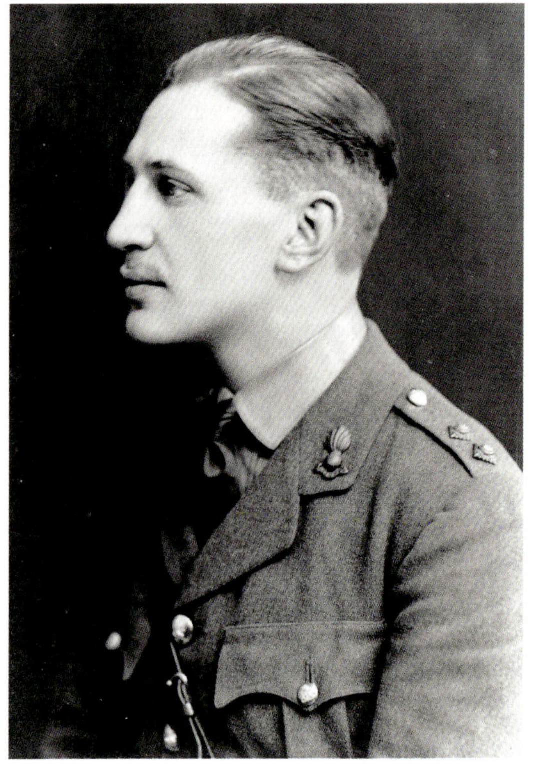

Johnstone (1928-1998) and Janet Johnstone (1928-1979), who became illustrators of books for children, Doris had a son, Captain Edward Murray Grahame Johnstone R.N. (1930-2017). The Zinkeisen sisters remained, however, first and foremost artists.

Nannies were employed and at the first available opportunity the children were despatched to boarding schools, in common with most of the offspring of the British upper crust at that time. In fact not long after having the twins Doris and her husband set off on a world cruise lasting many months leaving the girls with their nannies and Anna back in London. At that time it was accepted for well-heeled parents to ensure they were not held hostage by the demands of their children, who had instead to fit around the careers of their parents. Neither of the Zinkeisen sisters can be regarded as having been "traditional" stay-at-home mothers, as they most certainly regarded art not just as a job, but as a vocation.

During their careers, both Zinkeisen sisters produced poster and advertising designs for a range of businesses including, for example, Imperial Chemical Industries (ICI), the United Steel Companies Limited, and the London and North Eastern Railway (LNER) [Fig.3.33 – Fig.3.40; Fig.3.66 – Fig.3.77]. Interestingly the posters tended to include the name of the artists. So although the purpose of the posters was to sell goods and services, because the artwork used was not anonymous it simultaneously promoted the artists in the public domain and emphasised the artistic value of the designs.

Doris and Anna also produced numerous illustrations. It must be said, however, that it was Anna who dedicated more time than her sister to illustrating books. Likewise it was Anna, who early in her career accepted regular commissions to produce artwork for magazines, in particular *The Sketch*. These commercial design jobs were exacting and needed to be carried out to meet strict deadlines, but regular work equated to dependable pay. As a matter of fact Anna's weekly contributions of artworks for magazines in the late 1920s and 1930s are as close as she came to a more conventional permanent position. This early work producing illustrations would pave the way to significant commissions producing artwork for important medical texts, including *The Essentials of Modern Surgery* (1943) edited by Ranald Montagu Handfield-Jones (1892-1978) and Arthur Espie Porritt (1900-1994), *The Breast: Structure: Function: Disease* (1950) by Francis Donaldson Saner (1884-1975), and the general medical primer *Preparatory Anatomy and Physiology* (1949) by Bethina Alice Bennett O.B.E., DipN. Some of Anna Zinkeisen's medical drawings and paintings are in the archives of the Royal College of Surgeons of England in London [Fig.1.24].

It should be remembered that at this point in time medical drawings and paintings could be more accurate than photography, especially

Opposite top: Fig.1.38
Edward Grahame Johnstone and Doris Zinkeisen from a press clipping of 1929.
© Photograph courtesy of the estate of Doris Zinkeisen.

Opposite below: Fig.1.39
Guy Robert Nelson Heseltine, Anna Zinkeisen's husband.
© Photograph courtesy of Julia Heseltine.

in relation to colour. Anna found this phase of her artistic output totally engrossing and she was hands-on in her approach, quite literally painting from life during or just after operations she witnessed. Many of these medical works were exhibited in London at Foyles in 1947 and Parsons Gallery in 1953. Anna discovered beauty and fascination in producing medical artwork of individual organs, but Doris found this aspect of her sister's artistic endeavours stomach-churning. On one occasion Doris went to see her sister and on Anna's easel was a perfect drawing of a kidney. Whilst waiting for Anna, Doris could not resist drawing a piece of buttered toast beneath the kidney. Anna was not impressed.

Doris Zinkeisen could never relate to her sister's passion for painting parts of people's innards. She was attracted more to the theatrical world. Quite early in her career Doris launched herself into the design of costumes and sets for the theatre and film [Fig.1.40 – Fig.1.45]. Her creations ended up being worn by some of the greatest acting talents and entertainers of her age including Jack Buchanan (1890-1957), Sir John Gielgud (1904-2000), Brigitte Helm (1908-1996), Elsa Lanchester (1902-1986), Dame Anna Neagle (1904-1986), Baron Laurence Olivier (1907-1989), Sir Ralph Richardson (1902-1983), and Dame Sybil Thorndike (1882-1976) – to name but a few. Doris occasionally let slip that working with the distinguished thespians was always less troublesome than dealing with the wannabes, whom she sometimes found rather uppity and unprofessional.

In 1922, whilst still a student at the Royal Academy Schools, Doris showed up unannounced with a portfolio tucked under her arm and boldly put her foot in the door of the impresario Sir Nigel Playfair (1874-1934) and proactively asked him for a break. Playfair rated Doris's work highly and even employed her as an interior decorator when revamping his London home. This was widely featured in the popular women's magazines of the day. A further exciting perk working for Playfair, although perilous as it turns out, was the chance to fly to Prague to study *The Insect Play* by Karel Čapek (1890-1938) and Josef Čapek (1887-1945): a wonderful opportunity, only the aeroplane came down in the Black Forest... Doris lived to tell the tale. She made it to Prague to scrutinize the play's production after squelching through fields in high heels and catching a train, as if nothing serious had occurred.

Anna too experimented with theatre design, but never to the same degree as her sister. With theatre design it really does appear to be the case that Doris found her true métier in the same way that illustrating was more Anna's calling. As previously established Doris was an unashamedly flamboyant character and maybe this suited theatre design work

Opposite top left: Fig.1.40
The actress Jeanne Stuart, wearing the type of dress Doris Zinkeisen specialised in designing, making an entrance in the film *Leap Year* (1932).
© General Photographic Agency/Getty Images [3281960].

Opposite below left: Fig.1.42
Anna Neagle in the musical *Good Night, Vienna* (1932) in an elegant gown designed by Doris Zinkeisen.
© Everett Collection Inc./Alamy Stock Photo [HC1BDH].

Opposite top right: Fig.1.41
The actress Anna Neagle in the musical romance *The Little Damozel* (1933) in a costume designed by Doris Zinkeisen.
© Lebrecht Music and Arts/Alamy Stock Photo [ERHMCT].

Opposite below right: Fig.1.43
A sassy looking Anna Neagle in the title role of *Nell Gwyn* (1934) in an historically inspired outfit by Doris Zinkeisen.
© Everett Collection Inc./Alamy Stock Photo [HC2C6W].

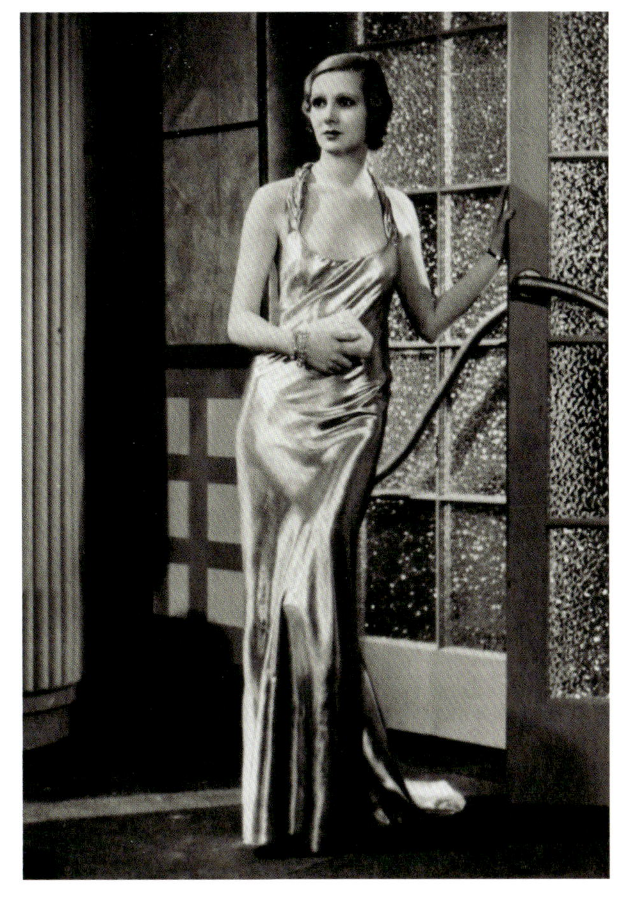

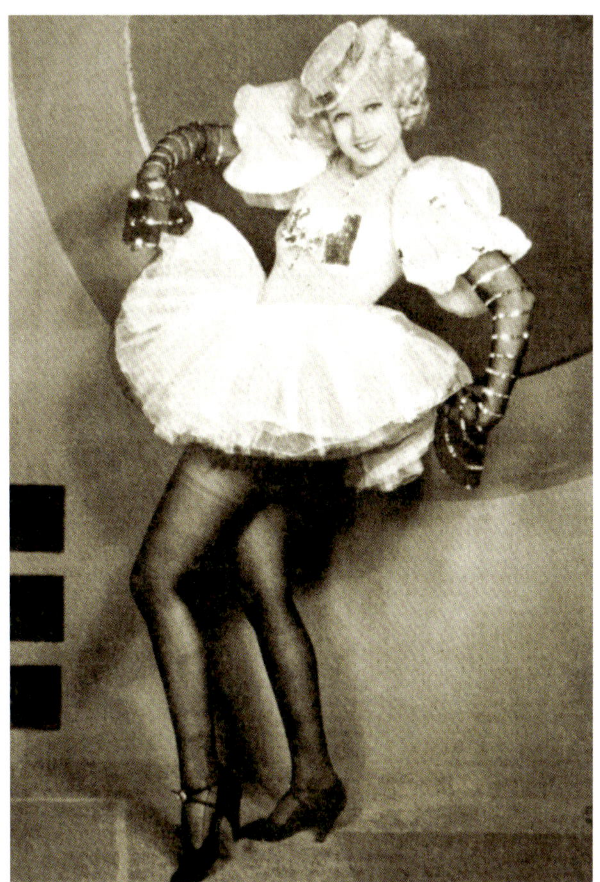

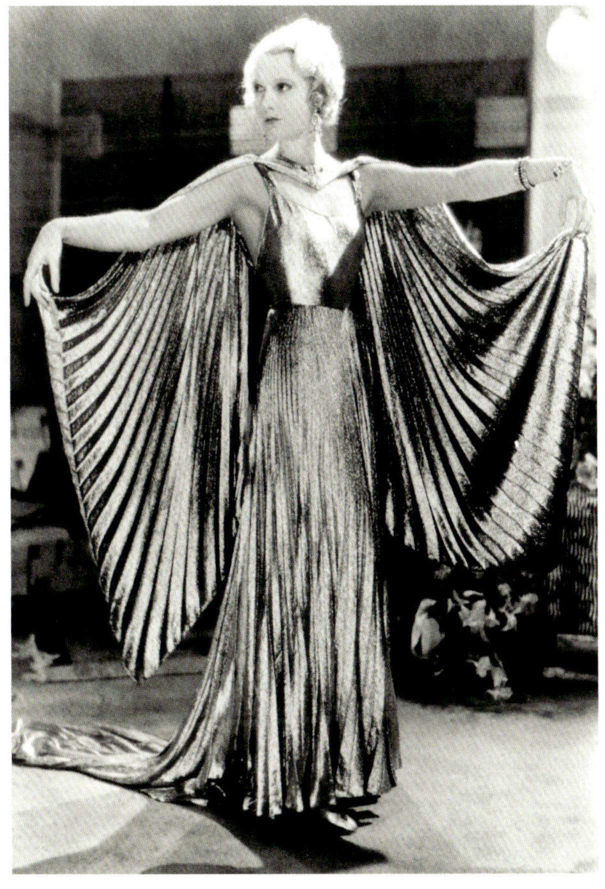

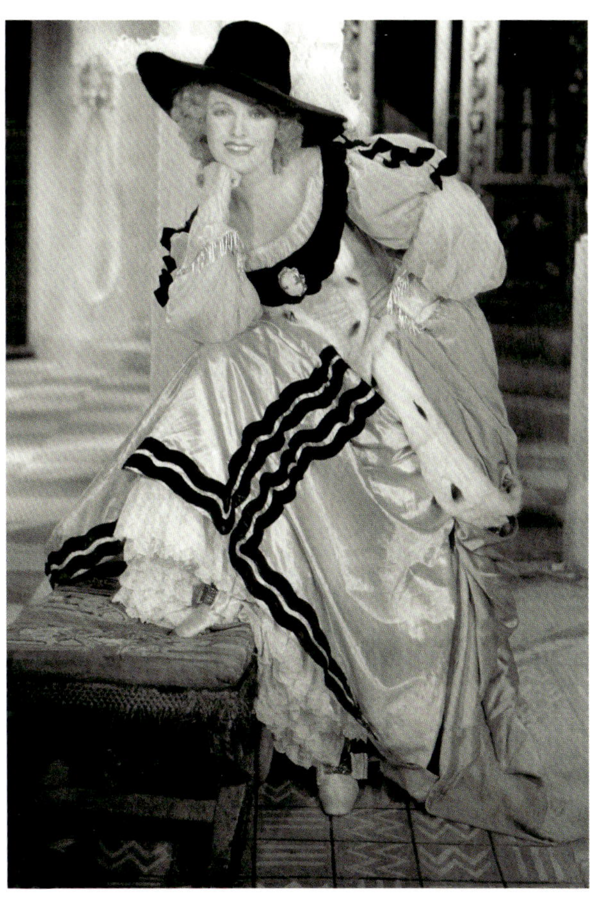

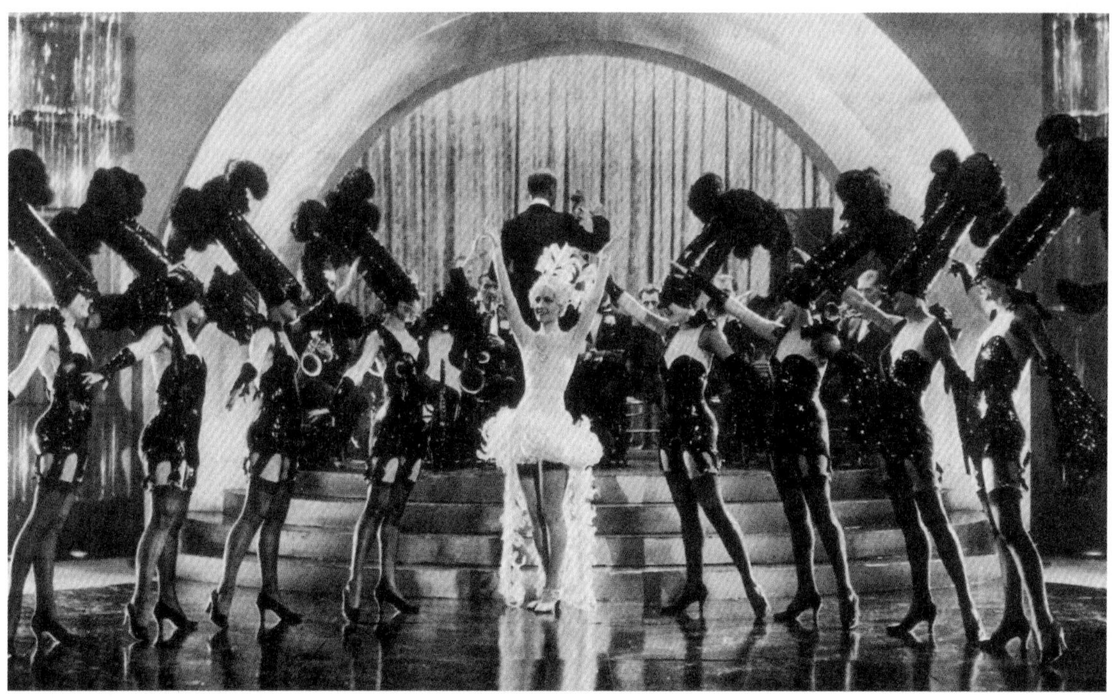

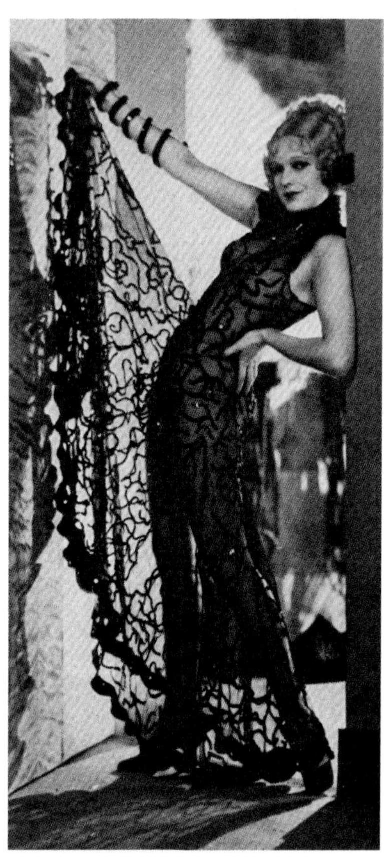

Above: Fig.1.44

Winifred Shotter (centre) framed by dancers in the cabaret scene from *A Night Like This* (1932) all dressed in slightly saucy costumes designed by Doris Zinkeisen.

Left: Fig.1.45

The actress Anna Neagle in an overtly outré diaphanous dress designed by Doris Zinkeisen for the film *The Little Damozel* (1933), which generated much publicity when the film was released.

Opposite left: Fig.1.46

Costume design by Doris Zinkeisen for the ballet *Twelfth Night* as performed by the International Ballet between the years 1943 to 1946.

Opposite right: Fig.1.47

Here the actor Anthony Eustrel (1902-1979) is paired with the dancer Mona Inglesby, both in costumes by Doris Zinkeisen for *The Masque of Comus* performed by the International Ballet between 1946 and 1948.

far better than Anna's reserved nature. Doris produced costume and stage sets for literally dozens of productions [Appendix 2]. She also became one of the chief designers for the dancer and choreographer Mona Inglesby (1918-2006), who was also the director of the International Ballet, a popular British touring ballet company between1941 and 1953 [Fig.1.46 – Fig.1.47]. Doris outlined some of her ideas on theatre design in her book *Designing for the Stage*, first published in 1938, but reprinted at least twice more in 1945 and 1948.

Doris Zinkeisen's costume and set designs for theatre were tailored to be as outlandish or traditional as the production required and were frequently quite risqué. Her work for Playfair caught the eye of another influential impresario, Sir Charles Blake Cochran (1872-1951), who engaged Doris to create costumes for his glittering revues, including those he produced together with the famous theatrical all-rounder Sir Noël Coward (1899-1973). These revues gave Doris the scope and freedom to come up with some fabulously wacky costumes. Another unusual fringe benefit in these early days working for Cochran was being requested by him to host parties in her name at venues, including the Savoy, but which he paid for. Apparently Cochran sometimes disliked feeling obliged to entertain particular individuals, or saddling them with the burden of reciprocation, so doing things this way enabled him to enjoy a function without giving anyone the cold shoulder.

Concerning the design of costumes, Doris not only had to sketch out and commit her conceptions to paper for the costumiers to follow, but was required to attend all the fittings also. The sheer numbers of these designs still extant and appearing from time to

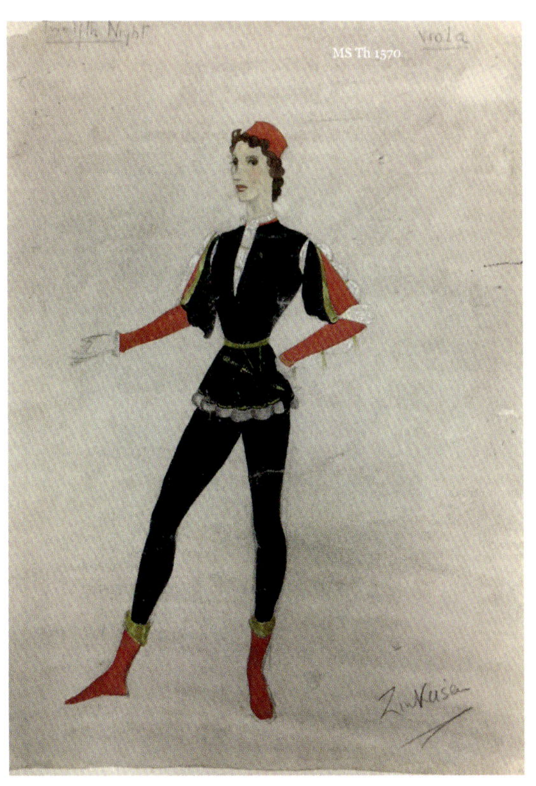

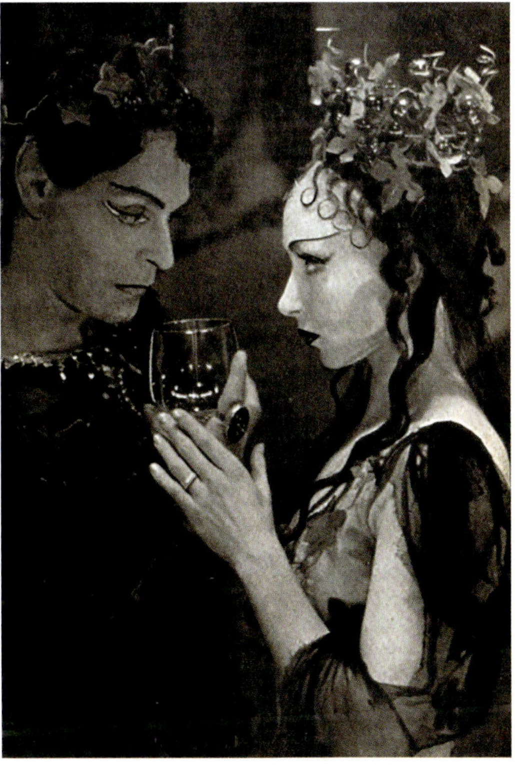

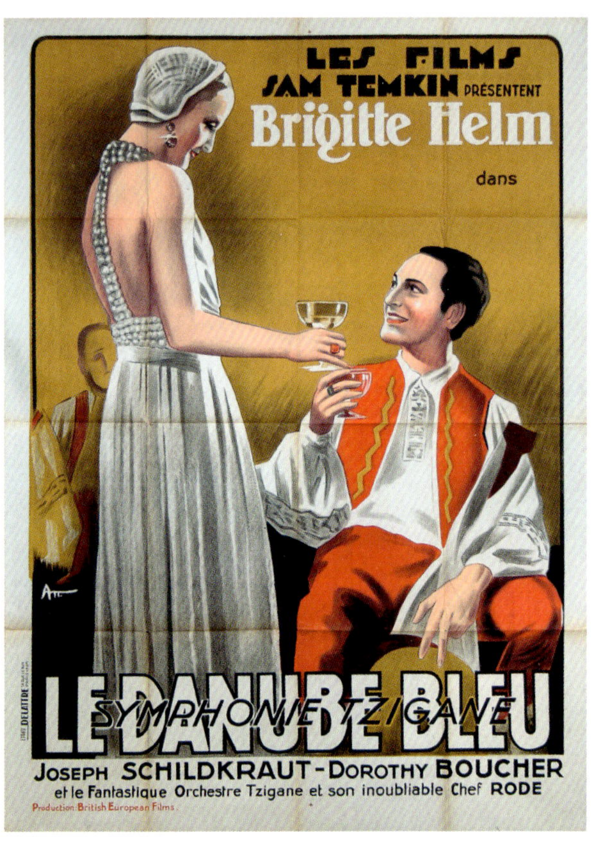
LES FILMS
SAM TEMKIN PRÉSENTENT
Brigitte Helm
dans
LE DANUBE BLEU
SYMPHONIE TZIGANE
JOSEPH SCHILDKRAUT - DOROTHY BOUCHER
et le Fantastique Orchestre Tzigane et son inoubliable Chef RODE
Production: British European Films

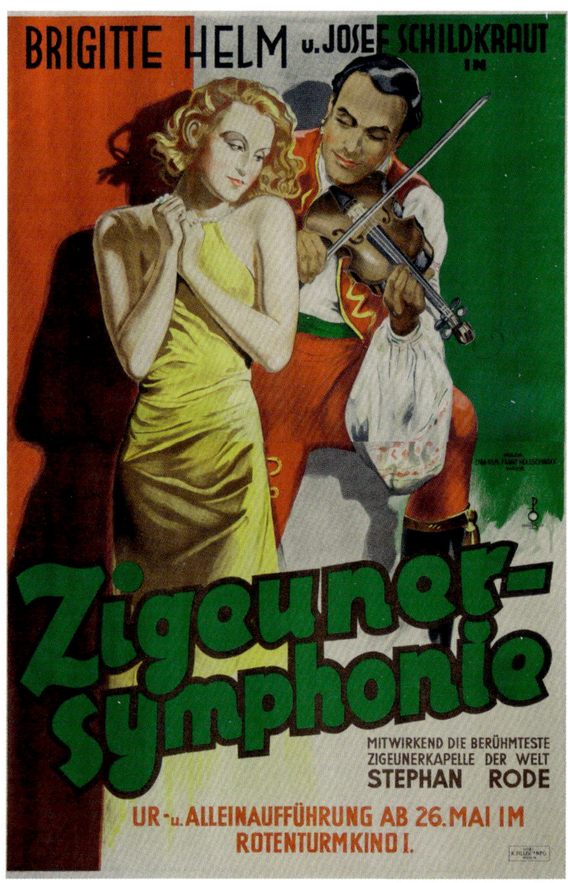
BRIGITTE HELM u. JOSEF SCHILDKRAUT
IN
Zigeuner-
symphonie
MITWIRKEND DIE BERÜHMTESTE
ZIGEUNERKAPELLE DER WELT
STEPHAN RODE
UR- u. ALLEINAUFFÜHRUNG AB 26. MAI IM
ROTENTURMKINO I.

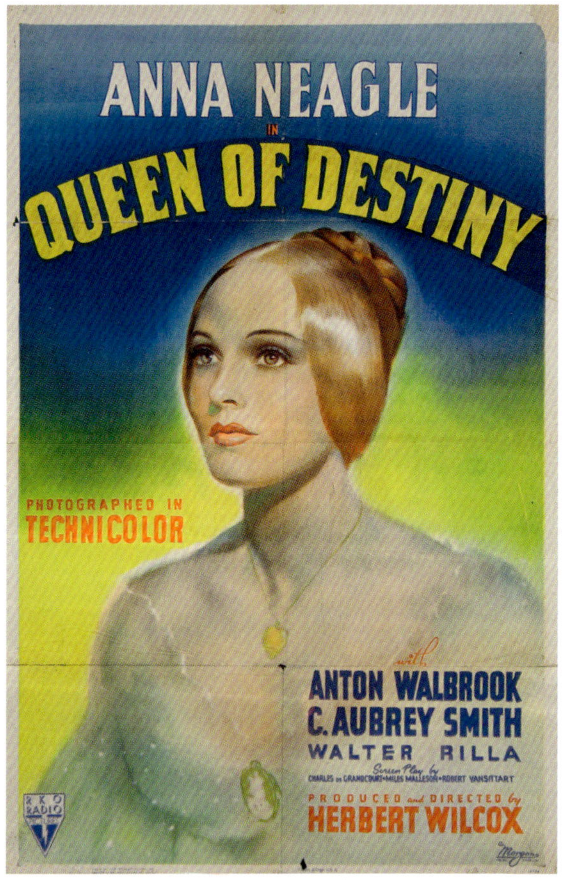
ANNA NEAGLE
IN
QUEEN OF DESTINY
PHOTOGRAPHED IN
TECHNICOLOR
with
ANTON WALBROOK
C. AUBREY SMITH
WALTER RILLA
PRODUCED and DIRECTED by
HERBERT WILCOX
RKO RADIO

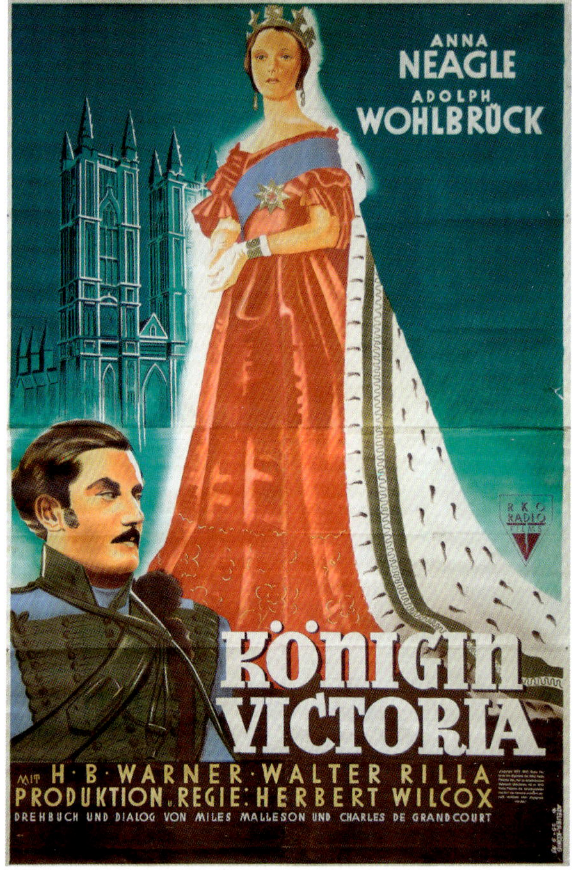
ANNA
NEAGLE
ADOLPH
WOHLBRÜCK
RKO RADIO
KÖNIGIN
VICTORIA
MIT H. B. WARNER · WALTER RILLA
PRODUKTION u. REGIE: HERBERT WILCOX
DREHBUCH UND DIALOG VON MILES MALLESON UND CHARLES DE GRANDCOURT

time at auctions is testimony to the scale of the task. A single production could require literally scores of designs. Many surviving examples of Doris's designs also have textile samples pinned to them, as she also had to hand-pick suitable fabrics, whilst being mindful of the cost too. Work had to be done to strict deadlines. Whilst designing costumes for the 1934 film *Nell Gwyn* Doris severely crushed and broke her pelvis in a riding accident; but to complete the commission she enlisted her sister, to whom Doris 'dictated' the designs, which Anna drew at her bedside in hospital. Doris could clearly always be relied upon to get the job done in one way or another. Doris's work for theatre was highly regarded and she found numerous opportunities to work on creations for the film sector.

Doris Zinkeisen's well-timed entrée into thespian circles during the interwar period synchronized with the emergence of a British film industry, which brought with it new and exciting possibilities. She went on to design costumes for at least eighteen films, chiefly during the 1930s, and in addition even provided the script for one of these, namely *The Blue Danube: A Rhapsody* [Appendix 1]. The majority of the films Doris worked on were for the film producer and director Herbert Wilcox (1892-1977).

The design of costumes for films brought with it some different challenges, remembering that the action was all captured at that time in black and white. In *The Morning Post* [12th December 1931] Doris mentions in an article she wrote the way in which she set about trying to put across to viewers in the medium of black and white film how the textiles appeared in real life: "All this involves the careful use of proportions of shades and the use of sharp contrasts. Material is matched against material, blacks against whites – and the exact proportion of blacks and whites has to be watched. Metals, too, are contrasted with dull surfaces, and so on." The films Doris Zinkeisen worked on were amongst the blockbusters of the 1930s [Appendix 1].

Doris Zinkeisen's role was not confined to costume design. Herbert Wilcox also gave Doris the task of providing the stars with makeovers, involving hair styling, use of make-up, speech and general deportment. For this reason, the 1930s press consulted Doris now and again on matters to do with fashion. What is more is that fashion is to be understood here in this context as a serious business. It was clearly understood at that time that the costumes could be a vital component of advertising and selling the film, remembering here that these films were in many instances translated and viewed in numerous countries. Doris's costume designs appeared in the

Opposite top left: Fig.1.48
Poster for the French language version of *The Blue Danube* (1932), a film for which Doris Zinkeisen created costumes and provided the storyline.

Opposite bottom left: Fig.1.50
Poster for the U.S. version of *Sixty Glorious Years* (1938), for which Doris Zinkeisen produced the costumes.

Opposite top right: Fig.1.49
Poster for the German language version of *The Blue Danube* (1932). See also Fig.1.48.

Opposite bottom right: Fig.1.51
Poster for the German language version of *Victoria the Great* (1937), another film Doris Zinkeisen designed the costumes for.

film advertisements on billboards and in magazines across the globe [Fig.1.48 – Fig.1.51]. Already in 1931 costumes designed by Doris for the stage were given additional economic significance when newspaper articles made big, if unsubstantiated, claims for their impact on stimulating parts of the flagging British textile trade. The point about encouraging a part of the manufacturing sector poignantly brings to mind the Great Depression of the late 1920s and 1930s.

When discussing theatrical costumes it is all too easy to forget the interwar period witnessed not just new opportunities, an increase in self-expression and consumer goods, and much decadence, but was also a time of disillusionment and hardship for many. The Great Depression resulted in a huge increase in unemployment and despair for millions. Whilst demand for many goods declined and there was contraction of production and bankruptcies amongst traditional businesses, the burgeoning film sector appeared to buck this trend and witnessed an increase in demand and thrived.

The flicks, or talkies were attracting audiences by the million. Filmgoers packed out the swish new picture palaces. Reasons for this social phenomenon are complex. There was perhaps an eagerness for some much needed escapism from the economic problems of the Great Depression and the menacing political tensions, which were brewing across the globe. Many, of course, were still reeling from the

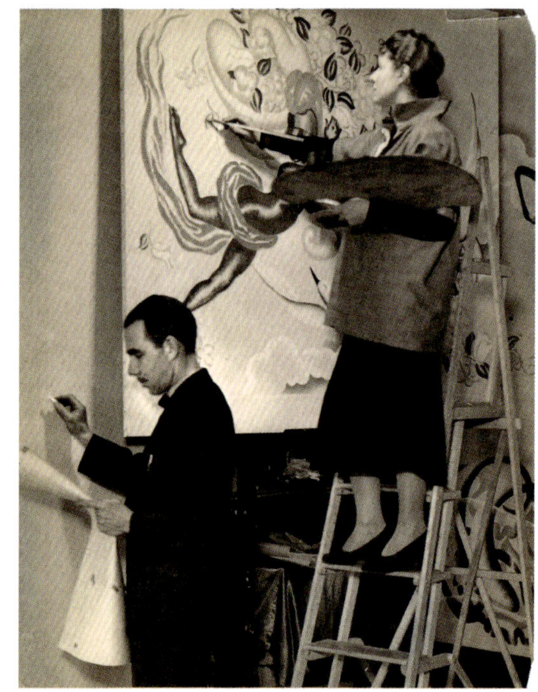

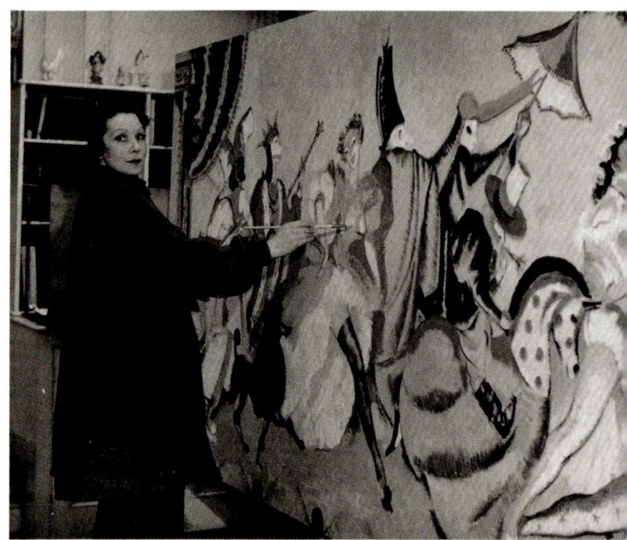

Top: Fig.1.52
Anna Zinkeisen and an assistant working on one of her murals for the *Queen Mary* ocean liner.

Above: Fig.1.53
Doris Zinkeisen in her London studio in the early 1930s at work on one of her murals for the Verandah Grill on the *Queen Mary*, as photographed by Harry Todd.

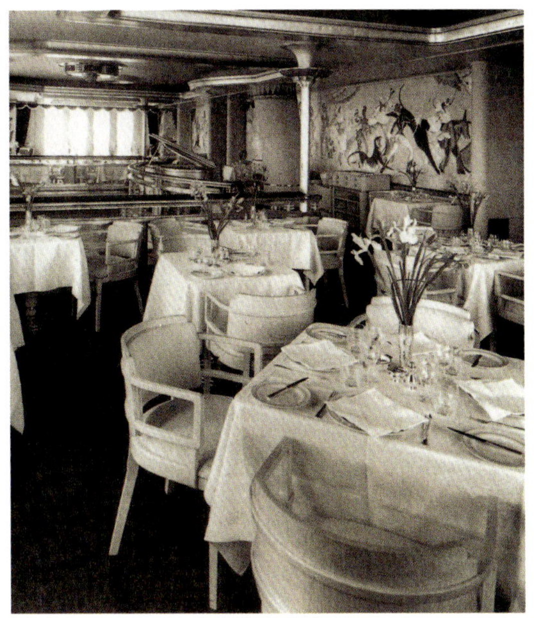

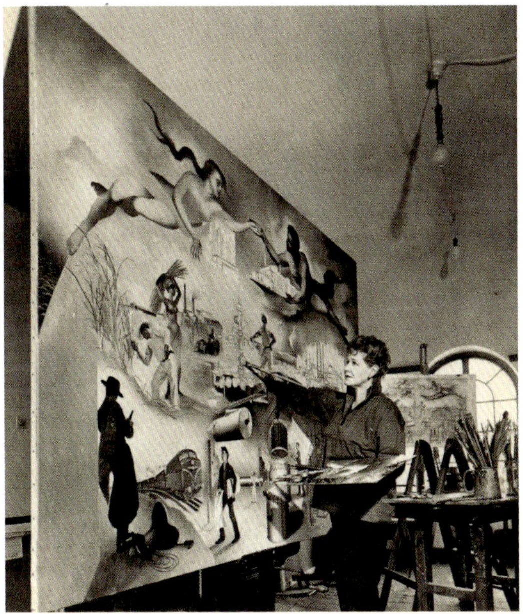

social and economic aftershocks of the First World War. Above all the cinema was able to cater for the public's need for reasonably priced entertainment to match both the purchasing power of consumers and their taste for a sense of glamour. Doris Zinkeisen's often lavish costumes can be seen in this context as her artistic contribution towards a panacea for a dispirited world once again about to enter into war. Interestingly, amongst the most prestigious assignments both of the Zinkeisen sisters were awarded was the opportunity to create huge murals for *R.M.S. Queen Mary* [Fig.1.52 – Fig.1.54; Fig.3.41].

In 1929 there was mass unemployment in shipbuilding and government subsidies were poured into projects like the *Queen Mary* to stimulate employment and trade. A feat of engineering, the *Queen Mary* was the world's biggest and fastest ocean liner and became a byword for luxury and streamlined refinement. In addition to ameliorating the economic despair felt by the shipbuilding sector in Clydebank, incidentally not far as the crow flies from where the Zinkeisen sisters were born, the vessel was intended to showcase the best of what Britain had to offer the wider world. The murals painted by the sisters for the *Queen Mary* were part of an ongoing floating art exhibition and included work by Vanessa Bell (1879-1961), Laura Knight, and Edward Wadsworth (1889-1949). Anna would go on to produce many more such large scale murals, including a ceiling at the Russell-Cotes

Top: Fig.1.54
General view from 1936 of the Verandah Grill on the *Queen Mary* with Doris Zinkeisen's mural in the background.

Left below: Fig.1.55
Anna Zinkeisen worked on large-scale murals throughout her career, as here in the 1950s.

Museum in Bournemouth, amongst others [Fig.1.55]. Doris's main mural was entitled *Entertainment*, a colourful and cheerful painting with a cheekily overt reference to her prominent work in show business [Fig.1.56]. Indeed the glamour of the entertainments sector can also be detected in the portraits produced by both of the Zinkeisen sisters.

Portraiture

Doris and Anna Zinkeisen painted many portraits during their careers. To this artistic category the sisters brought their very own idiosyncratic sense of panache. Posters bearing their names and hung in public places, magazine advertisements, the exceptionally wide press coverage relating to their designs for *R.M.S. Queen Mary* all generated further interest in the Zinkeisen sisters. This was assisted by Doris's association with the entertainments business. The seemingly trivial minutiae of their lives were deemed newsworthy.

One article gave its readers tips about Anna's lifestyle and her opinions on make-up. She "rides and hunts for pure pleasure"; and: "Using make-up has become second nature to her – even when working in overall and slacks or relaxing in the country she would feel slovenly without a complete, if simple, make-up." Both sisters were mad keen on riding and noted horsewomen, Doris winning numerous cups in competitions. *The Morning Post* described Doris as, "one of the best-dressed women of today" [13th June 1930]; whilst *The Overseas Daily Mail* informed us that: "Miss Zinkeisen is one of the fortunate women who retain a perfect figure without taking the least trouble about her diet. Her daily breakfast of bacon and egg, and coffee with cream, her love of all rich foods, and her habit of drinking half a pint of cream a day while on holiday, make less lucky women sigh with envy. Riding is her only form of exercise and she goes down into the country as often as possible for week-ends during the hunting season" [13th August 1932].

The foregoing quotations give a flavour of how the lifestyles enjoyed by the Zinkeisen sisters were reported. In truth both sisters worked extremely hard to fund this way of life, as it did not come cheap. The sisters themselves were not especially interested in such tittle-tattle, but they had entered into

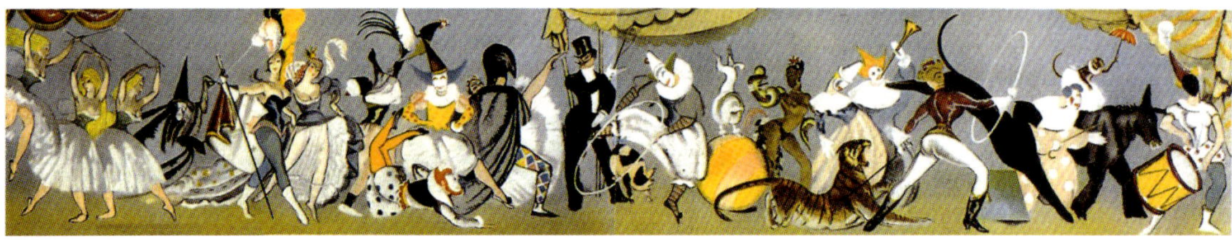

Above: Fig.1.56
Doris Zinkeisen's main mural for the *Queen Mary* was entitled *Entertainment* and directly relates to her work as a costume designer for theatre and film.

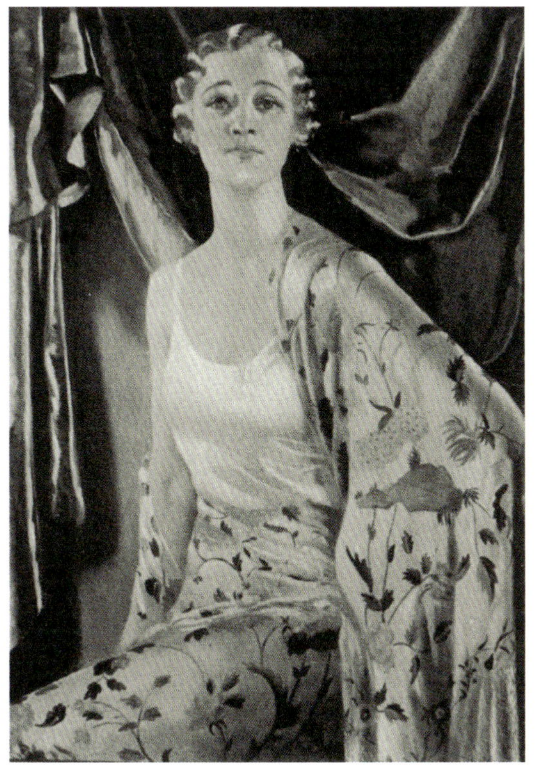

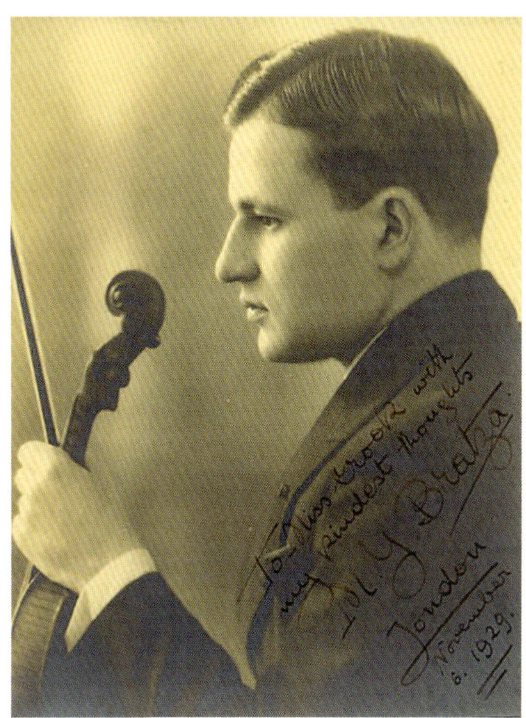

a kind of pact with the press, who gave them exposure, which, in turn, had the potential to lead to further commissions, including those for portraits.

The Zinkeisen sisters were in demand for their work as portraitists. Whenever and wherever they exhibited their stylish likenesses they were well received and were especially popular in the interwar era. These portraits were sometimes of the famous people of their day. For example Anna Zinkeisen captured likenesses of the actress Ursula Jeans (1906-1973) [Fig.1.57] and the virtuoso Serbian violinist Milan Yovanovitch Bratza (1904-1964) [Fig.1.58; Fig.3.28]. Doris Zinkeisen painted portraits of Elsa Lanchester [Fig.1.59; Fig.3.6], Anna Neagle [Fig.1.60], and the ragtime piano player Edythe Baker (c.1899-1971) [Fig.1.61 – Fig.1.62; Fig.3.8]. Doris also painted the director James Whale (1889-1957) [Fig.1.63 – Fig.1.64], who had been her fiancé in the early 1920s before he left for Hollywood, where he directed the 1930s cult classics *Frankenstein*, *The Invisible Man*,

Above: Fig.1.57
Anna Zinkeisen, *Ursula Jeans*, 1931, oil on canvas. Exhibited at the Royal Academy and Paris Salon. Ursula Jeans was a stage and film actress, who appeared in over thirty films between 1922 and 1965.
© Photograph courtesy of Julia Heseltine.

Above: Fig.1.58
Photograph of the Serbian born violinist Milan Yovanovitch Bratza. Bratza and Anna Zinkeisen formed a friendly bond and in his diaries he relates how he had to play to her during his sittings for his portrait to help inspire her. See also Fig.3.28.
© Private collection.

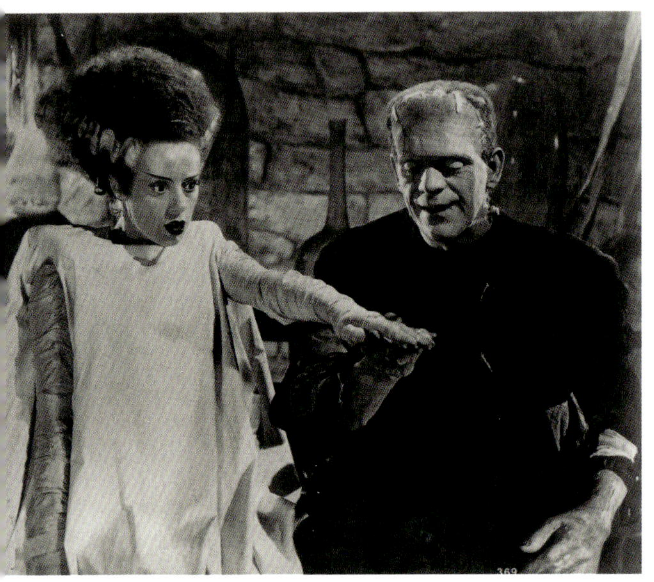

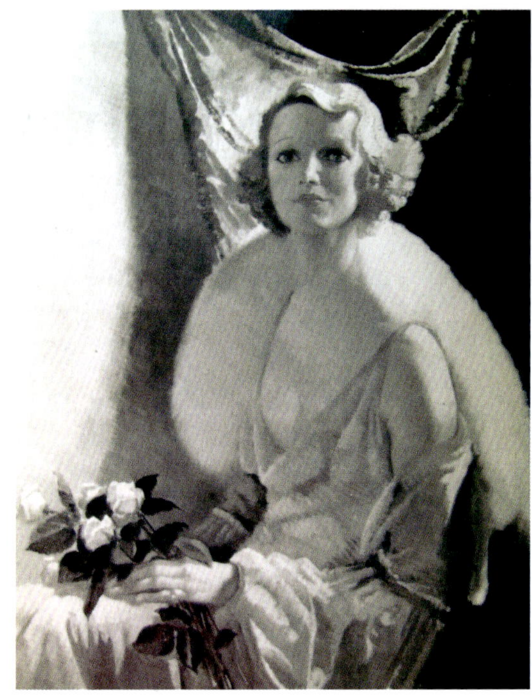

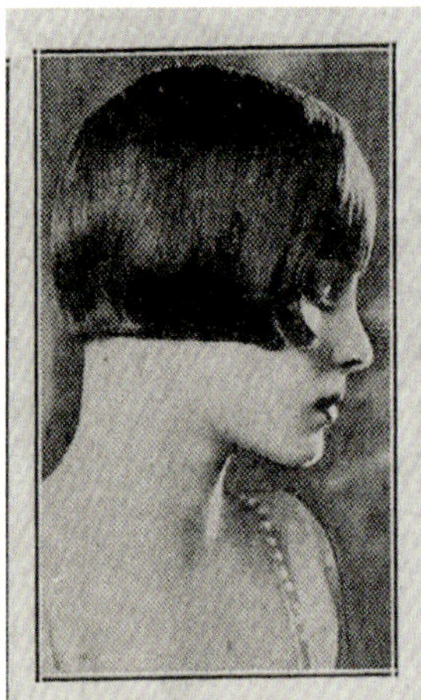

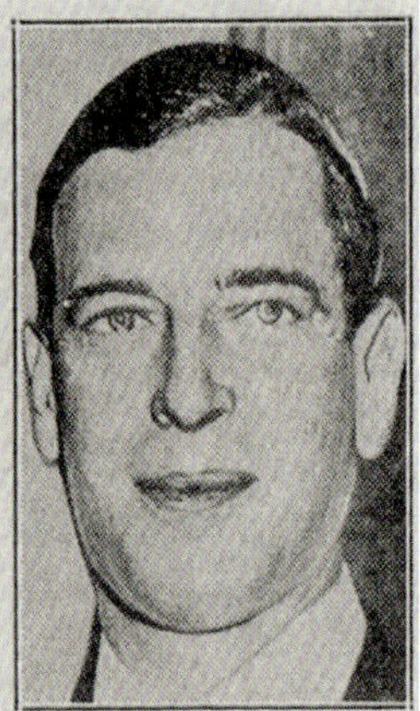

ACTIVE DUKE—Staid Londoners barely recovering from the romance of Edward and Mrs. Simpson were shocked recently when a British magazine gave two pages to the public appearance of the Duke of Kent, right, with two women, while his wife, the former Princess Marina of Greece, was at home awaiting the birth of a child. One of the women was identified as the svelte stage pianist, Edythe Baker, left, formerly of Kansas City, estranged wife of Gerard d'Erlanger, son of the British banker, Baron d'Erlanger.

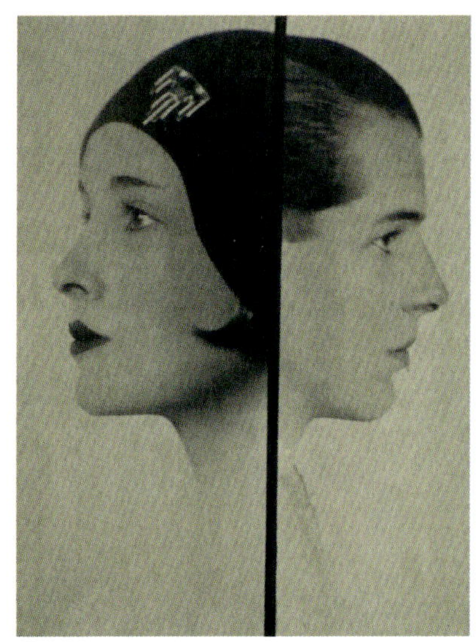

Top left: Fig.1.59
Elsa Lanchester (left) in her most famous role here paired off with the monster played by Boris Karloff in *The Bride of Frankenstein* (1935), a film directed by Doris Zinkeisen's former fiancé James Whale. Doris first met Whale and Lanchester in the early 1920s. See also Fig.3.6.

Top right: Fig.1.60
Doris Zinkeisen, *Anna Neagle*, *circa* 1932, oil on canvas.

Below left: Fig.1.61
Edythe Baker was a famous ragtime piano player, who became embroiled in scandal, as in this newspaper clipping.

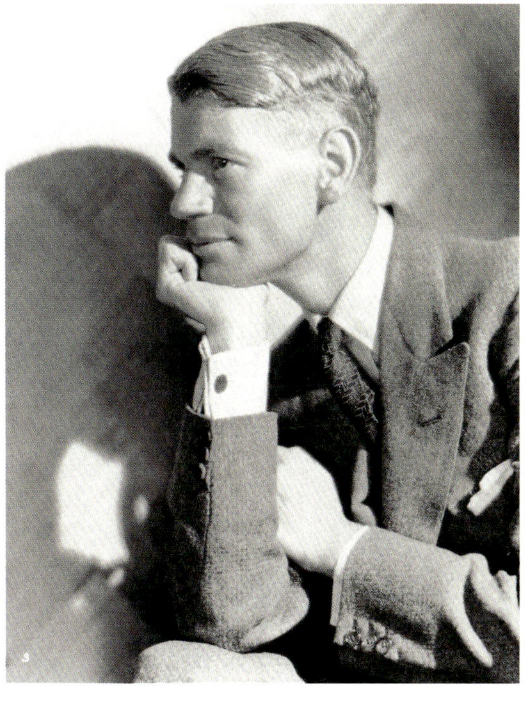

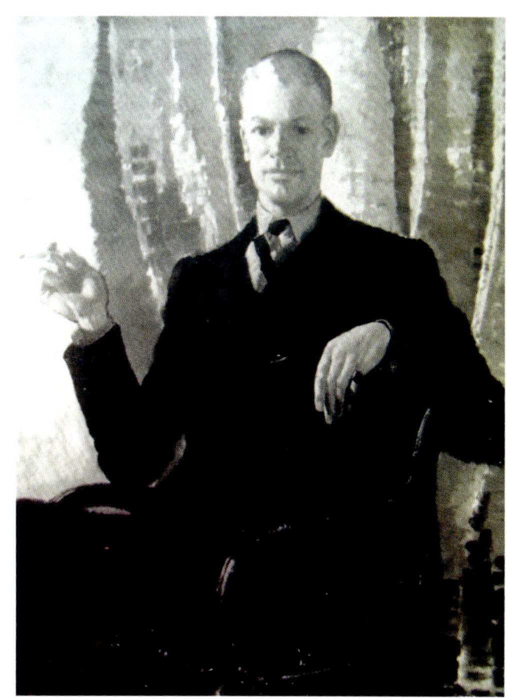

and *The Bride of Frankenstein*. Sadly, Doris was widowed whilst still young. Her husband died unexpectedly in 1946 from a tropical disease, caught on a business trip to Africa for a tobacco company. She never remarried, although she discovered there was no shortage of potential suitors.

After the death of her husband, Doris Zinkeisen had a friendship with a Harley Street Ear, Nose and Throat Surgeon named Michael Simon Horowitz (born *c.* 1898), a Polish émigré naturalized in 1947, but he later married the actress Faith Brook (1922-2012). The surgeon Geoffrey Parker (1902-1973), well-known for his book *The Black Scalpel* (1968), became very much a part of Doris's life and the wider Zinkeisen family, but did not become permanent. Then there was the handsome Oscar-winning actor Ray Milland (1907-1986), always fondly referred to as Spike, who is likewise said to be an old flame [Fig.1.65]. Doris was also propositioned by the émigré Russian choreographer and dancer Léonide Massine

Opposite below right: Fig.1.62
A clipping from a glossy magazine of Edythe Baker, here with Gérard d'Erlanger, the son of a wealthy aristocratic banker. Their marriage in 1928 was a press sensation, the media suggesting she had a predatory nature, pointing out Edythe was six years older than her husband, and that she was disapproved of by her father-in-law. See also Fig.3.8.

Above left: Fig.1.63
Publicity photograph from 1936 of Hollywood director James Whale, who was Doris Zinkeisen's fiancé in the early 1920s. Although Doris broke off the engagement with Whalebone (as she called him), probably sensing he was more attracted to men, the pair remained lifelong friends.

Above right: Fig.1.64
Doris Zinkeisen, *James Whale*, 1936, oil on canvas.

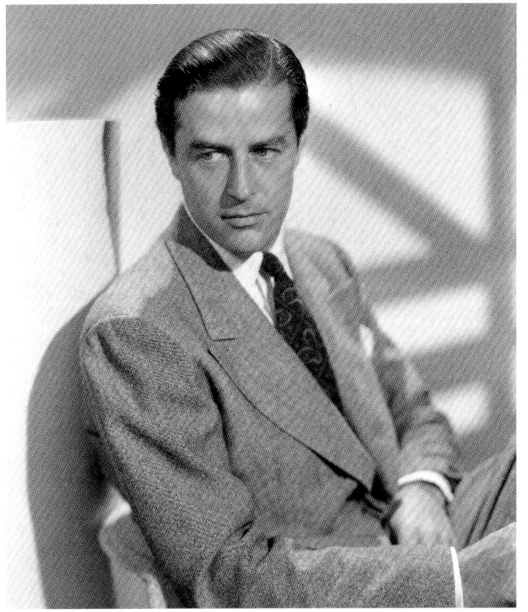

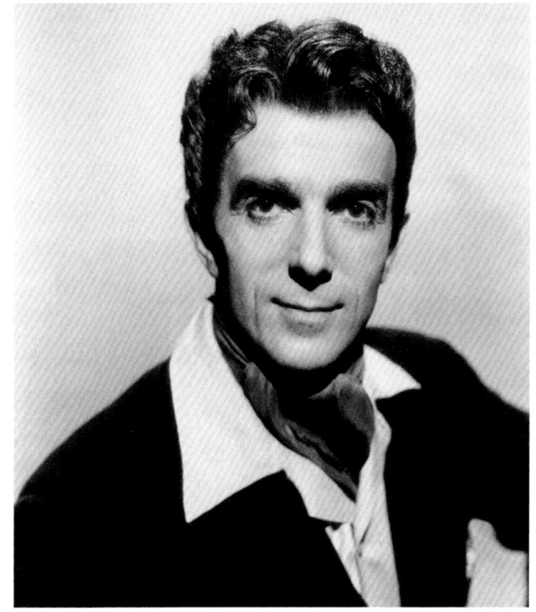

(1896-1979). She first encountered Massine when they both worked on Coward's and Cochran's revue *On with the Dance* in 1925. Both worked on the film *The Blue Danube* in 1932 and their paths crossed again when they had a professional involvement with Mona Inglesby's International Ballet touring company. Massine was, however, notorious for his numerous love affairs and although good-looking he was not, as Doris herself said, her "cup of tea", so she declined his advances [Fig.1.66]. The Zinkeisen sisters certainly moved amongst the "beautiful people" and had to deal with their mores.

Doris Zinkeisen did not paint and exhibit portraits to the same extent as in her earlier career after the Second World War, whereas it became the backbone of Anna's output. Portraiture evolved to become Anna's chief post-war artistic activity, although flower painting occupied much of her time too [Fig.1.67]. Anna's reputation as an important painter of flowers was sealed after she painted Her Majesty Queen Elizabeth II's "Coronation Bouquet", the symbolic flower arrangement Her Majesty The Queen carried at Her coronation service at Westminster Abbey in 1953 [Fig.1.68; Fig.3.88]. Anna's

Above: Fig.1.65
The actor Ray Milland was said to be an old flame of Doris Zinkeisen, who referred to him as Spike, in the years following her husband's death.
© Private collection.

Above: Fig.1.66
The legendary choreographer and dancer Léonide Massine was a notorious womanizer, who (unsuccessfully) propositioned Doris Zinkeisen. She remarked he was not her 'cup of tea' in that particular context, but worked harmoniously alongside him in several productions.
© Everett Collection Inc./Alamy Stock Photo [2ABEHD5].

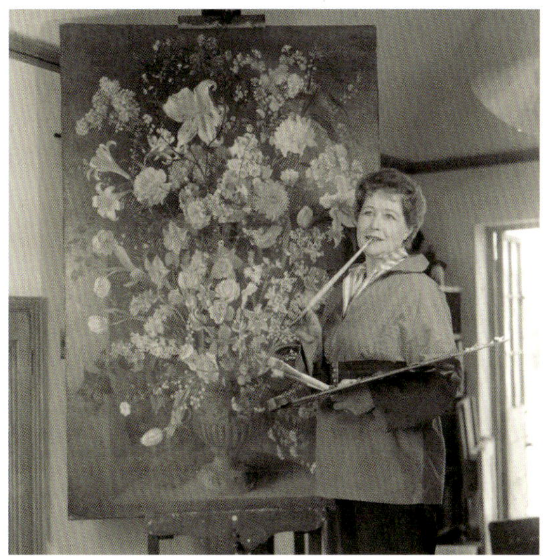

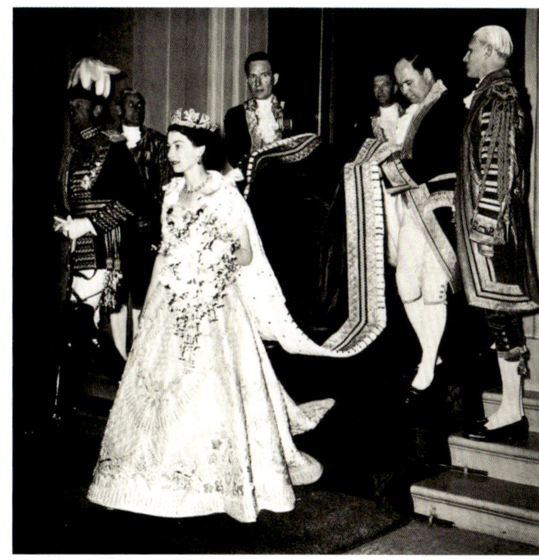

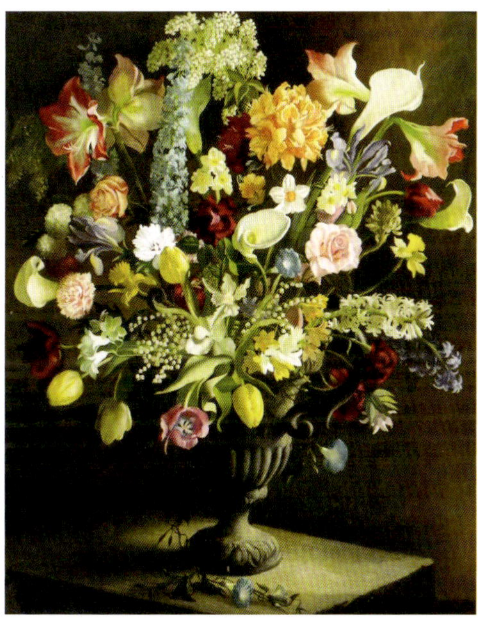

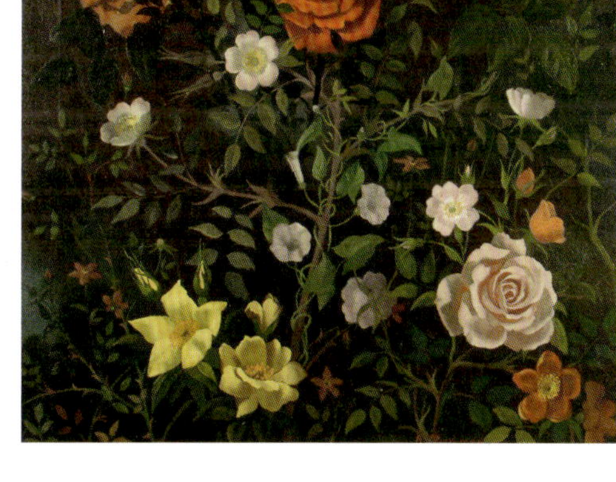

Top left: Fig.1.67
Anna Zinkeisen became an acclaimed painter of flower pieces, here snapped before one of her paintings in 1959.

Below left: Fig.1.69
An example of Anna Zinkeisen's early formal style of painting flower pieces from the 1940s.

Top right: Fig.1.68
Queen Elizabeth II on Her way to Her Coronation in 1953 holding the symbolic flower arrangement Anna Zinkeisen would famously later paint. See also Fig.3.88.

Below right: Fig.1.70
After Anna Zinkeisen's move to Suffolk in the mid-1960s her flower pieces became increasingly loose in relation to how they were arranged.

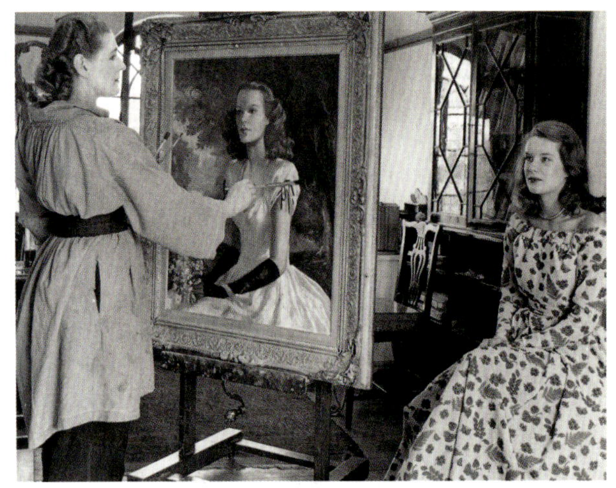
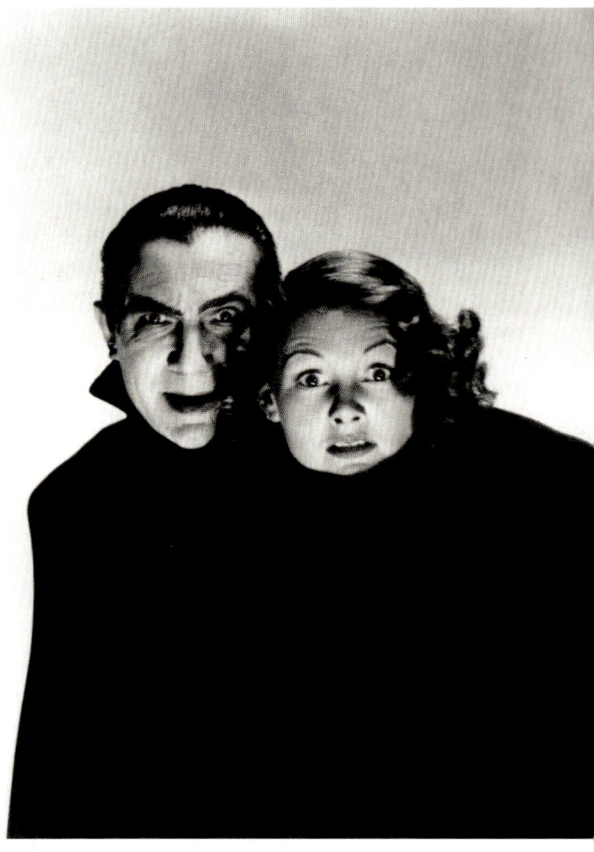
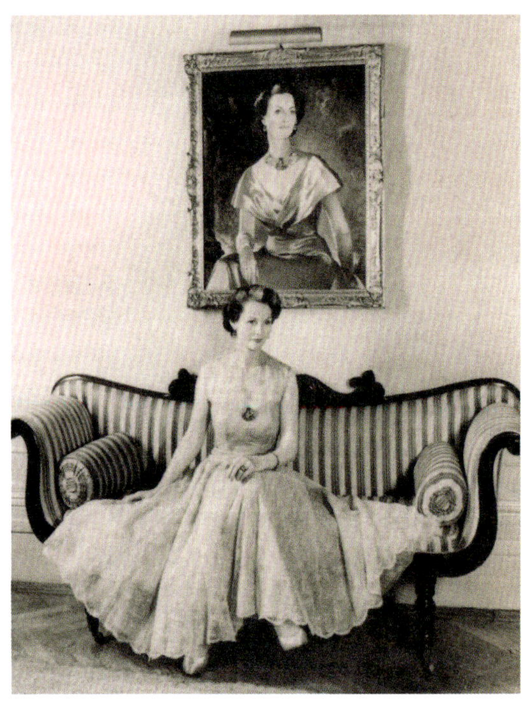
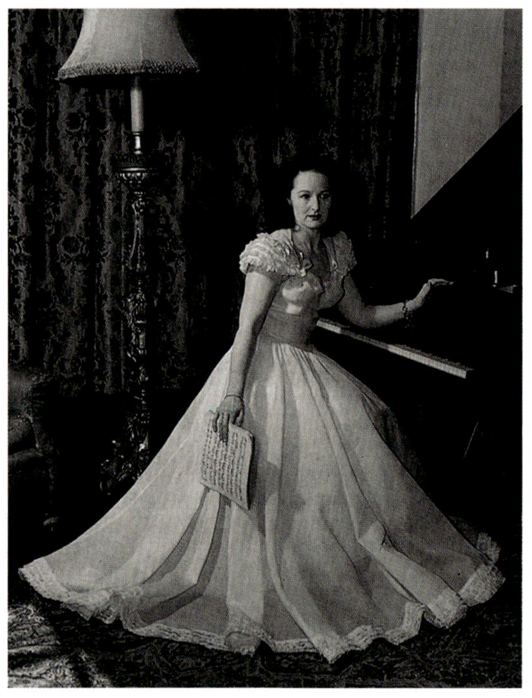

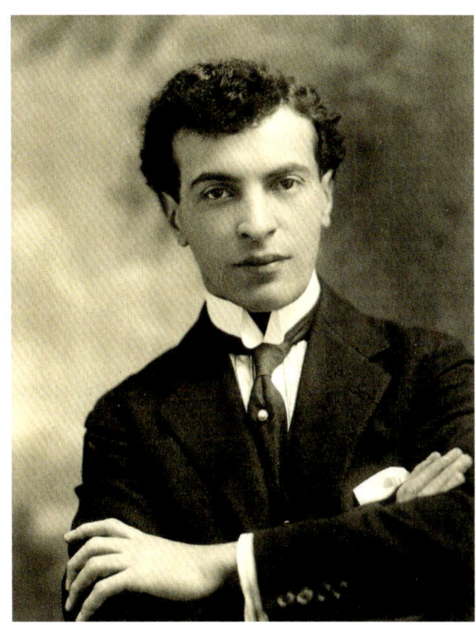

Opposite top left: Fig.1.71
Anna Zinkeisen painting the actress Sally Ann Howes, whose father, the entertainer Bobby Howes (1895-1972), was an acquaintance of Anna's and her husband. See also Fig.3.83.

Opposite top right: Fig.1.72
The actress Elizabeth Allan was a friend of Anna Zinkeisen. Allan is chiefly known today for her role opposite Bela Lugosi's much imitated interpretation of Dracula in *Mark of the Vampire* (1935).

Opposite bottom left: Fig.1.73
Elizabeth Allan seated in front of her portrait by Anna Zinkeisen, *circa* 1950s. See also Fig.3.85.

Opposite bottom right: Fig.1.74
The famous pianist Eileen Joyce always wore beautiful gowns when playing concertos and recitals. See also Fig.3.86.

Above: Fig.1.75
Benno Moiseiwitsch was widely appreciated for his interpretations of the Romantic composers and was known to both of the Zinkeisen sisters.

early flower pieces tend to be formal, whilst after she moved to Suffolk in the mid-1960s the arrangements become increasingly looser [Fig.1.69 – Fig.1.70]. The accuracy of these flower paintings means we can consider them to be a form of portraiture, insomuch as they capture likenesses.

Occasionally Anna incorporated props, including flowers, into her portraits. Anna continued to paint famous thespians and musicians after World War II. There are portraits of the popular 1940s film and stage actress Rosamund John (1913-1998) [Fig.3.84]; musical star of stage and screen Sally Ann Howes (b.1930) [Fig.1.71; Fig.3.83]; Hollywood screen goddess Elizabeth Allan (1910-1990) [Fig.1.72 – Fig.1.73; Fig.3.85]; as well as the legendary classical pianist Eileen Joyce (1908-1991) [Fig.1.74; Fig.3.86]. Incidentally, Anna also produced the illustrations for the best-selling imaginative book about Eileen Joyce's early life *Prelude* (1947) by Clare Hoskyns Abrahall (1900-1990), which was also turned into a film.

There is a tangible sense that musicians feature heavily in the social networks of the Zinkeisen sisters. In fact it would not have been unusual, for example, to find the great pianist Benno Moiseiwitsch (1890-1963), an émigré born in Odessa naturalised in 1937, playing piano in either of the sisters' homes [Fig.1.75]. Already in the years growing up in Pinner the Zinkeisen family appear to have come into the orbit of the composer and baritone singer Frederic Austin (1872-1952), best remembered today for his 1909 version of the Christmas carol *The Twelve Days of Christmas* [Fig.1.76]. Austin's arrangement, edited by Arnold Bennett (1867-1931), of *The Beggar's Opera* (1728) by John Gay (1685-1732) was produced by Nigel Playfair in 1920 and was hugely successful. It could well have been this family connection, which assisted in putting Doris on Playfair's radar. Doris would produce a poster for *Polly*, the sequel to Gay's ballad opera already mentioned, when it was produced in 1923; and create sets and costumes for Playfair's musical production of *The Way of the World* (1700) by the dramatist William Congreve (1670-1729), which was again composed and arranged by Austin in 1924. It is precisely because the Zinkeisen sisters were very much at home in London's artistic élite that they had access to opportunities to paint likenesses of the talented and famous, who felt unthreatened and equally at ease in their company too. The sisters used this privilege to their advantage and the public's curiosity surrounding their portraits perhaps provided them with an edge over some other artists and tacitly encouraged wealthy and aristocratic clients to loosen their purse strings and commission portraits from them. Living in a smart part of London by Regent's Park, Doris at 6 Chester Terrace and Anna a stone's throw away at 8 St Andrew's Place, would also have made their clients feel at home.

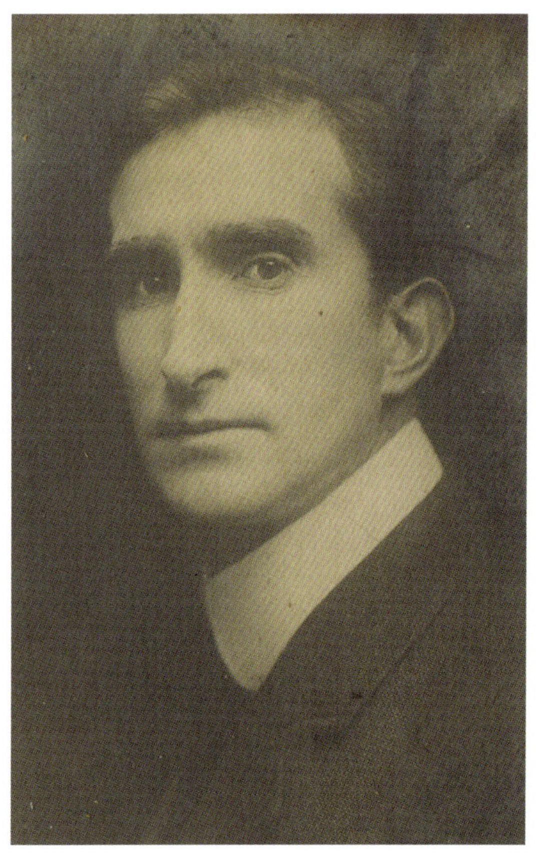

Above: Fig.1.76
The composer and baritone singer Frederic Austin was an old family friend of the Zinkeisen family. Austin's version of *The Twelve Days of Christmas* remains popular today.

Notes on Style and Subject Matter

The early portraits by the Zinkeisen sisters are noteworthy, not just for their sitters, but for their artistic flair and sophistication. An analogy can be drawn between the style of these portraits and jazz music. Just as jazz drew promiscuously upon many musical styles, so we see in the portraits of the Zinkeisen sisters an inclination towards what might be dubbed 'jazzy' characteristics in their compositions. The Zinkeisens often give their sitters unusual, showy poses inspired in an eclectic manner by medieval and ancient Egyptian art, as well as portraiture of the seventeenth and eighteenth centuries.

Colours are sometimes chosen by the sisters precisely because they jar with other colour tones on the canvas. They used this technique to strike the viewer's eye and create visual interest in a similar way to how the improvisation and syncopated rhythms (amongst other techniques) used by individual jazz musicians generates aural pleasure and maybe surprise. Their sitters exude urbanity. There are seldom shrinking violets or wallflowers here. Viewed collectively it can be difficult to tell the society beauties apart from the genuine stars of stage and film in the portraits by the Zinkeisen sisters. This is likely to be an important part of what some sitters were looking for. In fact there are instances where sitters wear garments designed by Doris [Fig.3.8; Fig.3.27]. So it can be said that portraits by the Zinkeisens encapsulate the extrovert nature of their generation.

On the whole the portraits, posters, and illustrations by the Zinkeisen sisters tend to be forthrightly figurative and represent people and things as they appear in real life. Anna's early flower paintings are clearly inspired by Dutch and Flemish flower pieces of the seventeenth and eighteenth centuries. Compared today with the work of an artist like Georgia O'Keeffe (1887-1986), whose strikingly individualistic close-up style of painting flowers has in the meantime become widely known and much emulated, Anna's flower pieces appear conventional. Over a period of many decades, however, Anna continued to find inspiration in the myriad of shapes, colours, and textures offered by nature. In these flower paintings Anna not only showed off her dazzling technical skills in observation and painting, but hoped to rouse the senses of viewers to what she found so compelling. Anna also wrote in an article for the *Nursing Mirror* [12th May 1950], recalling here that she had much experience as an auxiliary nurse, that flower paintings (amongst other subjects) could make excellent decorations for hospital walls; as they could be subconsciously restful and provide much needed distraction. Placed in this context, and maybe more generally too, Anna's flower paintings assume a profound psychological significance. This is a manifestly different and quite divergent aim from her boldly surrealist style paintings.

Both Doris and Anna painted a number of surrealistic pictures in the 1940s [Fig.3.66 – Fig.3.74]. In these works the sisters continue to use conventional painting techniques, but to create dream-like imagery. In some of them unexpected objects are found placed in incongruous settings. These paintings are fascinating to find in the oeuvres of the Zinkeisen sisters and it is a shame neither opted to allow such ingenuity to permeate their other work. We are left to imagine for ourselves what a Doris Zinkeisen stage set, or Anna Zinkeisen portrait might have looked like if influenced by surrealism. Most interestingly all their surrealist paintings were produced as commissions from industry to be ultimately used for posters and magazine advertisements. To date it is not clear whether they chose this style themselves, or if it was a requirement set out by the terms of their engagement. Whatever the case may be, these paintings demonstrate much flair and a willingness to experiment and actively engage in a different style of painting from their habitual one at a time of prolific avant-gardism.

The Zinkeisen sisters chose not to persevere with their foray into a more experimental mode of expression and returned to their traditional approach, although they continued to exercise their powers of imagination to the full. Their emphasis after the Second World War was on clean draughtsmanship, colour, and form. Anna is quoted in the *Toronto Globe* [19th April 1951] as saying: "It does not matter whether art be conservative or radical if it is sincere and if the artist's talent be large enough." Her manifesto here is reassuringly broad and suited her era. The Zinkeisens lived in an age of remarkable creativity. The flourishing artistic experimentalism in twentieth-century Britain produced a vast array of art to cater for every conceivable taste, at times decorative, at others conceptually complex, or both together; and the Zinkeisens formulated their own distinctive style.

Whilst Anna Zinkeisen focused on portraits and flowers after the Second World War, Doris turned her attention increasingly to painting romantic scenes and those centred on history [Fig.3.91 – Fig.3.94]. After moving to Suffolk in 1966 to be closer to her sister, who already had a home there [Fig.2.2], every so often Doris also found inspiration in stories concerning Suffolk history [Fig.3.100]. Anna also produced such paintings, but it became the mainstay of Doris's artistic output. These idealized evocations can be suggestive of bygone periods with a focus on Regency, *fin-de-siècle*, and Edwardian elegance with occasional Rococo influences. Their content sometimes overlaps with that found in the work of Raoul Dufy (1877-1953), or the story-telling aspect of those faux-naïve costumed matchstick characters populating the paintings of Helen Bradley (1900-1979). Doris mines her knowledge of horses for scenes of carriages and her experience of designing for the stage for paintings of dancers [Fig.3.78

– Fig.3.82]. In fact these later paintings are extremely closely linked to all those costume dramas she worked on. Doris's work for the entertainments sector was vital to her so it is not surprising to find it reflected in her art and she even named her horses and dogs after productions she had worked on, for example: her grey horse is named Quaker Girl after a musical; whilst Comus the spaniel is named after a ballet.

In numerous later paintings Doris Zinkeisen creates a world of glamour. This is most evident in the triple portrait purchased for the Ipswich Borough collections [Fig.2.1]. The sitters of the Christchurch Museum portrait by Doris rarely dressed like debutantes in such finery. So what we are seeing is a particular kind of fantasy. This art can be regarded as a reaction against modernist abstraction and other contemporary trends, such as the expressionist 'Kitchen Sink' realist school of the 1950s. So in an inverted way Doris was actually commenting on post-war art.

The avoidance of disturbing content and focus on producing a decorative effect in vivid colours became Doris Zinkeisen's stock-in-trade and was well received. In 1954 the critic and editor G. S. Whittet gave Doris's work a glowing write up in *The Studio* [No.148]:

"At the Fine Art Society Recent Paintings by Doris Zinkeisen provided a gaiety and charm that is absent from many exhibitions nowadays. Flower pieces, scenes of social life at the races, in the café, dancers dressing, actors on the stage (one of Doris Zinkeisen's recent commissions was the décor of the Noël Coward musical show *After the Ball*) all of these in bright colour and deft handling provided a degree of decorative impressionism that made them highly desirable 'props' for a domestic setting. One might wish that more artists would paint for the lounge instead of the cellar."

Doris continued to paint in this vein for the rest of her life only setting aside her brushes a few days before she passed away [Fig.1.77]. As her eyesight deteriorated, so too did her brushwork. Later paintings remain characteristically decorative, but the precision

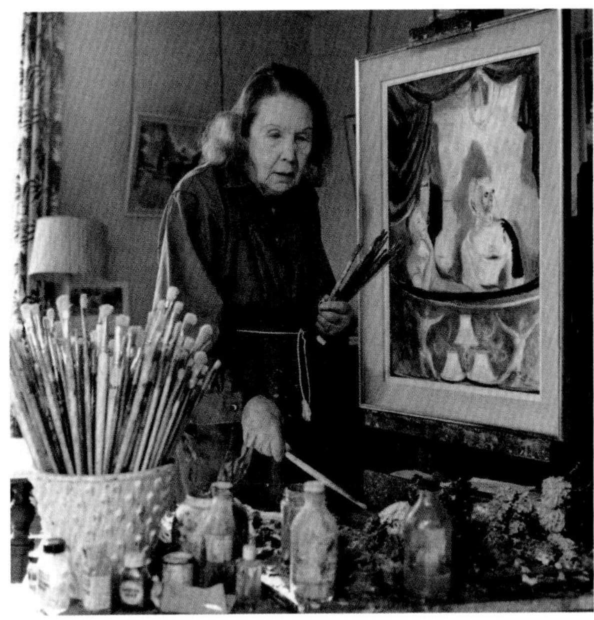

Above: Fig.1.77
Here the photographer Lucinda Douglas-Menzies has captured Doris Zinkeisen working in her studio in 1990 less than a year before she passed away.

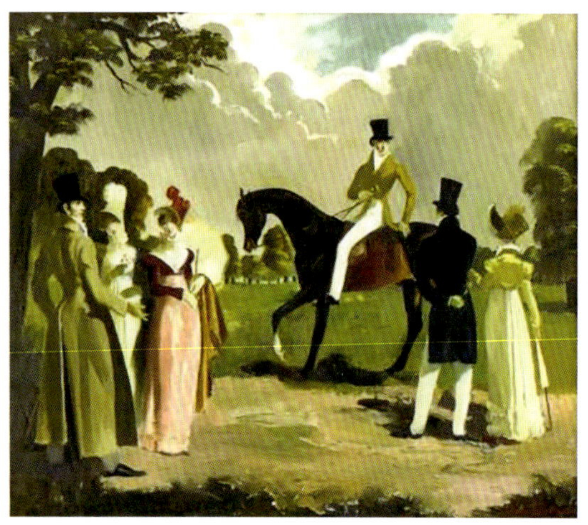

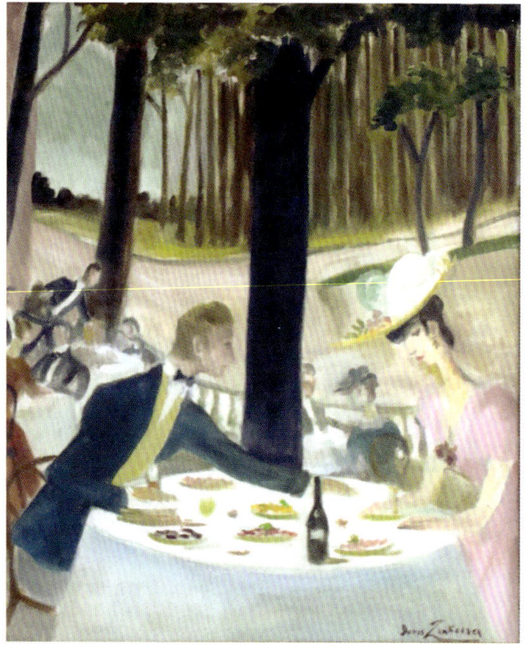

of her earlier compositions is understandably absent [Fig.1.78 – Fig.1.79]. Because Doris rarely dated her paintings, this increasing looseness in her handling of paint is the only clue as to when a particular picture might have been produced. Here again, however, it is impossible to be precise about dates.

Anna Zinkeisen also hardly ever dated her canvases. In the absence of other evidence, such as an invoice, a picture in a magazine, a title in an exhibition catalogue, it remains a highly speculative venture to cite specific dates in relation to individual works. Signatures help here a little. Early signatures from the 1920s by Anna tend to be more elongated than thereafter [Fig.3.2]; whilst the earliest signatures of Doris tend to be more angular than those from the 1920s onwards [Fig.1.81 – Fig.1.83]. At least two early works survive by Doris with monograms [Fig.1.80; Fig.3.1]. Both sisters tended to use red or black to sign their oil paintings. Doris produced literally thousands of costume designs and most of these are unsigned. These were not usually done on the finest quality paper, as they were work in progress. Pinholes from when attached to Doris's drawing board or the costume makers' workshop walls are usually clearly visible. Many costume designs show the signs of rough treatment, such as folds. During the Second World War an incendiary bomb fell on Doris's home in London. Hundreds of

Above: Fig.1.78
Doris Zinkeisen, *The Morning Stroll*, 1949, oil on canvas. There is a great deal of detail and precision in this painting when compared to Fig.1.79.
© Nigel Castell-Reepham Antiques/Nicholas Wells-Nicholas Wells Antiques.

Above: Fig.1.79
Doris Zinkeisen, *Café Rendezvous*, *circa* 1985, oil on canvas. Doris's later paintings remain superbly decorative, but her brushwork becomes looser as is the level of 'accuracy' (note the elongated necks). These clues can assist in deciding whether a painting is early or late, given that they were rarely dated. See also Fig.1.78.
© Private collection.

costume designs were saved from the fire, but bear the scars of war for they suffered water damage. Others show signs of foxing, that is they have brownish spots of discolouration. If you find a costume design in mint condition it might just be too good to be true.

In recent years several suspect paintings have passed through the auction rooms. One to do the rounds is an oil painting after a work by the doyenne of Art Deco, Tamara de Lempicka (1898-1980), to which someone has added Doris Zinkeisen's signature. Several paintings have surfaced on the art market with the label 'in the manner of' either Doris or Anna Zinkeisen attached to them, but these vague attributions should be taken with a pinch of salt. One or two have decidedly dodgy, or tampered with signatures. A local legend in the area where the Zinkeisen sisters were born in Scotland has it that some small ceiling paintings in a church there are by them, but they are unlikely to be in the hand of either of the sisters on stylistic grounds and in the absence of supporting documentation. Further examples of paintings are marketed as 'in pristine condition', but have in actual fact undergone extensive restoration.

Both conservation (involving preservation and repair) and restoration (which includes renovating and retouching) can be necessary and positive courses of action, particularly if it rescues a painting from oblivion and provided it is done sympathetically. However, there does need to be honesty from the art market and acceptance from collectors around this issue. There is added confusion caused by some prints. It would seem that particularly during the 1950s numerous print runs were made of Zinkeisen paintings. Most of these are easily identifiable as prints, but some were oleographs, which are a specific type of lithograph commonly using a canvas support to imitate oil paintings. This particular form of print can even have quite realistic textured surfaces emulating impasto, where the thick application of paint stands out from the surface, surprisingly well. The uninitiated often insist these are 'original' paintings. If buying a Zinkeisen do be sure to use a reputable dealer with a track record and preferably with membership of LAPADA or BADA, the associations helping to maintain high standards in the art and antiques market.

Conclusion

Some questions simply remain a mystery. How is it possible that the Zinkeisen sisters, who were so famous and popular in their own lifetimes, could sink into obscurity and find their work out of the limelight? This connects with a broader debate as to why there are hardly any women artists with established places in the canon of art history, let alone a part of national consciousness, in the mode of John Constable (1776-1837), or Thomas Gainsborough (1727-1788). Whatever the reasons, it remains certain that the work of the

Zinkeisen sisters is amongst the more stylish of what twentieth-century British art has to offer, particularly their paintings and designs from the 1920s through to the 1950s: indeed, much of their work visually captures this zeitgeist as infallibly as the written word does in those sharp, satirical novels about the British Bohemian upper-classes by, for example, Evelyn Waugh (1903-1966), Nancy Mitford (1904-1973), or Anthony Powell (1905-2000). The exuberance of the Zinkeisen sisters' work was a visual tonic in troubled times. Indeed the designs, paintings, and biographies of the sisters add some lustre to a period marred by economic, social and political instability. Some of their paintings are eyewitness visual accounts documenting and describing what they saw during the Second World War; whilst the costume design work by Doris assists in an understanding of popular public taste in entertainment at the time it was created. Both beautiful and talented, the sisters were the publicists dream duo and a little partial to self-mythologizing. What is more they enjoyed the limelight, which they had worked so hard for, and were at ease hobnobbing with famous musicians, actors, tycoons, aristocrats, royalty, and émigrés stranded in Britain by circumstances beyond their control. Fatigued by London the sisters both settled in rural Suffolk for a quieter existence, although continued to paint with a vengeance. Their aesthetics did not attempt to embrace international modernism and entirely break with the past in search for a new mode of artistic expression. Despite this, the work of the Zinkeisen sisters was pioneering in other ways.

They were amongst a minority, who kicked against traditional attitudes towards women and their perceived role and forged successful careers for themselves. With considerable panache the Zinkeisen sisters sashayed their way past initial, highly gendered opposition to realise their dreams of becoming award-winning, celebrated, professional artists. The Zinkeisen sisters were all determination and ambition with immaculately lipsticked smiles. In these times much of their oeuvres can add visual zest to an historical understanding of their jazz age heyday, together with its mores and tastes, just as the triple portrait recently purchased by the Colchester and Ipswich Museums Service, to be discussed in more detail in the next section by Emma Roodhouse and Nicola Evans, is emblematic of opulent 1950s chic.

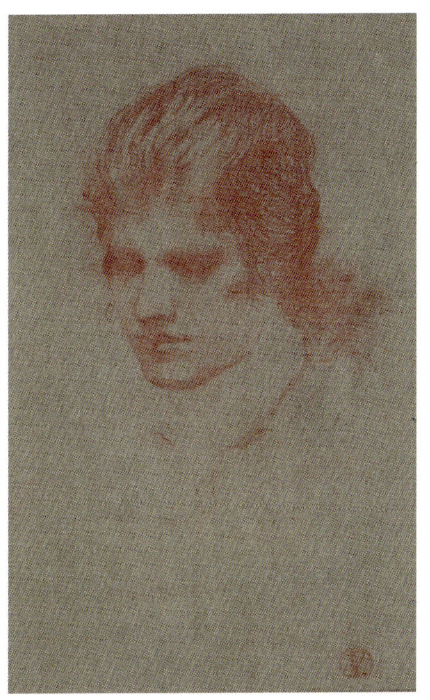

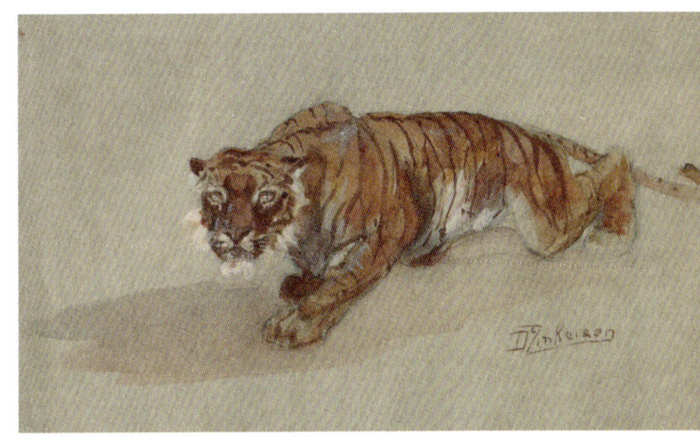

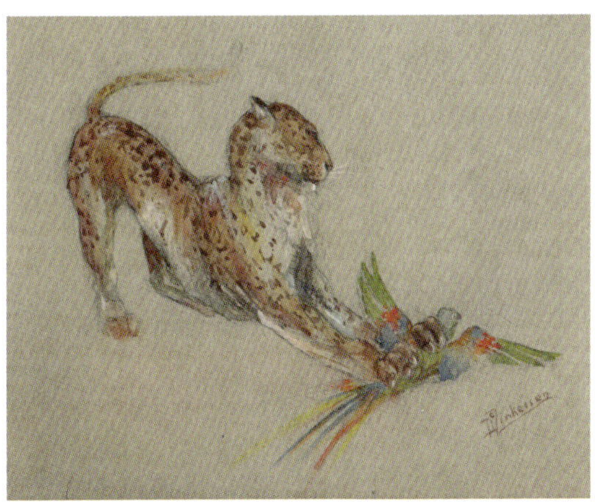

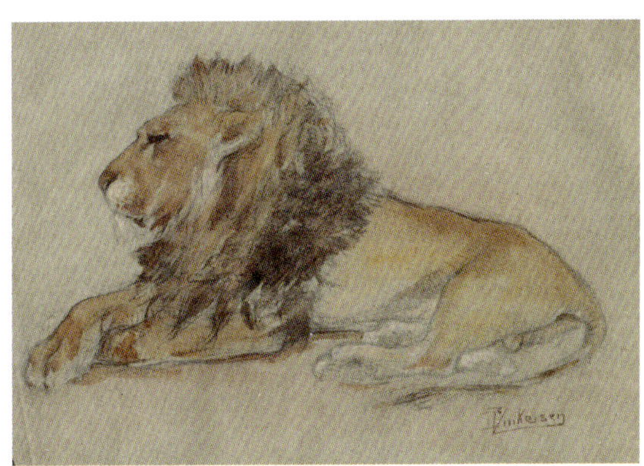

Top left: Fig.1.80
Doris Zinkeisen, *Head Study of a Girl, circa* 1912-1914, red chalk on paper.
Note the unusual monogram. See also Fig.3.1.
© Photograph courtesy of Julia Heseltine.

Bottom left: Fig.1.82
Doris Zinkeisen, *Leopard, circa* 1912-1914, watercolour on paper.
© Photograph courtesy of Julia Heseltine.

Top right: Fig.1.81
Doris Zinkeisen, *Tiger, circa* 1912-1914, watercolour on paper.
Early works bear a more angular signature.
© Photograph courtesy of Julia Heseltine.

Bottom right: Fig.1.83
Doris Zinkeisen, *Lion, circa* 1912-1914, watercolour on paper.
© Photograph courtesy of Julia Heseltine.

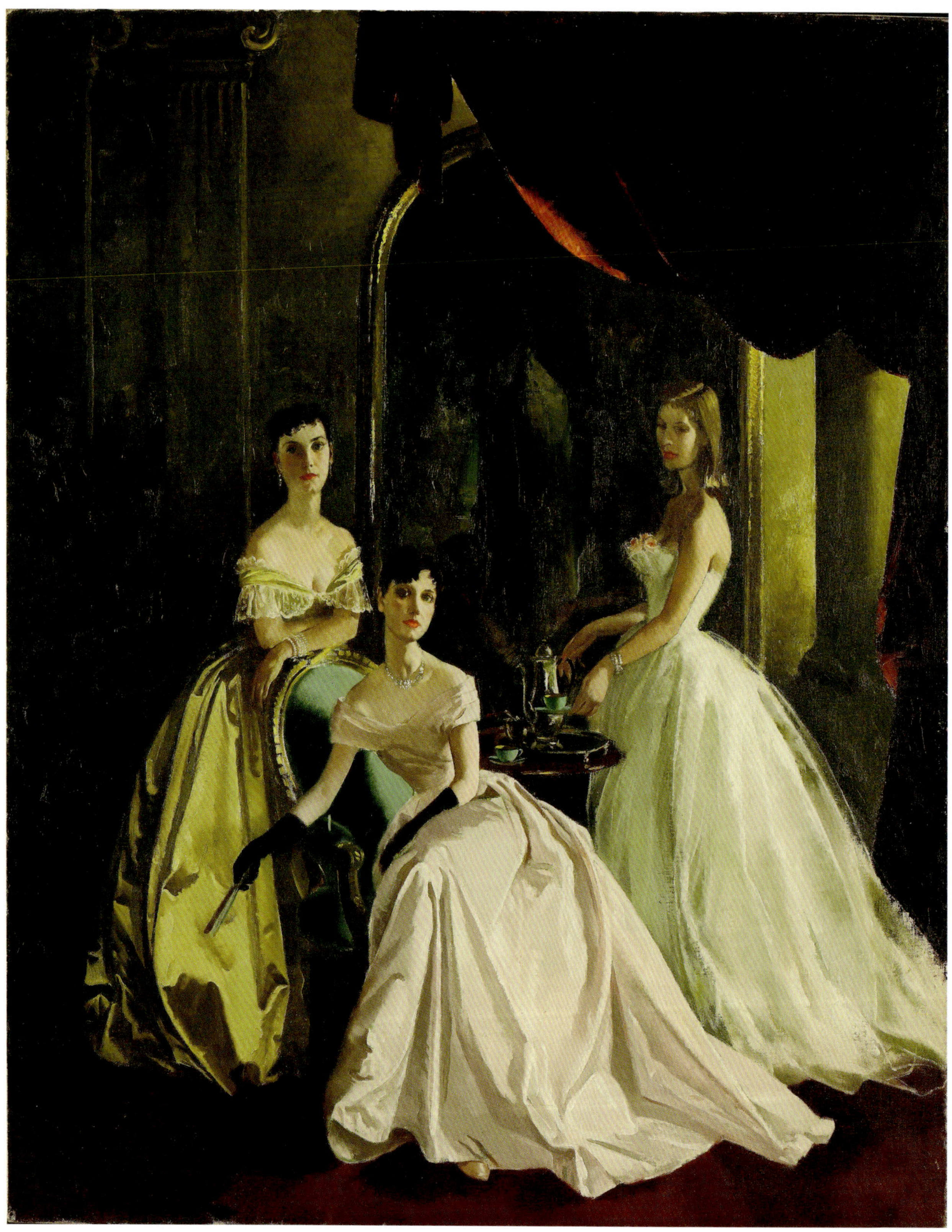

Part II
A Conversation Piece by Doris Zinkeisen

Emma Roodhouse & Nicola Evans

Introduction

In this chapter the curator Emma Roodhouse relates how the triple portrait by Doris Zinkeisen came to be acquired by the Colchester and Ipswich Museums Service to add to the Ipswich Borough collections [Fig.2.1]. The conservator Nicola Evans of KSH Conservation Limited gives the inside story behind the condition of the picture at the time of purchase and the subsequent conservation work required to prepare the painting for display. Emma Roodhouse also provides information about the sitters. The painting has close associations with the conversation piece, in that the composition consists of a group of figures, in this instance with family ties, shown here in majestic indoor surroundings. In common with numerous eighteenth-century conversation pieces by artists including, for example, Arthur Devis (1711-1787), the Christchurch Mansion Zinkeisen painting shows the sitters engaged in an everyday occupation, as they appear to be about to have some coffee. This particular conversation piece is unequivocally a group portrait and bears a label with its title in Doris's handwriting on the reverse, namely *The Misses Janet and Anne Grahame Johnstone and Miss Julia Heseltine*, but more on this to follow.

Emma Roodhouse on Christchurch Mansion's Zinkeisen

In 2014 I curated an exhibition at Ipswich Art Gallery entitled *Once Upon a Time: East Anglian Children's Book Illustrators*. At the core of this exhibition was a large selection of work by Janet Johnstone and her twin Anne Grahame Johnstone that the Museum Service had acquired in 2011. This was made possible by a very generous donation from a private collector of work by the twins and meant for the first time Ipswich could highlight the important story of the two artists, who had not been previously represented in the collection.

The exhibition research highlighted the considerable number of illustrators to have come out of Ipswich Art School, or else

Left: Fig.2.1
Doris Zinkeisen, *The Misses Janet and Anne Grahame Johnstone and Miss Julia Heseltine*, *circa* 1954, oil on canvas.

had close ties to the East Anglian region. I was amazed to discover that a number of these significant artists such as Edward Ardizzone (1900-1979), Helen Oxenbury (b.1938), Margaret Tempest (1892-1982), Nick Butterworth (b.1946), and James Mayhew (b.1964) to name but a few, were not always represented in the Ipswich collection. On finding out more about Janet and Anne's life I also came to know more about the work of their mother Doris Zinkeisen and their aunt, Anna Zinkeisen. Both of these Suffolk-based artists, who had such distinguished careers, were again not represented in the Ipswich art collection. It was at that point I became determined to try to add work by the Zinkeisen sisters to the collection.

I did not realise when I made that declaration to try and acquire a Zinkeisen or two for the collection in Ipswich that it might take a long time to find a suitable work. I would scan auctions and private sales, but it was a fortunate opportunity that I answered the phone at the Ipswich Museum one afternoon in 2019 as it led to the Museum securing the triple-portrait by Doris. The telephone call was from the Johnstone family, who had a painting by Doris Zinkeisen they were considering selling and asked if Ipswich Museum might be interested in it? I leapt at the chance and immediately asked for digital photographs to be emailed. The painting was of Doris's daughters and niece and could not be more appropriate for the collection. The portrait of the twin sisters Janet Johnstone (1928-1979) and Anne Grahame Johnstone (1928-1998) together with their cousin Julia Heseltine (b.1933) reveals the story of a phenomenal family of women artists, who all came to call Suffolk their home. Anna Zinkeisen and her daughter Julia Heseltine moved to Looms Cottage in Burgh, near to Grundisburgh and Woodbridge in the mid-1960s, where they had a purpose-built studio erected to work from [Fig.2.2; See also Foreword]. Enchanted by Anna's and Julia's new life in rural Suffolk, Doris and her daughters followed suit and left London for good in 1966 after finding The White House in Badingham, where the three of them had their studios. As Julia and the twins are the sitters in the triple portrait it is pertinent to find out a little more about them.

Julia Heseltine

There can be no doubt that Julia learned a great deal about painting from her mother and was inspired by her – see here also Julia's foreword to this book. She attended the Byam Shaw School of Art in Kensington and then

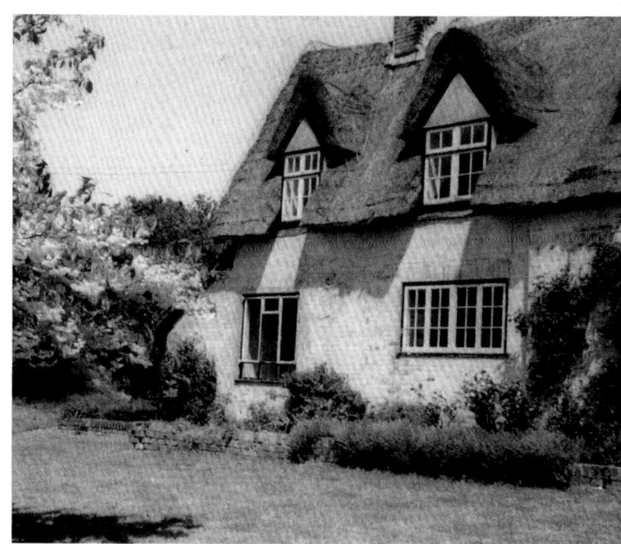

Right: Fig.2.2
Looms Cottage, Anna Zinkeisen's idyllic Suffolk home when she lived and worked there in the 1960s together with her daughter, Julia Heseltine.
© Photograph courtesy of Julia Heseltine.

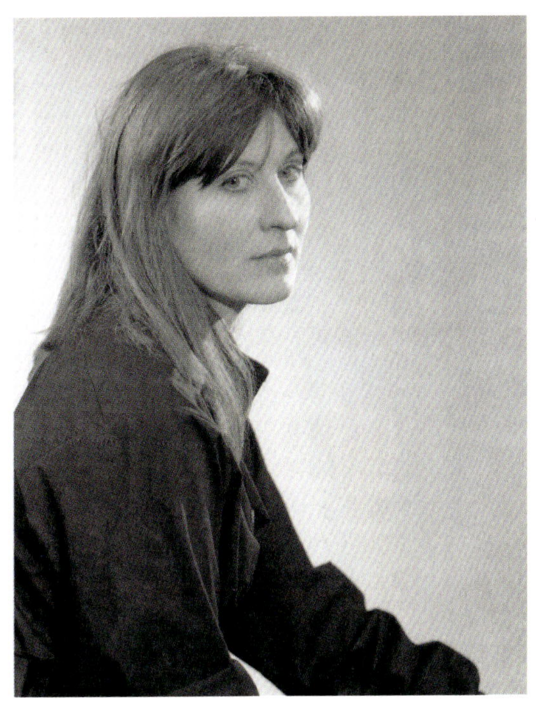

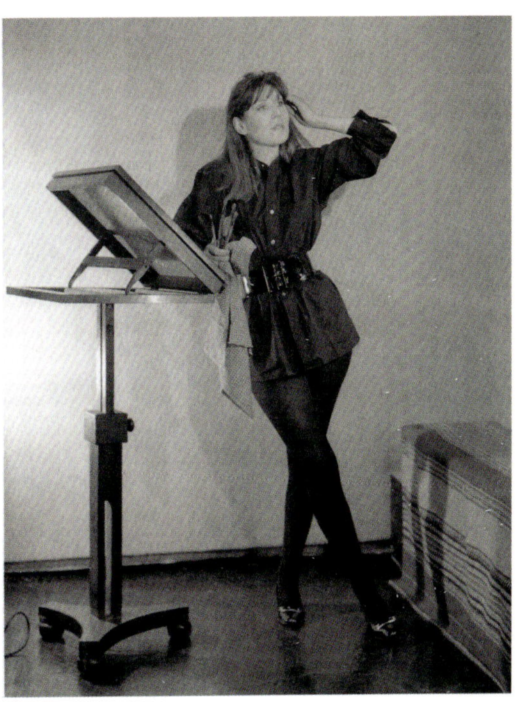

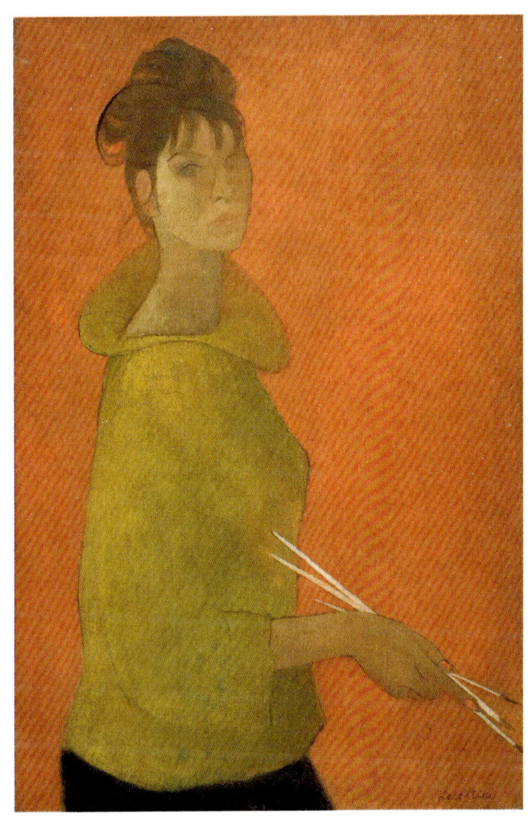

Above left: Fig.2.3
Julia Heseltine in her student years.

Above right: Fig.2.4
Julia Heseltine during her King's Road in Chelsea years.

Right: Fig.2.5
Julia Heseltine, *Self-portrait*, *circa* late 1950s, oil on canvas.
Julia painted herself in a very different way to her mother and aunty. See also Fig.3.95 and Fig.3.96.

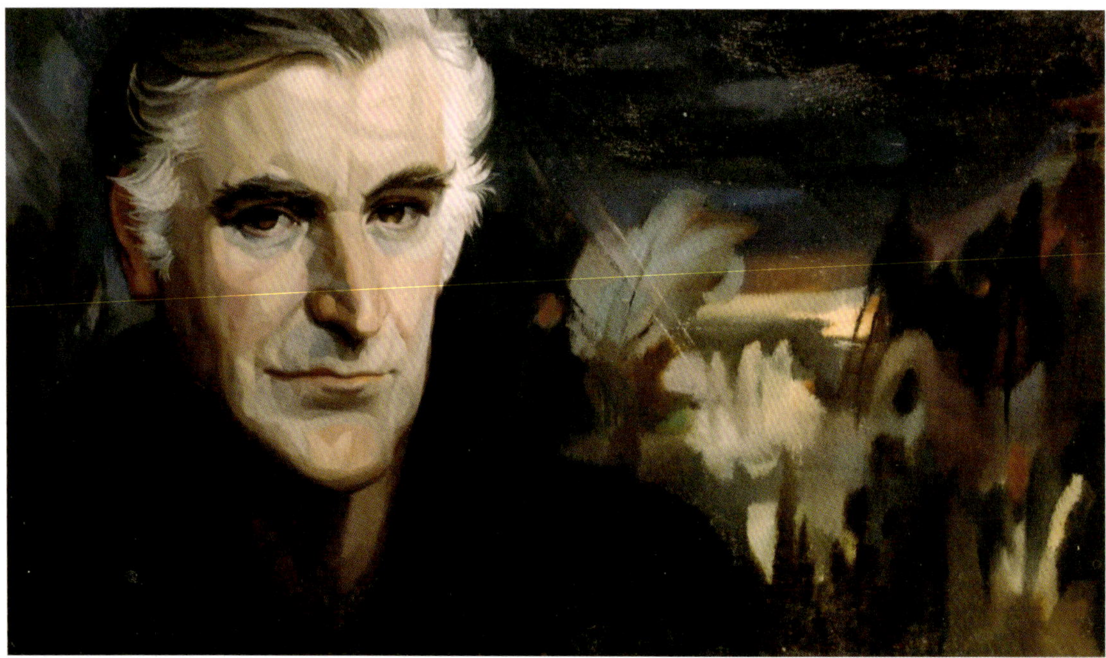

followed in her mother's footsteps by attending the Royal Academy Schools in London between 1952 and 1957. During these student years in the 1950s and in the early 1960s Julia was very much part of the Bohemian art scene centred on the King's Road in Chelsea, although at the first available opportunity she sought a quieter existence in Suffolk [Fig.2.3 – Fig.2.5]. She has exhibited at the Royal Academy Summer Exhibitions and at galleries in London and Suffolk.

As a portraitist Julia has received numerous commissions including the actress Joan Plowright (b.1929), the poet Ted Hughes (1930-1998), and a group portrait of the politician Alan Clark (1928-1999) and his family, to name but a few [Fig.2.6]. Her real passion, however, is painting landscapes. These largely Suffolk-inspired paintings frequently have a mysterious and disquieting undercurrent, as in her recent works focusing on global warming. Their dream-like quality can also be tinged with humour [Fig.2.7 – Fig.2.9].

The Johnstone Twins

Both Janet and Anne were inspired to become artists by their mother. They began their more formal art education just after the Second World War at St Martin's School of Art. Their

Above: Fig.2.6
Julia Heseltine, *Ted Hughes*, undated, oil on board.

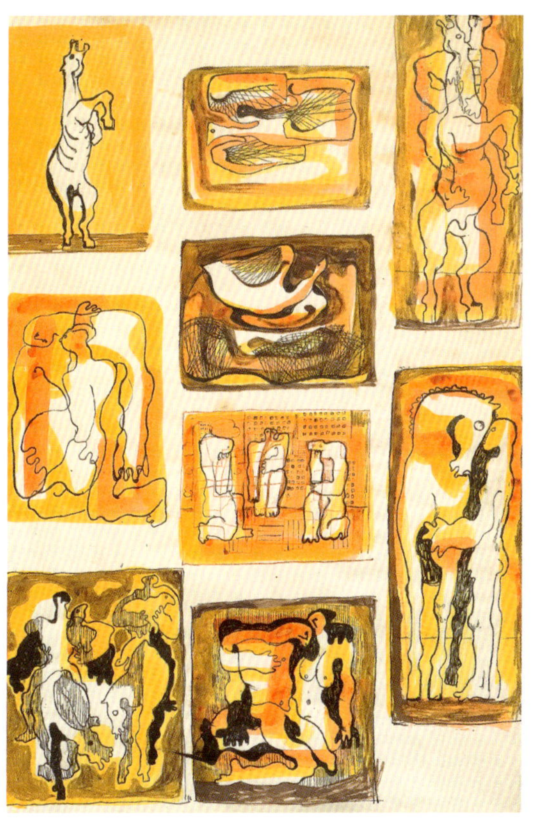

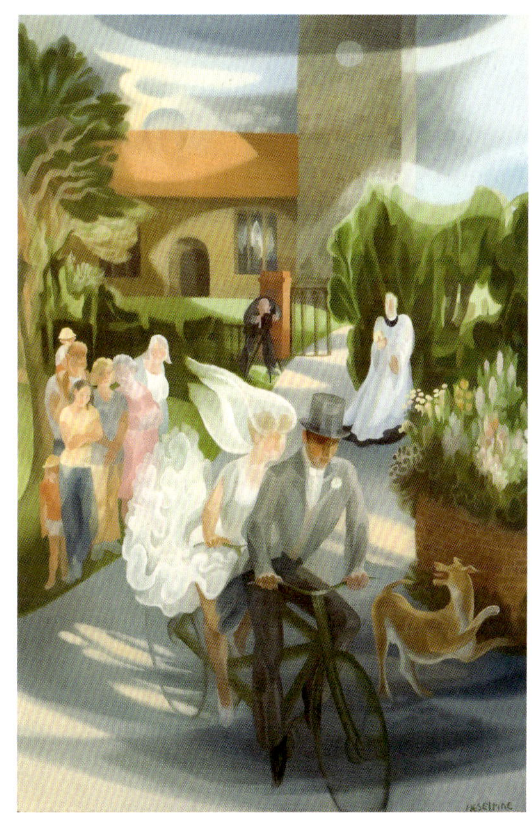

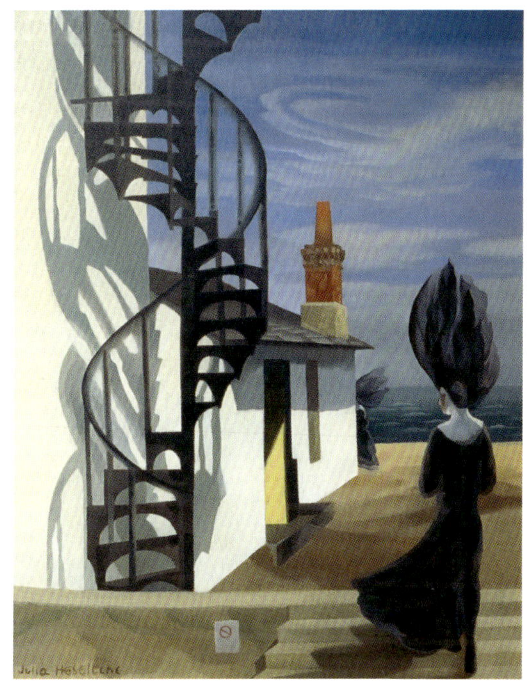

Above left: Fig.2.7
A page from one of Julia Heseltine's student sketch books.
© Photograph courtesy of Julia Heseltine.

Above right: Fig.2.8
Julia Heseltine, *Daisy's Wedding, Tuddenham Church, Suffolk*, undated, oil on board.
© Photograph courtesy of Julia Heseltine.

Right: Fig.2.9
Julia Heseltine, *Nuns on Aldeburgh Beach*, undated, oil on board.
© Photograph courtesy of Julia Heseltine.

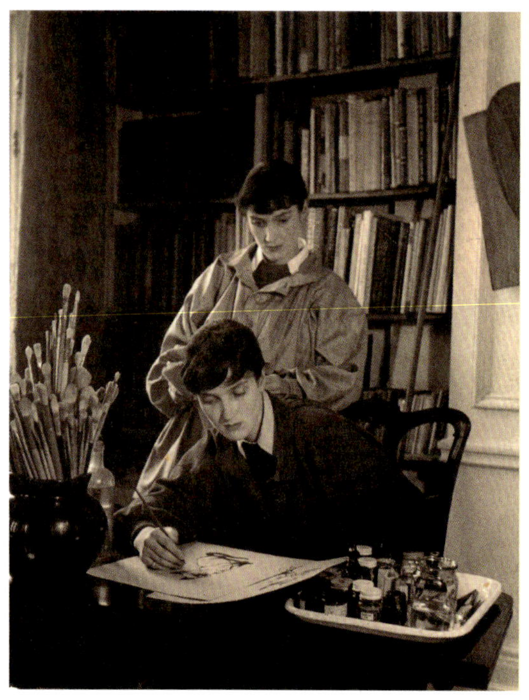

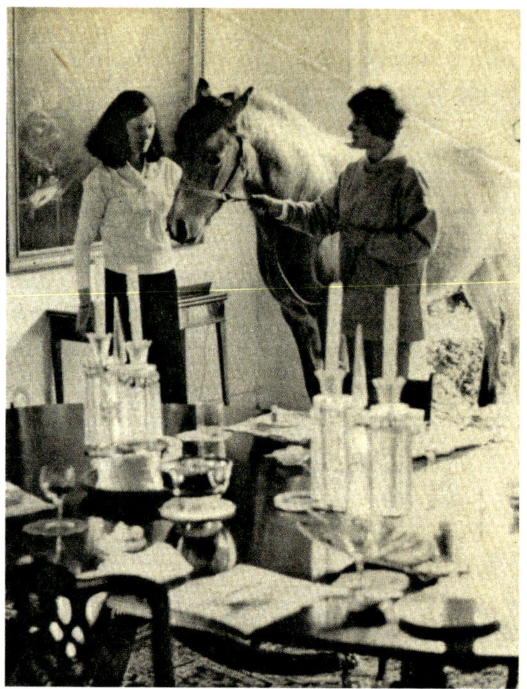

careers really took off in 1950 and they went on to become two of the most prolific illustrators of children's books in twentieth-century Britain and still found time to produce, amongst other things, card designs.

The illustrations by the Johnstone twins can often appear whimsical, which to a large extent reflects their own sense of fun [Fig.2.10 – Fig.2.11]. It is, therefore, no surprise to discover the twins were amongst several artists to be employed to illustrate children's favourites including Andy Pandy and Bill and Ben the Flower Pot Men. A good deal of their work is anthropomorphic, as toys and animals have human attributes, although ascribing human characteristics to non-human things is familiar territory in children's books generally [Fig.2.12 – Fig.2.16]. The period detail of their historical costumes found in many of their illustrations is clearly an influence from their mother, which is hardly surprising as they lived together under the same roof. Living in Suffolk was perfect for the twins as they could keep lots of pets, including ponies [Fig.3.97]. In fact the twins were more normally attired in jodhpurs or slacks, so their representation in Doris's triple portrait is quite an anomaly.

Above: Fig.2.10
Johnstone twins in their studio, *circa* late 1950s.

Above: Fig.2.11
Anne Grahame Johnstone (left) and Janet Johnstone (right) together with their pony, Victoria, in the dining room of The White House in Badingham, Suffolk *circa* 1976.

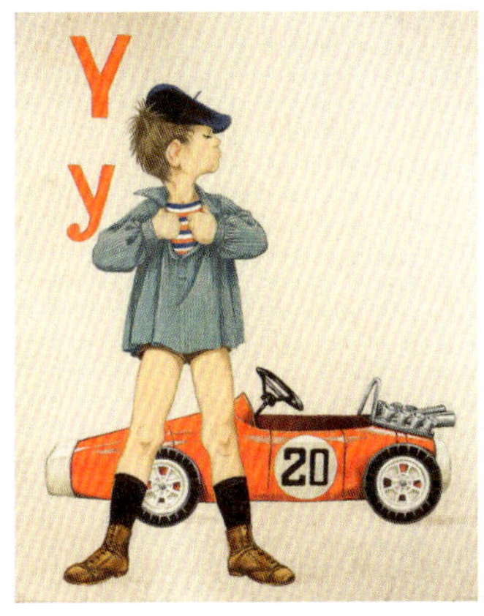

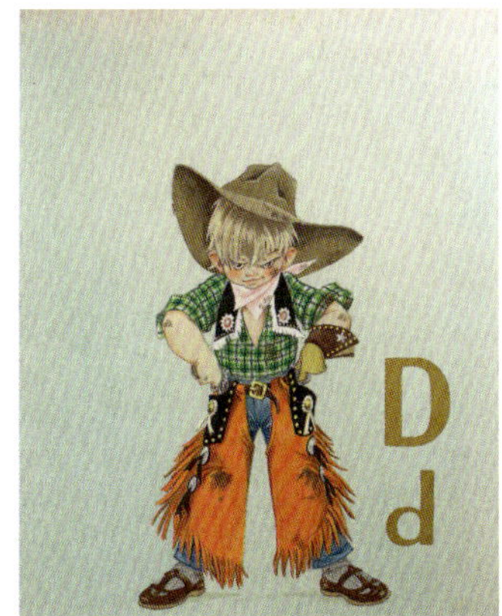

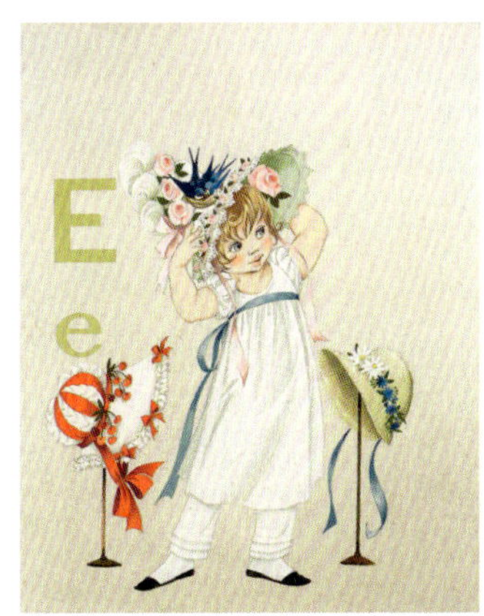

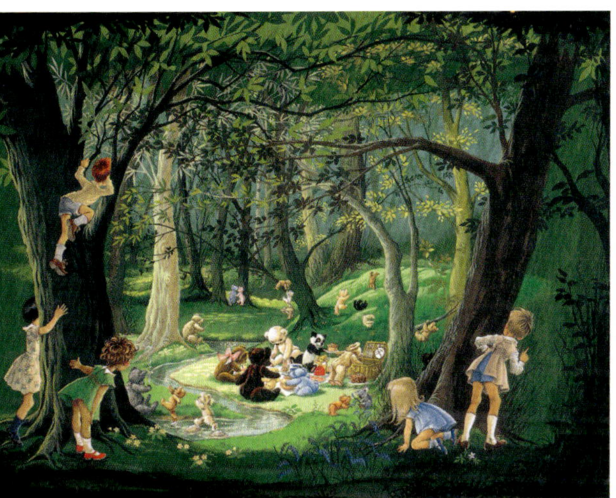

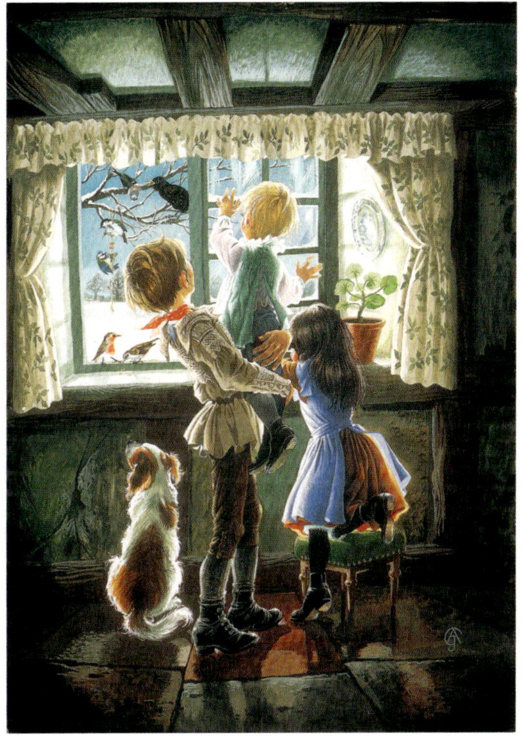

Above left: Fig.2.12
Janet Johnstone and Anne Grahame Johnstone, illustration of 'Y' from: *A Book of Children's Rhymes and Verse*, 1973.
© Photograph courtesy of the estate of Doris Zinkeisen.

Above centre: Fig.2.13
Janet Johnstone and Anne Grahame Johnstone, illustration of 'D' from: *A Book of Children's Rhymes and Verse*, 1973.
© Photograph courtesy of the estate of Doris Zinkeisen.

Above right: Fig.2.14
Janet Johnstone and Anne Grahame Johnstone, illustration of 'E' from: *A Book of Children's Rhymes and Verse*, 1973.
© Photograph courtesy of the estate of Doris Zinkeisen.

Below left: Fig.2.15
Anne Grahame Johnstone, *Teddy Bears' Picnic*, undated, gouache on paper.
© Photograph by courtesy of The Great British Card Company.

Below right: Fig.2.16
Anne Grahame Johnstone, *Children and Dog Birdwatching at a Window*, undated, gouache on paper.
© Photograph by courtesy of The Great British Card Company.

More on the Portrait and Funding the Acquisition

The Christchurch Mansion Zinkeisen painting can certainly be dated to the 1950s. A very similar oil sketch appears to have been displayed in 1954 at the Fine Art Society, although it lacks the detail of the Christchurch Mansion portrait and the figures are too vague to be called portraits. The painting dates, therefore, to a time when all three sitters were on the cusp of making names for themselves in the world of art.

The oil on canvas group portrait is an impressive painting of three young women dressed in formal ball-gowns. The dark-haired twins are shown close to each other. Janet in a yellow gown trimmed with lace off-the-shoulder, worn with looped pearls around her wrist and sparkling drop earrings. She leans on the back of a gilt and green velvet chair, on which her sister perches. Anne is swathed in a pale pink silk dress that descends to the bottom edge of the canvas. It is made more dramatic with the long black gloves she wears to highlight her pale skin and a closed fan dangles from her right hand. Unlike Janet she has no bracelets or earrings but just a sparkling necklace.

Julia Heseltine is dressed in a white tulle off-the-shoulder gown that has pink roses nestled in the bodice. Julia is the only sitter not looking directly out of the painting. Instead she is in the act of holding a coffee cup and potentially pouring some from the silver pot, although there are only two cups and they have been selected to match the chair's green upholstery. The painting is arranged rather like a stage set, with Doris Zinkeisen the designer posing the 'actors' and setting the props.

Janet, Anne, and Julia were models for their mothers in many works of art and this painting is a staged moment [Fig.2.17; Fig.3.87; Fig.3.95 – Fig.3.97]. The heavy dark red swag of curtain that takes up the top right corner reminds us of a theatre curtain pulled back at the beginning of a play. Classical columns frame the scene and the large mirror in the background shows a glimpse into the world outside the frame reflected. At the time this painting was captured Janet and Anne had not yet illustrated the first edition of *The Hundred and One Dalmatians* (1956) by Dodie Smith (1896-1990), arguably their first major breakthrough; whilst Julia was still a student at the Royal Academy Schools. Ball-gowns, formal coffee mornings or soirées and jewels were a world away from their daily reality. Julia Heseltine in recalling the time this was painted wrote: "We were used as models a lot and perhaps this was for a play or a film. But it wasn't what we would normally wear."

In the 1950s, when this painting was created, Doris Zinkeisen was designing costumes, sets, and props for several productions that had 'high society' as their theme, including the musical *After the Ball* by Noël Coward (1899-1973) performed during

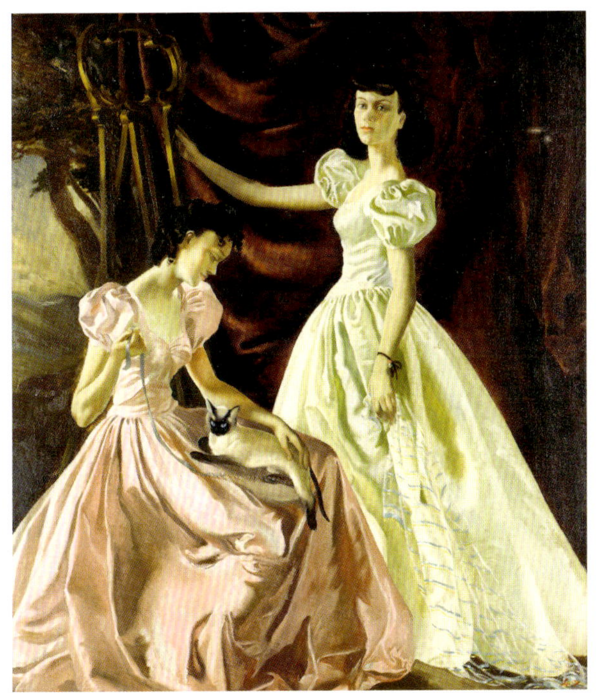

the 1953 to 1954 season – remembering here Coward's dislike of the then newly emerging 'Kitchen Sink' school in writing, which certainly would have mirrored Doris's own lack of enthusiasm for similar trends in painting. So the triple portrait has certainly been influenced by Doris's work for the theatre at that time and might also, in part, be seen as a visual homage to haute couture and exclusive high fashions. The painting bears a label for the Royal Society of Portrait Painters and could well have been displayed at the annual exhibition. Both Doris and her sister joined the Royal Society of Portrait Painters in 1964, but prior to this they would have been able to exhibit work as non-members through open submission. Incidentally the label also provides the full title of the work and the artist's address at that time, 50 Albert Court, where she lived between 1946 and 1966 when she moved to Suffolk. This picture had remained in the family since it was painted and was on display in the family home in Suffolk for many years. The family were very keen that it could permanently reside in Suffolk, to represent Doris and her wider family.

When any item is presented as a possible acquisition our Museum Service has to follow certain procedures to assess the object. Every accredited Museum Service has a collections development policy that outlines the current collections and the criteria for what it will, or will not collect. The painting by Doris Zinkeisen fitted the collections criteria for being by a relevant Suffolk-based artist and was of sitters with strong Suffolk connections. Notwithstanding the painting's immaculate provenance, the one area which was of concern was the condition the painting was in, as it had a tear in the canvas and was discoloured through decades of dirt. This issue with conservation did not outweigh the fact that this was a once in a lifetime opportunity to acquire a painting by a significant artist. The case for acquiring the painting was made to our internal committee of the collections working group, but how to raise the funds to acquire the painting?

Above: Fig.2.17

Anna Zinkeisen, *Janet Johnstone and Anne Grahame Johnstone*, 1950s, oil on canvas.

Ipswich is very fortunate in having a supportive and active Friends charity that contributes regularly to fundraising for acquisitions, conservation, and exhibitions. A case was put forward to the Friends of the Ipswich Museums (FOIM) and they very kindly supported the acquisition. Two other funds were possible options to assist with the purchase. The Art Fund, a national charity for art, and The Arts Council England/V&A Purchase Grant Fund, supports purchases of non-nationally funded organisations in England and Wales. Applications had to be written, valuations gathered, together with a detailed condition report and independent assessments of the painting which looked at, for example, the condition of the stretcher, the canvas, and the state of the ground and paint layer, in addition to a comprehensive proposal of recommended treatments.

Once submitted it was a matter of waiting and hoping that a good enough case had been presented. I am eternally thankful to the Johnstone family for their patience and support during this process, which some might regard as bureaucratic and involving too much red tape, but is in actual fact very necessary when public money is at stake and there is a need for complex conservation work to be professionally evaluated. Then during the first Covid Lockdown during 2020 the Art Fund and V&A Purchase Grant Fund confirmed they would support the purchase of the painting. It was officially secured for the public collection at Ipswich. The next part of the painting's story would be to send it for conservation, which was kindly funded by the Friends of the Ipswich Museums. The conservation was carried out by KSH Conservation Limited, a leading company in such work, whose client base includes some major public galleries and museums around the world including, for example, the Metropolitan Museum in New York, the National Gallery in London, and the National Galleries of Scotland, to name but a few. Conservator Nicola Evans of KSH Conservation Limited tells us in the following sections what was involved in preparing the painting for display. The triple portrait will now be able to tell an important story about Doris Zinkeisen and the sitters; it might also contribute to our understanding of British art in the 1950s and provide inspiration, learning, and enjoyment for a wide range of people who visit Ipswich.

Nicola Evans on Conservation of the Zinkeisen Painting

First some general remarks about the portrait. The stretcher is English, commercially made, and of a standard 50 x 40 inch 'portrait' size – one that the artist probably bought dismantled from her local art supplier. The Belgian linen canvas, however, appears to have been prepared with an off-white ground or 'priming' and cut and stretched up by the artist herself. The ground reaches to three cut edges

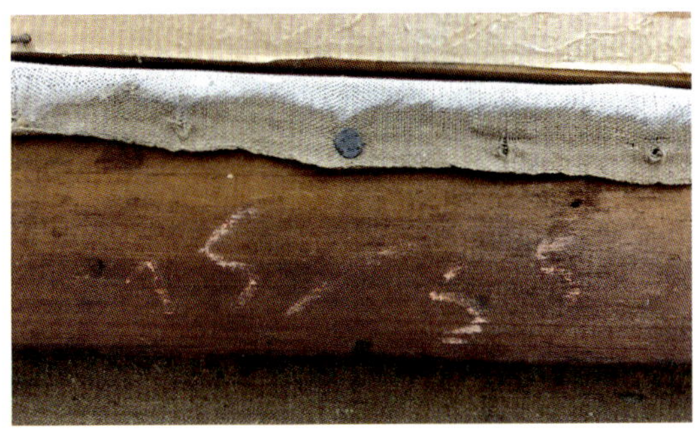

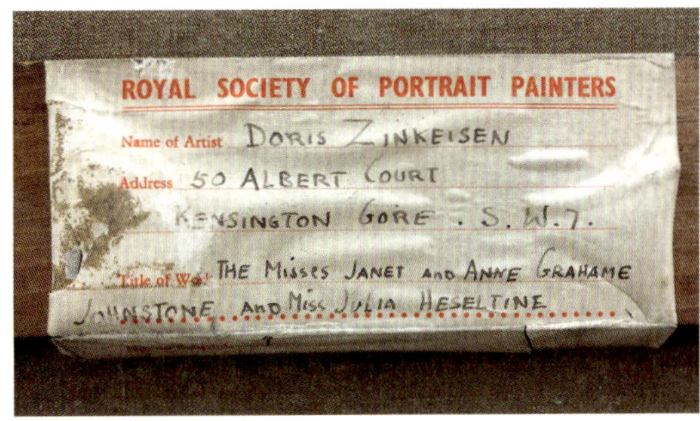

of the canvas turnover, but the top turnover edge displays the canvas bolt's selvedge edge, which is un-primed and has cusping and a previous set of empty tack holes [Fig.2.18]. This indicates that Doris Zinkeisen stretched and primed a much larger canvas initially, and then cut smaller pieces off to be used for smaller painting sizes.

Although the artist's colour palette is relatively limited, with the light hues of the ladies' dresses set against a more muted background, the paint layer is extremely lively through having been applied in a variety of ways. Broad strokes sweep across the canvas with a loaded brush, or palette knife, which in other areas give way to thinly applied washes. Elsewhere paint passages have been scraped back, leaving visible traces of colour in the interstices and the ground visible on the raised weave. These passages are frequently juxtaposed by heavy impasto with the edge of the palette knife preserved in the thick paint.

The feel of immediacy in this portrait is created by rapid and expressive brush work. The paint layer remains brushy and unpolished around the edges, with the ground left visible at the perimeters, as well as in several exposed flashes seen throughout the composition. Doris Zinkeisen was a member of The Royal Society of Portrait Painters in London and it appears that she exhibited this painting there on an undated occasion, or else submitted the work as a non-member prior to joining – see the label on reverse [Fig.2.19].

Condition of the Painting Prior to Restoration

When acquired by the Colchester and Ipswich Museums Service to add to the Ipswich Borough collections this painting had a few conservation issues, which needed addressing. Consequently it was brought to KSH Conservation Limited's studio in Norfolk. The most pressing issue was to treat the mould present on the painted surface and in the interstices of the canvas weave. Although relatively minor, the mould spots were widespread and speckled the entire paint surface on the front. If left, damage caused

Above: Fig.2.18
Top edge of the canvas turnover on reverse, showing an un-primed selvedge edge with cusping and prior tack holes.
© Photograph courtesy of KSH Conservation Ltd.

Above: Fig.2.19
Royal Society of Portrait Painters' exhibition label attached to the cross bar of the stretcher on reverse.
© Photograph courtesy of KSH Conservation Ltd.

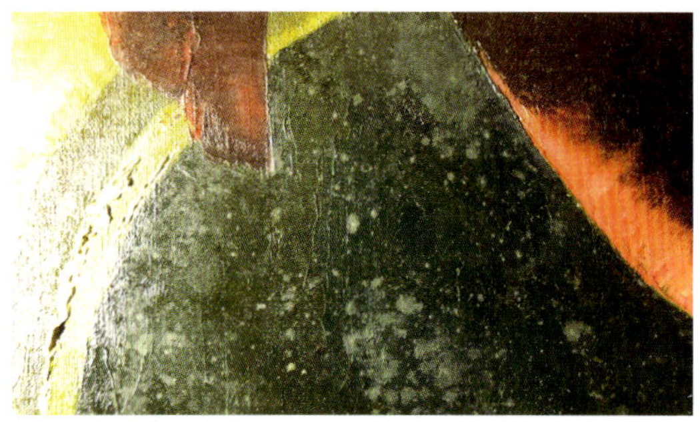

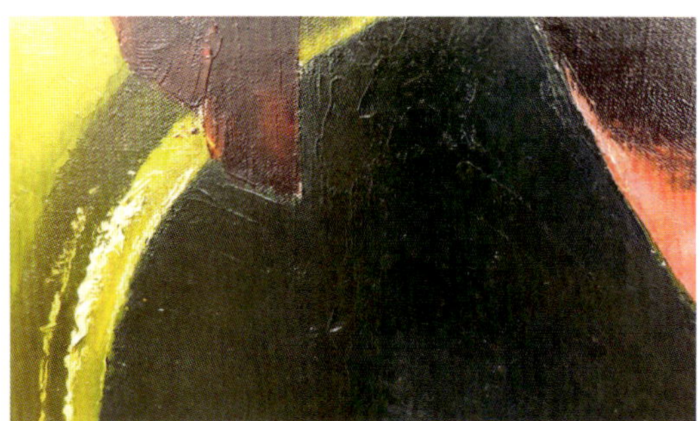

by the mould filaments would become more extensive and so harder to treat. Paintings, like most objects made from organic materials, are susceptible to mould growth if exposed to adverse conditions. The mould on this painting had left the paint in the affected areas matt and blanched, with passages of the painting that should have appeared saturated taking on a flat, milky appearance [Fig.2.20 – Fig.2.21].

It was not immediately apparent whether there was a varnish layer present on top of the paint layers due to the uneven surface appearance. However, when examined under ultra-violet light (a form of technical illumination commonly used to reveal information about the surface condition of a painting), the surface fluoresced green, indicating that a thin natural resin varnish had been applied by the artist before the paint layer was fully dry. As a result, the varnish had been absorbed by the wet paint layer in certain paint passages and this, combined with the damage caused by the mould, was contributing to the uneven surface appearance of the painting.

Although there were several other minor issues which required attention, the other main issue was that the painting had received an impact from the reverse. This blow had resulted in a tear, but because the canvas is still relatively young and flexible (over time canvas becomes more brittle as it degrades), the canvas threads elongated before finally giving way and breaking. This stretching resulted in a localised bulge in the canvas surrounding the tear [Fig.2.22 – Fig.2.23]. Additionally, the overall tension of the canvas was extremely slack. Half of the tensioning keys (which are usually present in the corners of a stretcher) were missing and so the stretcher had been unevenly 'keyed out', further contributing to some significant planar deformations around the edges and at the corners [Fig.2.24].

Conservation Treatments Carried Out

Once unframed, the painting was cleaned front, back, and sides to remove both mould and surface dirt, as over time, other pollutants contained within a dirt layer will cause

Above top: Fig.2.20
Detail showing severe mould and subsequent blanching of the paint layer.
© Photograph courtesy of KSH Conservation Ltd.

Above bottom: Fig.2.21
Area once mould removed and the paint layer has been re-varnished.
© Photograph courtesy of KSH Conservation Ltd.

Opposite top: Fig.2.22
Tear and surrounding deformation from the front.
© Photograph courtesy of KSH Conservation Ltd.

Opposite second down: Fig.2.23
Area after the tear had been mended, the paint loss filled, and the fills retouched to match the surrounding paint.
© Photograph courtesy of KSH Conservation Ltd.

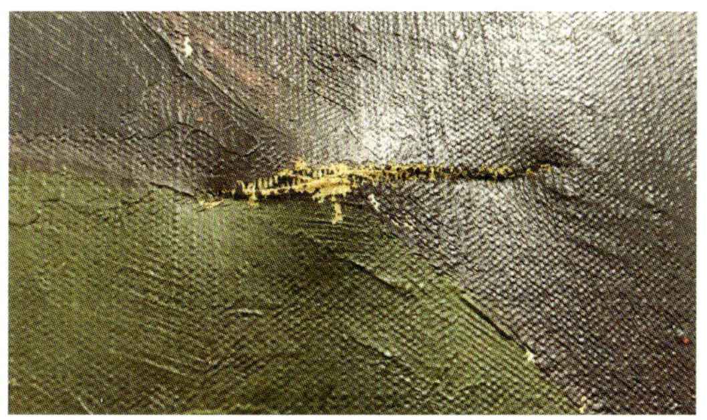

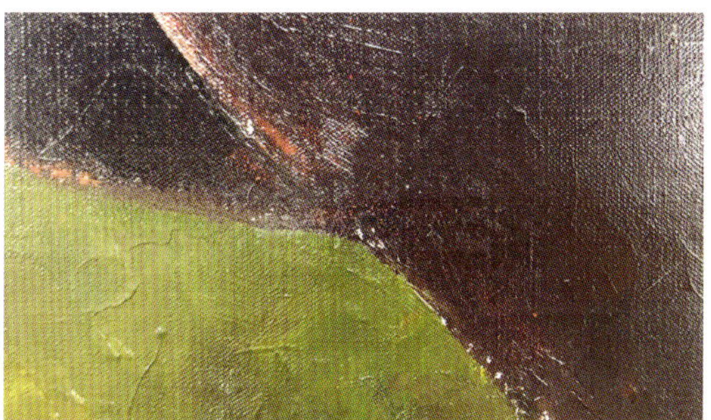

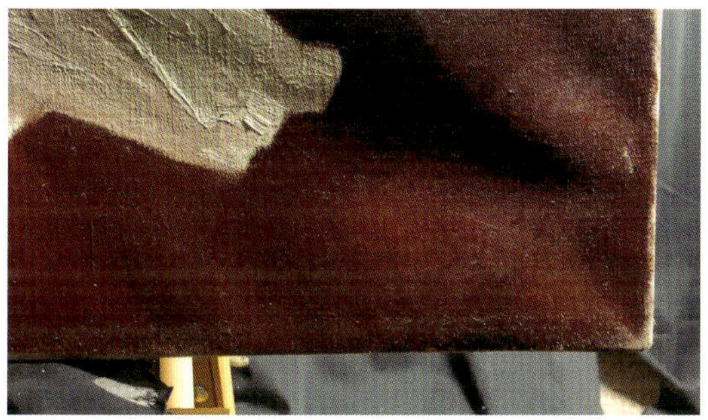

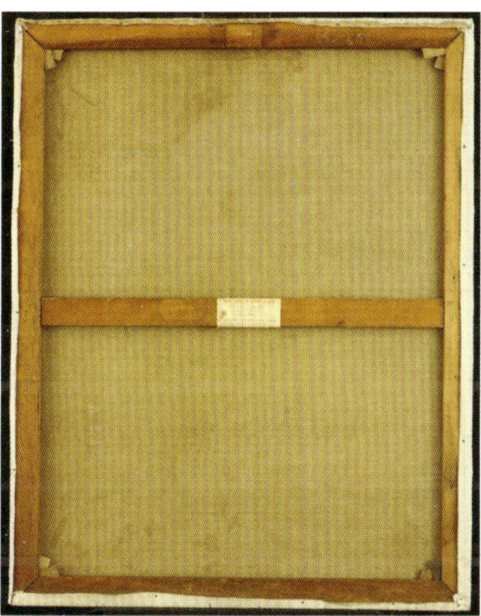

accelerated degradation processes. An alcohol solution was used to kill the mould spores within the canvas fibres on reverse [Fig.2.25].

The bulge surrounding the tear was reduced by carrying out controlled gentle humidity treatments. This aided the re-alignment of the broken threads. Using a microscope, the broken threads could then be carefully re-woven and adhered back together. After the tear had been mended further humidity treatments were carried out to completely remove the deformation surrounding the tear.

The painting had previously been framed in a late twentieth-century gilt frame without glazing, or a protective backing. As a result, dirt had been able to accumulate on the front and back of the painting, and the exposed canvas was subject to an impact from the reverse resulting in a tear. It is now re-framed in a new, custom-made frame that is both stylistically more in keeping with the painting, as well as one more able to house it safely. The latter protections include UV filtered glass to protect the painted surface from air pollutants (dirt) and light exposure (which can result in fading of some pigments and more rapid aged discolouration of paint films); and an inert, transparent and lightweight protective backing is also fitted on the reverse.

After all this meticulous, time-consuming and specialist care and attention the painting is now finally on display for all to enjoy as part of the Ipswich Borough collections in Suffolk.

Left third down: Fig.2.24
Planar deformations (buckles) in the bottom right corner of the slack canvas.

Left: Fig.2.25
After treatment, unframed, reverse. Normal light.

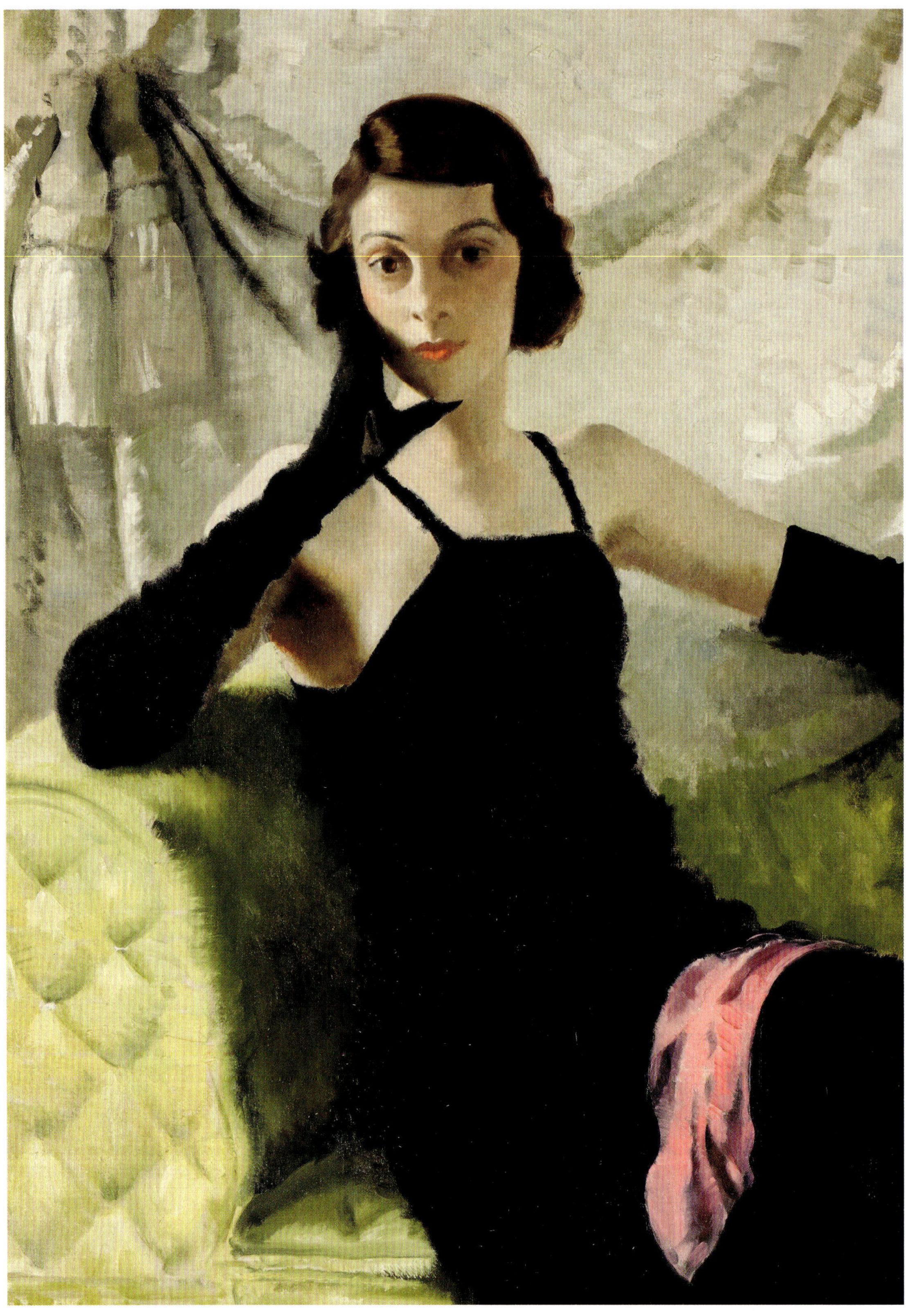

Part III
Gallery of Pictures

Introduction

The pictures in this third section of the book come from many different places, which are outlined together with their captions. Any omissions are inadvertent and will receive appropriate redress and be corrected in future editions, provided the publisher and author are notified in writing. The choice of pictures presented here and throughout is governed by personal preference of the authors and was subject to their availability. The images are arranged as far as is realistically practicable in chronological order, rather than thematically, as in portraits, landscapes, posters and so on. As previously alluded to, the Zinkeisen sisters rarely dated their paintings so without confirmation from other sources this process is imprecise and relies heavily on conjecture. The eagle-eyed will notice that although the media are recorded the dimensions are omitted. Details on sizes were unavailable for many of the works illustrated here, so for the purposes of uniformity none are given. The reproductions presented here are a first-rate selection of works by the Zinkeisen sisters, although there is a bias towards works from the golden age of their output from the 1920s up to and including the 1950s. It is hoped the illustrations will be a useful resource for those interested in the Zinkeisens, or with a general curiosity about twentieth-century British art.

Left: Detail of Fig.3.45

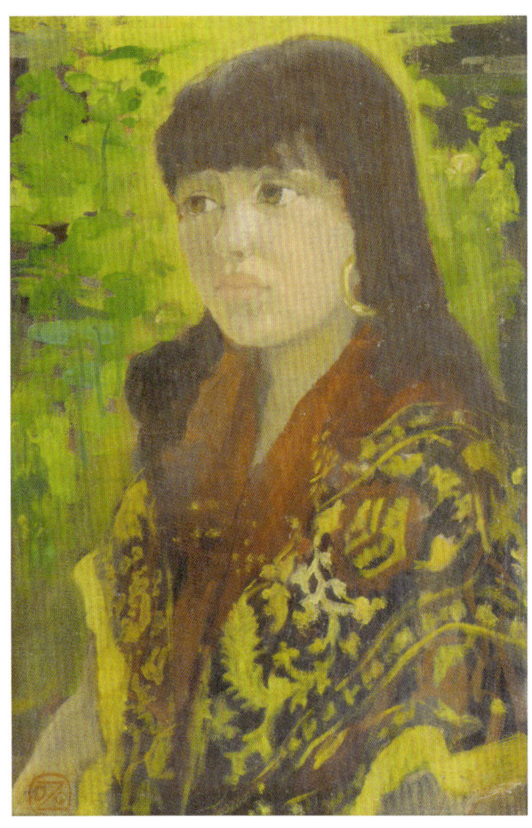

Fig.3.1
Doris Zinkeisen, *Portrait of Anna, circa* 1910-1912, oil on canvas.
© Photograph courtesy of Sotheby's.

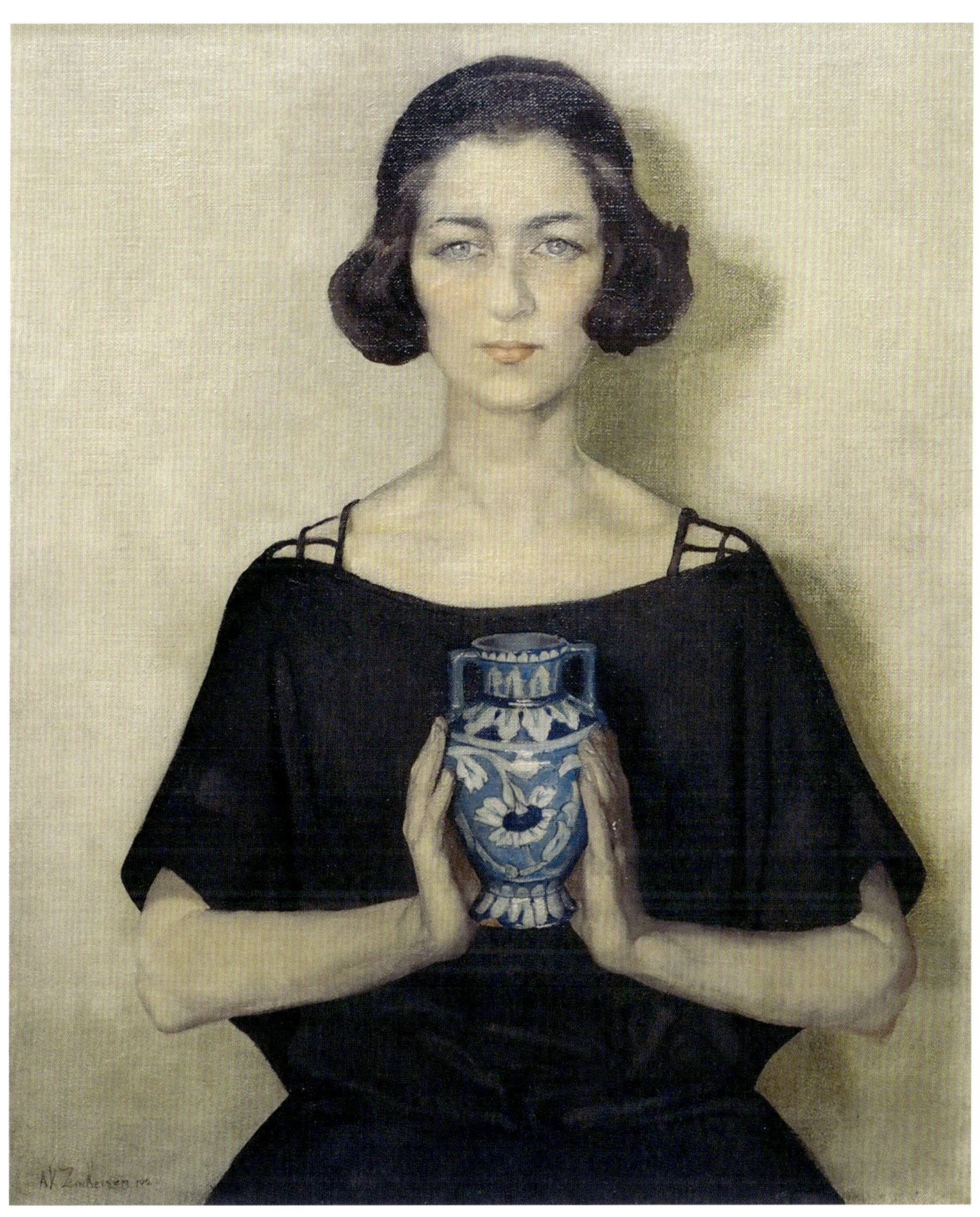

Fig.3.2
Anna Zinkeisen, *The Blue Persian Urn: Portrait of Audrey*, 1921, oil on canvas.

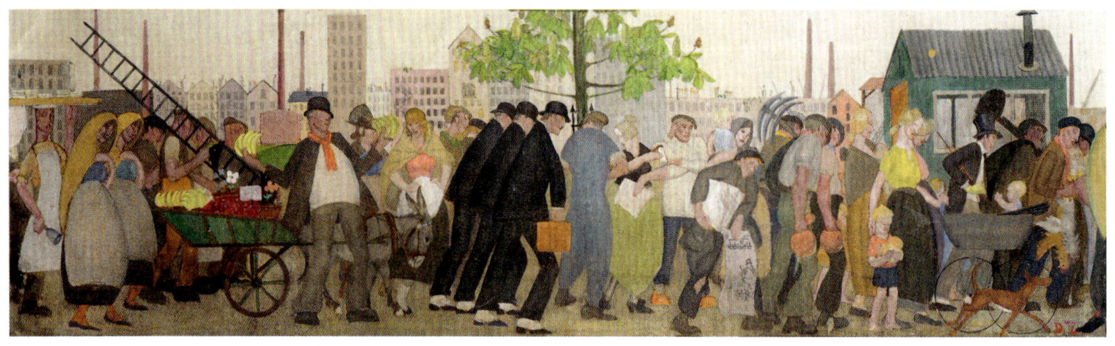

Fig.3.3
Doris Zinkeisen, *Design for a Mural: The People of London*, *circa* 1916-1920, oil on board.

Fig.3.4
Anna Zinkeisen, *Portrait of Doris*, 1923, oil on canvas.

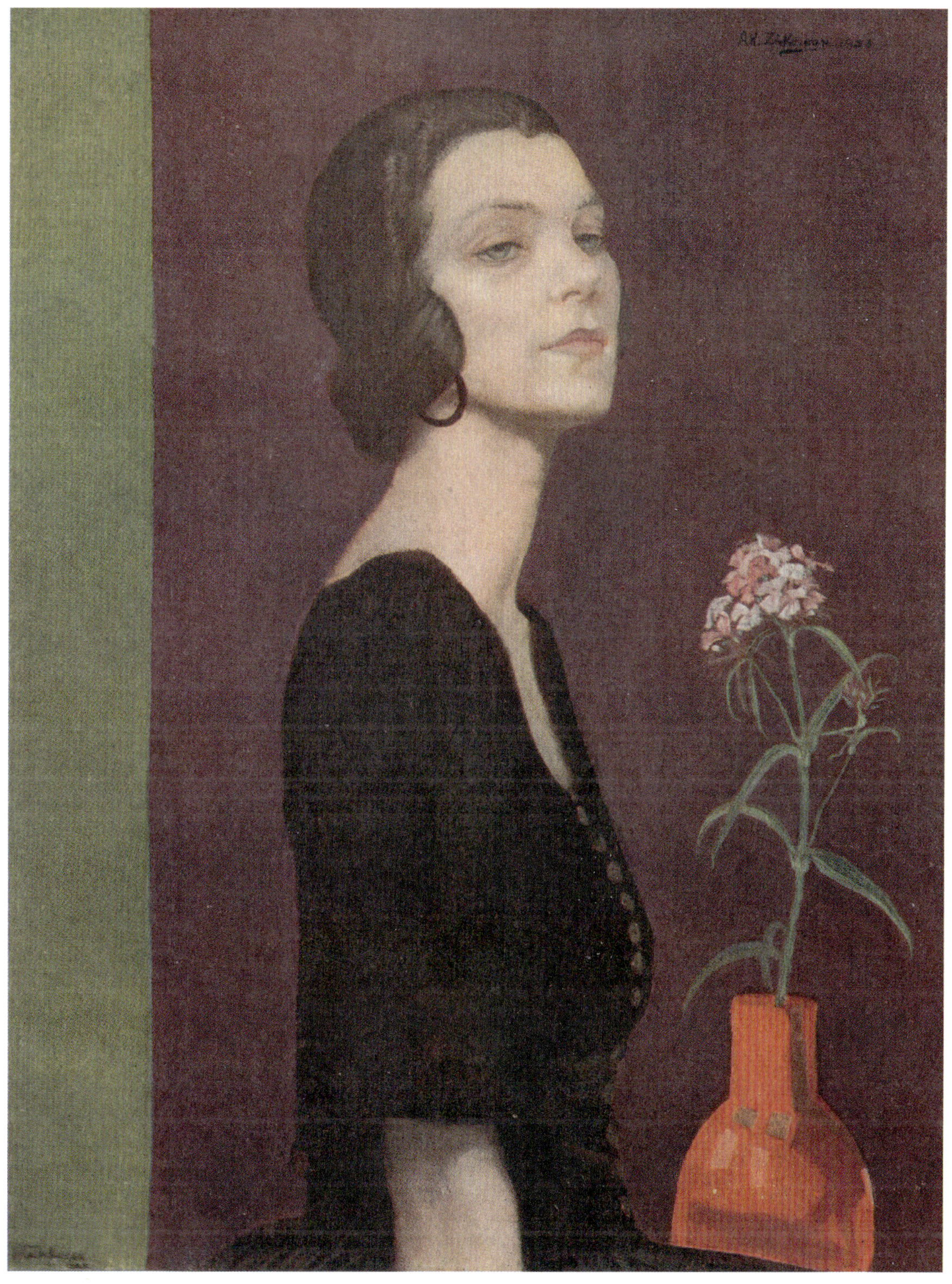

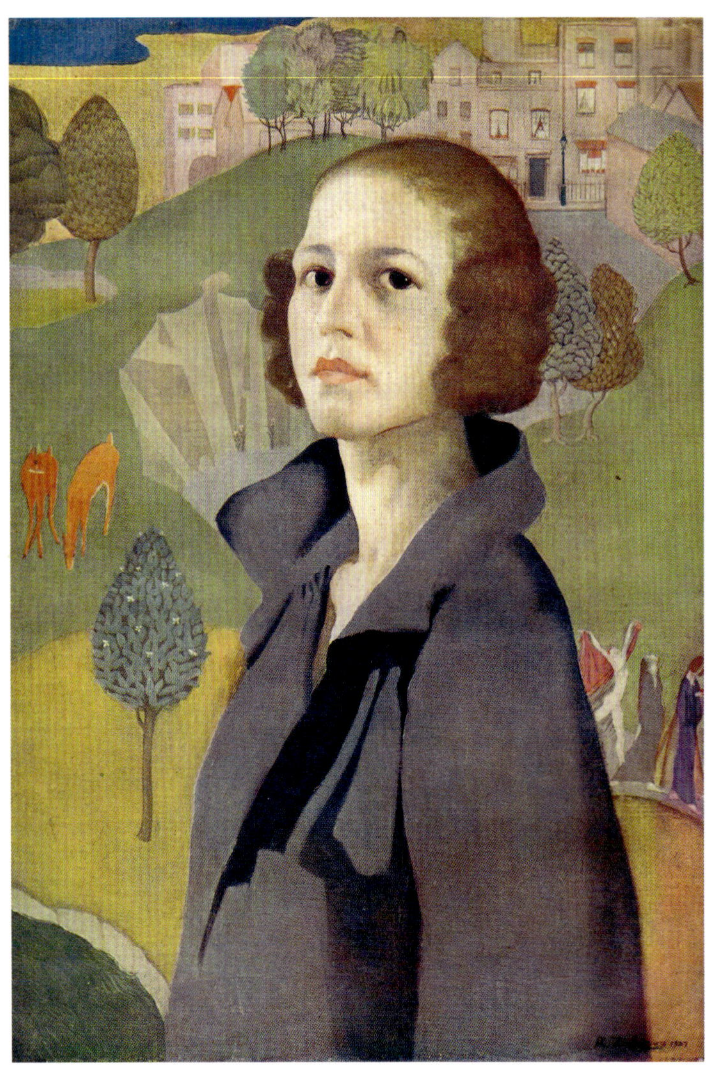

Fig.3.5
Anna Zinkeisen, *Self-portrait*, 1923, oil on canvas.

Fig.3.6
Doris Zinkeisen, *Elsa Lanchester, circa* 1925, oil on canvas.
Exhibited at the Royal Academy and Paris Salon. See also Fig.1.59.

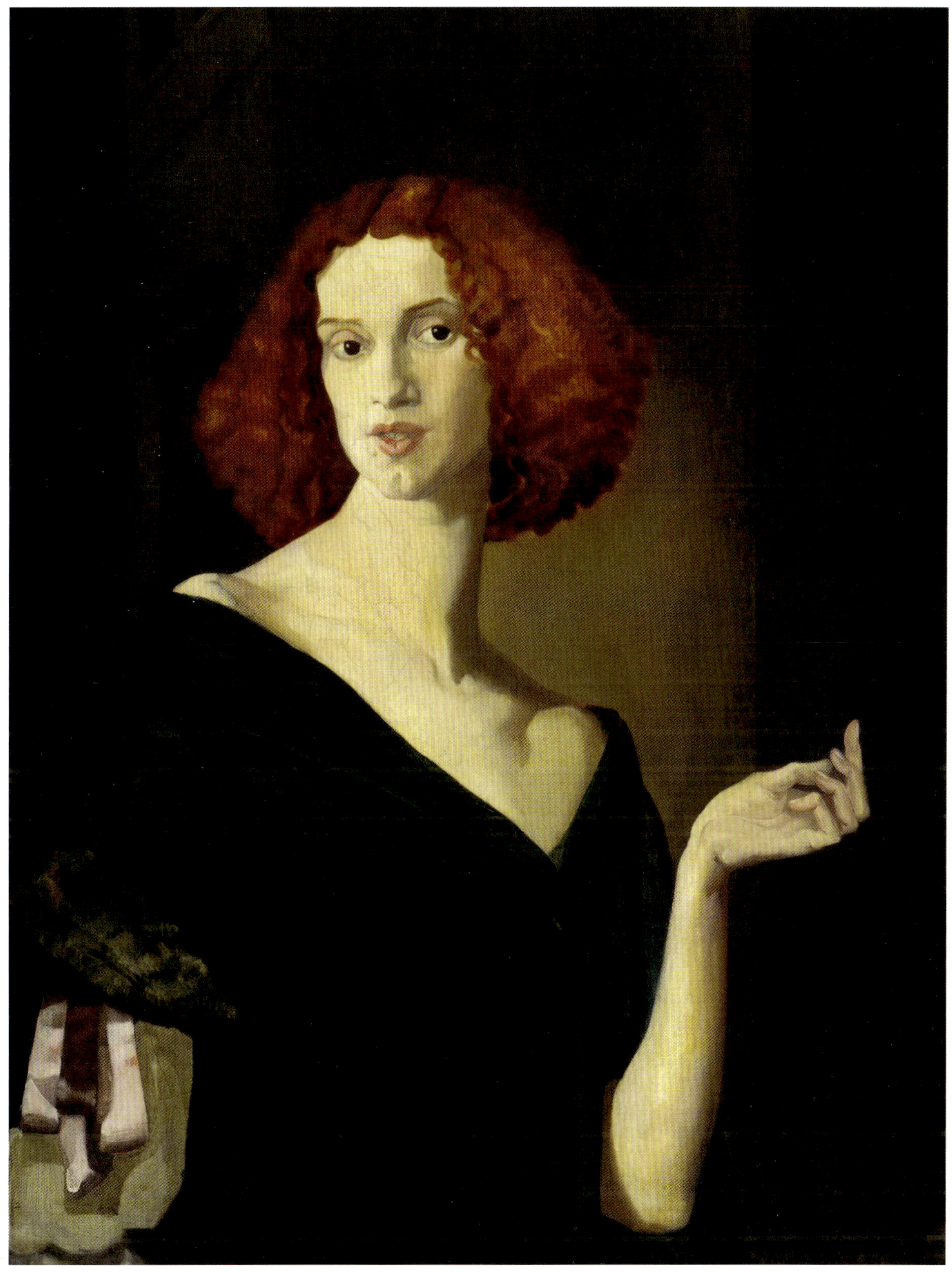

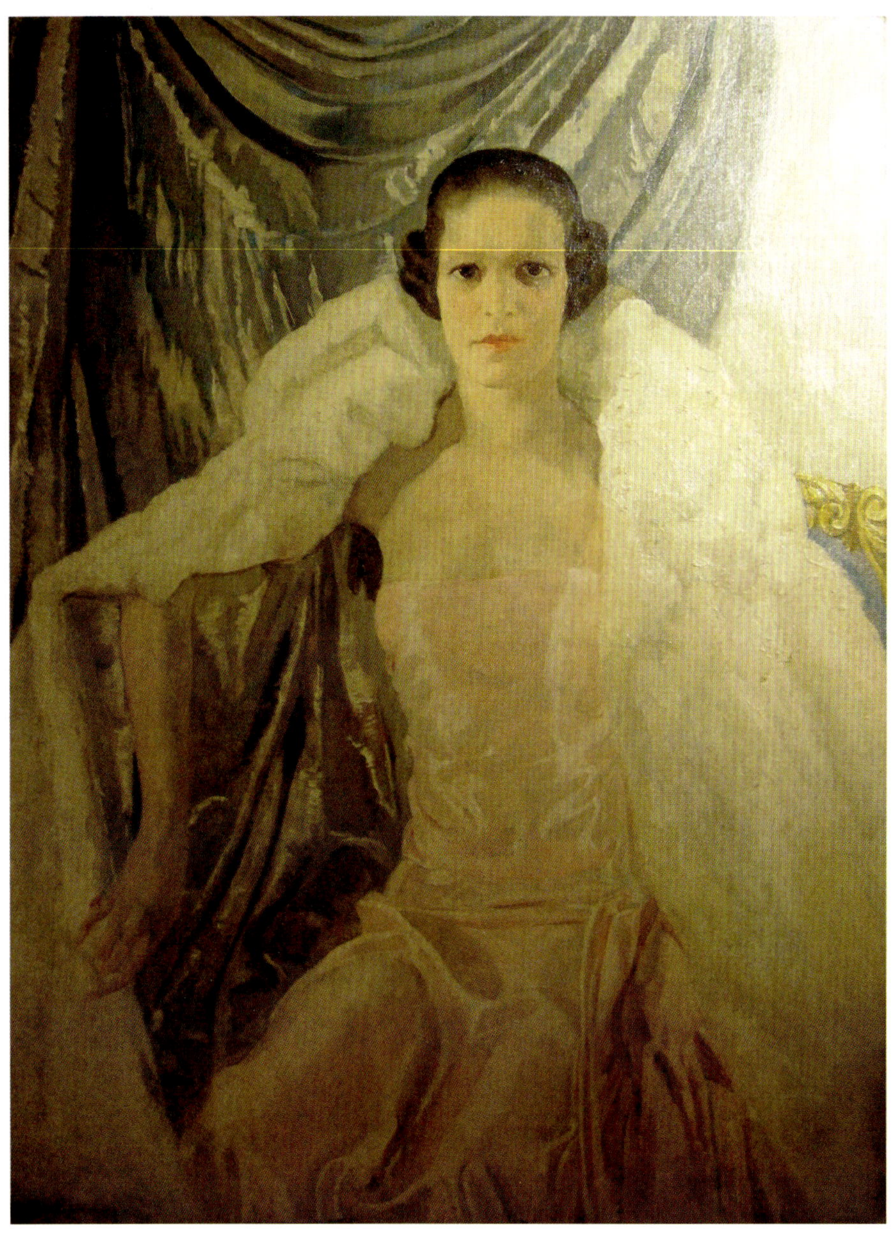

Fig.3.7
Doris Zinkeisen, *Anna*, 1927, oil on canvas.

Fig.3.8
Doris Zinkeisen, *Edythe Baker*, 1928, oil on canvas. Exhibited at the Royal Academy and Paris Salon (Bronze Medal). Edythe almost certainly wears a costume designed by Doris Zinkeisen. See also Fig.1.61 and Fig.1.62.

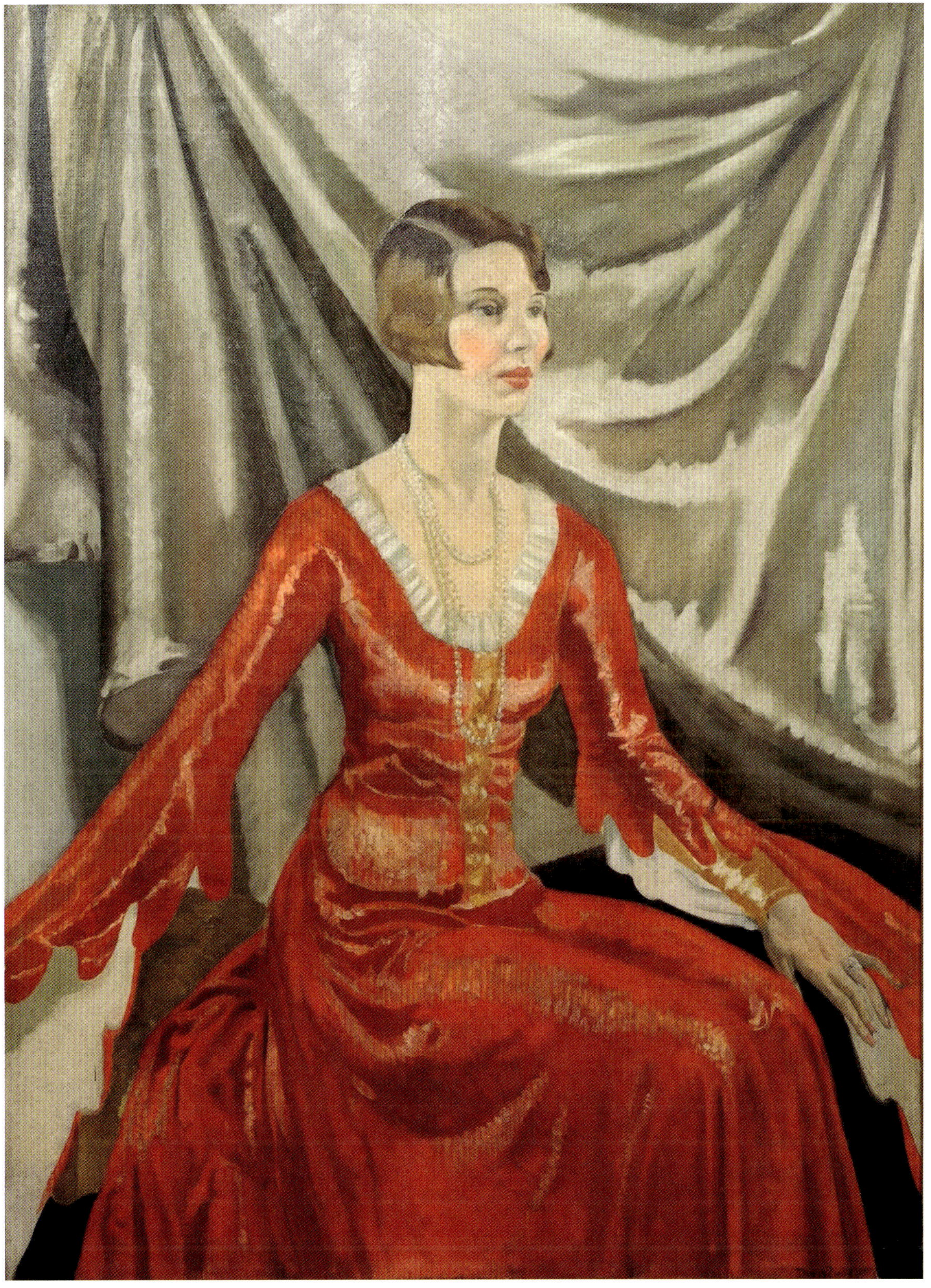

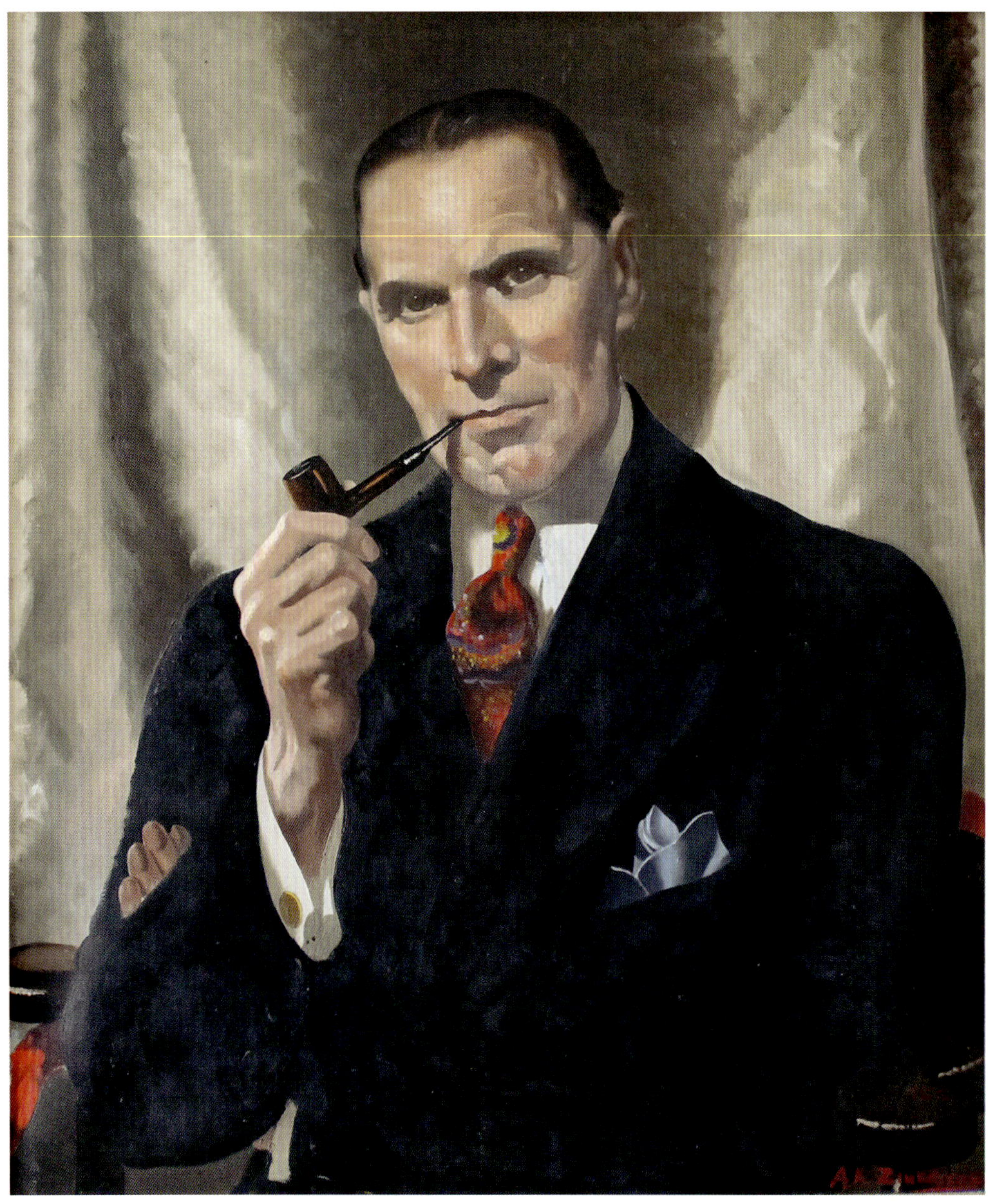

Fig.3.9
Anna Zinkeisen, *Stanley Beeton*, 1927, oil on canvas. Stanley Beeton (1874-1941) was a prominent electrical engineer involved in electric trams in Madrid and Dublin, in addition to several electricity companies. He later bought an estate in Hertfordshire, farmed, and hunted.

Fig.3.10
Anna Zinkeisen, *The Olympians*, 1927, oil on canvas.

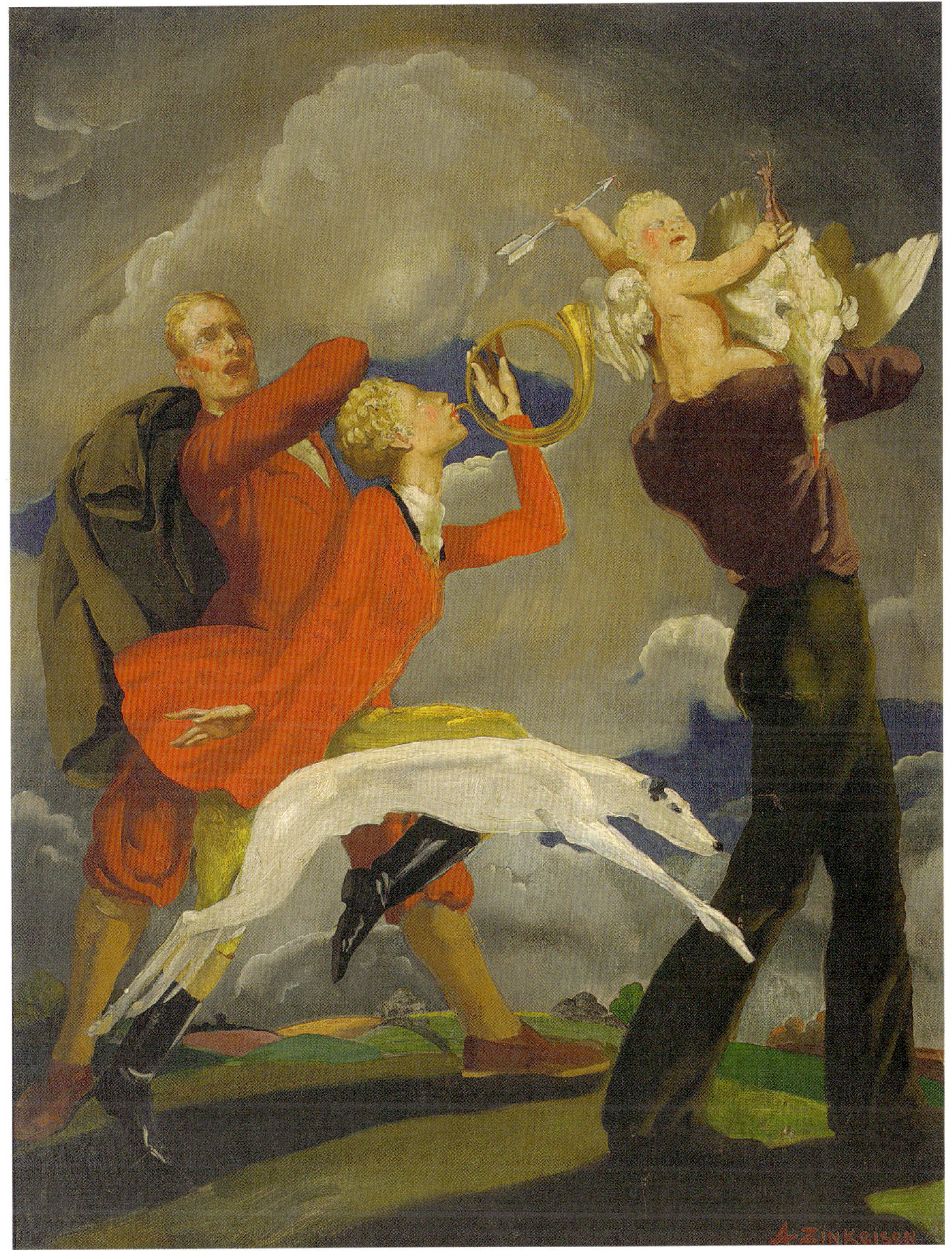
A ZINKEISEN

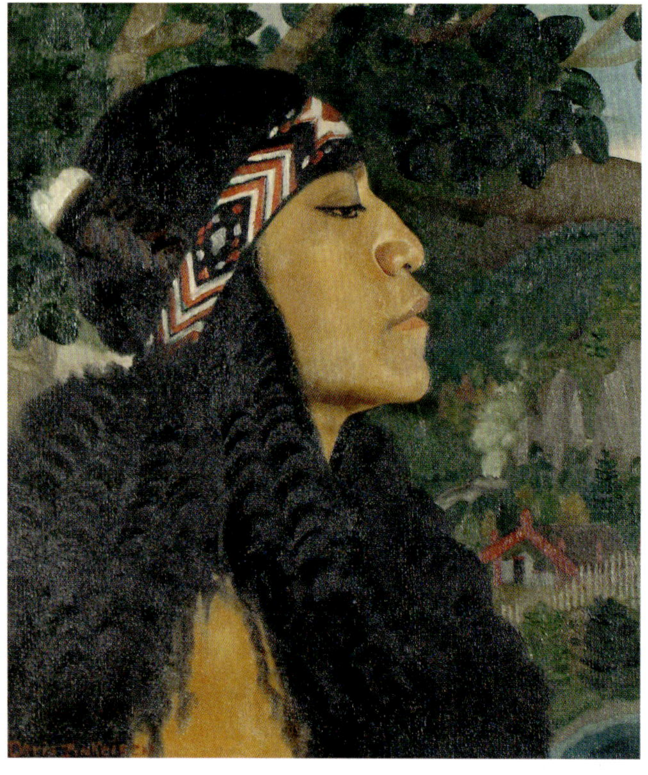

Fig.3.11
Doris Zinkeisen, *Ana Hato*, 1929, oil on canvas. Exhibited at the Paris Salon as *Ann, the Māori Girl*. Ana Hato (1907-1953) was New Zealand's most famous Māori singer and first Māori recording star, whom Doris met and heard sing when in New Zealand in 1929 when she captured this remarkably accurate portrait.

Fig.3.12
Doris Zinkeisen, *Self-portrait*, 1929, oil on canvas. Exhibited at the Royal Academy and Paris Salon.

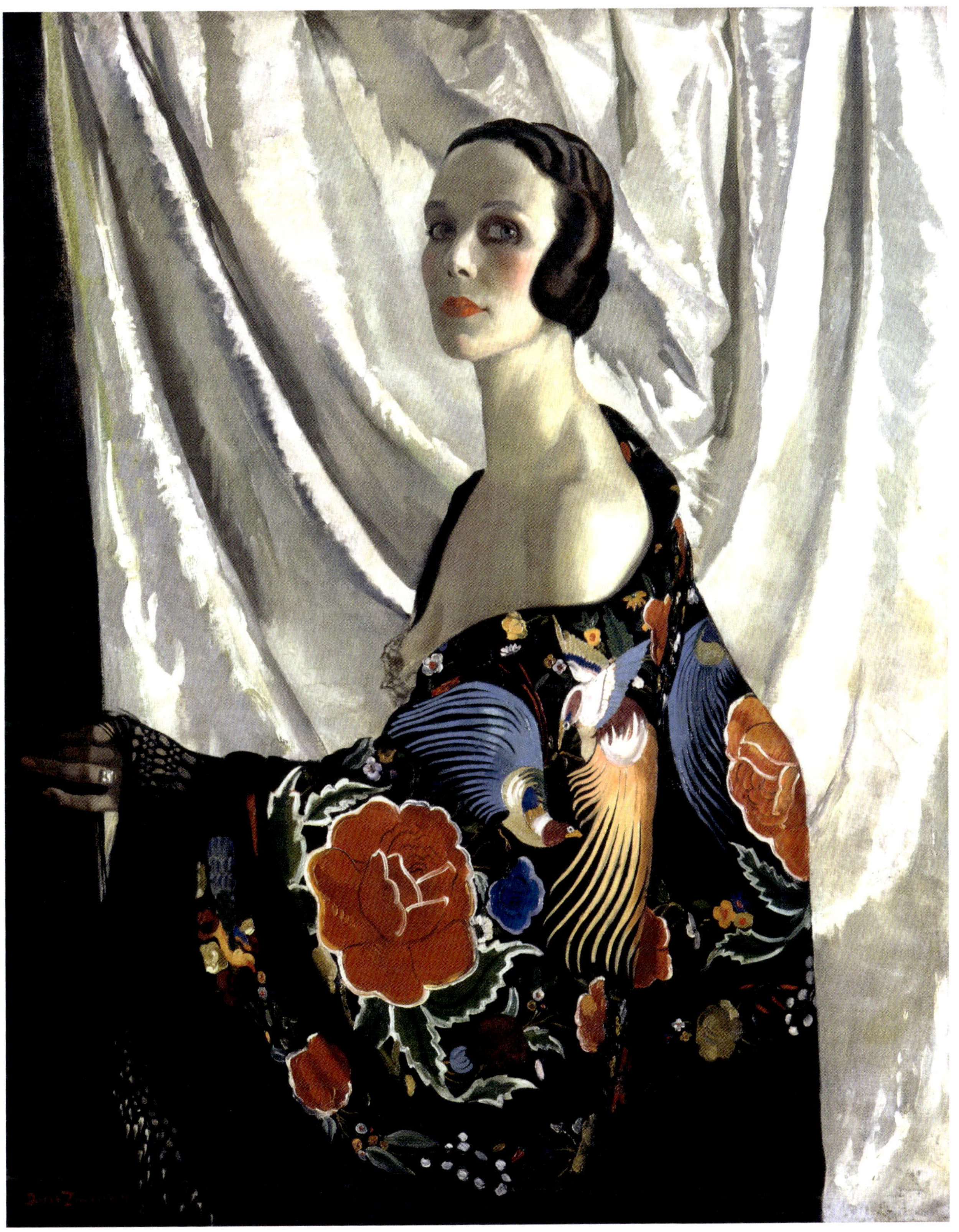

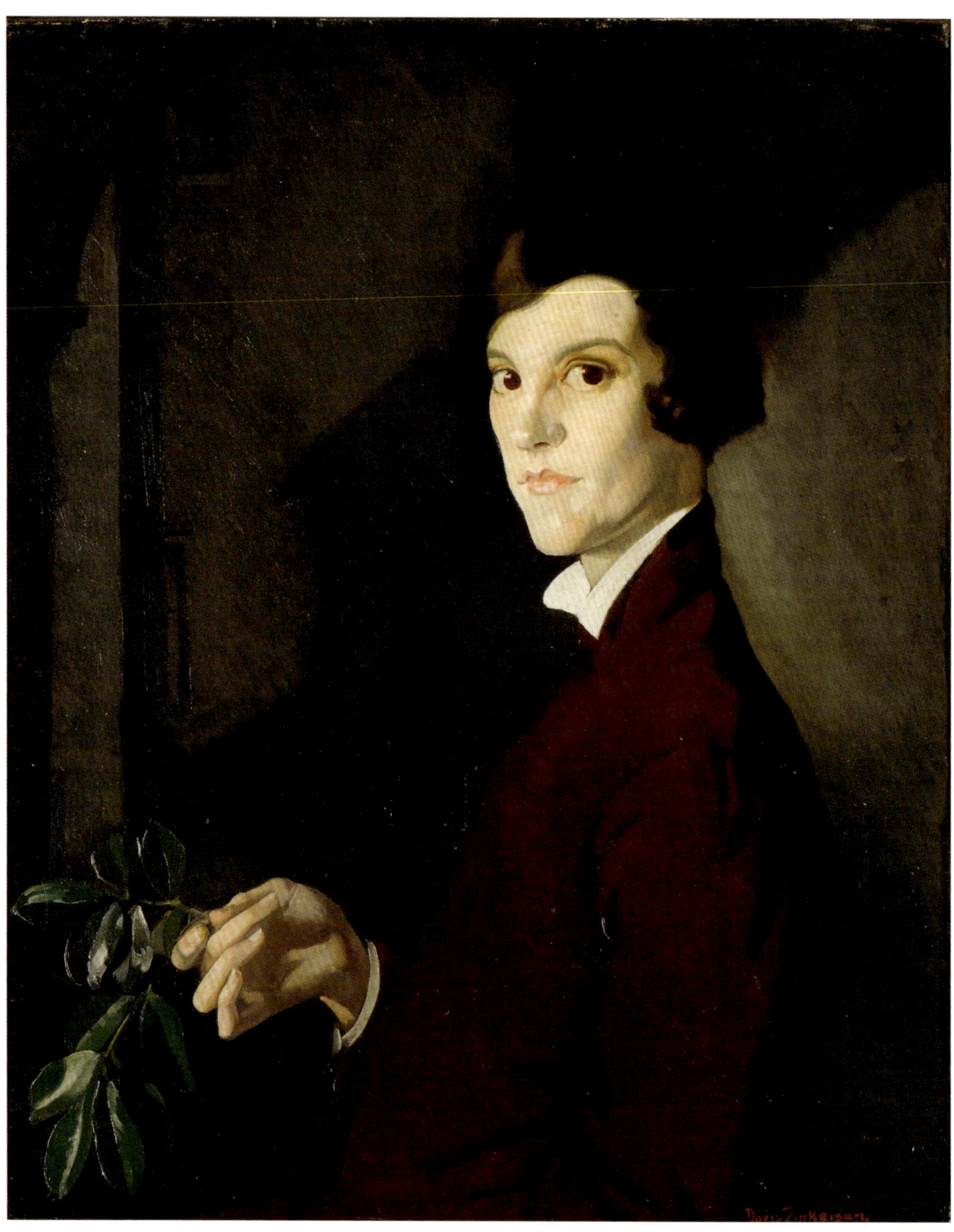

Fig.3.13
Doris Zinkeisen, *Edith Weaver*, 1930, oil on canvas. Exhibited at the Paris Salon (Silver Medal) as *The Girl with the Laurels*. It is not certain, but the sitter may be the daughter of the Australian conservative parliamentarian Reginald Weaver (1876-1945), who married manufacturer Terence Gwyer M.B.E. at St Alban's Cathedral, England, in 1937 and might have met the artist when she visited Australia in 1929.

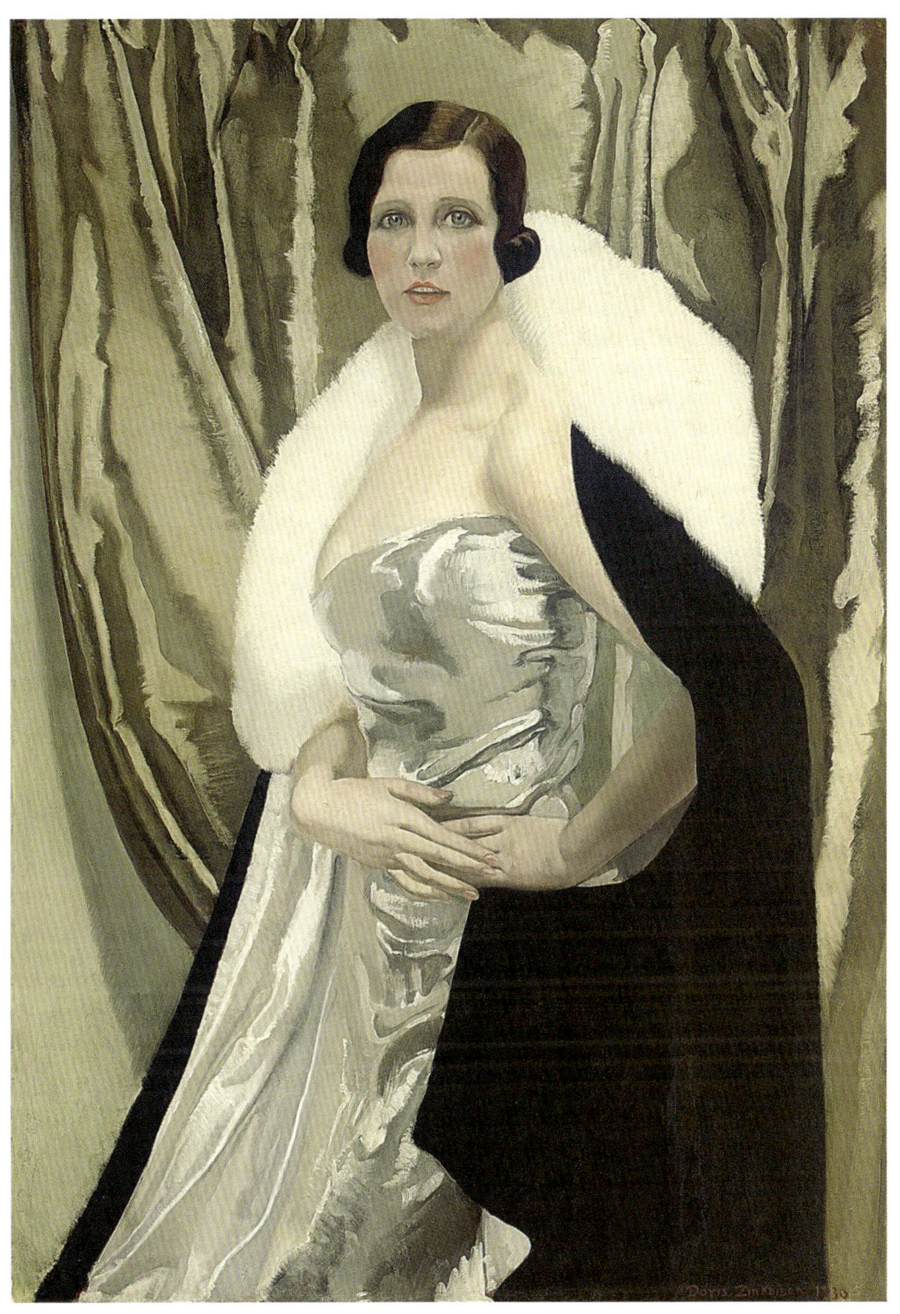

Fig.3.14

Doris Zinkeisen, *Mrs Irwin Buxton*, 1930, oil on canvas.

Exhibited at the Royal Academy.

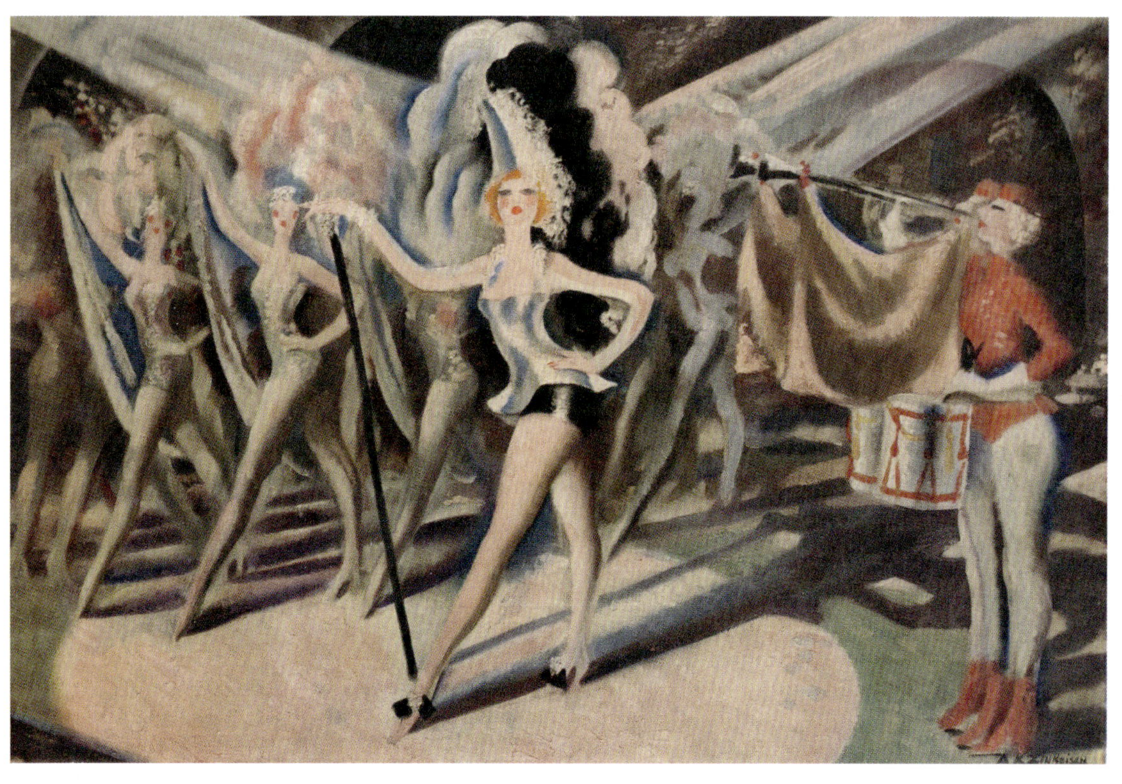

Fig.3.15
Anna Zinkeisen, *Cabaret Scene*, *circa* 1930, oil on canvas.

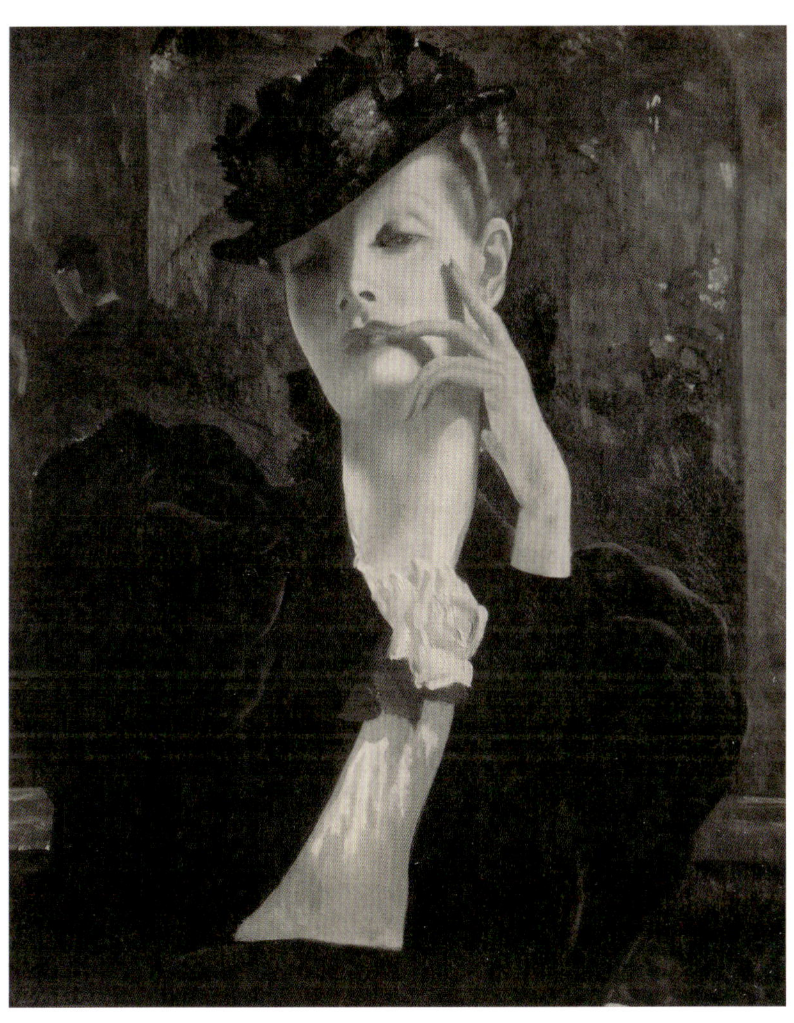

Fig.3.16

Anna Zinkeisen, *The Fair Lady*, 1930s, oil on canvas.

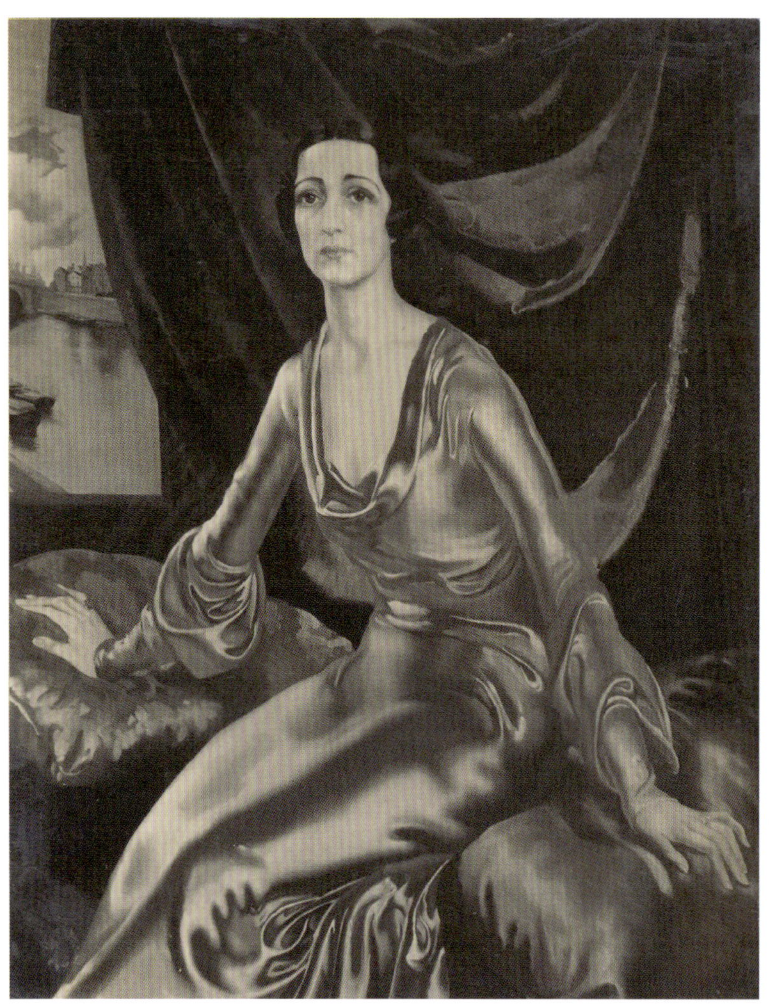

Fig.3.17
Anna Zinkeisen, *Mrs Ralph Woodford St Hill*, 1931, oil on canvas.
Exhibited at the Royal Academy.

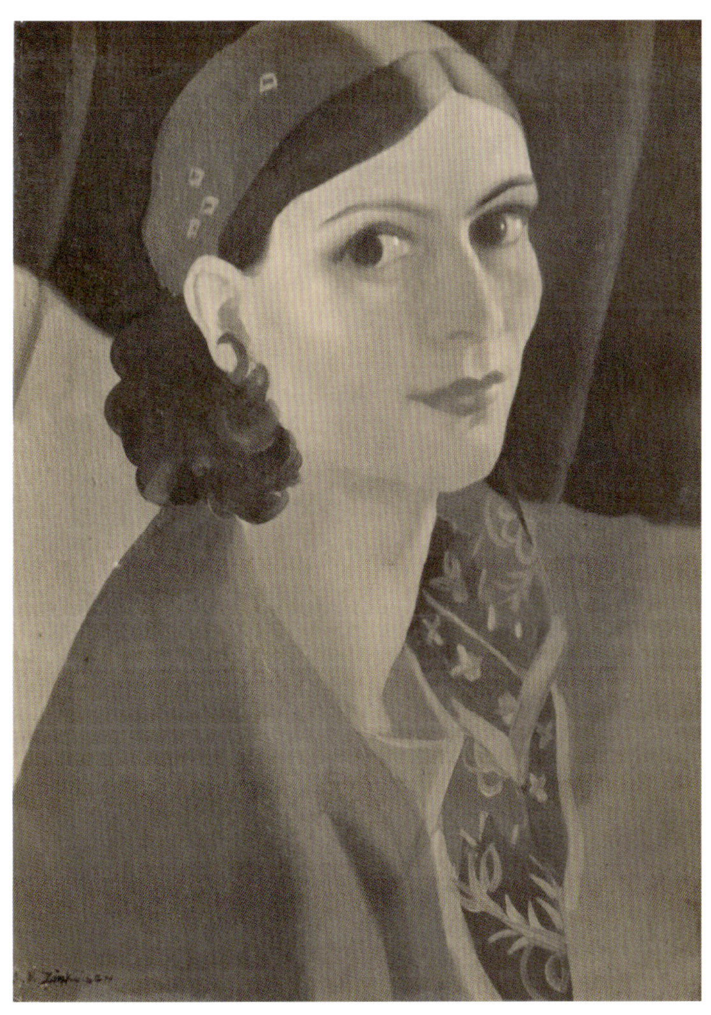

Fig.3.18
Anna Zinkeisen, *Diana*, 1930s, oil on canvas.

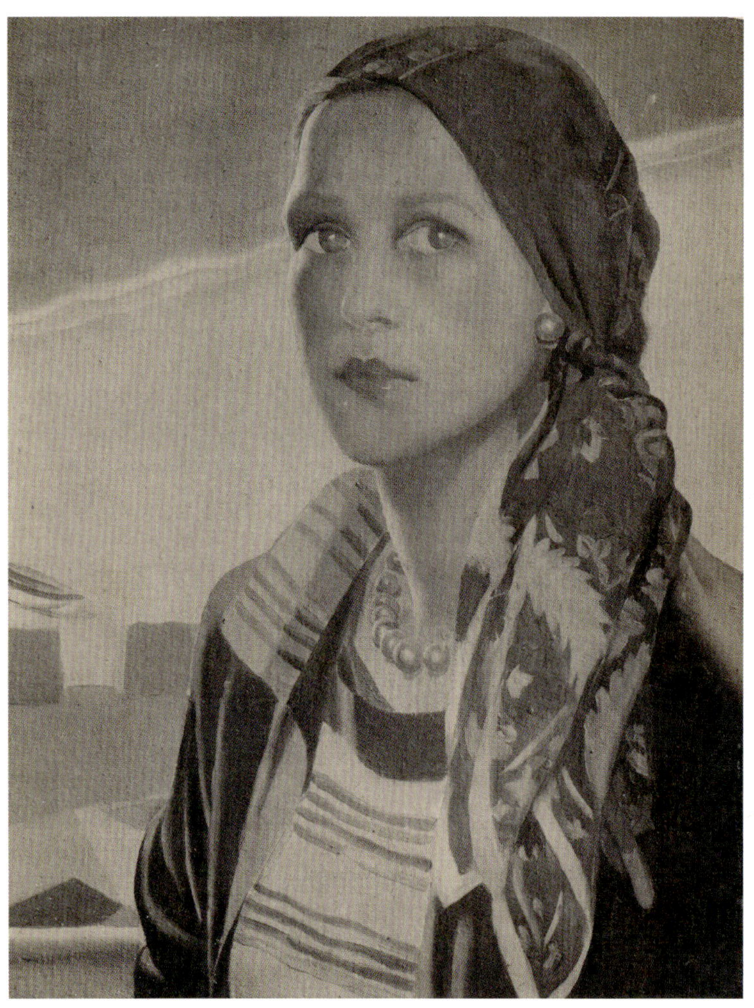

Fig.3.19
Anna Zinkeisen, *Lady with a Headscarf before a Beach*, 1930s, oil on canvas.

Fig.3.20
Anna Zinkeisen, *Mrs David Heneage*, 1930s, oil on canvas.

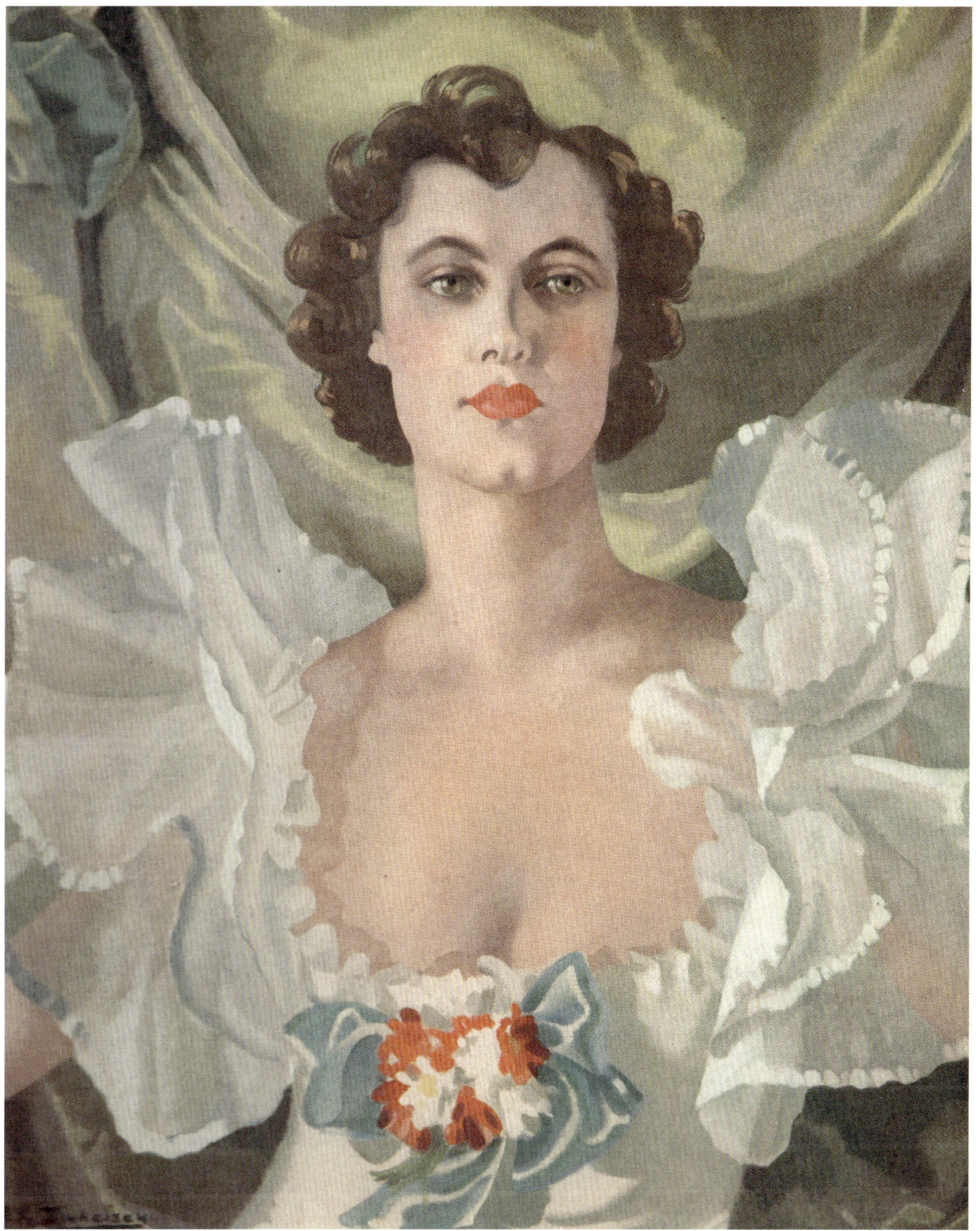

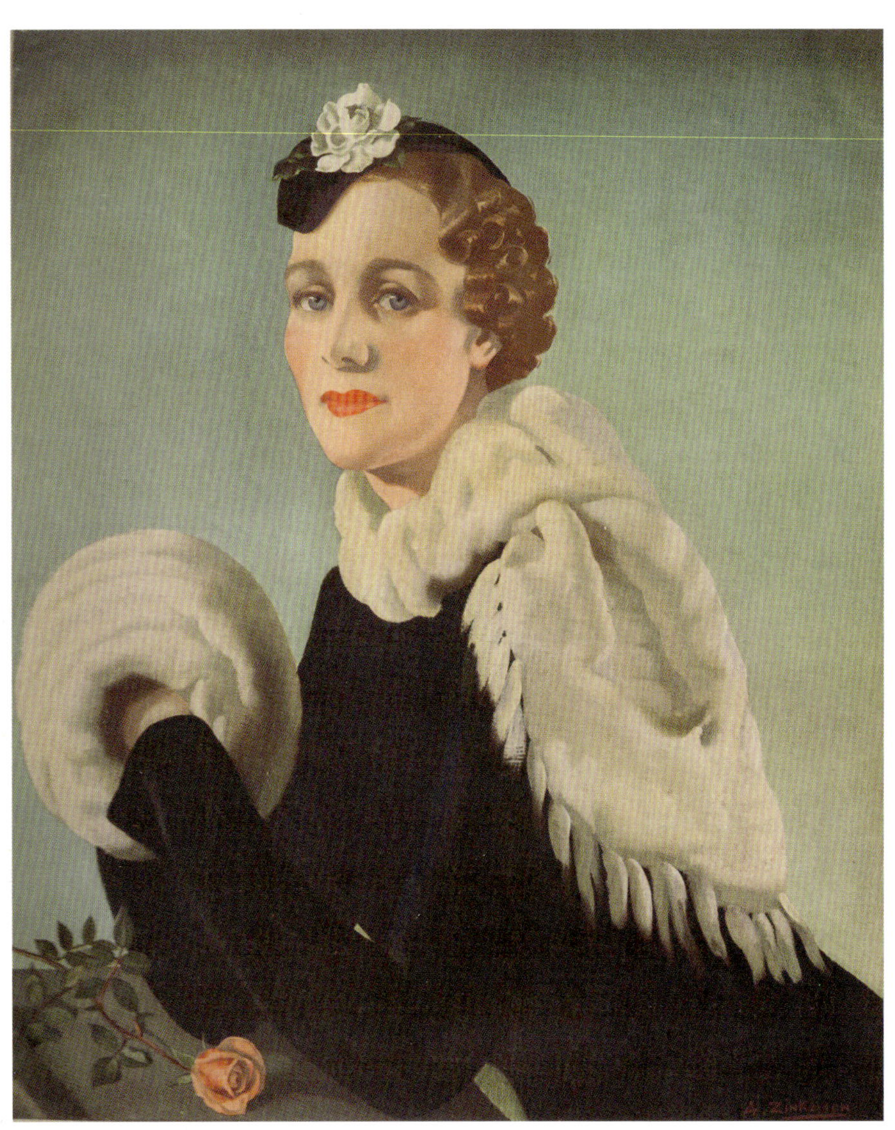

Fig.3.21
Anna Zinkeisen, *Mrs Eric Preston*, 1930s, oil on canvas.

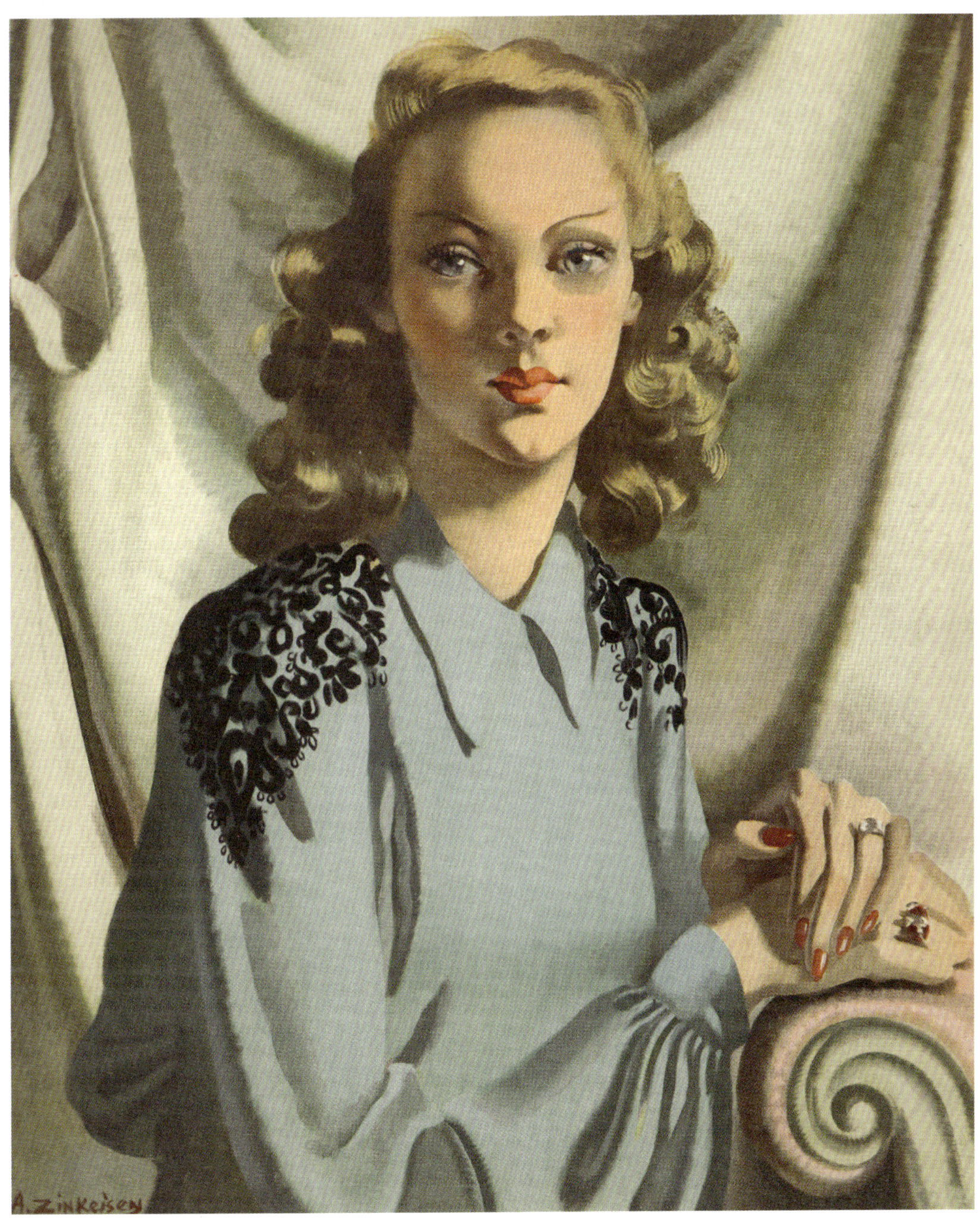

Fig.3.22
Anna Zinkeisen, *The Viscountess Errington, circa* 1942, oil on canvas.

The sitter is the Hon. Esmé Mary Gabriel Harmsworth (1922-2011) the daughter of the 2nd Viscount Rothermere, who married Viscount Errington (1918-1991), later the 3rd Earl of Cromer, in 1942. She was a former Lady-in-Waiting to the Queen.

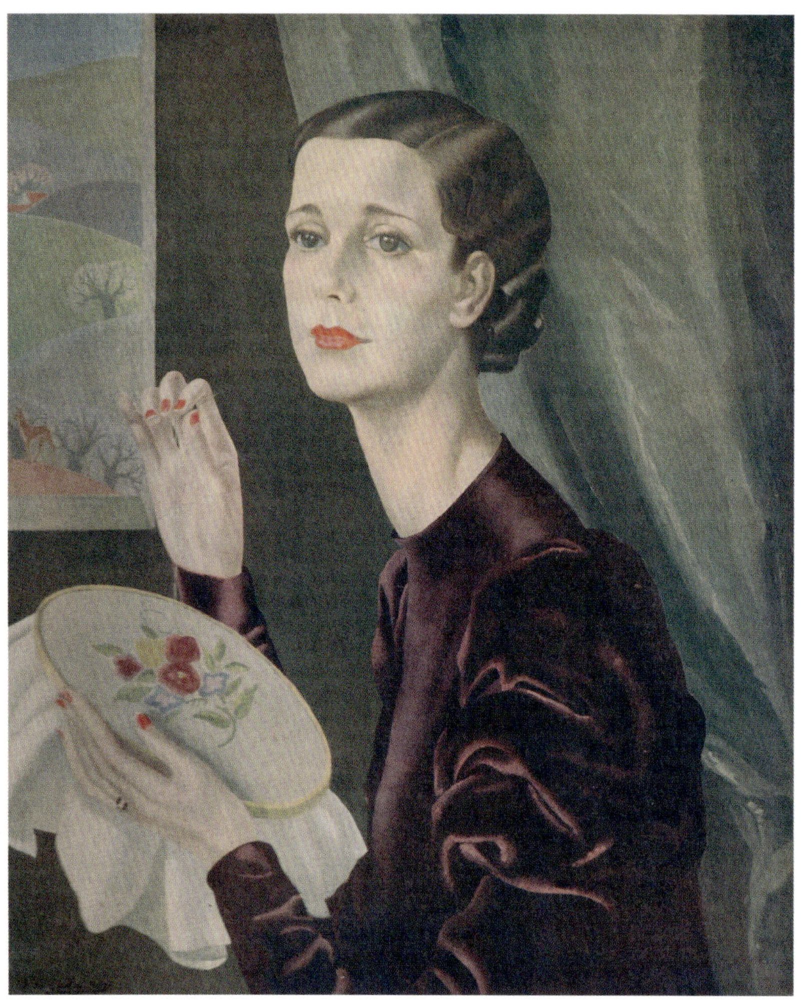

Fig.3.23
Anna Zinkeisen, *The Lady Doria Childe*, *circa* 1930, oil on canvas.

This portrait is of Lady Doria Hope (1908-1942), who was the daughter of the Duke of Newcastle. Although she died young at just thirty-four, she managed to fit in two marriages, firstly to Freddie Childe in 1930 (which helps to date this portrait), and secondly to Stefan Neumann in 1936.

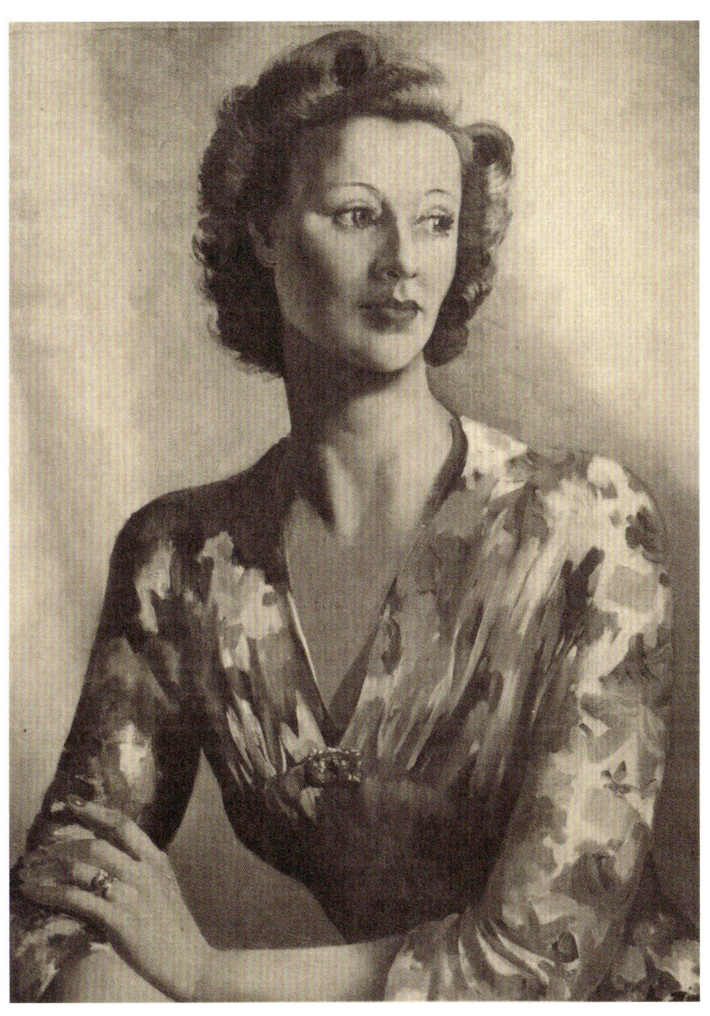

Fig.3.24
Anna Zinkeisen, *Miss Eileen Peel*, 1930s, oil on canvas. The likeness is of the actress Eileen Peel (1909-1999), who appeared in numerous cinema and television films between 1932 and 1976.

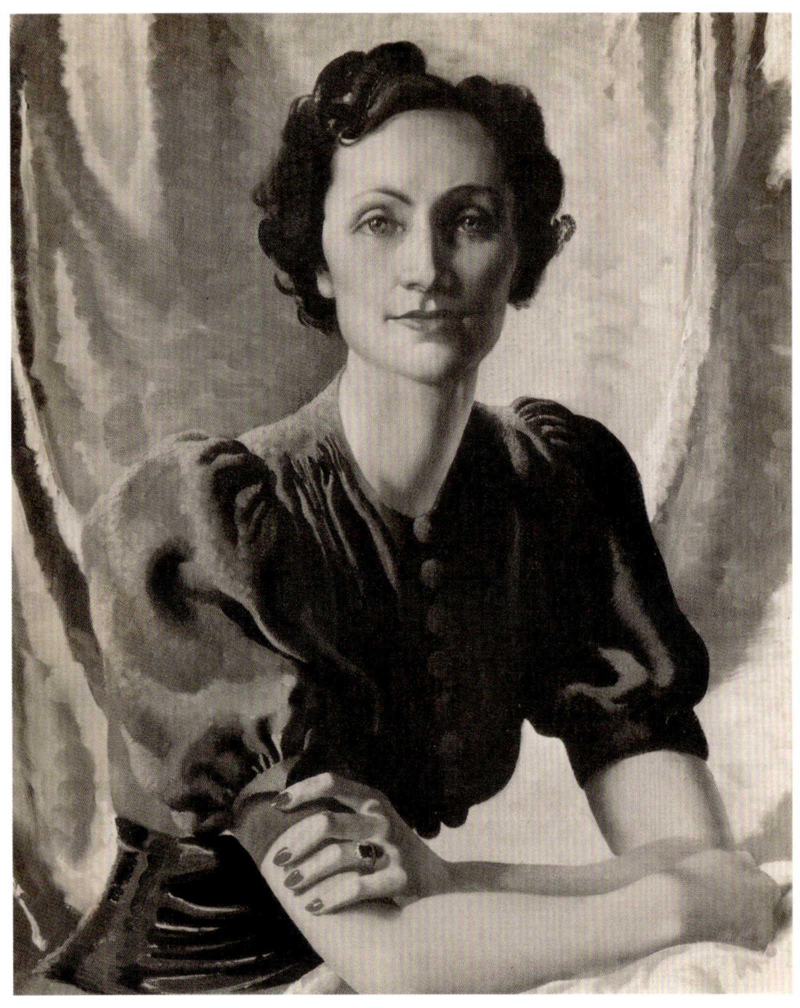

Fig.3.25
Anna Zinkeisen, *Mrs Philip Symmington*, 1930s, oil on canvas.

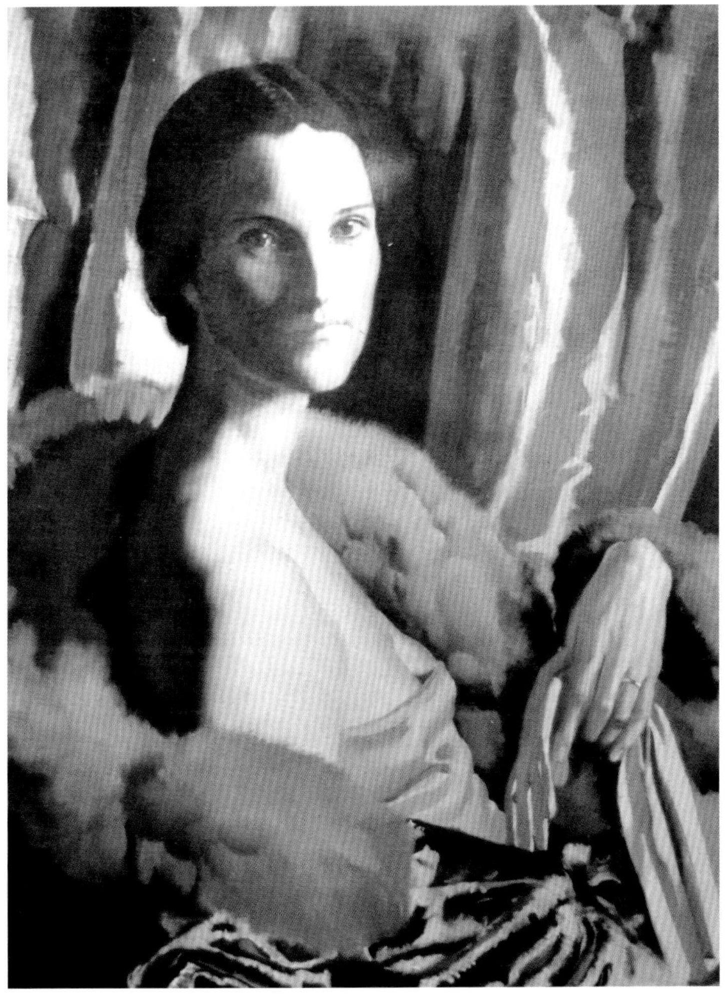

Fig.3.26
Doris Zinkeisen, *Mrs Roland Dangerfield*, 1931, oil on canvas.

Exhibited at the Royal Academy and Paris Salon. The sitter's name was Margot, who in 1929 married Roland Dangerfield (1897-1964), a prominent individual in the printing business. The colouring and draughtsmanship were much admired when it was exhibited.

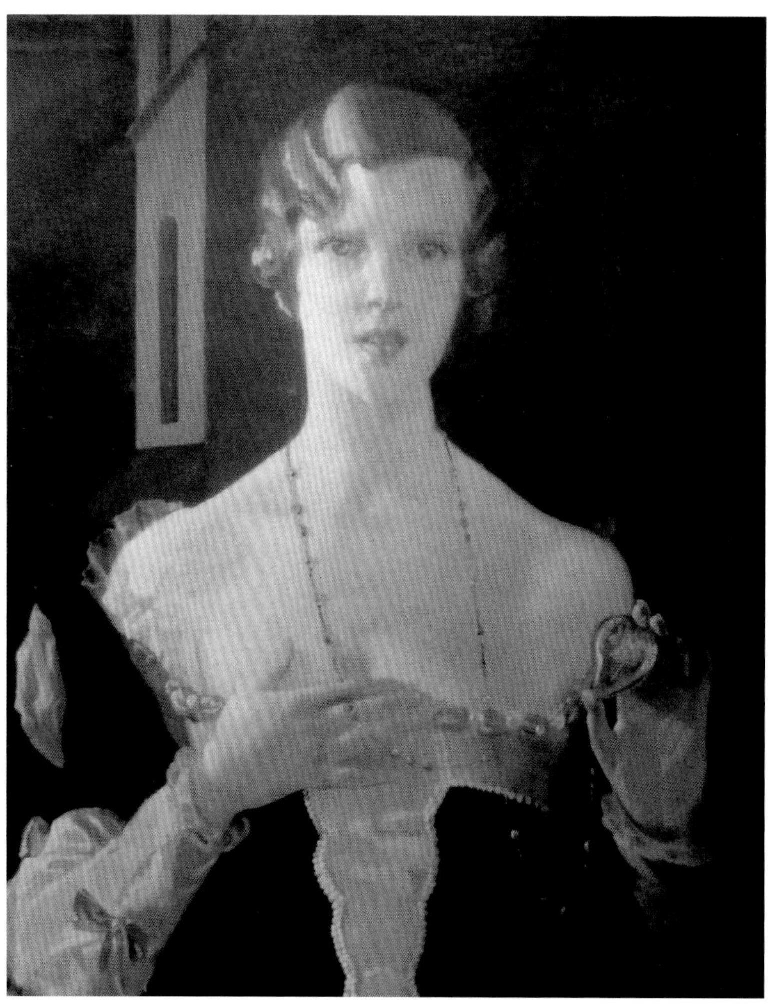

Fig.3.27
Doris Zinkeisen, *Vivien St George in Costume*, 1932, oil on canvas.
Exhibited at the Royal Academy. Vivien St George (1912-1975) was the love child of the artist Sir William Orpen and Evelyn St George (1870-1936), herself the daughter of the financier George Fisher Baker (1840-1931) – one of the richest men in America during his lifetime. During their scandalous long affair the couple were referred to as 'Jack and the Beanstalk', as Orpen was far shorter than the willowy Evelyn, who happened also to be eight years older than him. Vivien seems similarly to have led an adventurous private life and was married three times. This portrait by Doris was much admired by the critics in

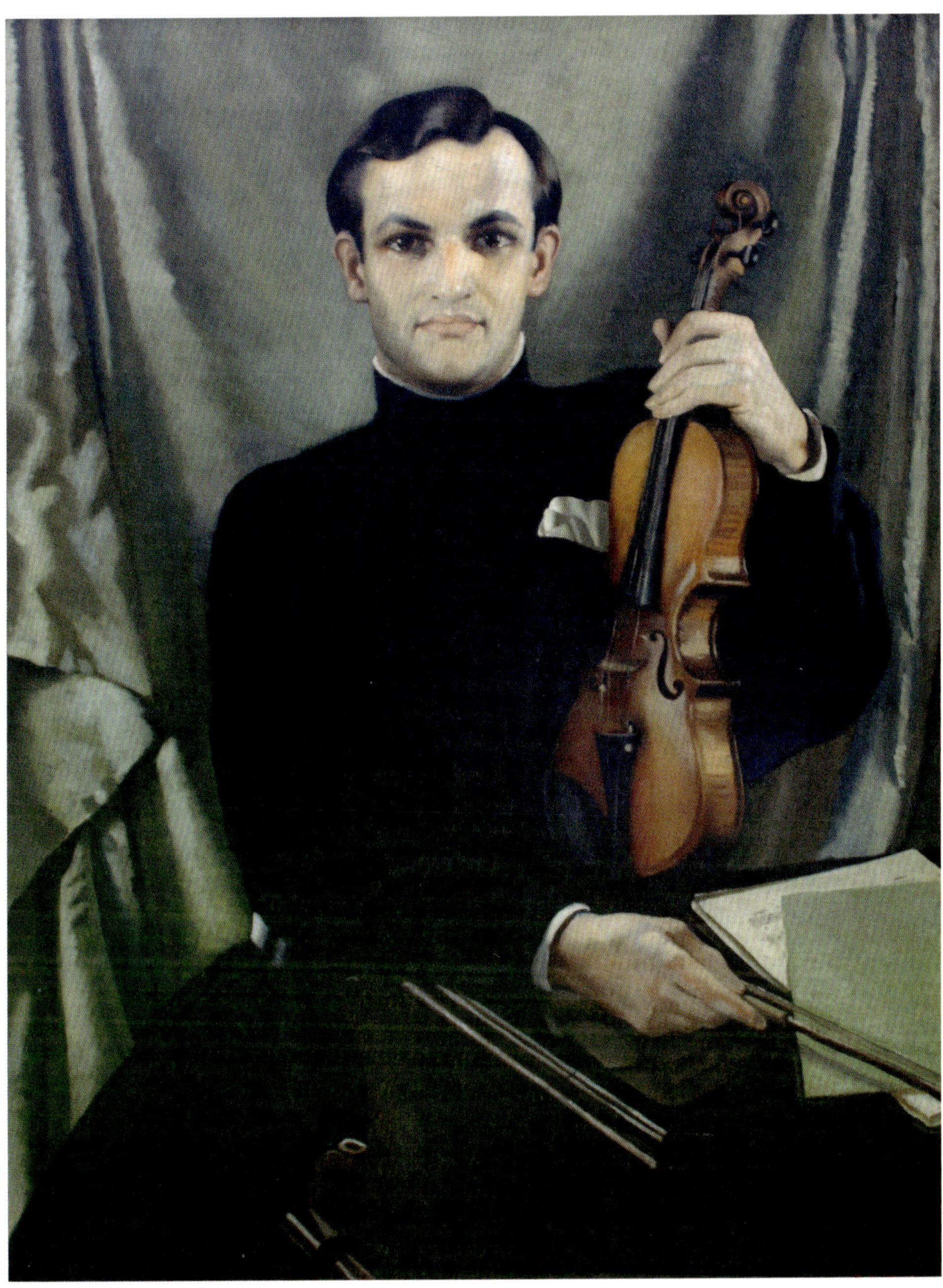

the press. Despite the modern coiffure, Vivien is dressed in the period costume designed by Doris and worn by the actress Chili Bouchier (1909-1999) in the 1931 film *Carnival*. The necklace is a hugely significant piece and was discussed in detail by jewellery expert Geoffrey Munn on *The Antiques Roadshow*.

Fig.3.28

Anna Zinkeisen, *Milan Yovanovitch Bratza*, 1932, oil on canvas.

Exhibited at the Paris Salon. See also Fig.1.58.

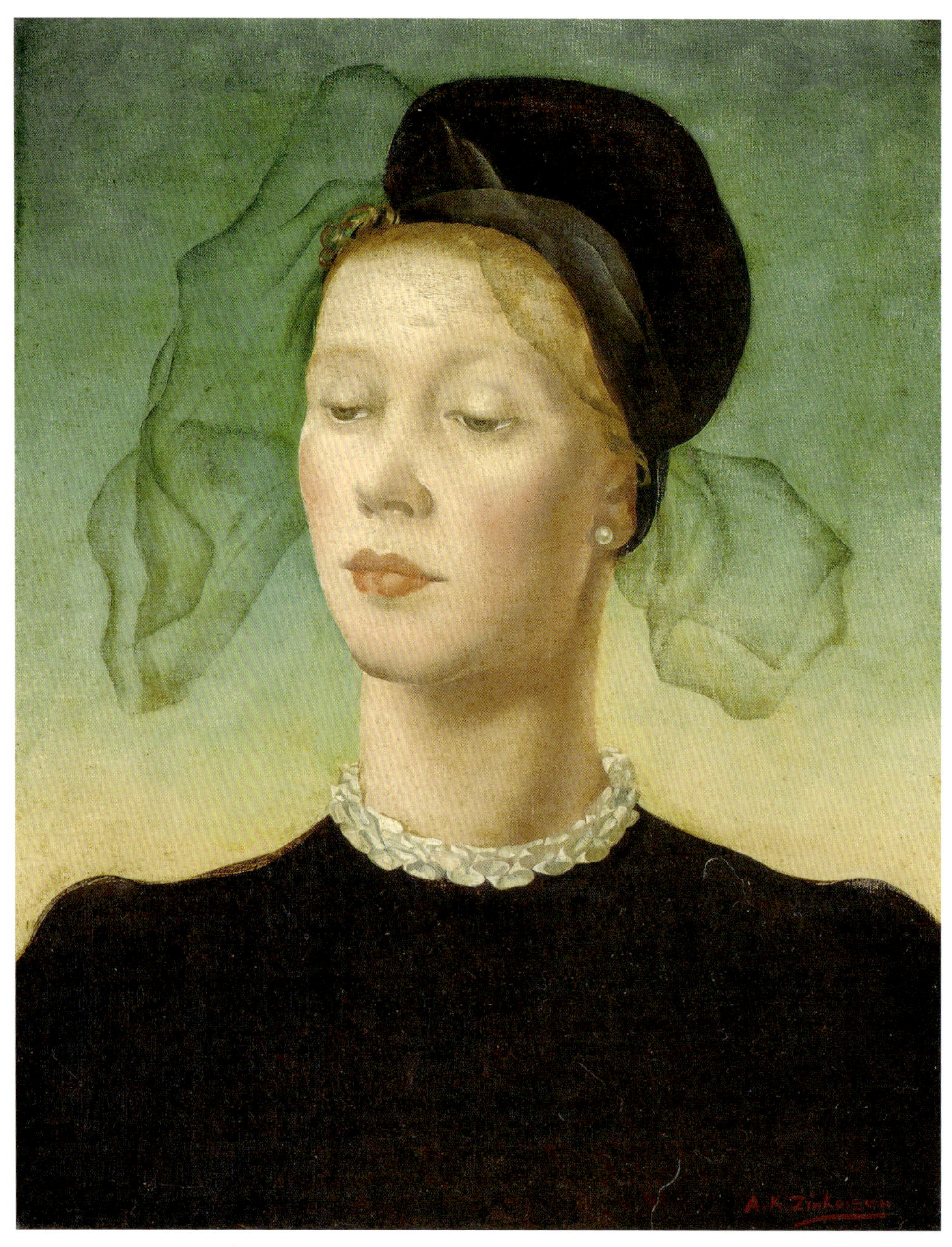

Fig.3.29

Anna Zinkeisen, *The Lady in Black*, 1930s, oil on canvas.

© Private collection/Christie's Images/Bridgeman Images [CH6317747].

Fig.3.30

Anna Zinkeisen, *Doris*, 1934, oil on canvas.

© Photograph courtesy of the estate of Doris Zinkeisen.

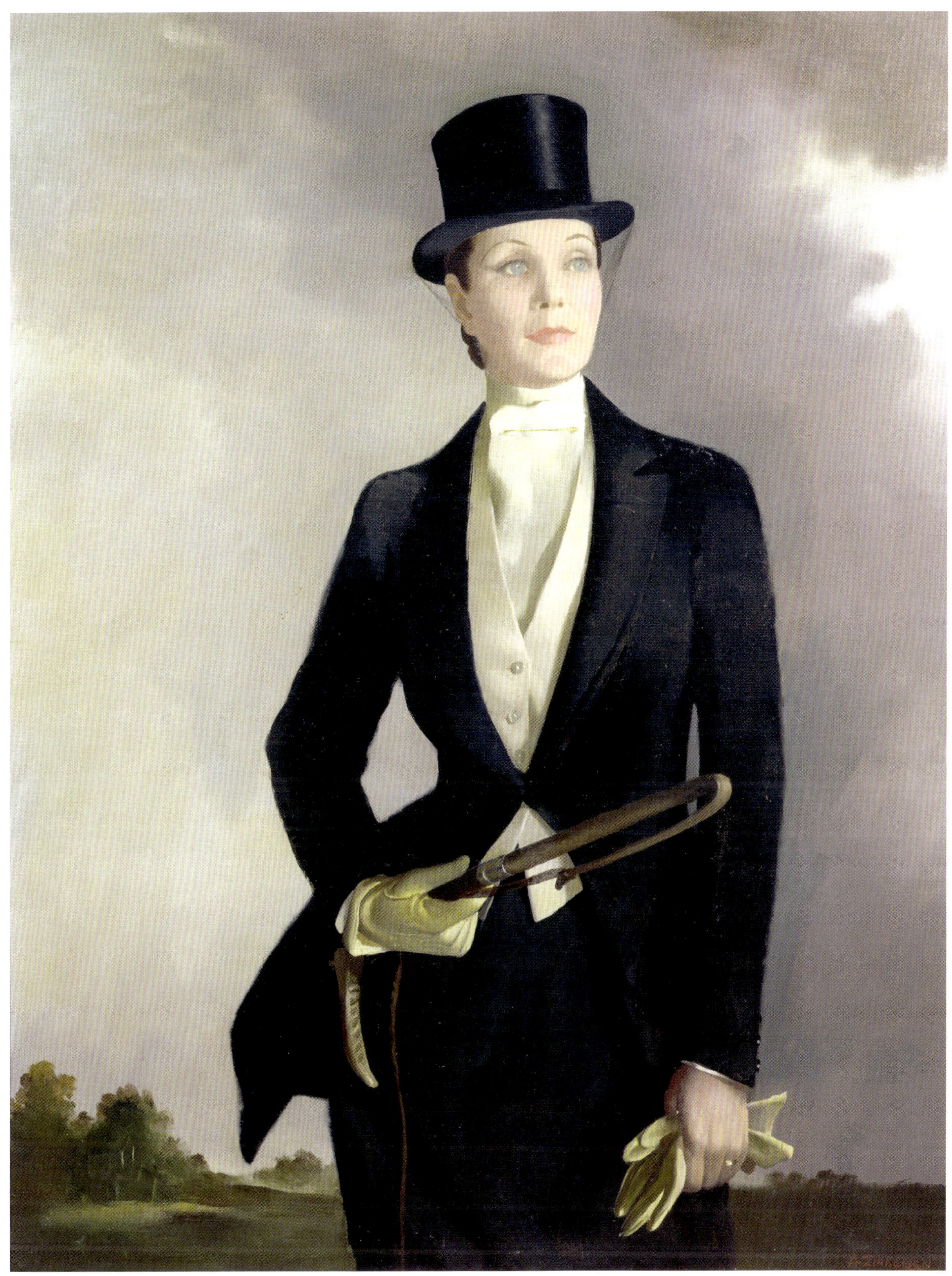

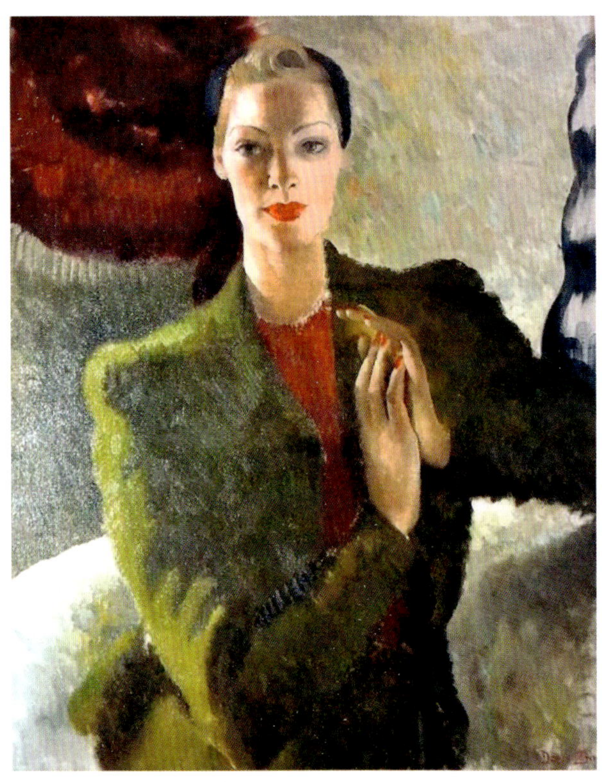

Fig.3.31
Doris Zinkeisen, *The Green Outfit*, 1930s, oil on canvas.

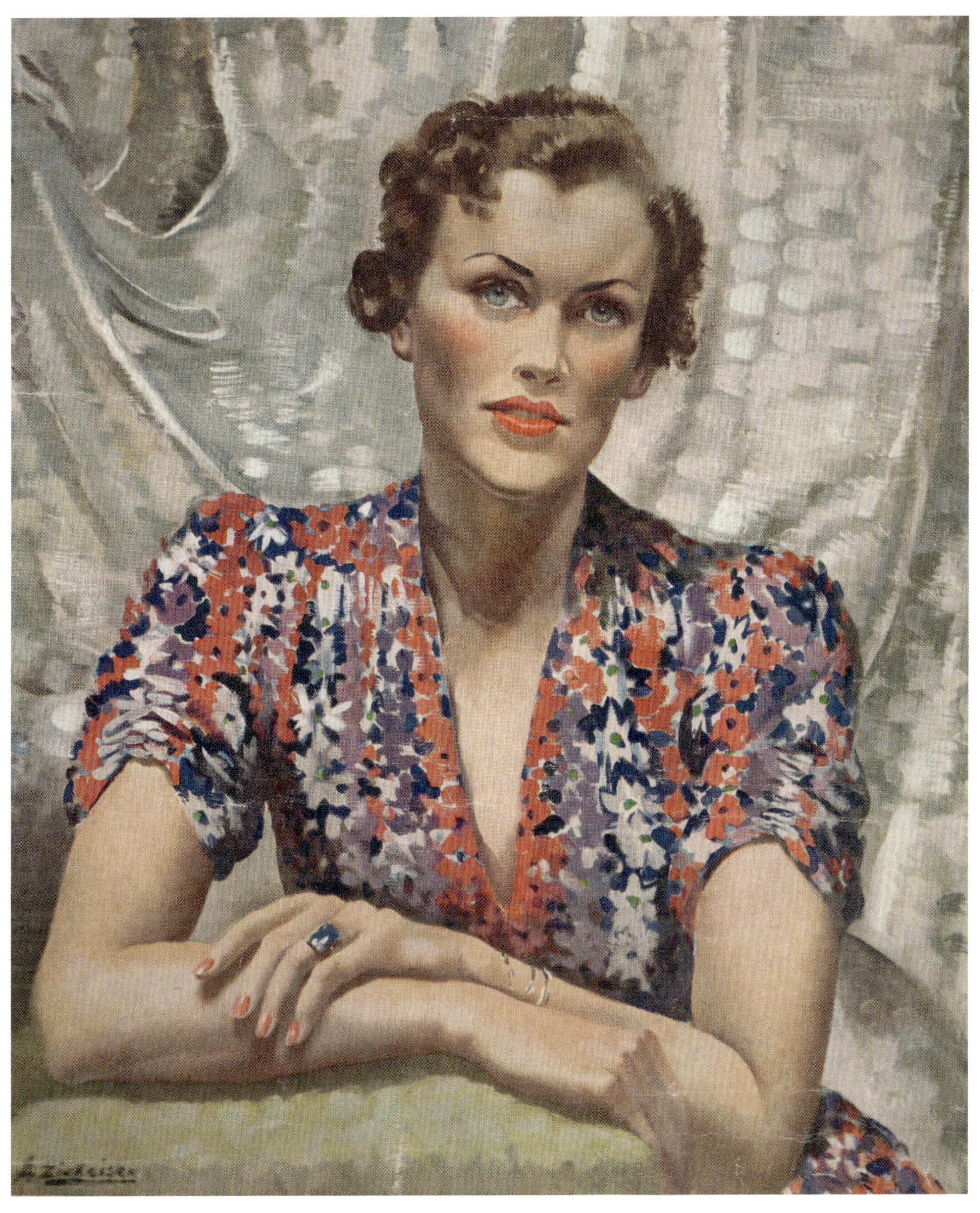

Fig.3.32
Anna Zinkeisen, *The Floral Dress*, 1930s, oil on canvas.

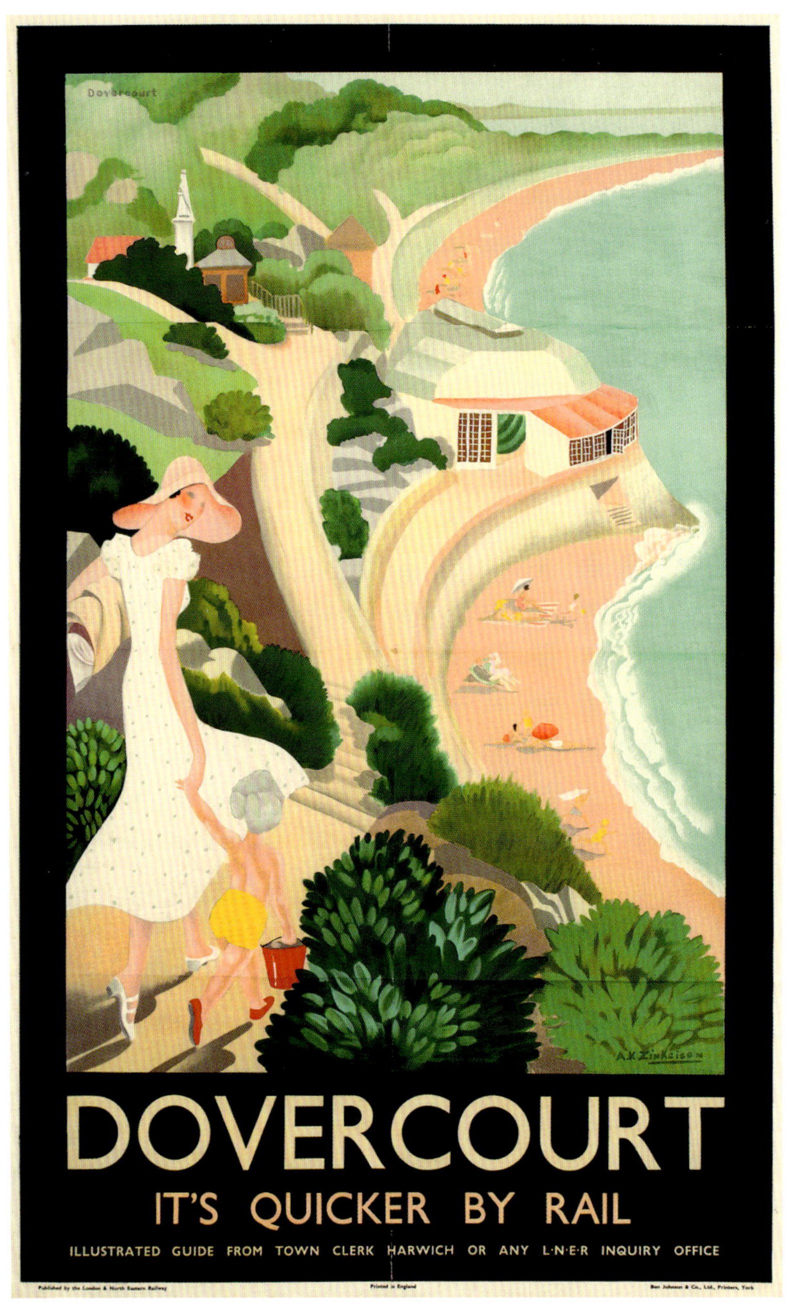

Fig.3.33

Anna Zinkeisen, *Dovercourt Poster*, 1933, colour lithograph.

© Private collection/Christie's Images/Bridgeman Images [CH6317757].

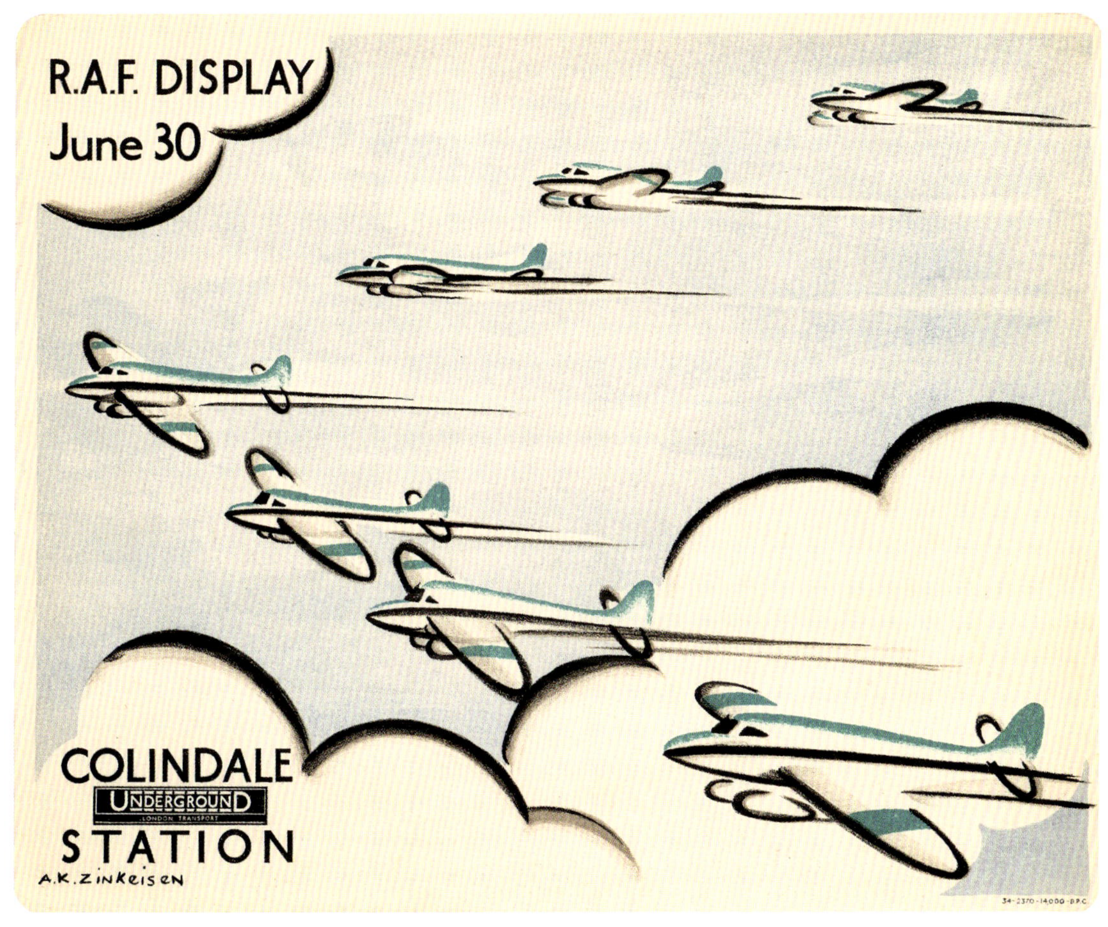

Fig.3.34
Anna Zinkeisen, *London Underground Transport Poster advertising an R.A.F. Display*, 1930s, colour lithograph.
© Private collection/Christie's Images/Bridgeman Images [CH1198196].

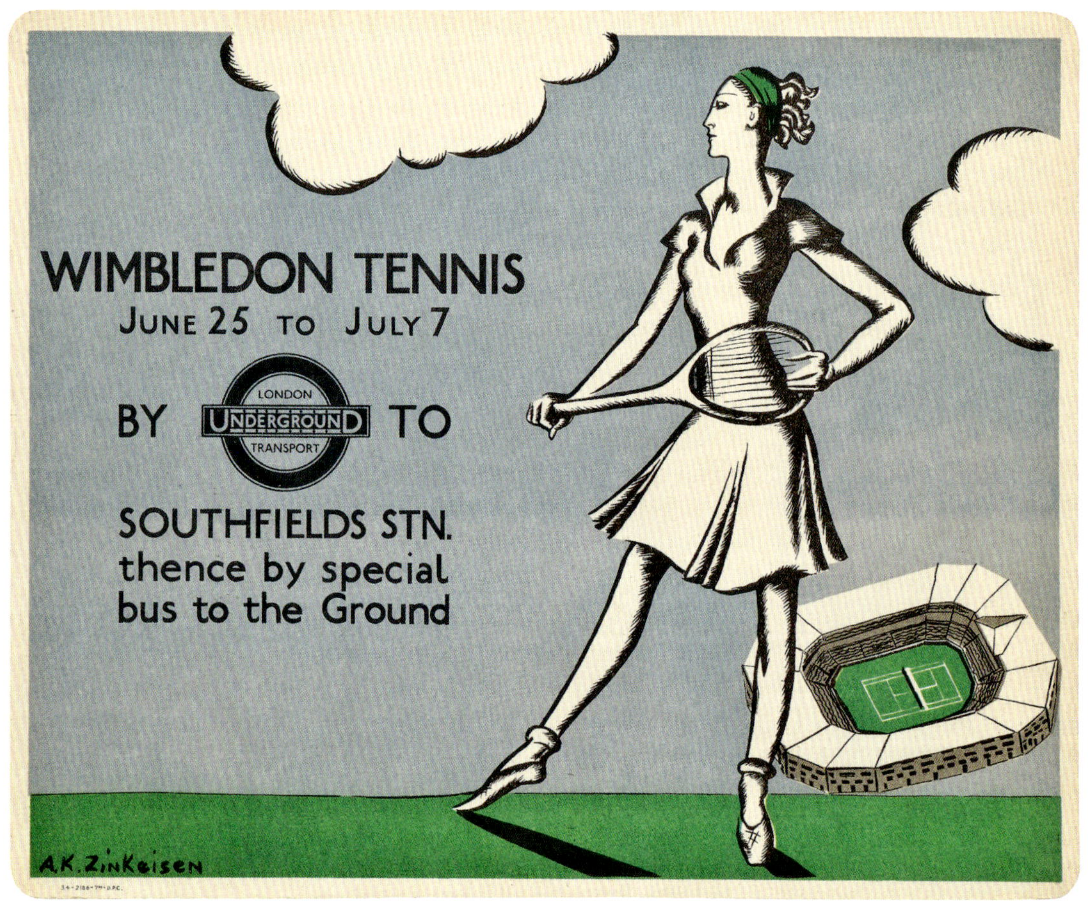

Fig.3.35
Anna Zinkeisen, *London Underground Transport Poster advertising Tennis at Wimbledon*, 1930s, colour lithograph.

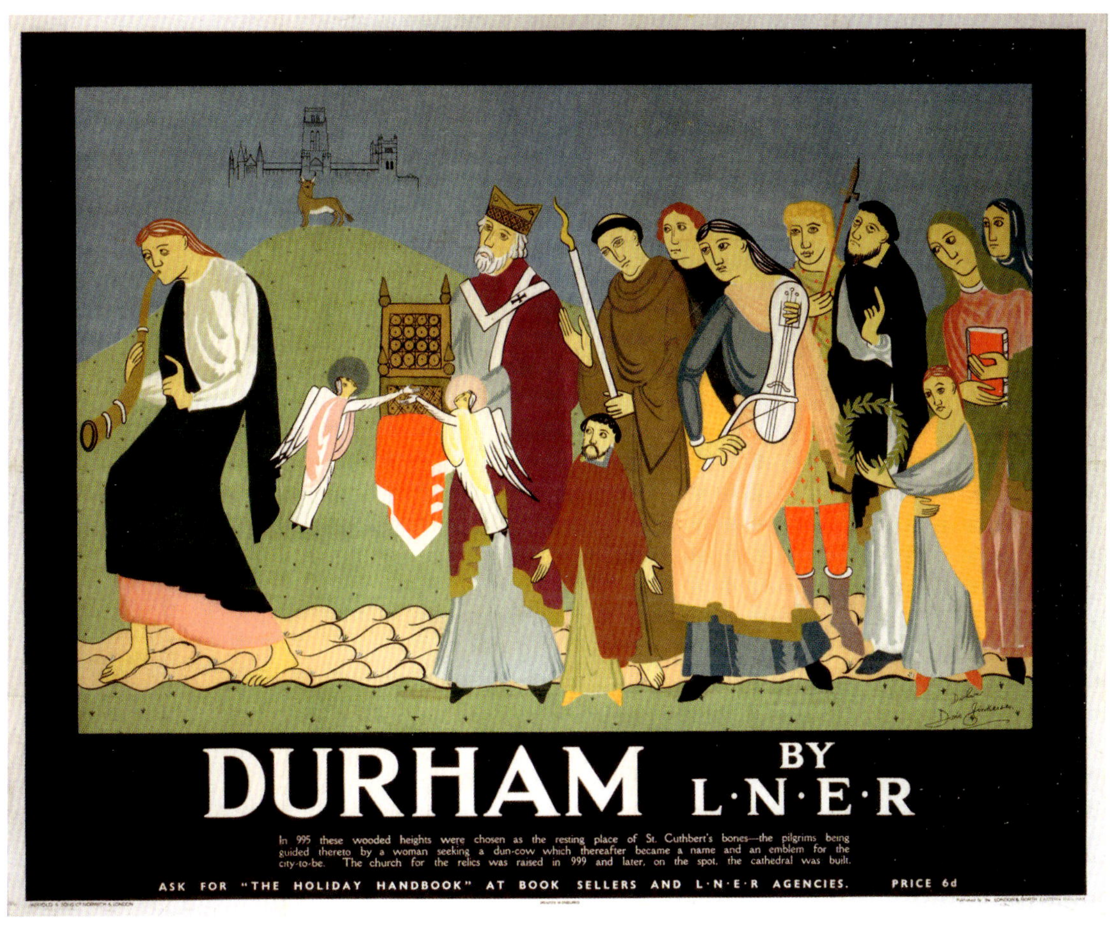

Fig.3.36
Doris Zinkeisen, *London and North Eastern Railway Poster advertising Durham*, 1930s, colour lithograph.

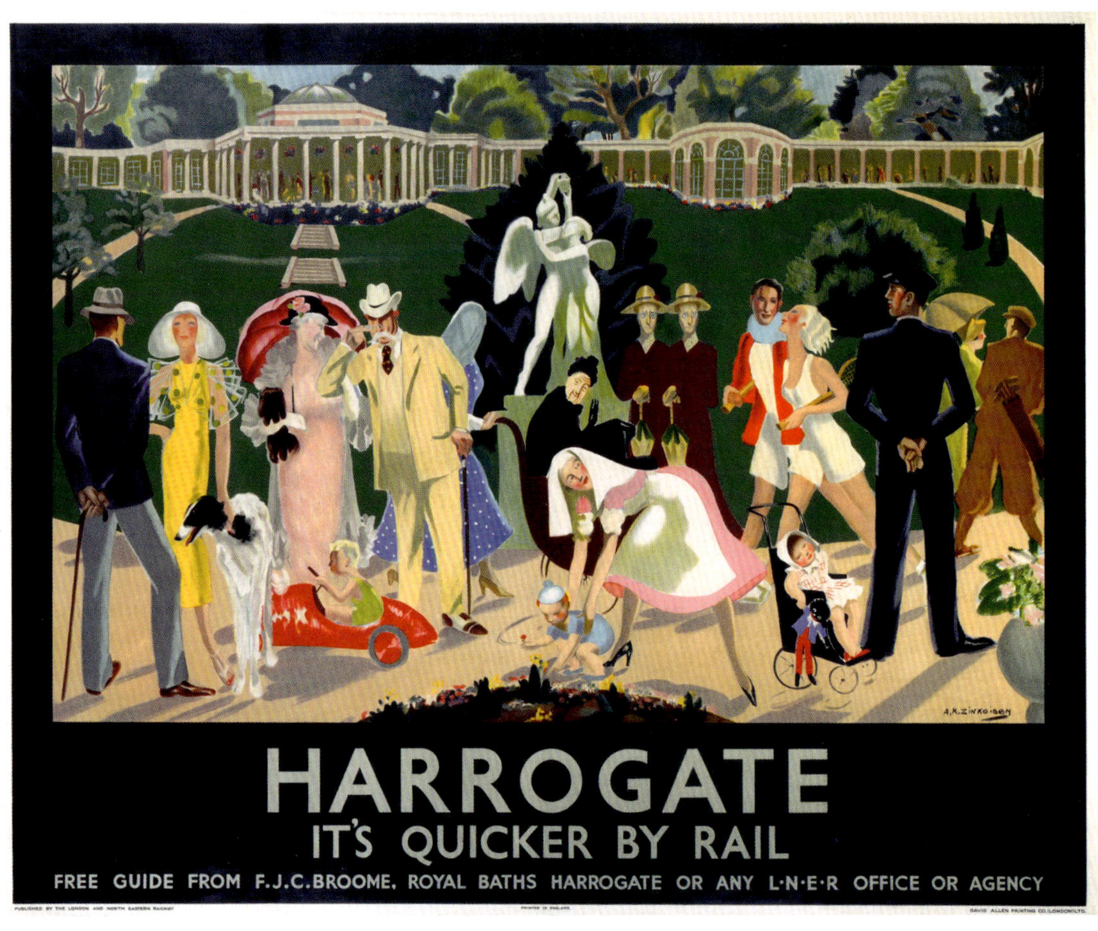

Fig.3.37
Anna Zinkeisen, *London and North Eastern Railway Poster advertising Harrogate*, 1930s, colour lithograph.

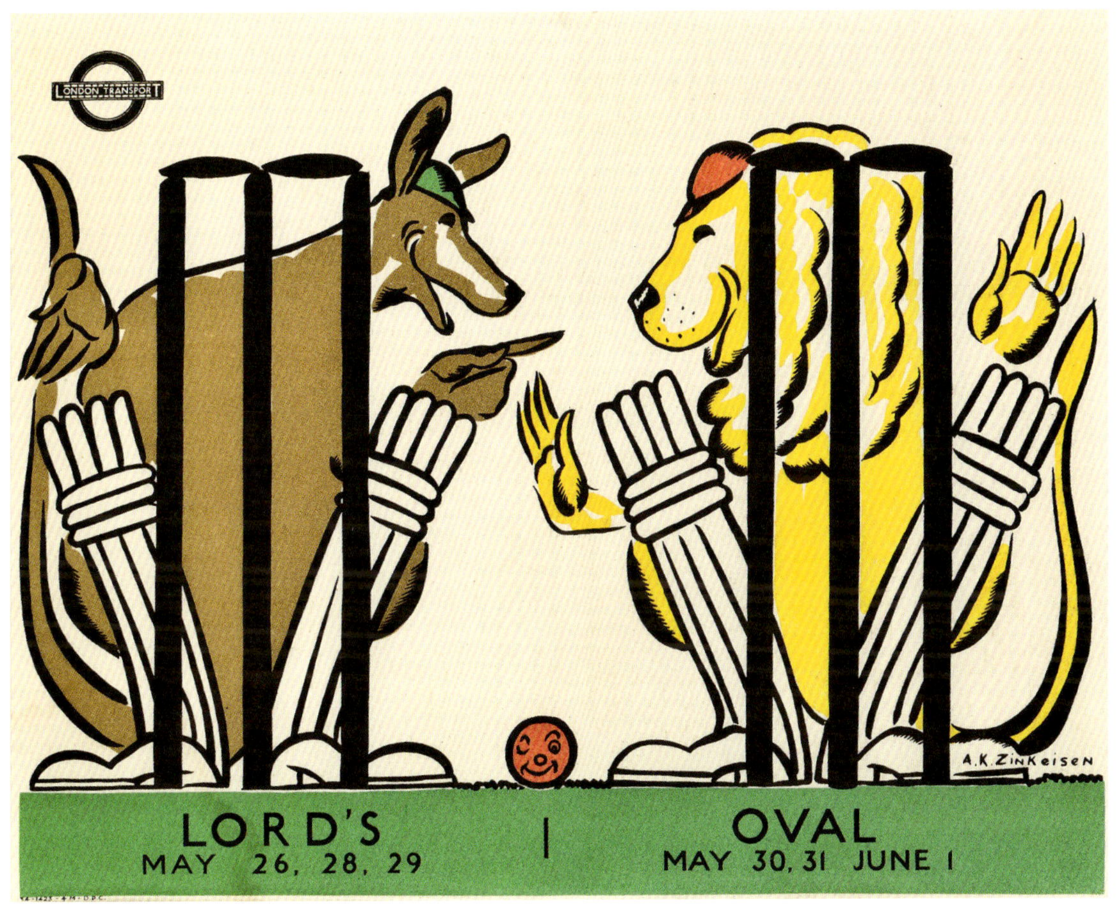

Fig.3.38

Anna Zinkeisen, *London Transport Poster advertising Cricket at Lord's Oval*, 1930s, colour lithograph.

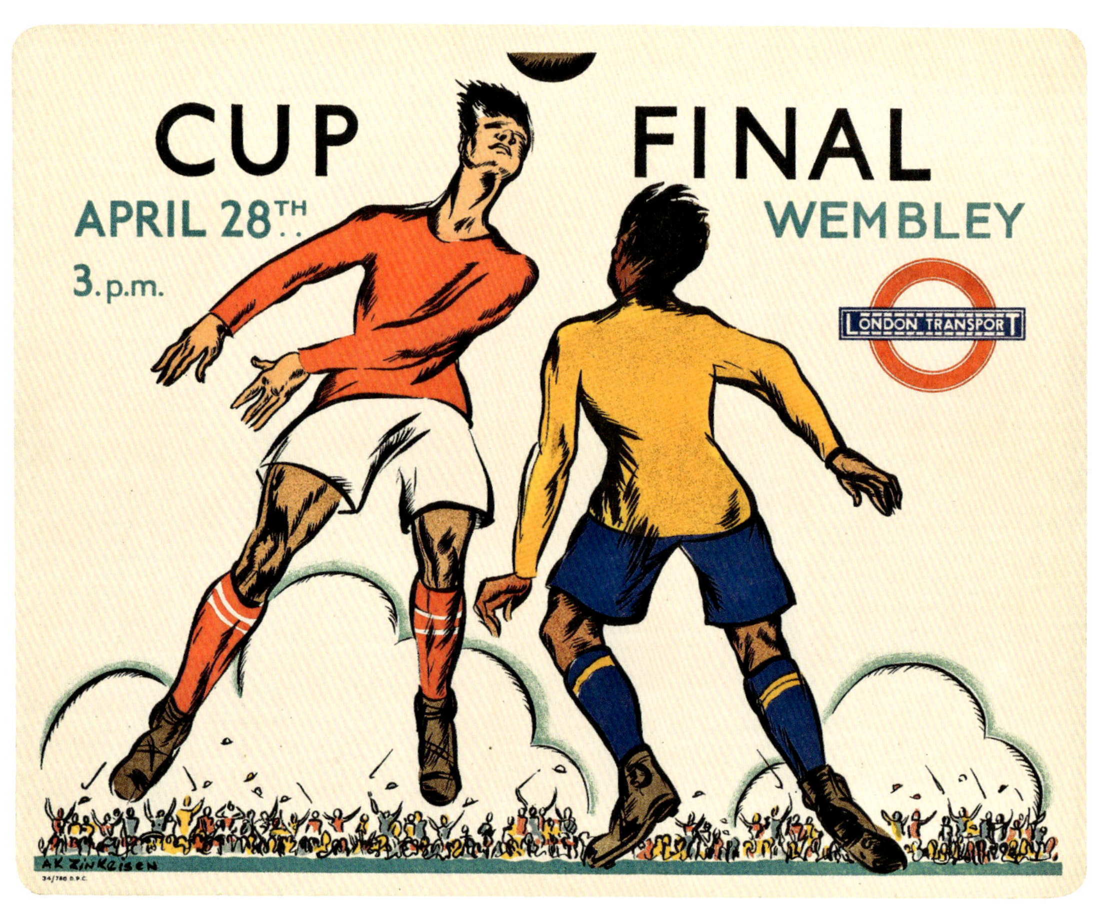

Fig.3.39
Anna Zinkeisen, *London Transport Poster advertising Football Cup Final at Wembley*, 1930s, colour lithograph.

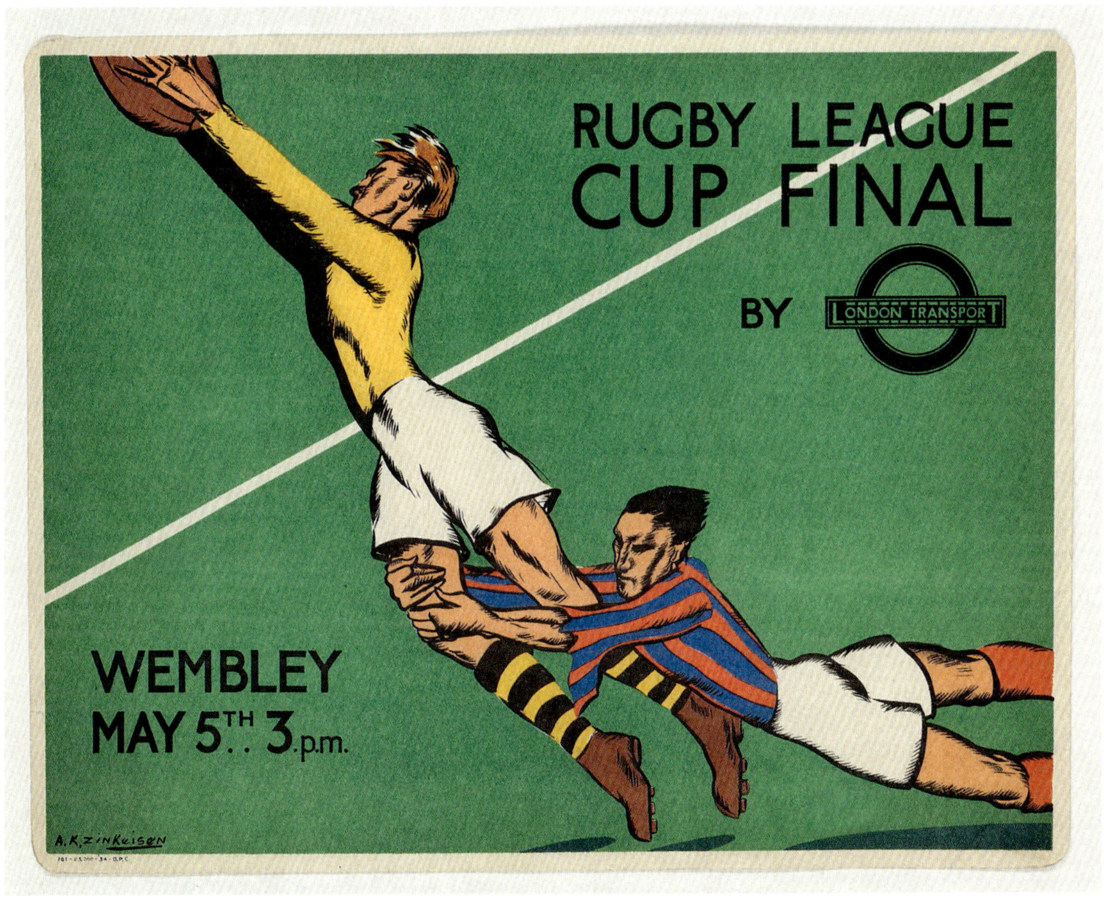

Fig.3.40
Anna Zinkeisen, *London Transport Poster advertising Rugby League Cup Final at Wembley*, 1930s, colour lithograph.

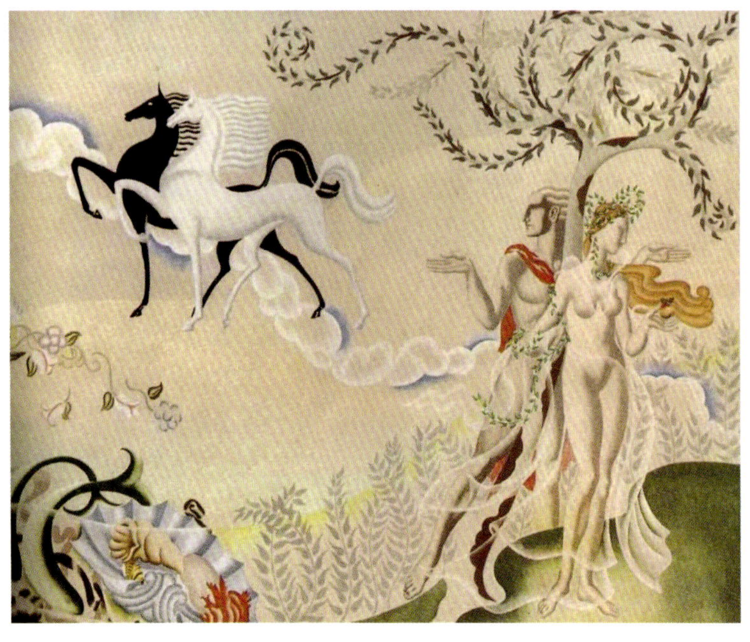

Fig.3.41
Anna Zinkeisen, *Mural for R.M.S. Queen Mary*, 1934, oil on canvas.

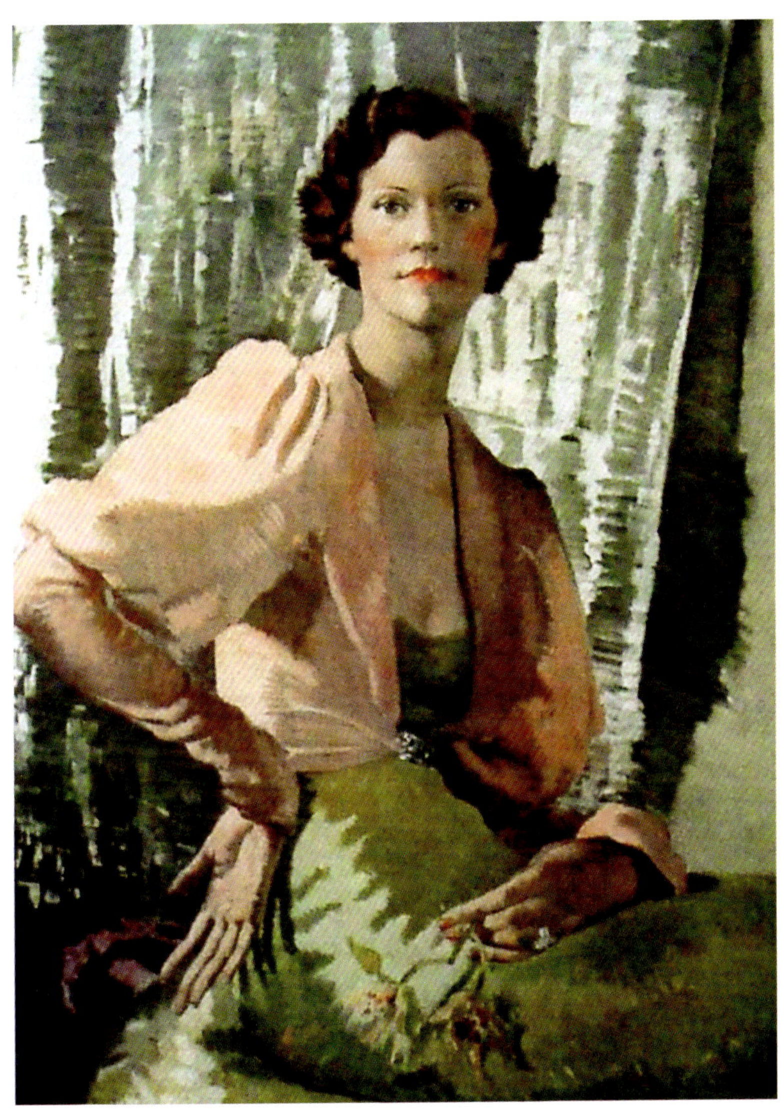

Fig.3.42
Doris Zinkeisen, *Mrs Harold Taylor,* 1934, oil on canvas.
Exhibited at the Paris Salon.

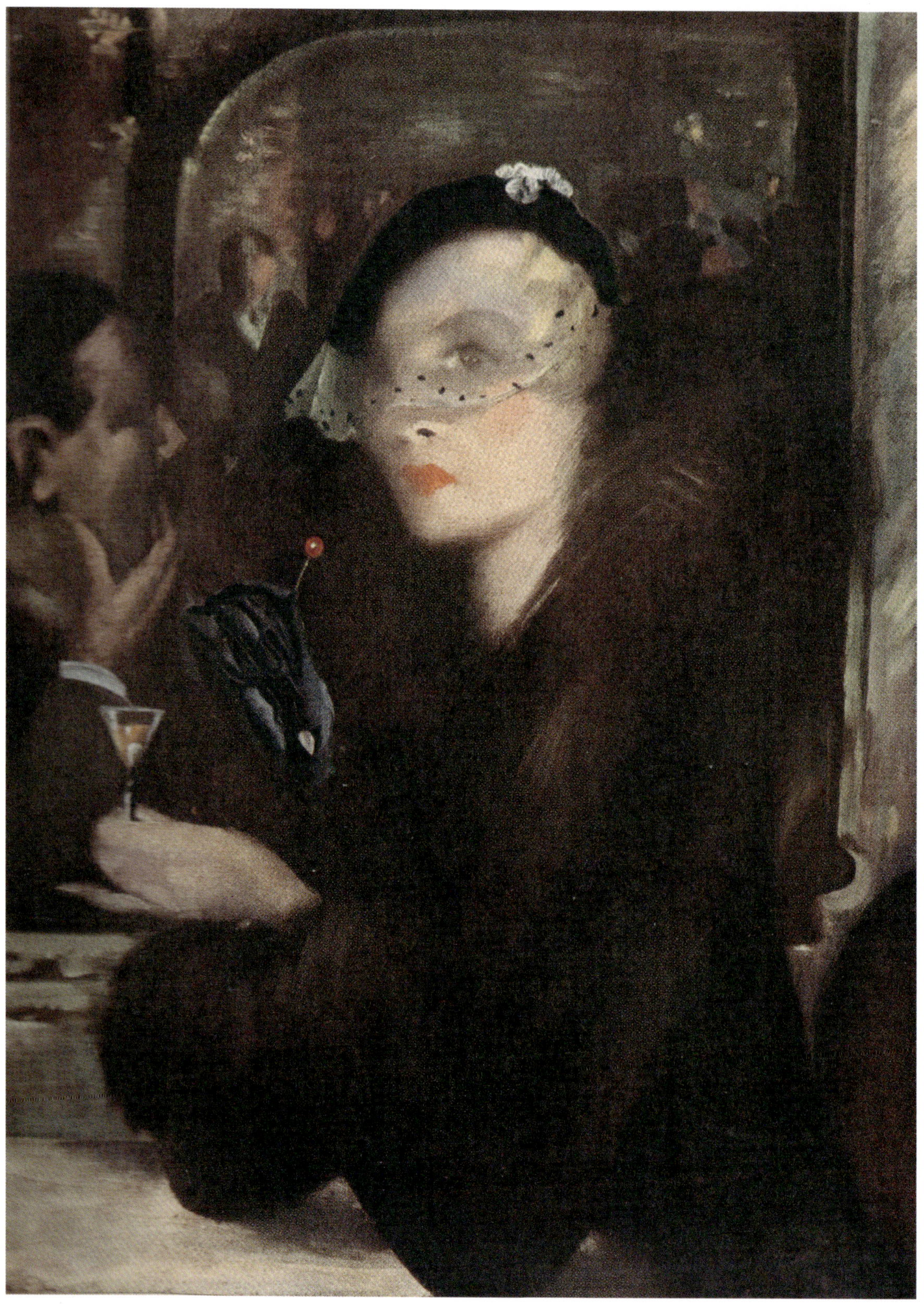

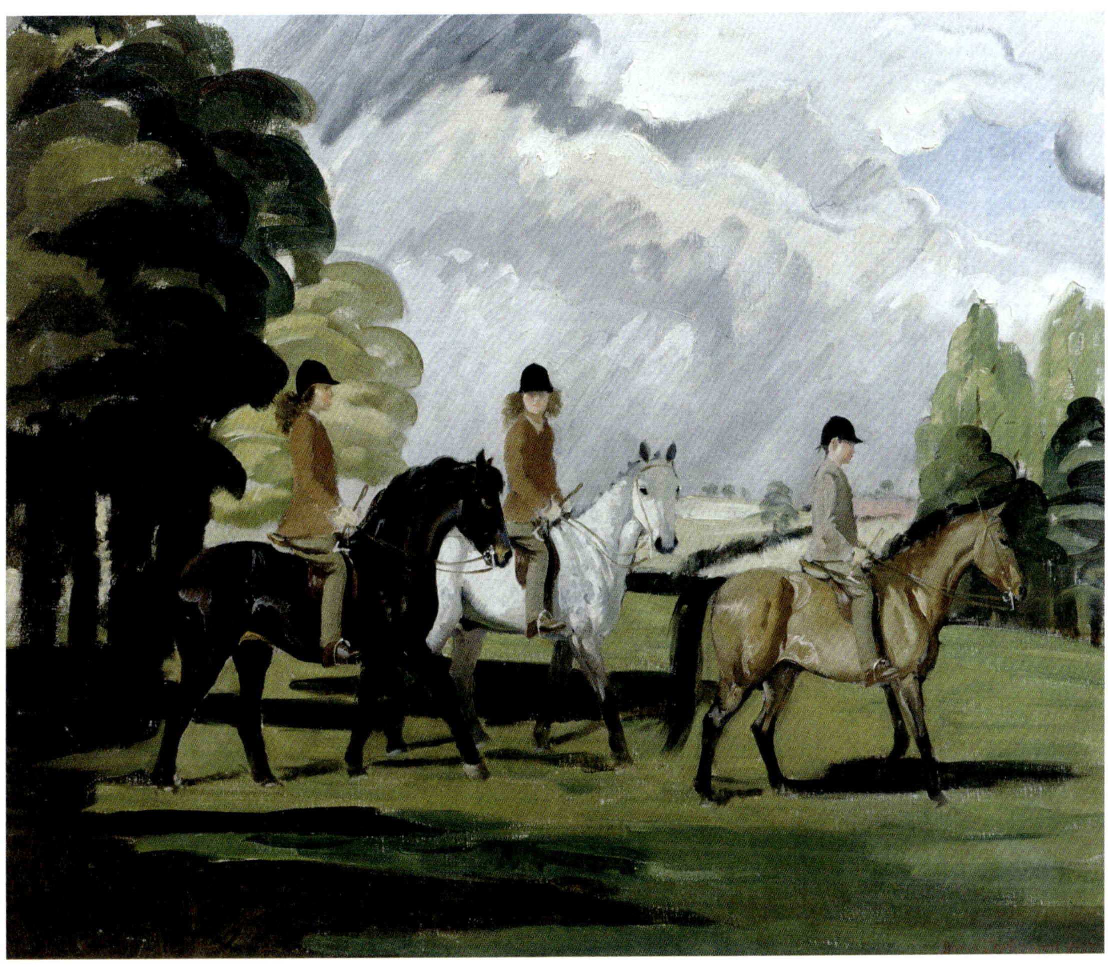

Fig.3.43
Anna Zinkeisen, *Manhattan*, 1936, oil on canvas.
The Manhattan referred to in the title is not the borough of New York, but the cocktail made of Italian vermouth, American bourbon whiskey, and a dash or two of bitters (alcoholic spirits) stirred with cracked ice, strained, and served with a maraschino cherry, that is a cherry preserved in sweet maraschino liqueur made from Dalmatian cherries. This picture was also made into a limited edition print.

Fig.3.44
Doris Zinkeisen, *Janet, Anne, and Murray Johnstone, the Artist's Children, on their Ponies*, 1937, oil on canvas.

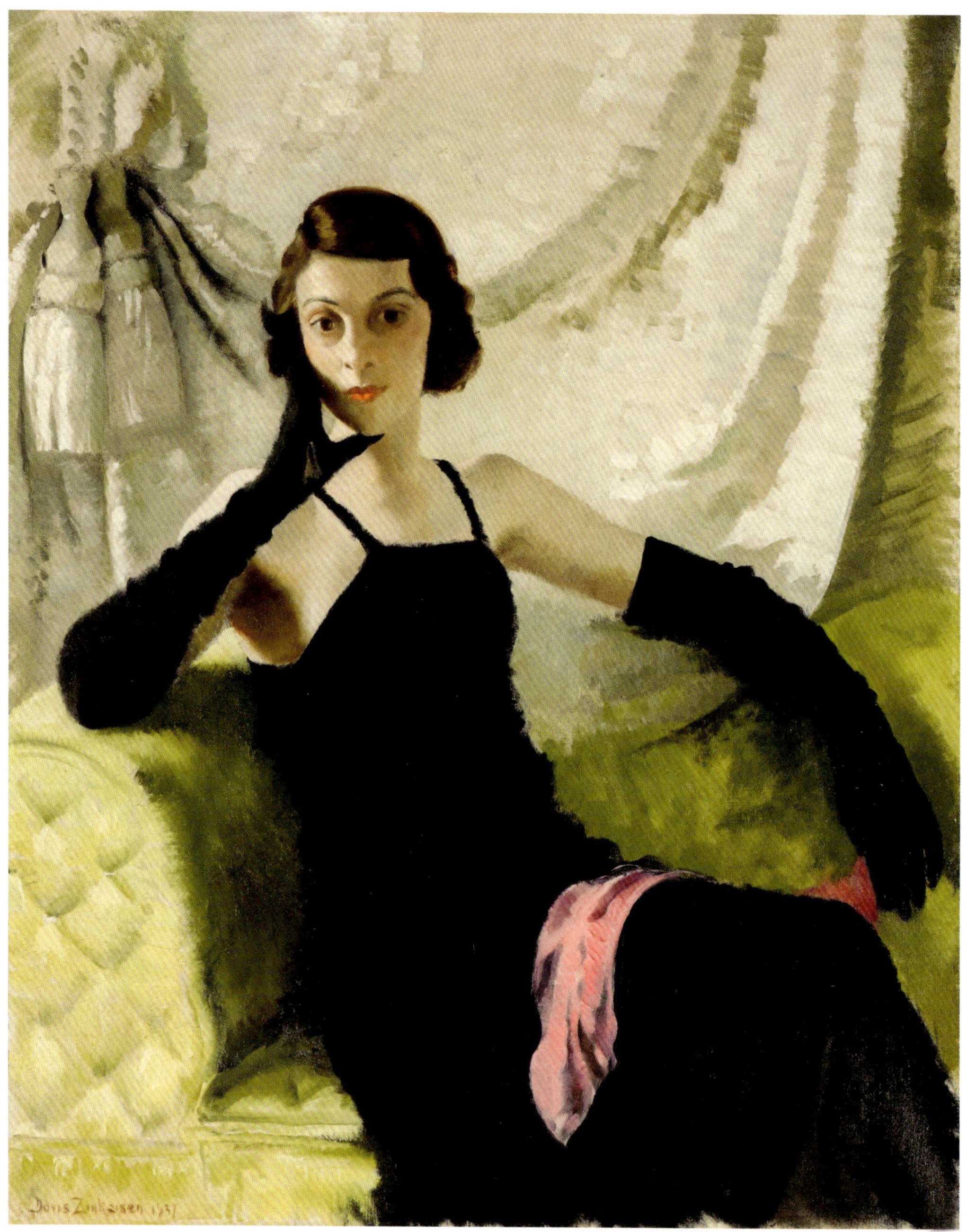

Fig.3.45
Doris Zinkeisen, *The Black Dress: Mrs Sanders Watney*, 1937, oil on canvas.
Sanders Watney (1908-1983) was a bigwig in the brewing sector, a director of Watneys, Coombe and Reed, and an old friend of Doris and her husband, with a shared passion for horses and carriages – Sanders was a founder and president of the British Driving Society in 1957. Given that this portrait is dated 1937 it is probably Sanders' first wife, Helen Marjorie Guthrie, whom he married in 1935, but divorced in 1945. Doris also painted a double portrait of Sanders with his second wife Marylian (known as Biddy) driving one of their carriages with horses. Marylian was a noted horsewoman and author of several books on horsemanship.

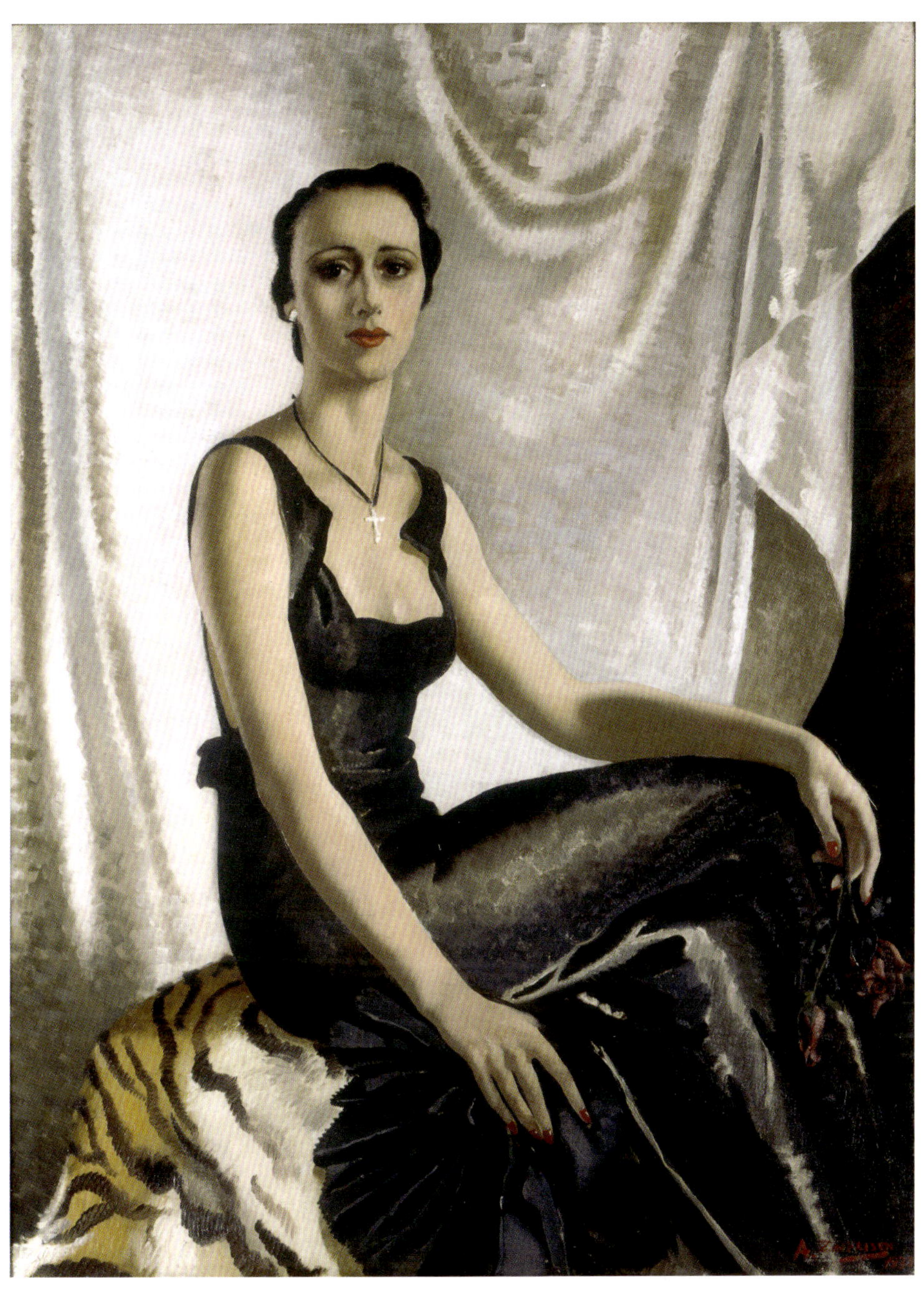

Fig.3.46
Anna Zinkeisen, *Consuela Kennedy in Evening Dress*, 1937, oil on canvas.

Consuela Kennedy (1907-1975) hailed from Ecuador and was a socialite mixing in circles which included thespians such as Laurence Olivier and Vivien Leigh. She also managed to notch up three marriages.

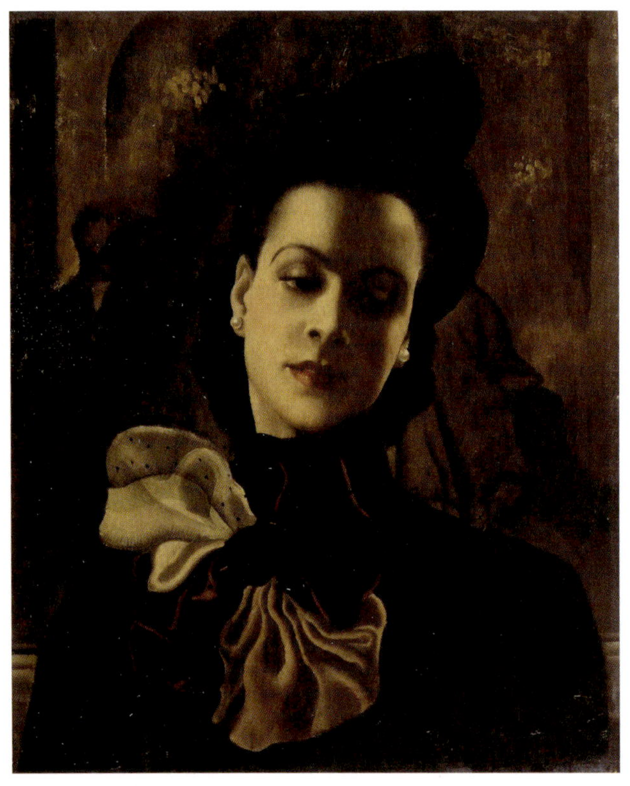

Fig.3.47
Anna Zinkeisen, *The Dark Lady*, 1938, oil on canvas.

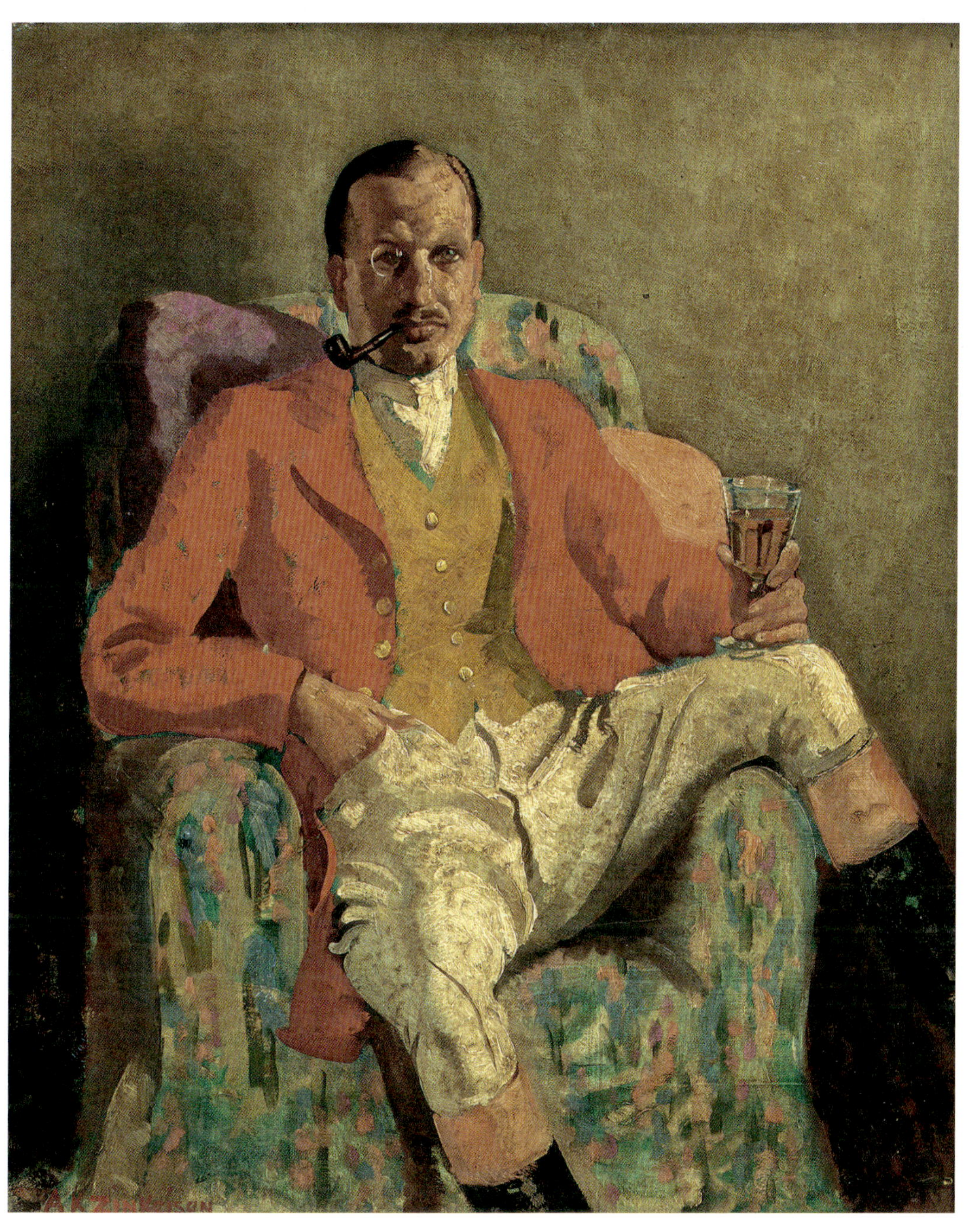

Fig.3.48
Anna Zinkeisen, *Colonel Guy Robert Nelson Heseltine M.C., the Artist's Husband*, 1930s, oil on canvas.

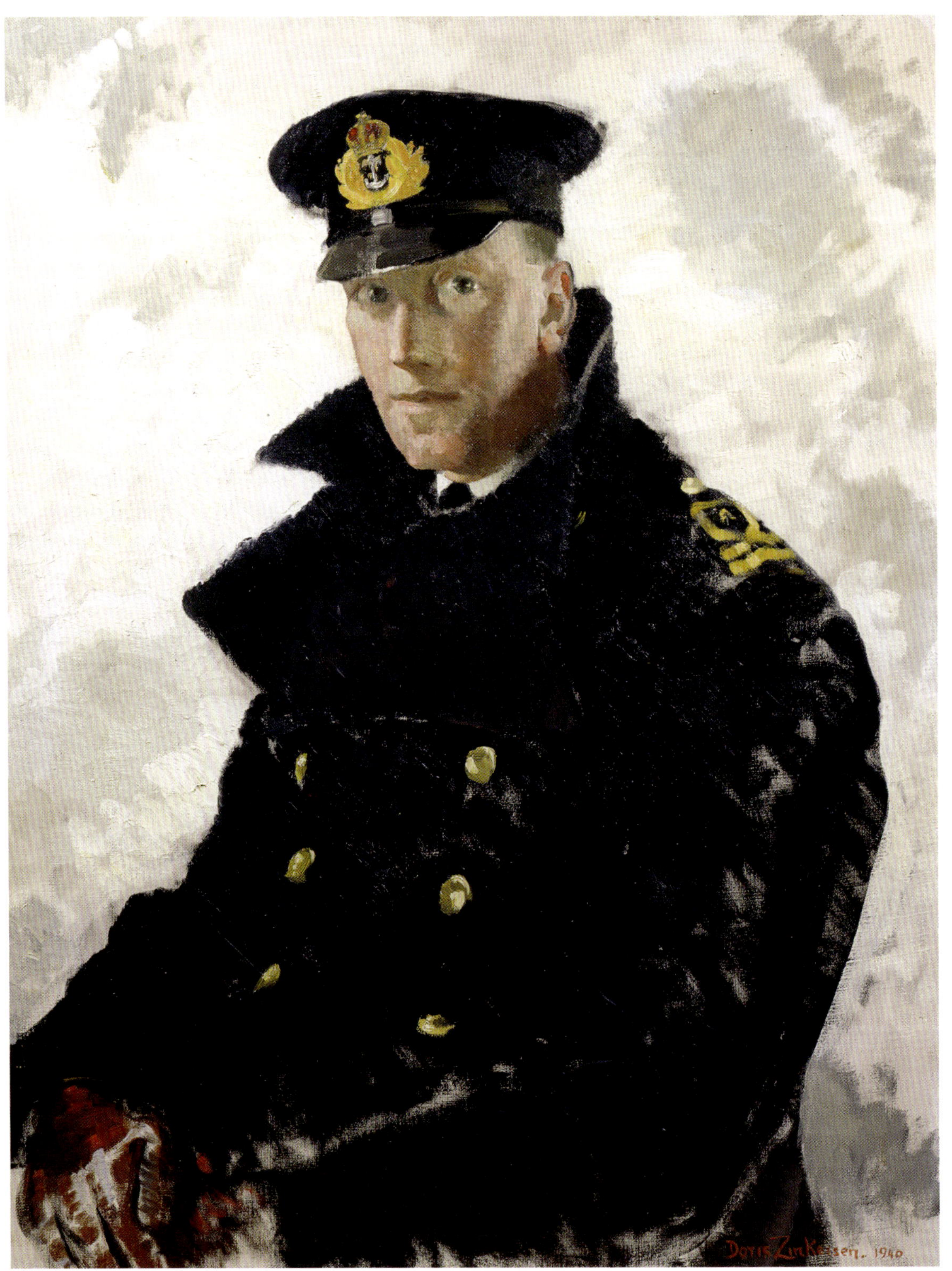
Doris Zinkeisen. 1940

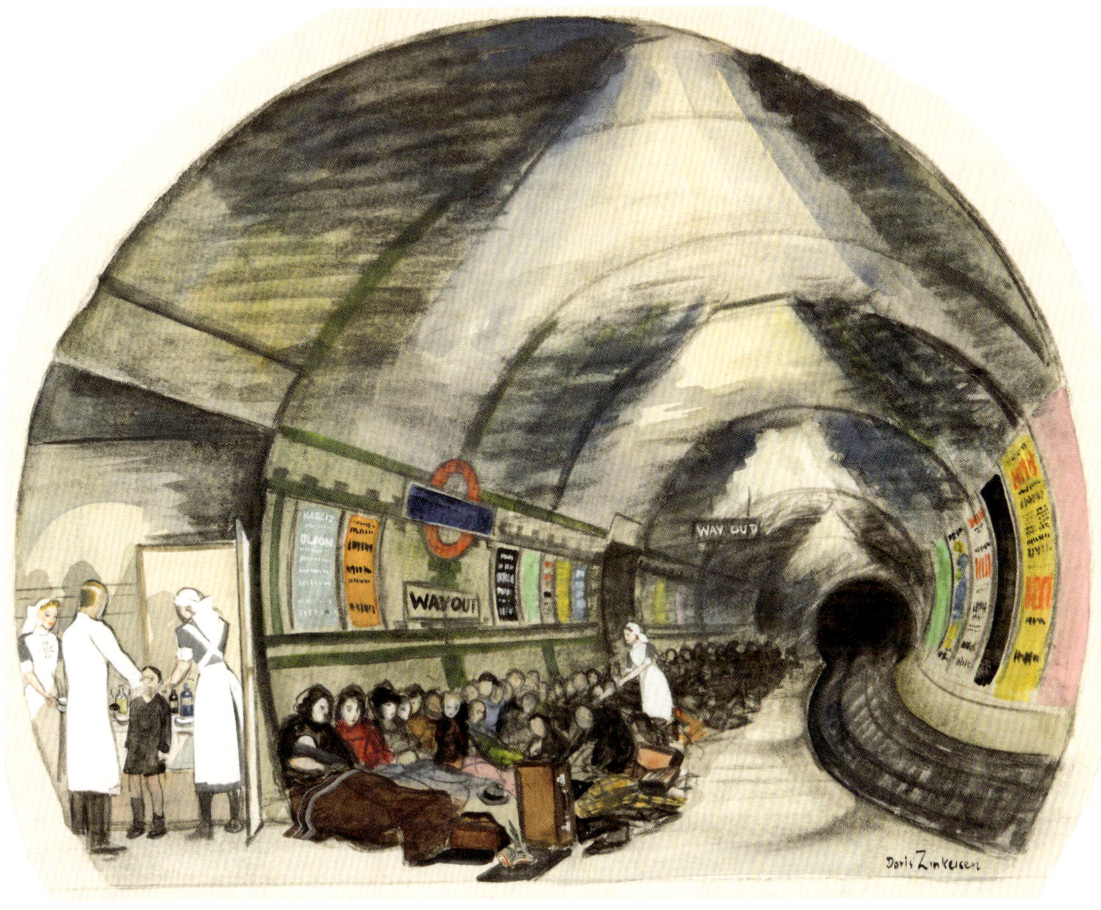

Fig.3.49
Doris Zinkeisen, *Captain Edward Grahame Johnstone D.S.C., R.N.V.R., the Artist's Husband*, 1940, oil on canvas.
Exhibited at the Royal Academy.

Fig.3.50
Doris Zinkeisen, *St John Ambulance Brigade at Work in a London Underground Station*, *circa* 1940-1941, watercolour and gouache on paper.

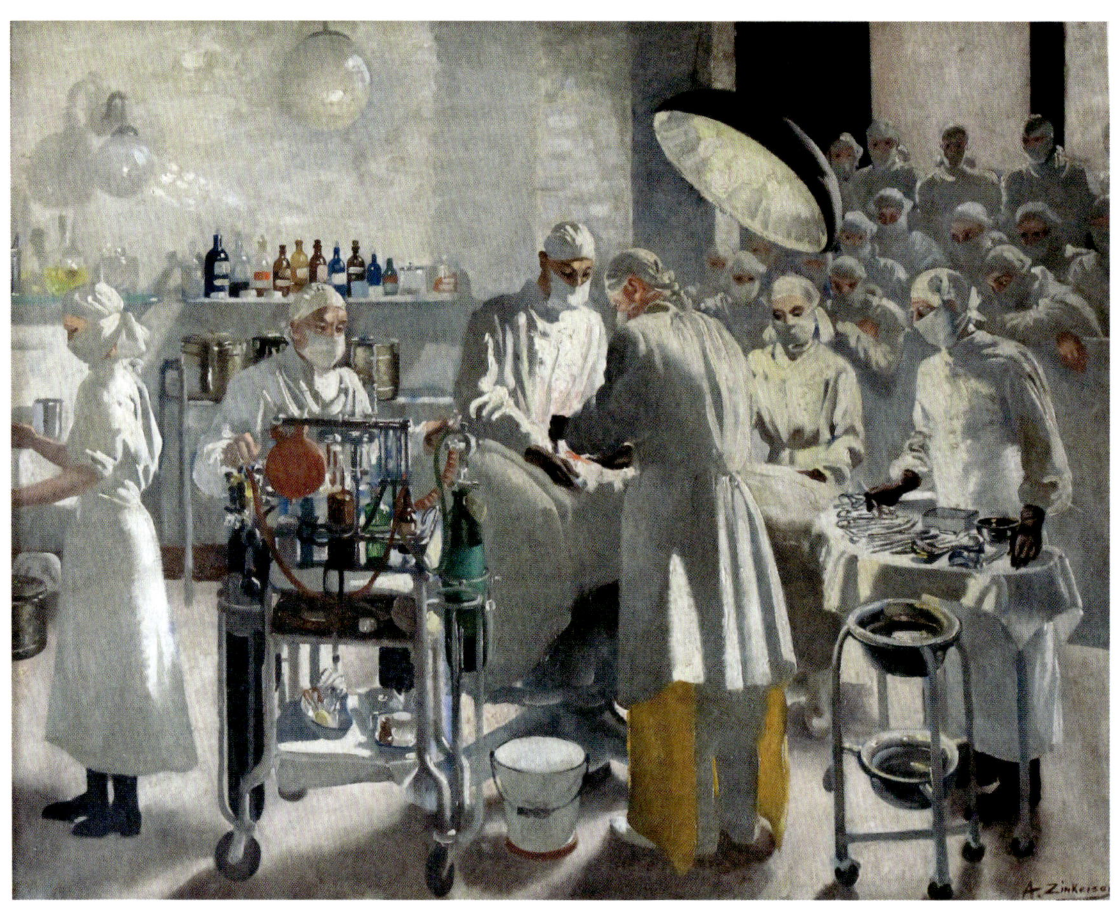

Fig.3.51
Anna Zinkeisen, *Operation in Progress: St Mary's Hospital, Paddington*, 1941, oil on canvas.
Formerly in the collection of ICI.
© Photograph courtesy of Paul Mayhew Fine Art.

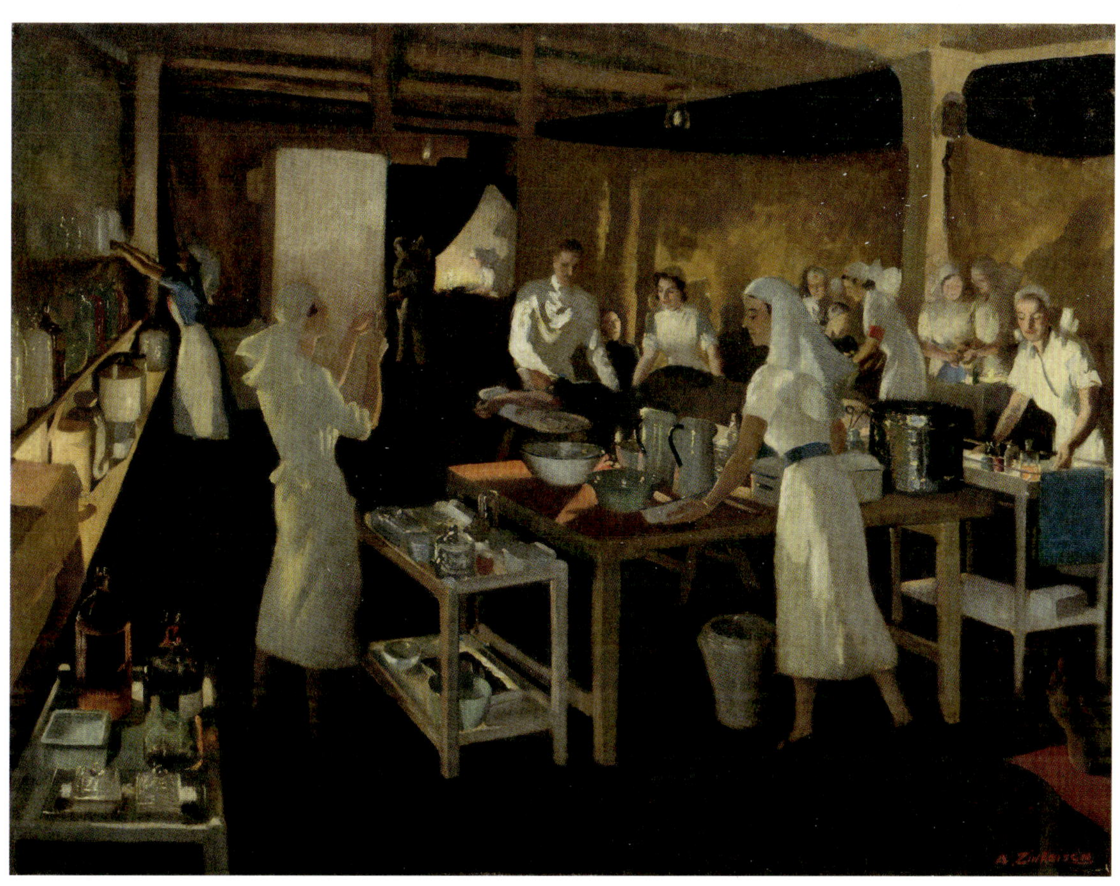

Fig.3.52
Anna Zinkeisen, *St Mary's First Aid Post by Candlelight*, 1941, oil on canvas.
Exhibited at the Royal Academy. The sketch for the scene represented here was captured during an actual air raid.

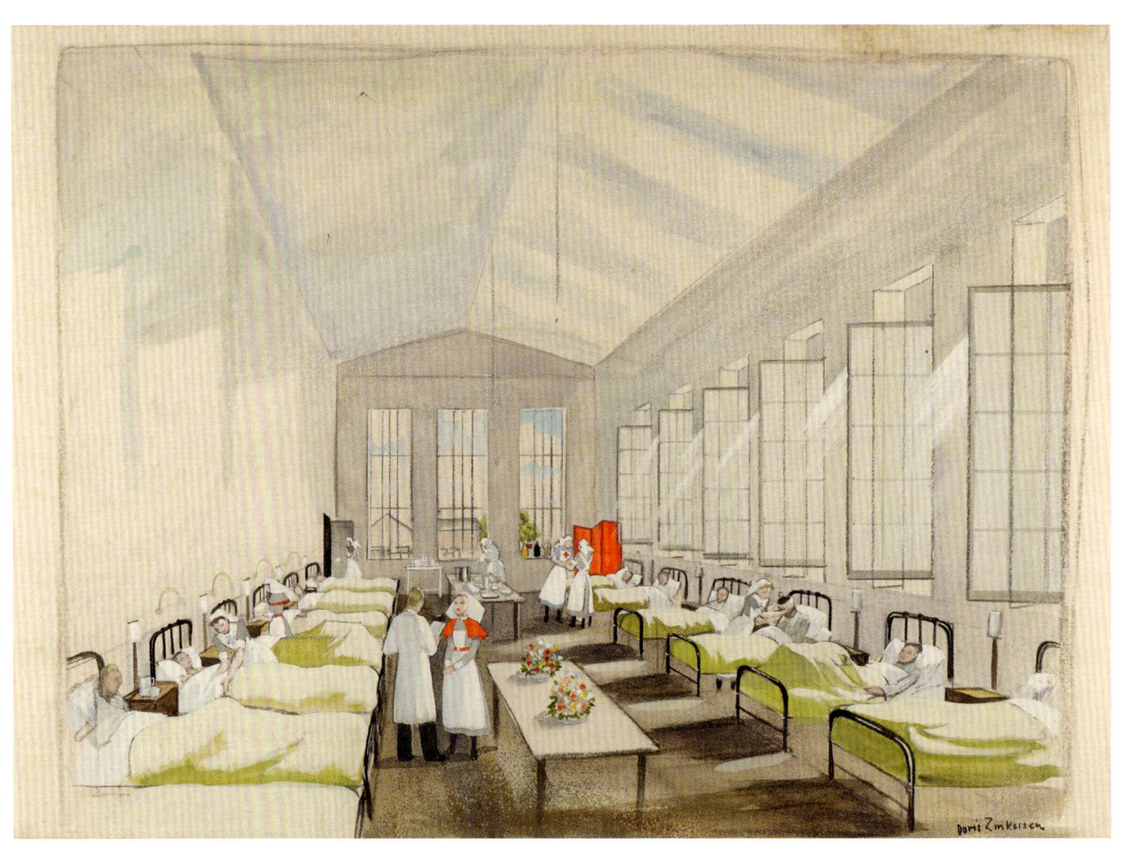

Fig.3.53

Doris Zinkeisen, *Diorama Design of a Hospital Ward in a Military Hospital staffed by St John and Red Cross Nurses, circa* 1942, watercolour and gouache on paper. See also Fig.1.21.

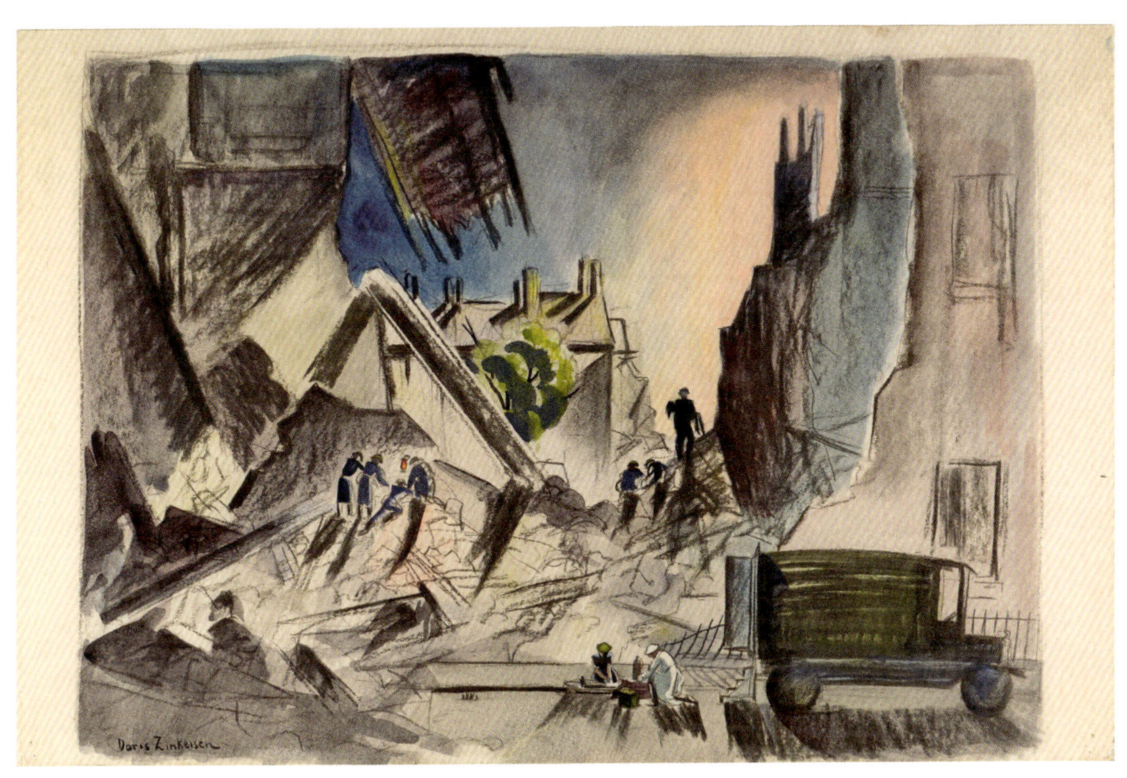

Fig.3.54
Doris Zinkeisen, *Diorama Design of a Mobile Unit at Work in an Air Raid*, *circa* 1942, watercolour and gouache on paper.
See also Fig.1.20 and Fig.1.22.

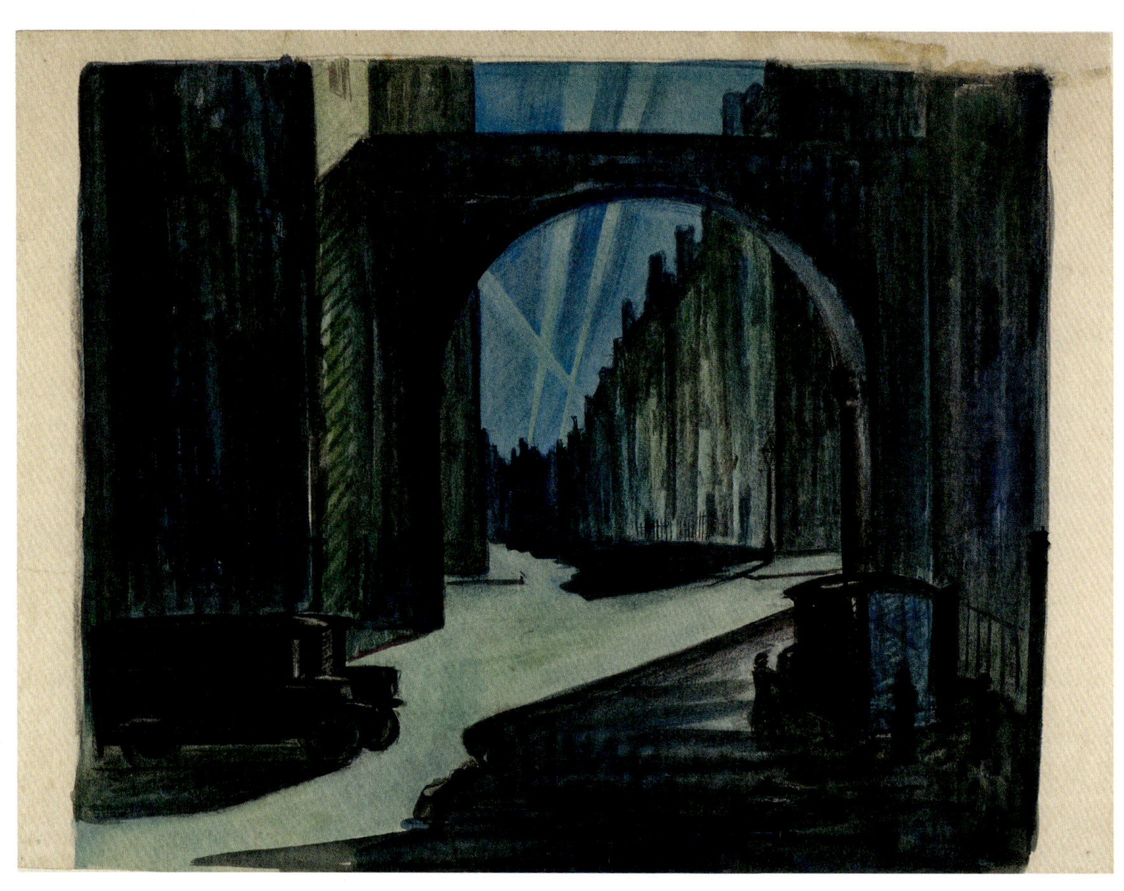

Fig.3.55
Doris Zinkeisen, *Diorama Design of Night Air Raid on London*, *circa* 1942, watercolour and gouache on paper.

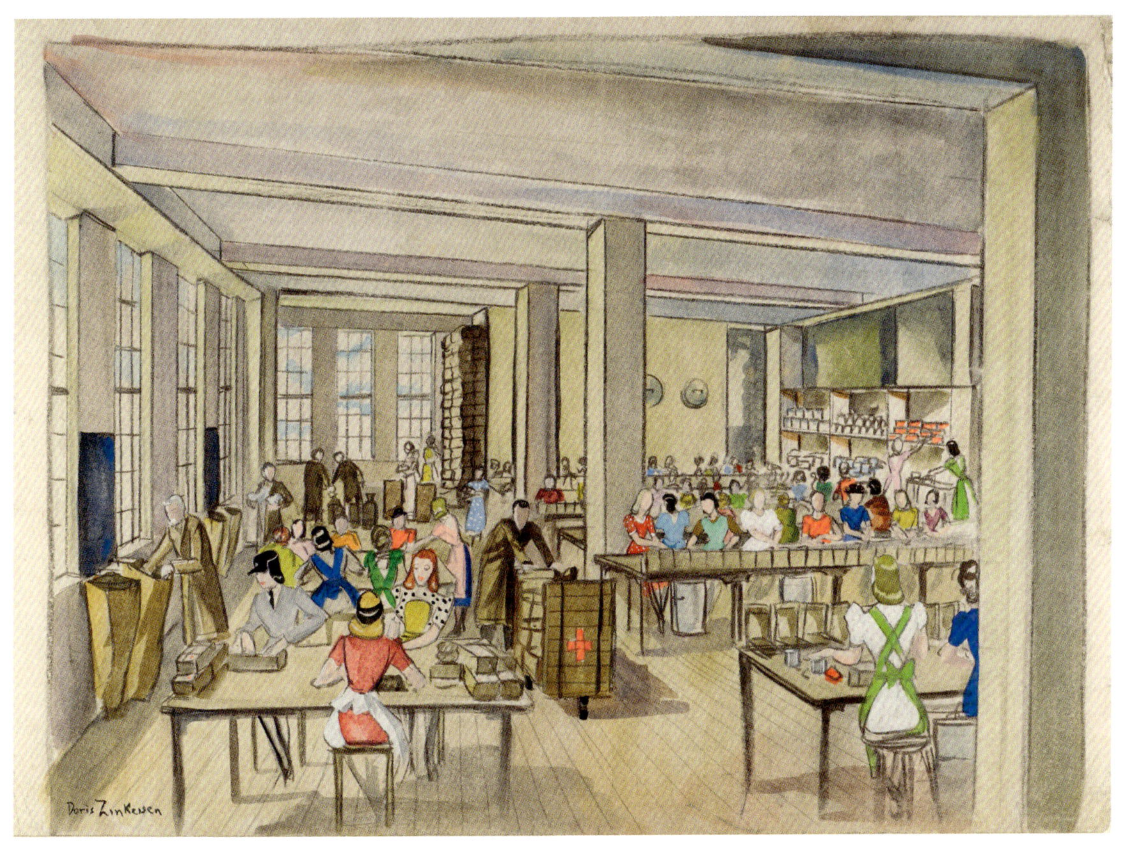

Fig.3.56

Doris Zinkeisen, *Diorama Design Showing the Packing of Parcels for Prisoners-of-War, circa* 1942, watercolour and gouache on paper.

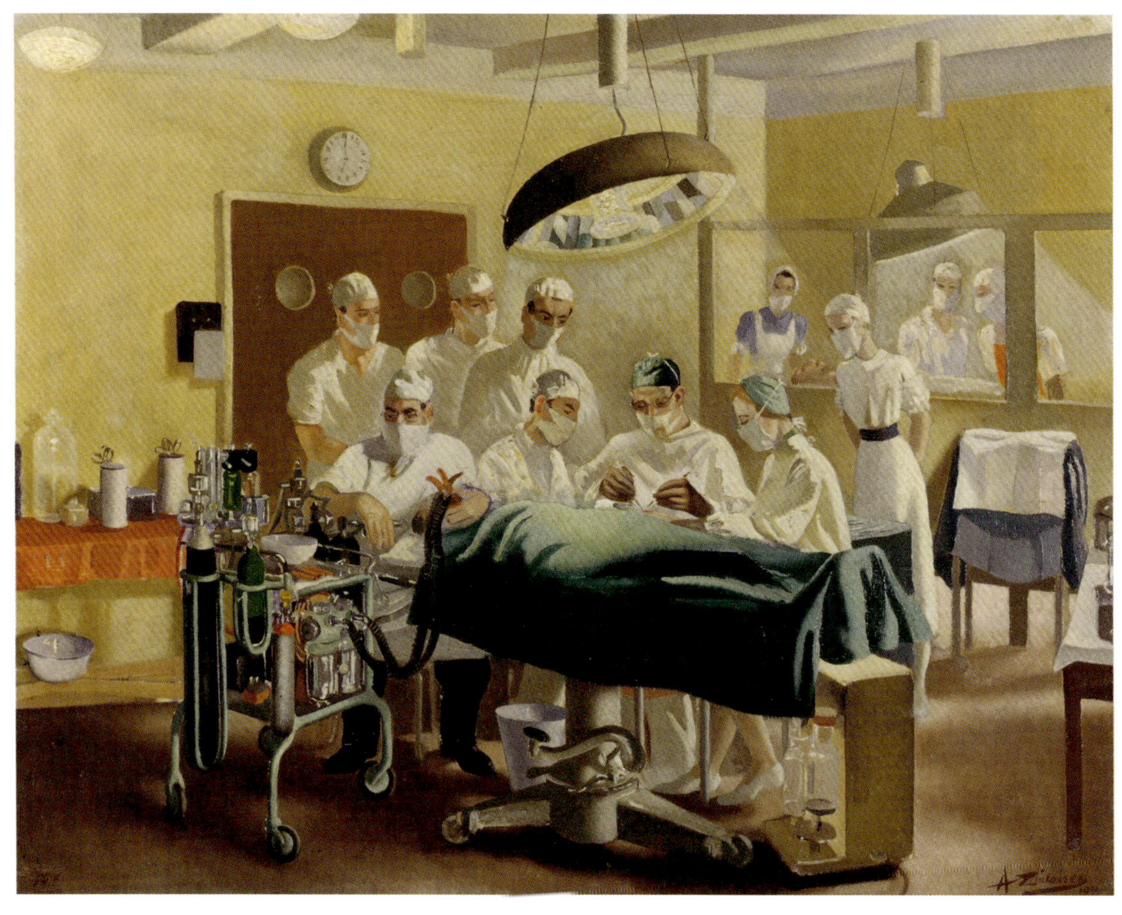

Fig.3.57
Anna Zinkeisen, *East Grinstead Team: Sir Archibald McIndoe Operating*, 1944, oil on canvas.

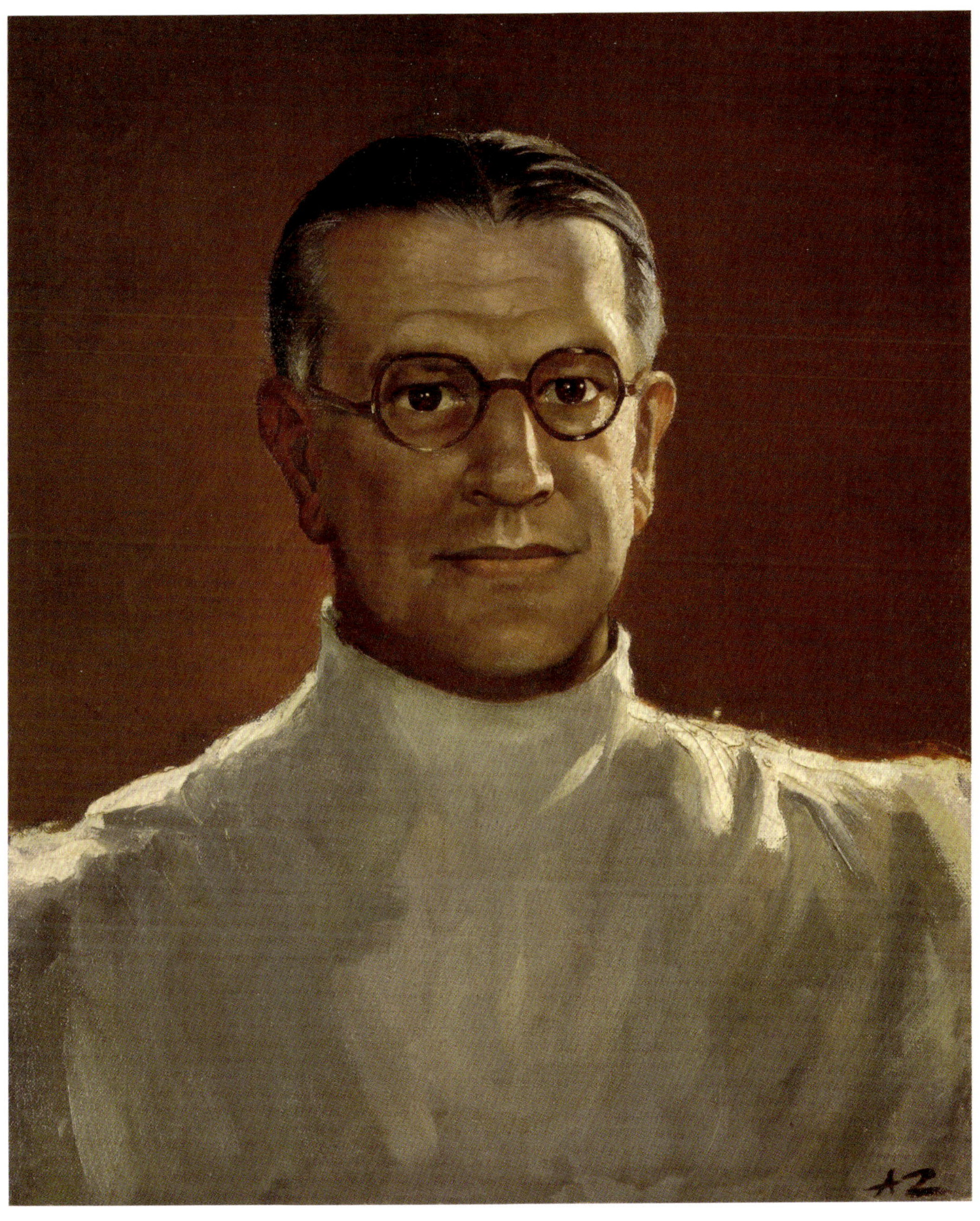

Fig.3.58
Anna Zinkeisen, *Sir Archibald Hector McIndoe*, *circa* 1944, oil on canvas.

McIndoe (1900-1960) became famous during the Second World War for his skills as a plastic surgeon, in particular on the burned faces and bodies of Royal Air Force airmen, who were nicknamed 'McIndoe's Guinea Pigs', as well as his focus on the rehabilitation of his patients. Anna saw him in action in the operating theatre at East Grinstead. See also Fig.3.57.

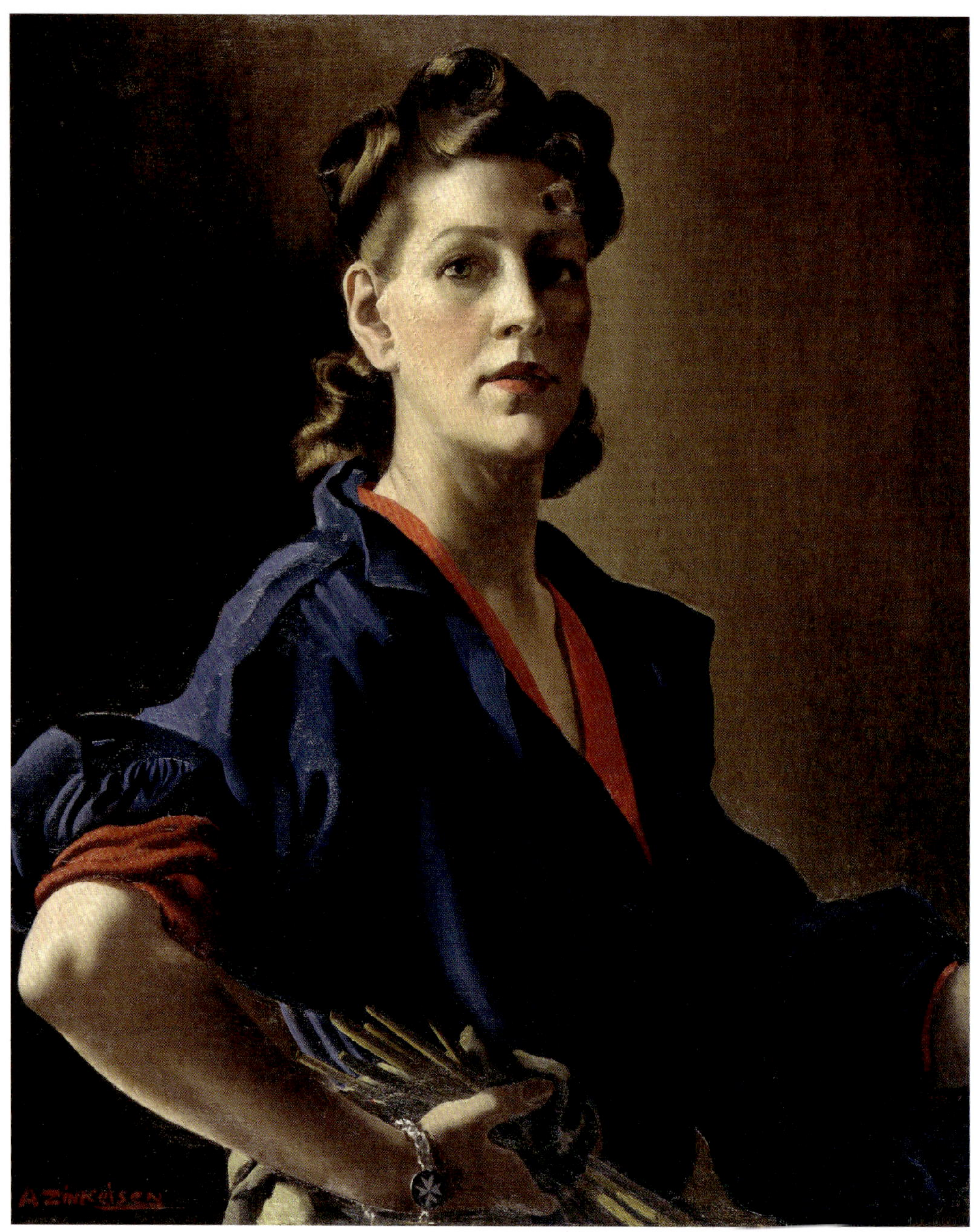

Fig.3.59

Anna Zinkeisen, *Self-portrait*, *circa* 1944, oil on canvas. The brushes relate to Anna's work as an artist, whilst her bracelet, with its Maltese Cross (a symbol of the Order of St John), draws attention to her nursing role with the St John Ambulance Brigade during the Second World War.

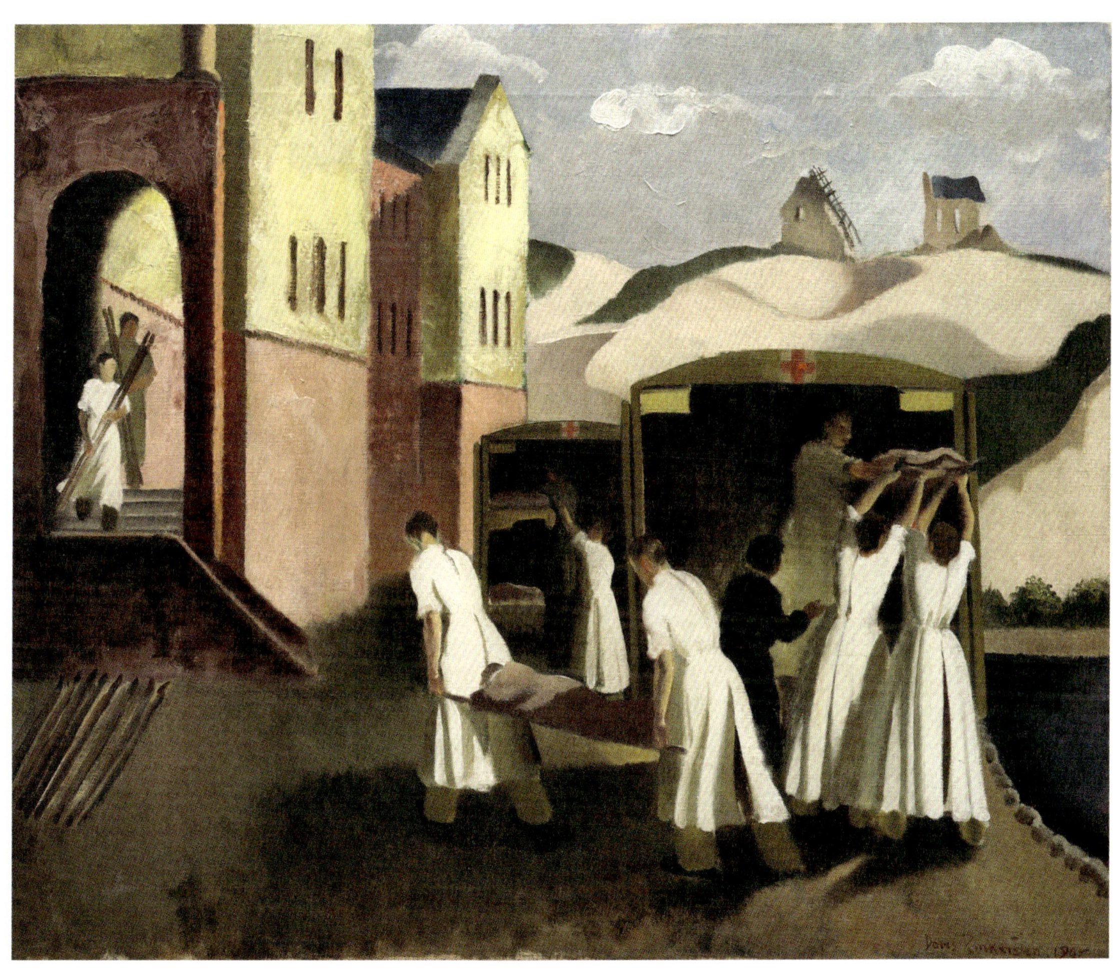

Fig.3.60
Doris Zinkeisen, *No.115 British General Hospital, Ostende: Unloading Wounded*, 1945, oil on canvas.

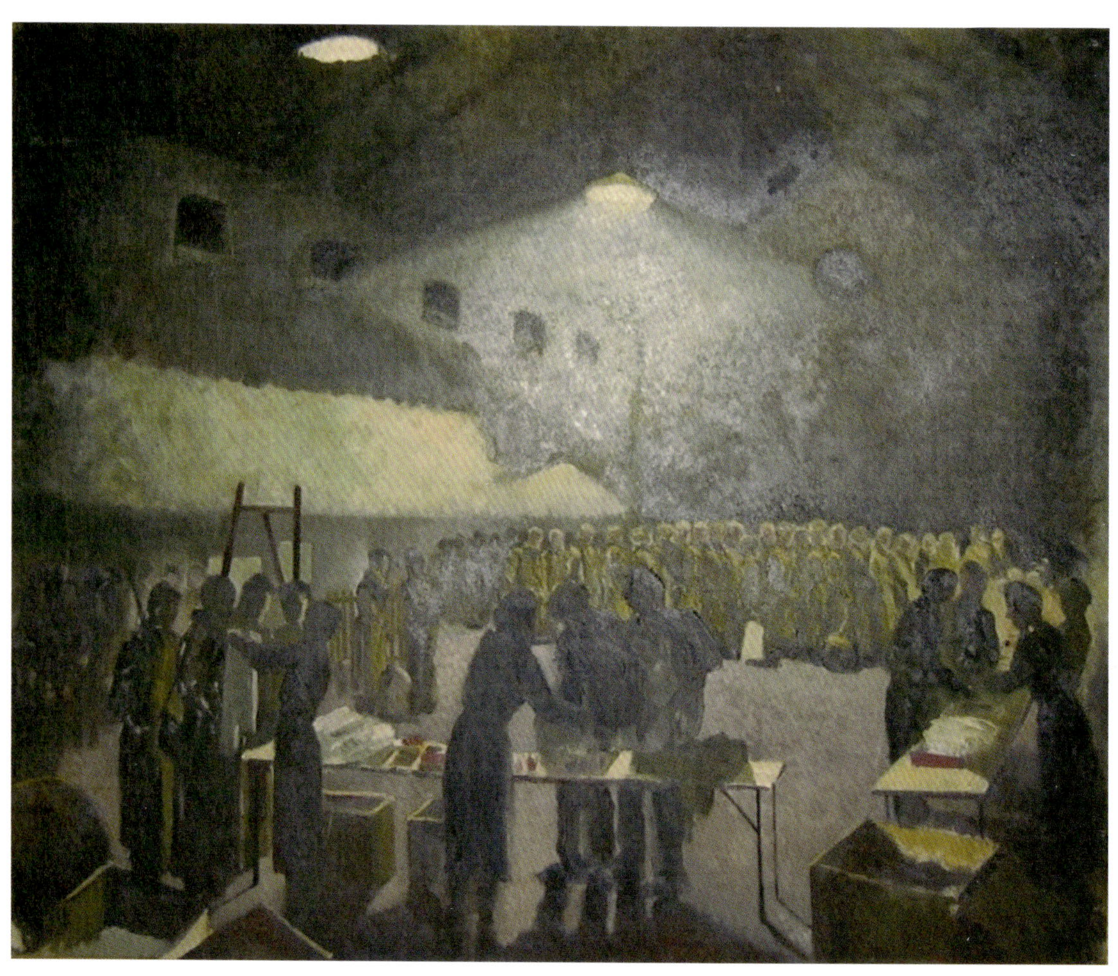

Fig.3.61
Doris Zinkeisen, *British Red Cross Relief Team issuing Gift Bags to Prisoners-of-War in Brussels before they return Home*, 1945, oil on canvas.

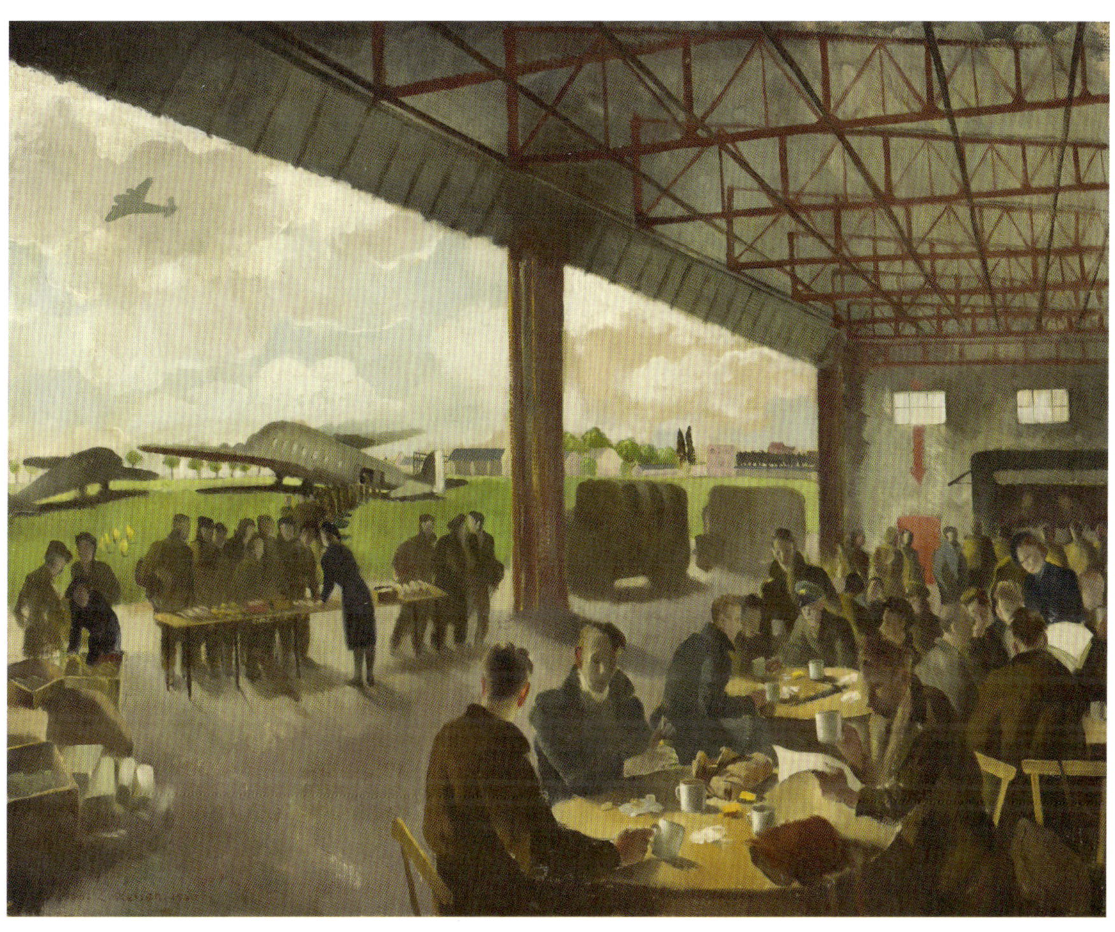

Fig.3.62
Doris Zinkeisen, *Feeding Liberated Prisoners-of-War before they are flown Home: Brussels Airport*, 1945, oil on canvas.

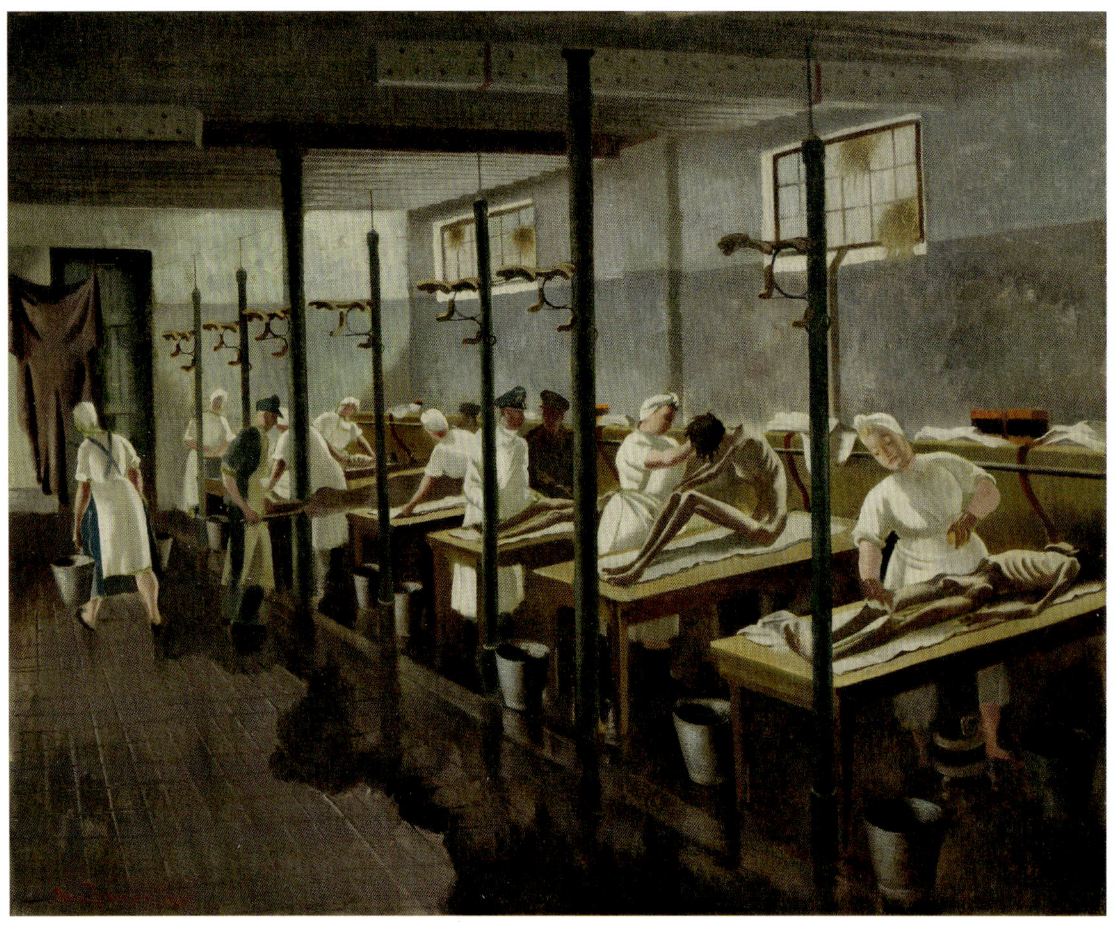

Fig.3.63
Doris Zinkeisen, *Human Laundry, Belsen*, 1945, oil on canvas.
Here Doris contrasts the emaciated bodies of the survivors of the concentration camp with the fat German nurses, who are cleaning them.

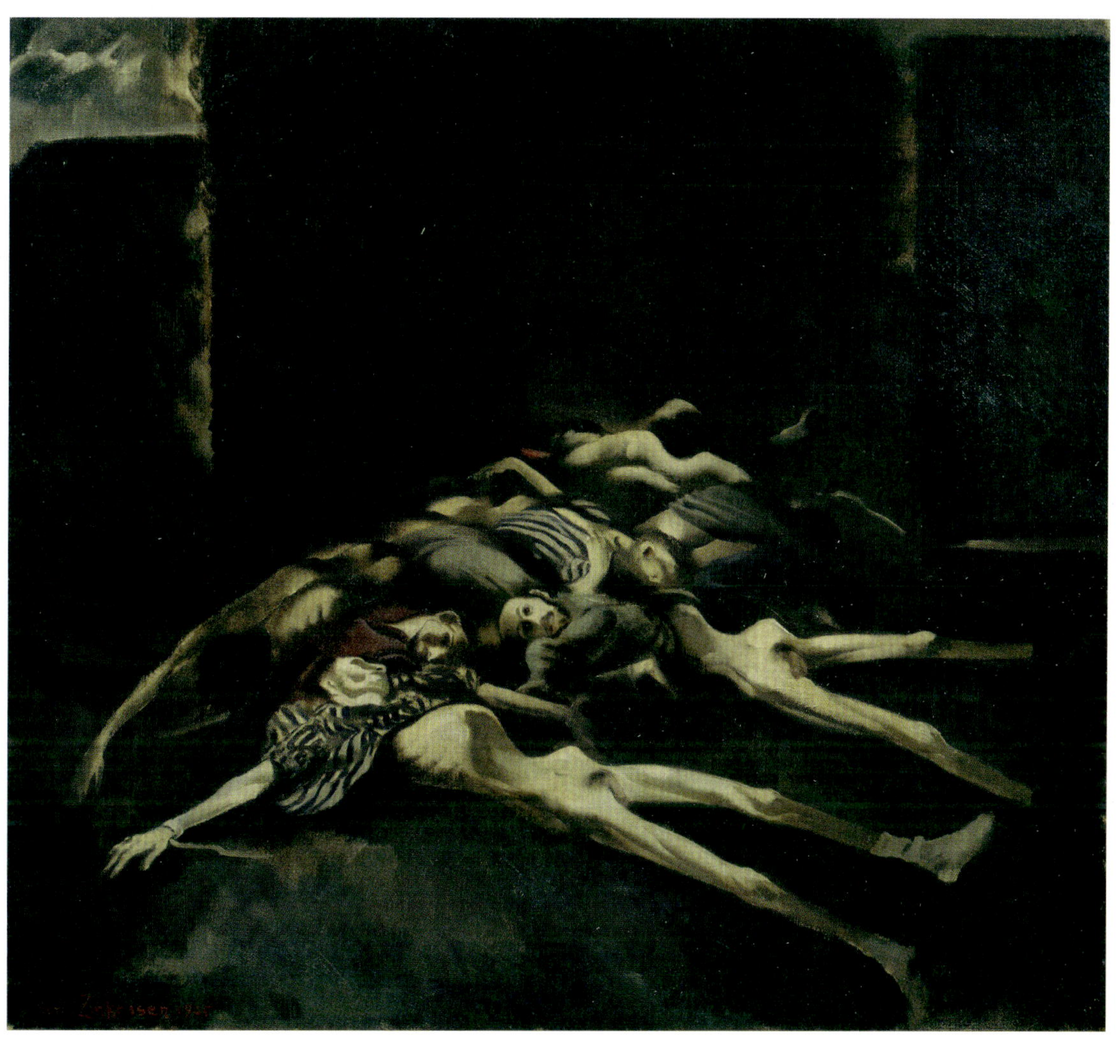

Fig.3.64
Doris Zinkeisen, *Belsen, April 1945*, 1945, oil on canvas. Doris had recurring nightmares about what she witnessed at Belsen throughout the rest of her life. What the paintings cannot capture, however, is the stench of rotting flesh. In her letters home Doris wrote how the corpses numbering in their thousands lay in heaps all over the concentration camp, as in her painting.

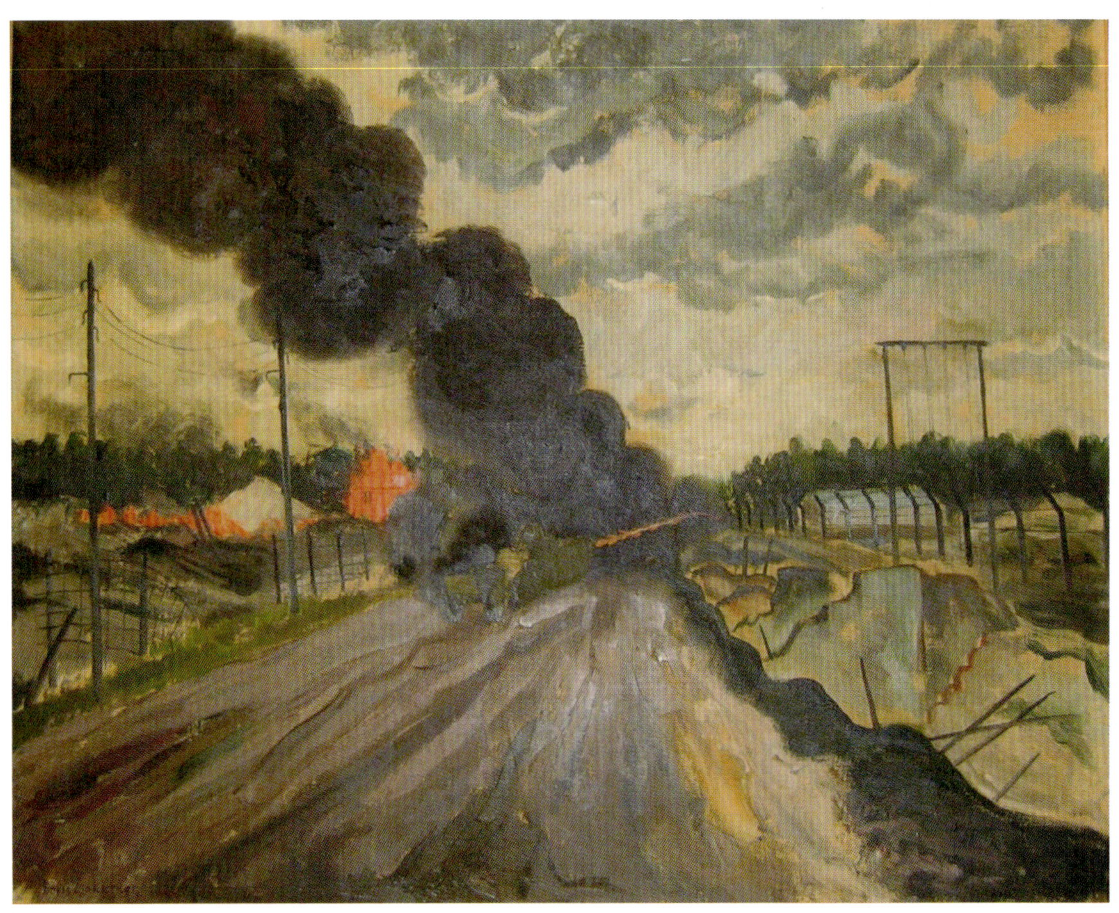

Fig.3.65
Doris Zinkeisen, *Burning of Belsen Concentration Camp*, 1945, oil on canvas.
In the centre of the composition is a tank with a flame thrower moving down a track burning everything in its path. The poles to the right are in actual fact the gallows used for executions.

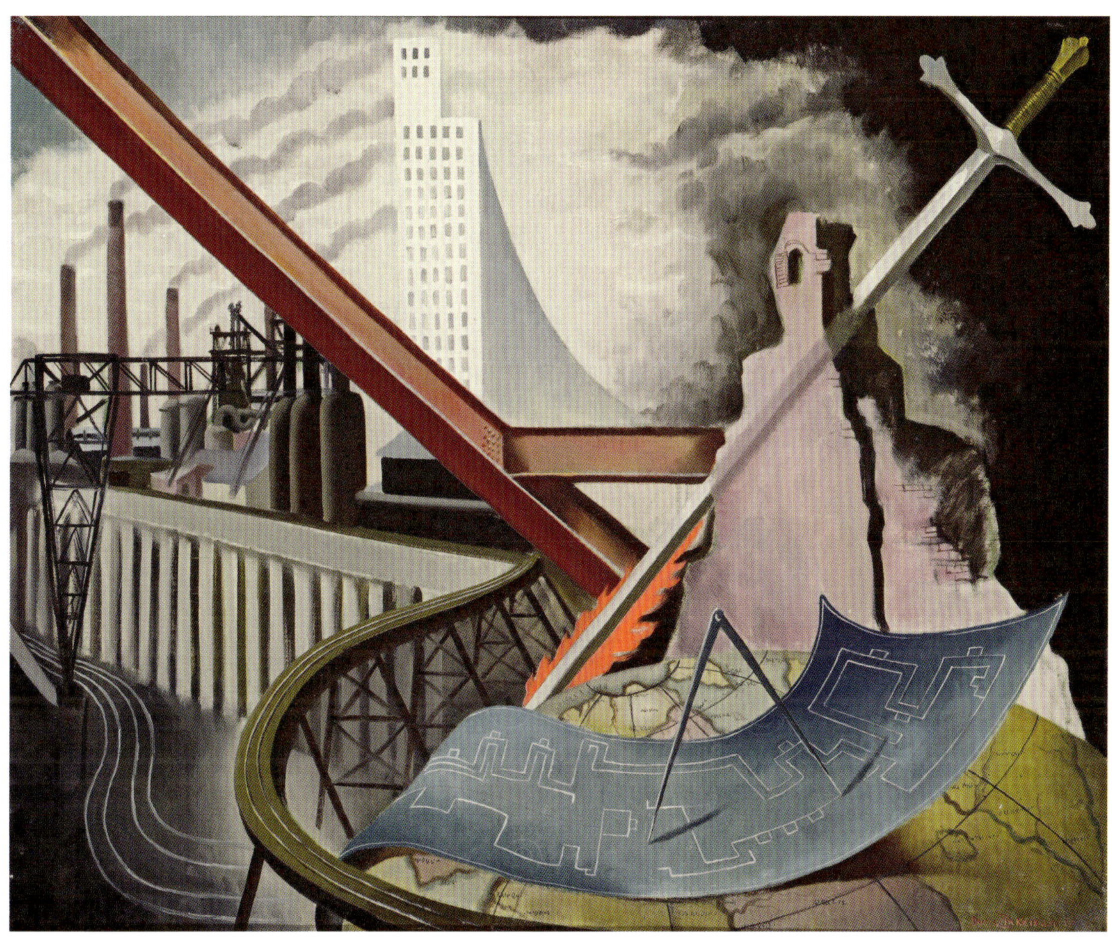

Fig.3.66
Doris Zinkeisen, *The Flaming Sword of Industry*, 1946, oil on canvas.
Number four from the advertising series *This Present Age* painted for The United Steel Companies. Used in magazines the series were also collected together in a limited edition book of one-hundred copies published in 1946. There are a total of twelve paintings in the series, six by each sister. See also the next three reproductions.
© Private collection/Peter Nahum at The Leicester Galleries/ Bridgeman Images [PNH419791].

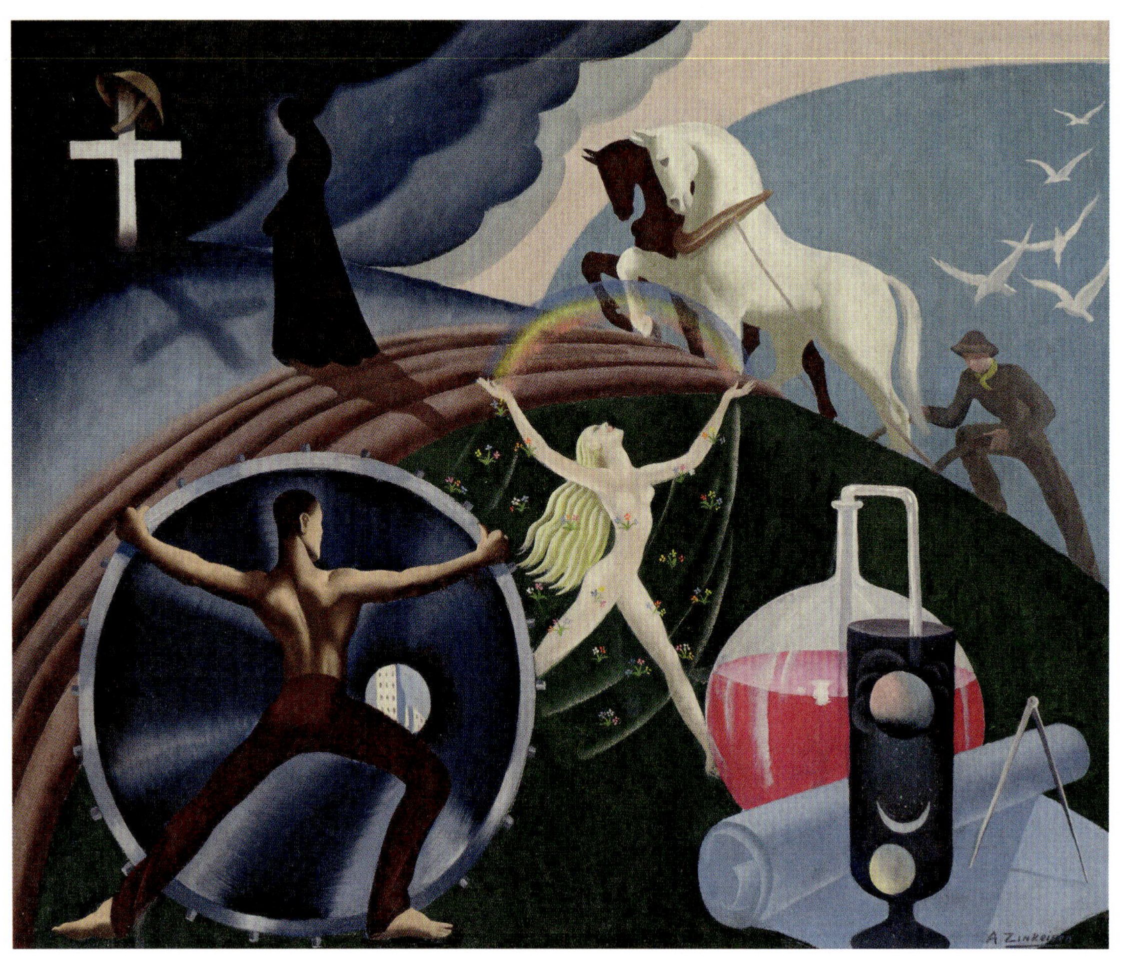

Fig.3.67
Anna Zinkeisen, *The Unity of Purpose in Peace*, 1946, oil on canvas.
Number three from the advertising series *This Present Age* painted for The United Steel Companies. See also Fig.3.66, Fig.3.68, and Fig.3.69.

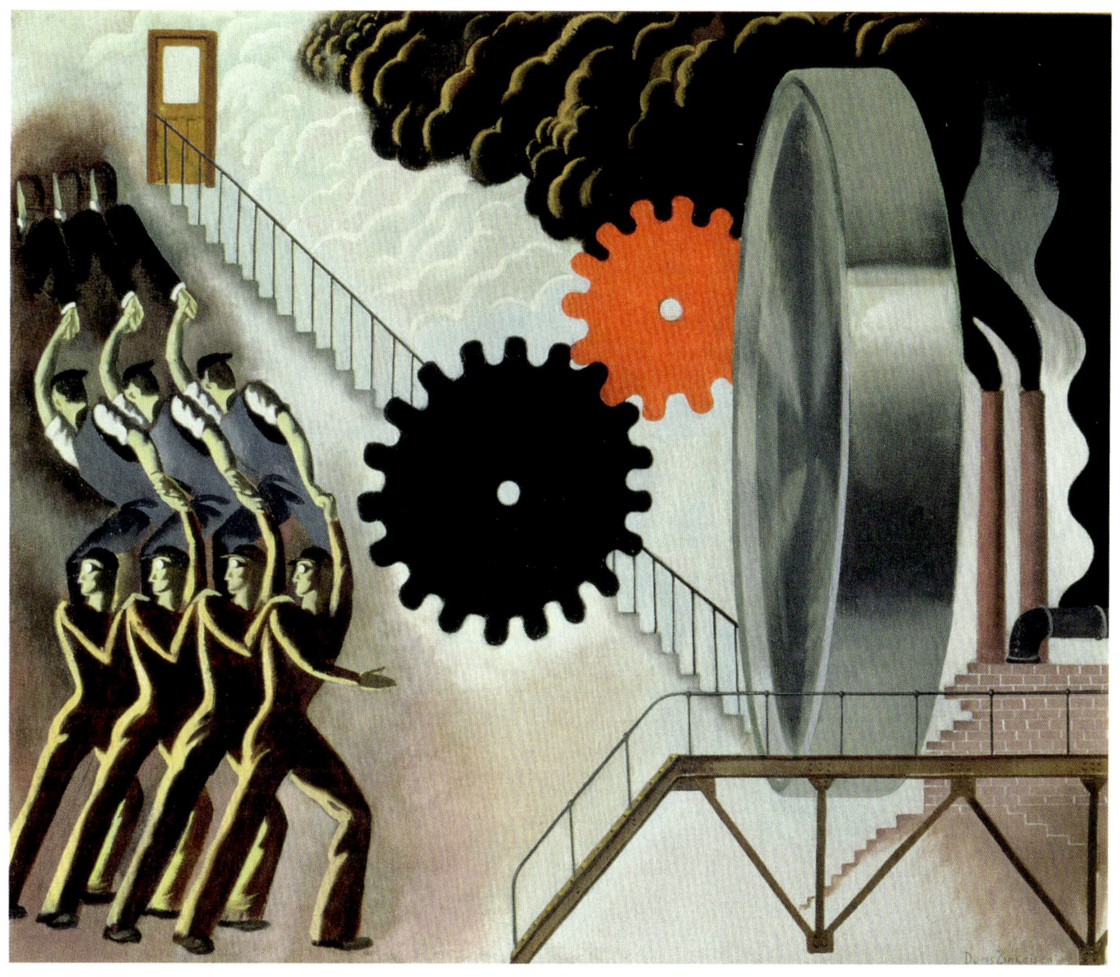

Fig.3.68
Doris Zinkeisen, *The Relations of Management and Labour*, 1946, oil on canvas.
Number two from the advertising series *This Present Age* painted for The United Steel Companies. See also Fig.3.66, Fig.3.67, and Fig.3.69.

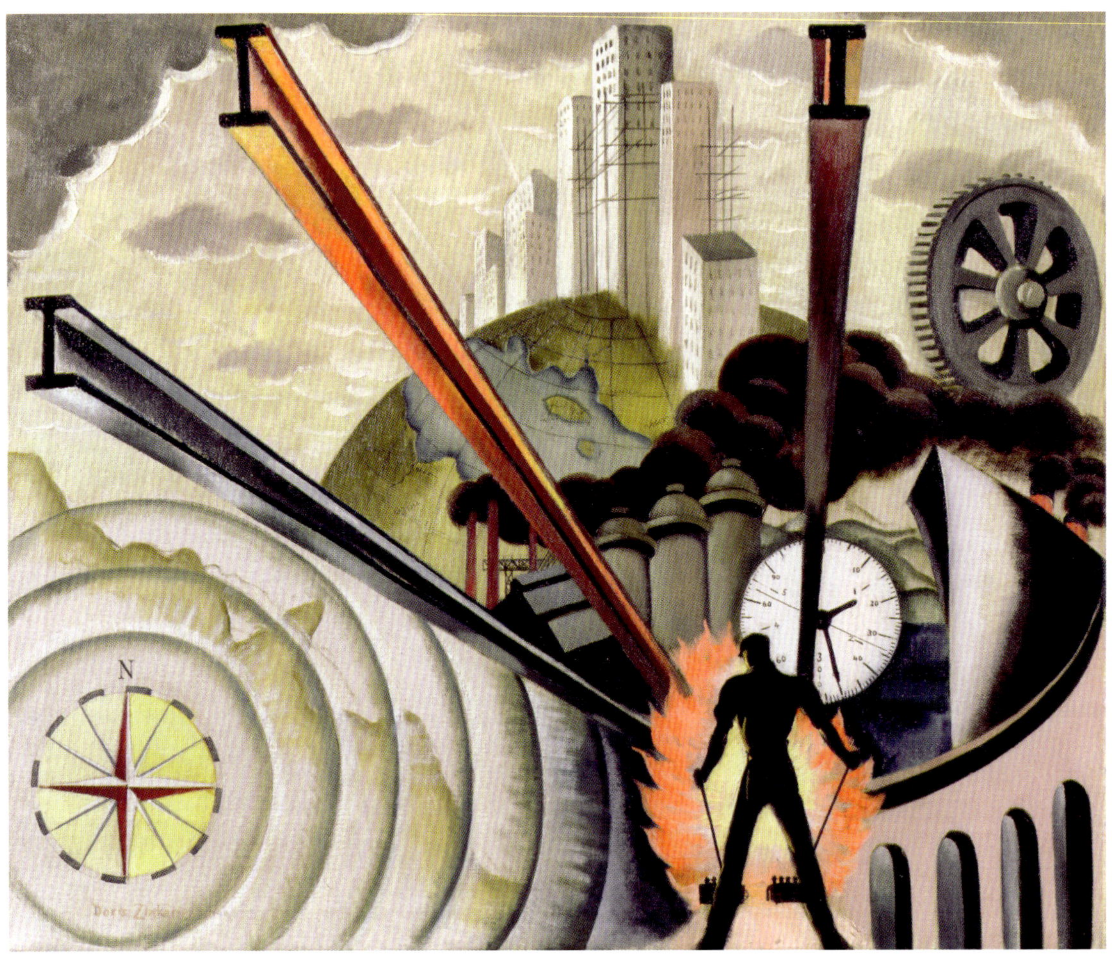

Fig.3.69

Doris Zinkeisen, *Industrial Power*, 1946, oil on canvas. Number twelve from the advertising series *This Present Age* painted for The United Steel Companies. See also the three preceding reproductions.

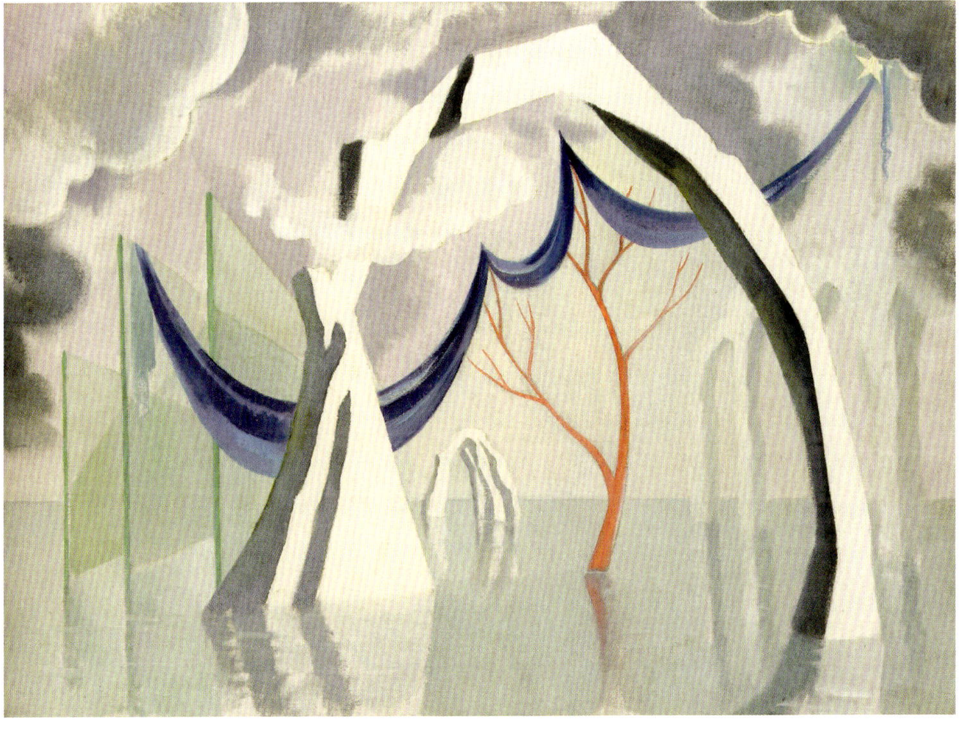

Fig.3.70
Anna Zinkeisen, *Monastral Blue*, mid to late 1940s, oil on canvas.
One from a series of commissions from The Imperial Chemical Industries (ICI) in connection with advertisements for plastic materials and dyestuffs, in this particular instance a new blue pigment used in paints and dyes, which was brought into production at ICI during 1935.

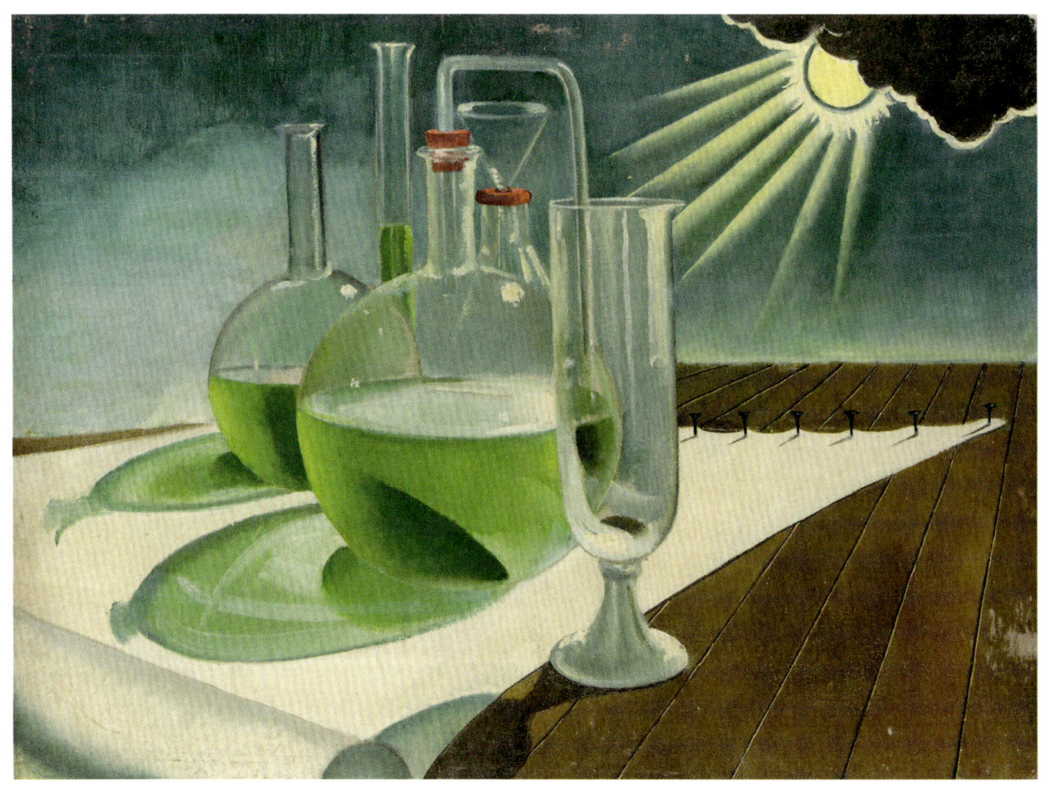

Fig.3.71
Anna Zinkeisen, *'Caledon' Jade Green*, mid to late 1940s, oil on canvas.
An Imperial Chemical Industries commission to celebrate the work of its chemists in the development of the dyestuff giving the painting its name.

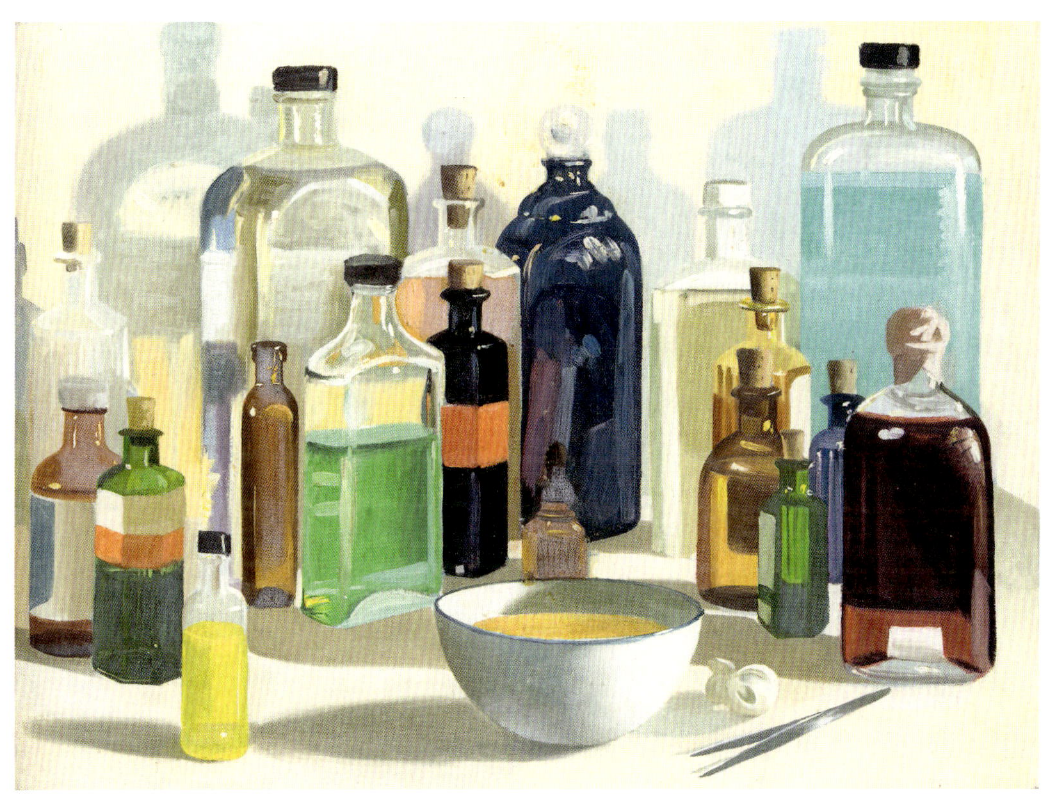

Fig.3.72
Anna Zinkeisen, *Antiseptics*, mid to late 1940s, oil on canvas.

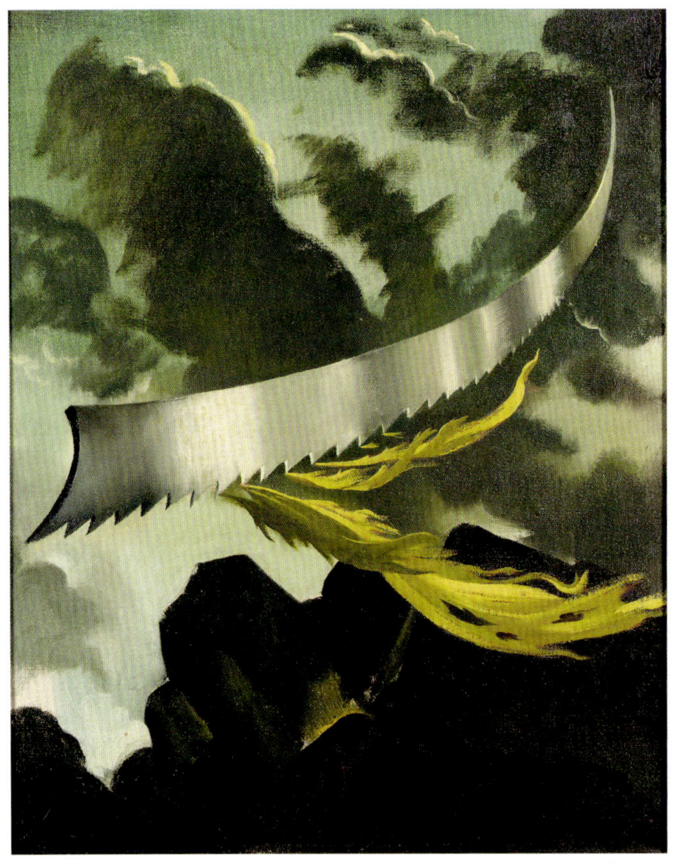

Fig.3.73
Doris Zinkeisen, *Wear and Tear*, mid to late 1940s, oil on canvas.
Previously in the corporate collection of The Imperial Chemical Industries (ICI), the painting relates to the Technical Services.
© Photograph courtesy of Sotheby's.

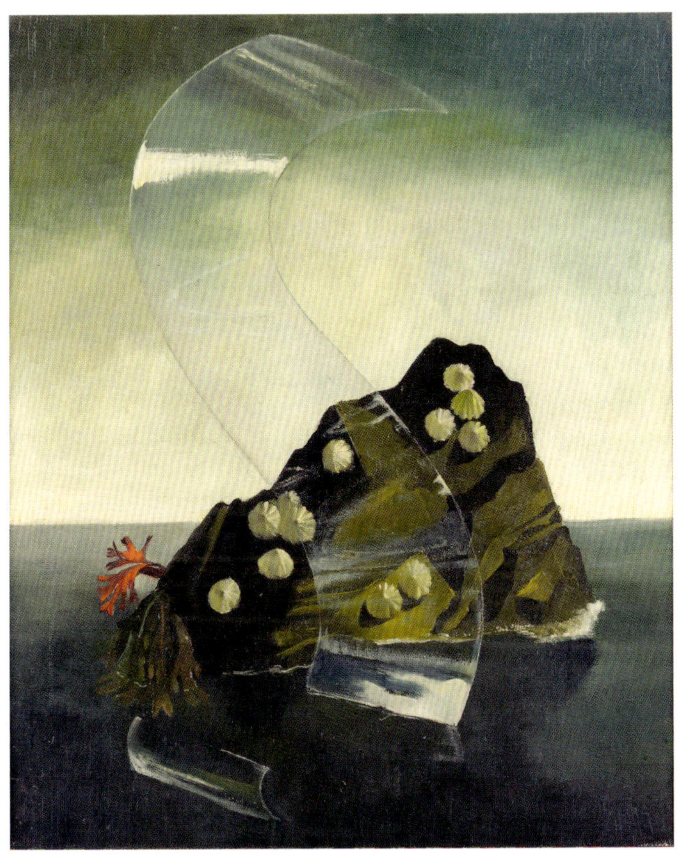

Fig.3.74
Doris Zinkeisen, *Limpet Ink*, mid to late 1940s, oil on canvas.
A commission from The Imperial Chemical Industries (ICI) and formerly in its collection, a painting presumably relating to a new greenish-blue dyestuff and possibly also a plastic material. Does the see-through (or limpid) 'S' represent the 'synthetic', or 'surreal' nature of the chemically produced moulded material?

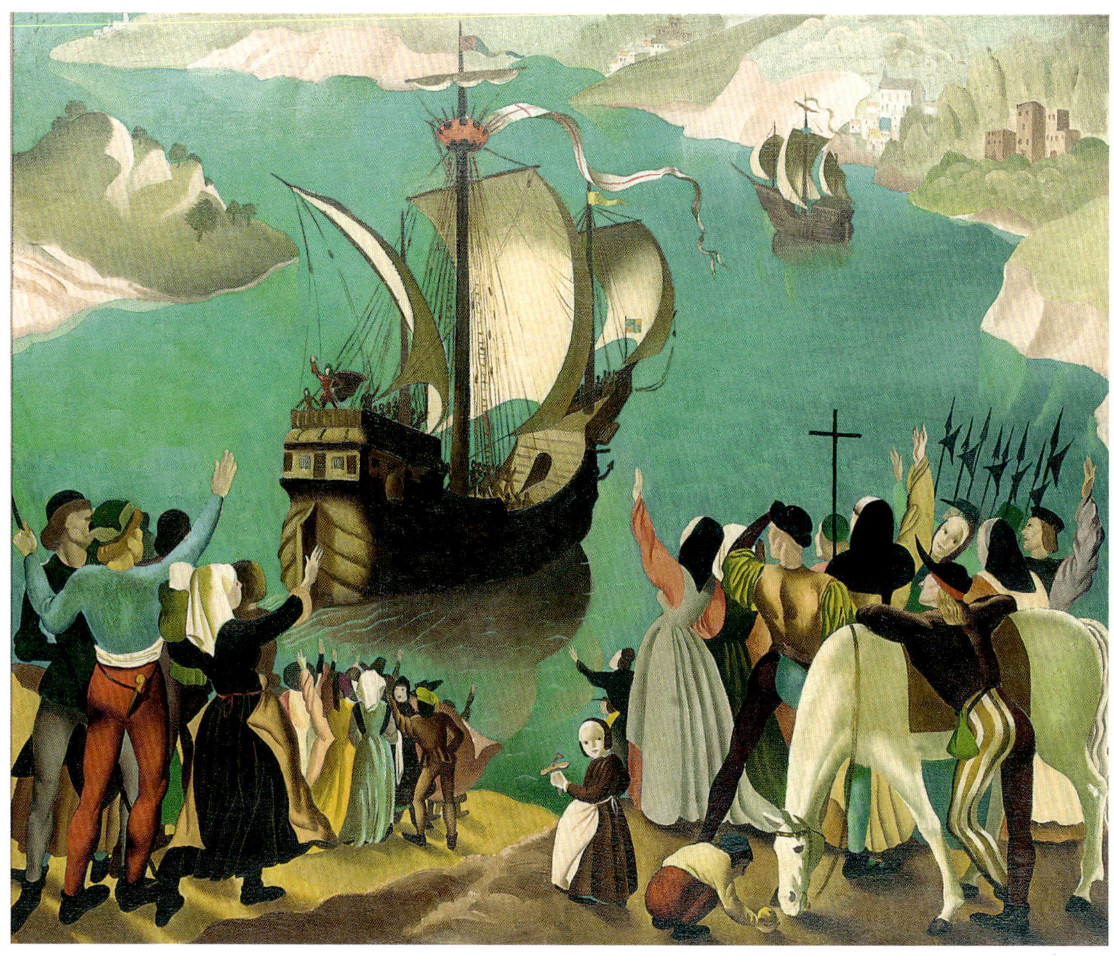

Fig.3.75
Anna Zinkeisen, *Bristol Ships Manned by Bristol Men*, 1948, oil on canvas.
One from a series of twelve advertisements by nine different artists (the Zinkeisen sisters contributing two each) for The United Steel Companies. This painting is number five of the series, which was published as a collection in 1948 entitled *Trade Winds* in a limited edition of just one hundred and fifty copies. See also the two following reproductions.

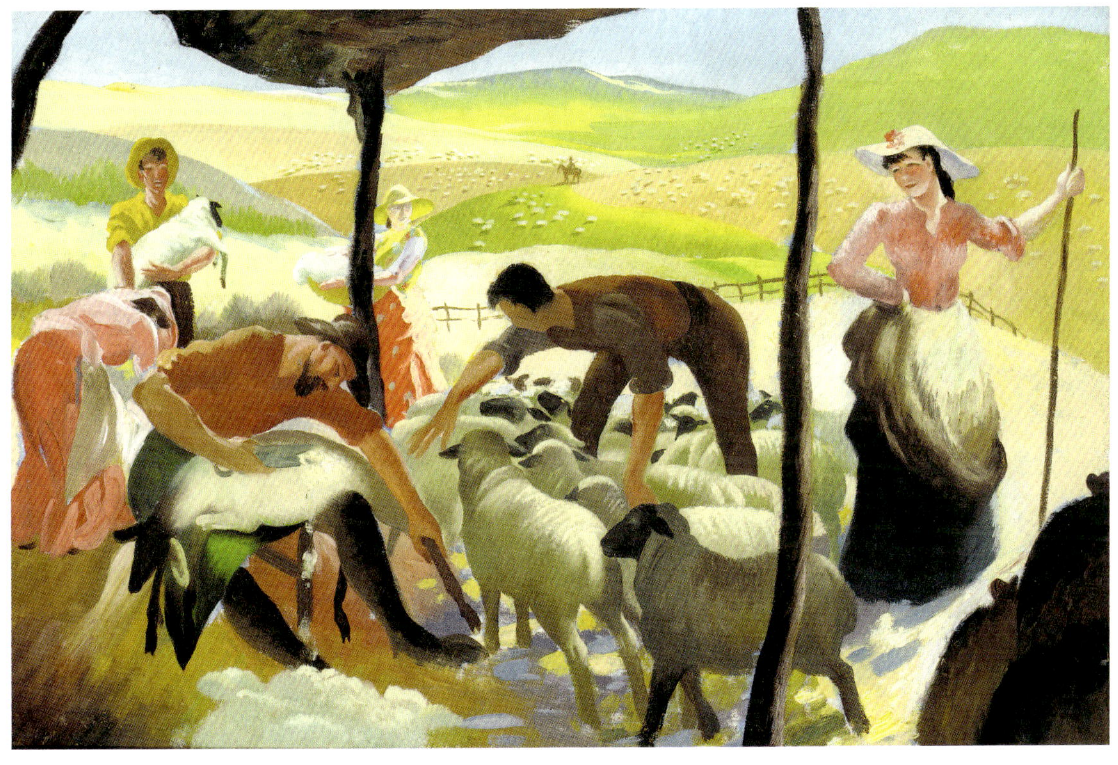

Fig.3.76
Anna Zinkeisen, *The Wool Race*, 1948, oil on canvas. Number eleven from the *Trade Winds* series for The United Steel Companies. See also the preceding and following reproductions.

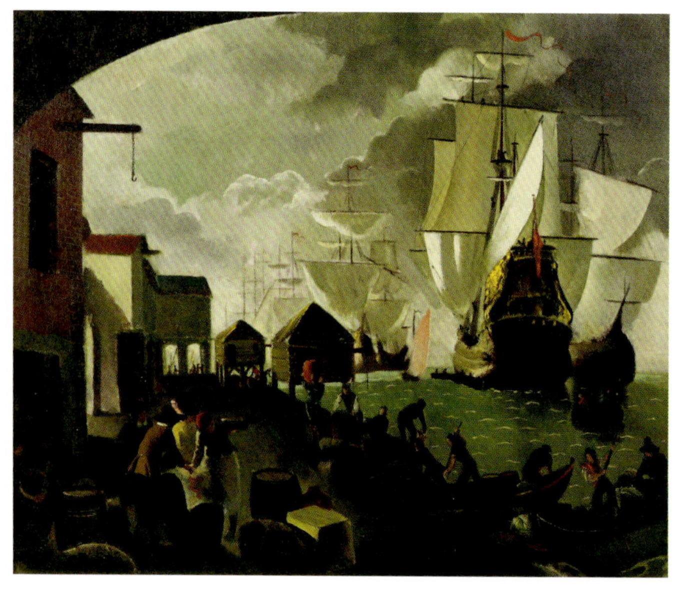

Fig.3.77
Doris Zinkeisen, *The Merchant Adventurers*, 1948, oil on canvas.
Number six in the *Trade Winds* series for The United Steel Companies. See also the two preceding reproductions.

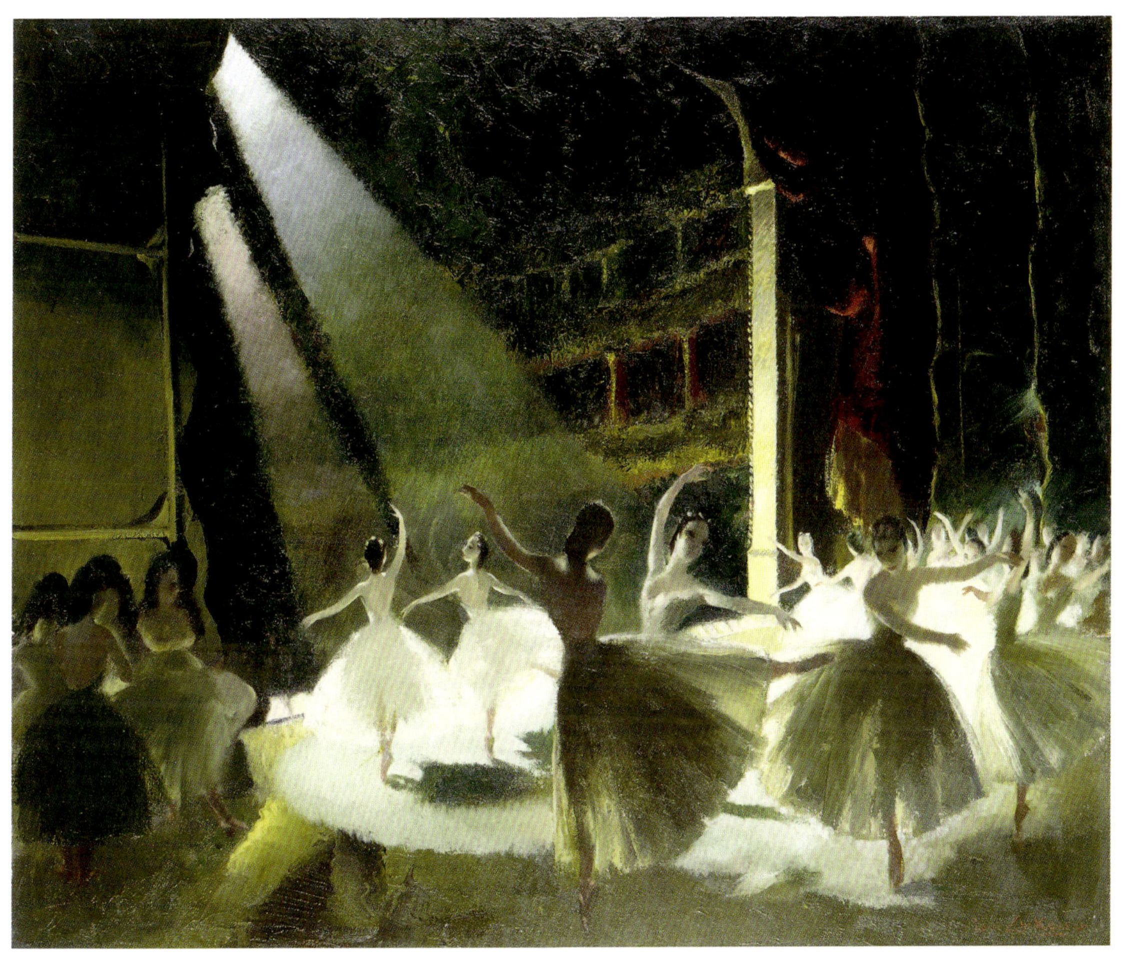

Fig.3.78

Doris Zinkeisen, *The Rehearsal*, *circa* 1949-1950, oil on canvas.

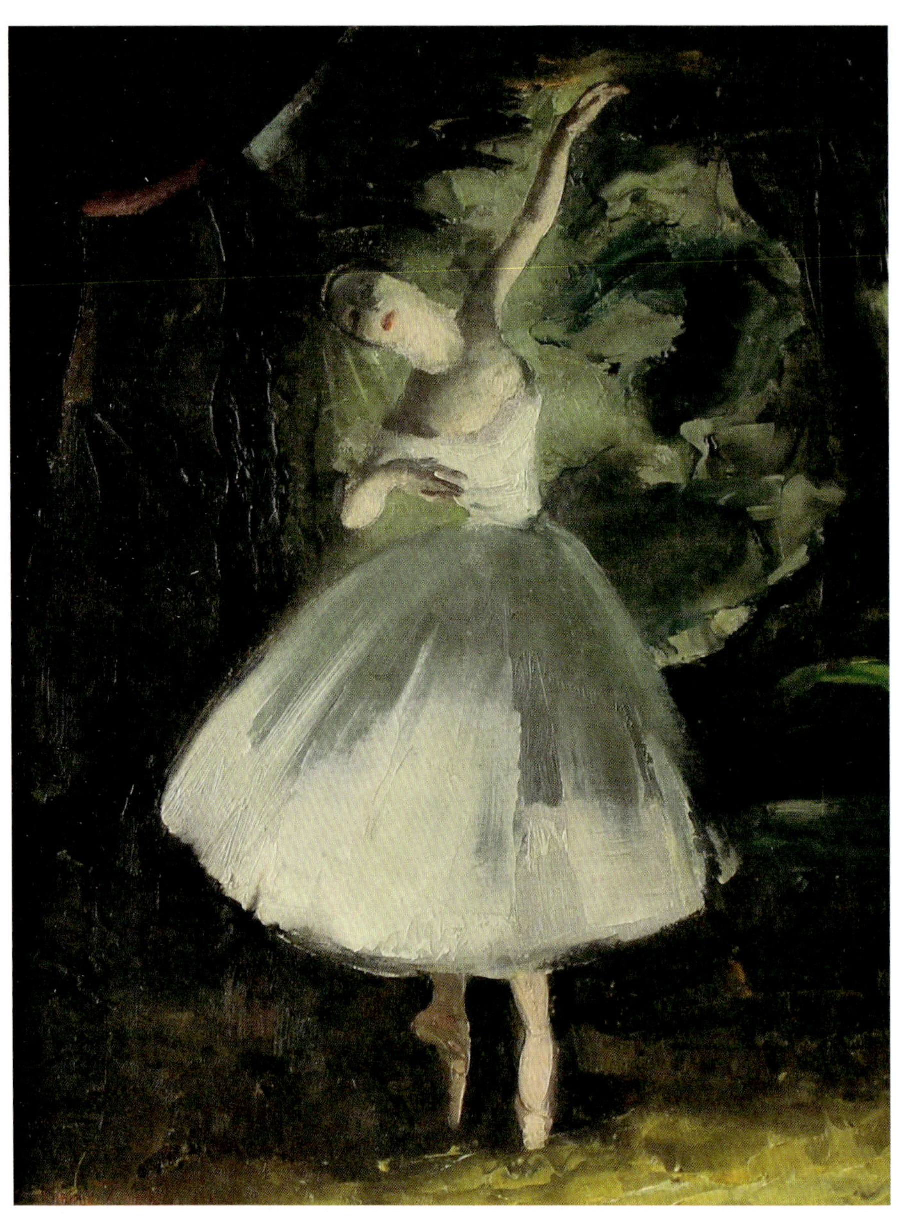

Fig.3.79
Doris Zinkeisen, *Ballet Dancer*, 1949, oil on canvas.

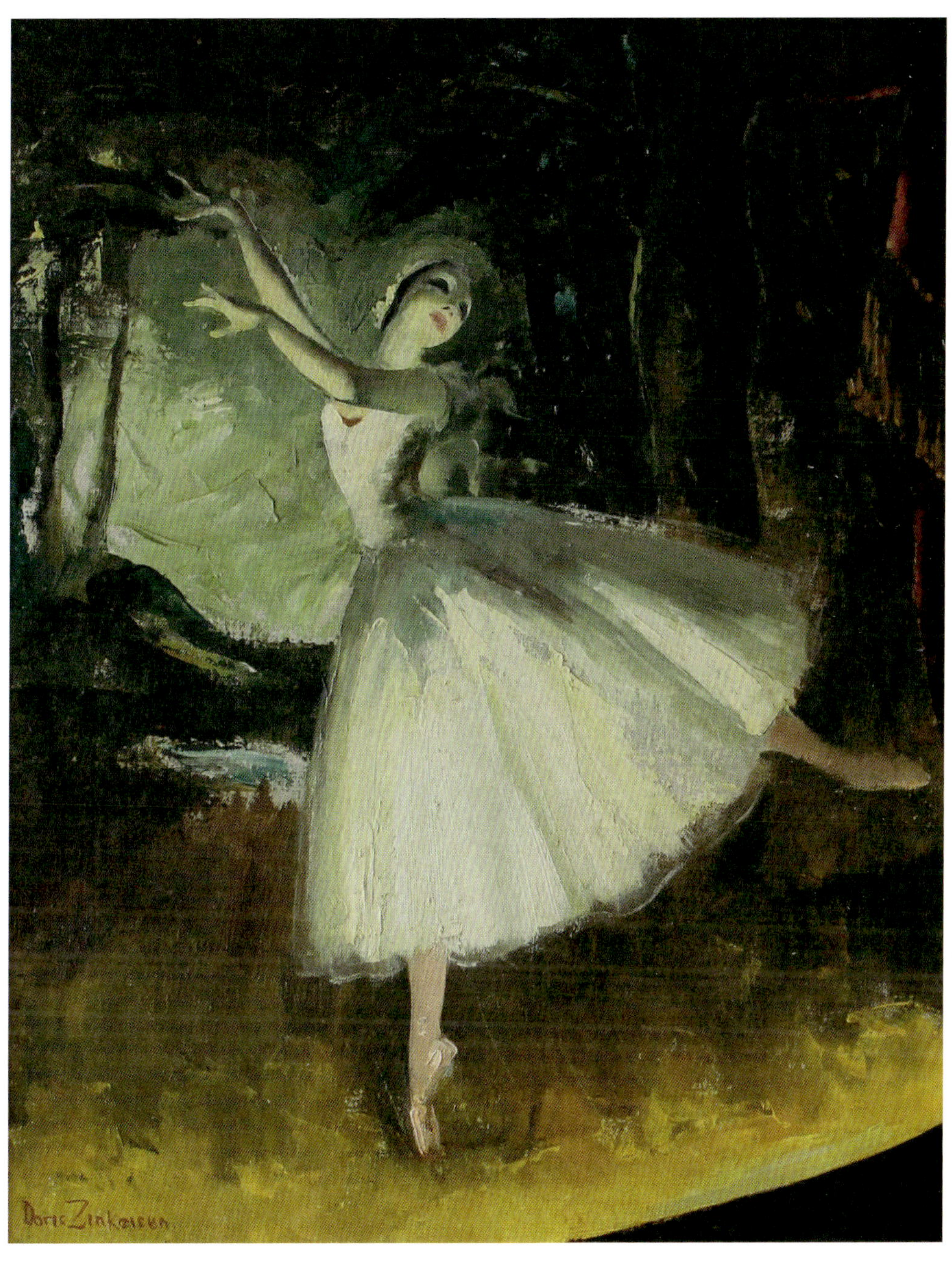

Fig.3.80
Doris Zinkeisen, *The Ballerina*, 1949, oil on canvas.

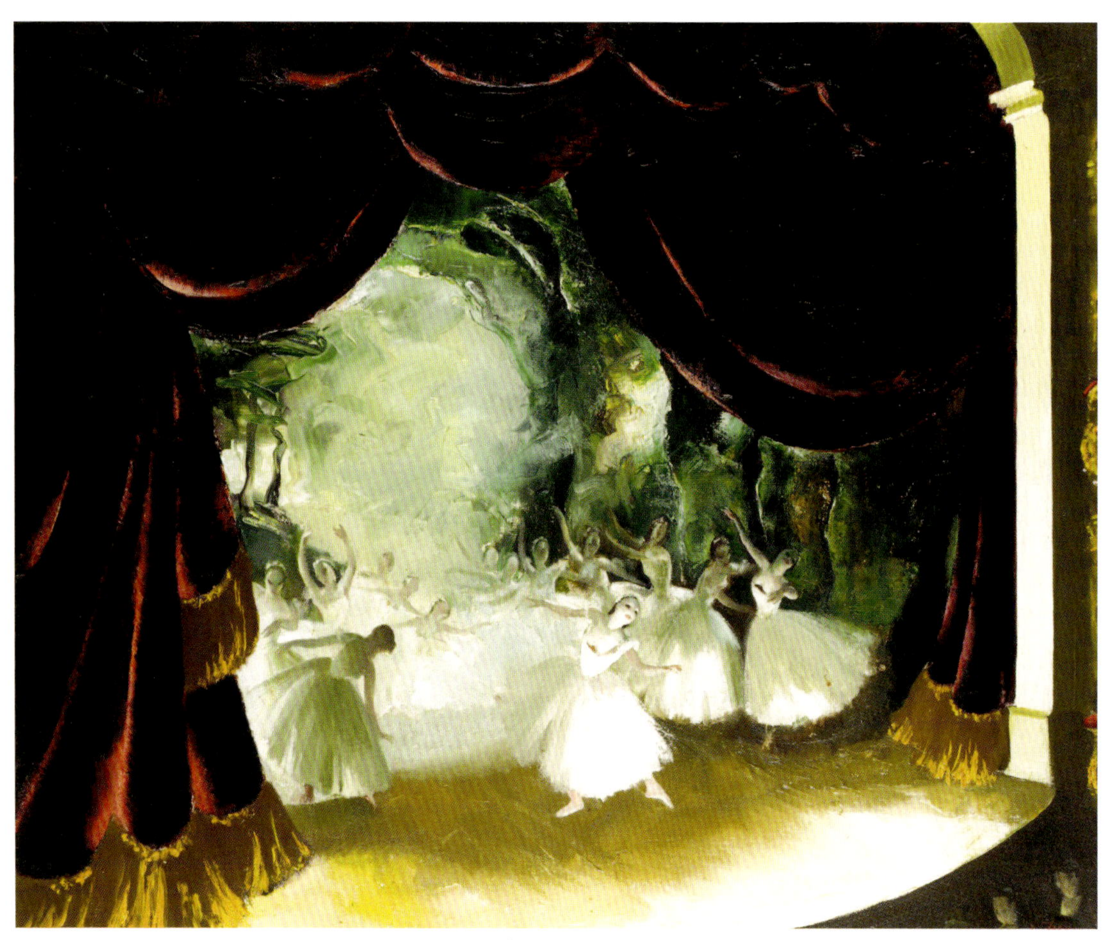

Fig.3.81
Doris Zinkeisen, *Les Sylphides*, *circa* 1949-1950, oil on canvas.

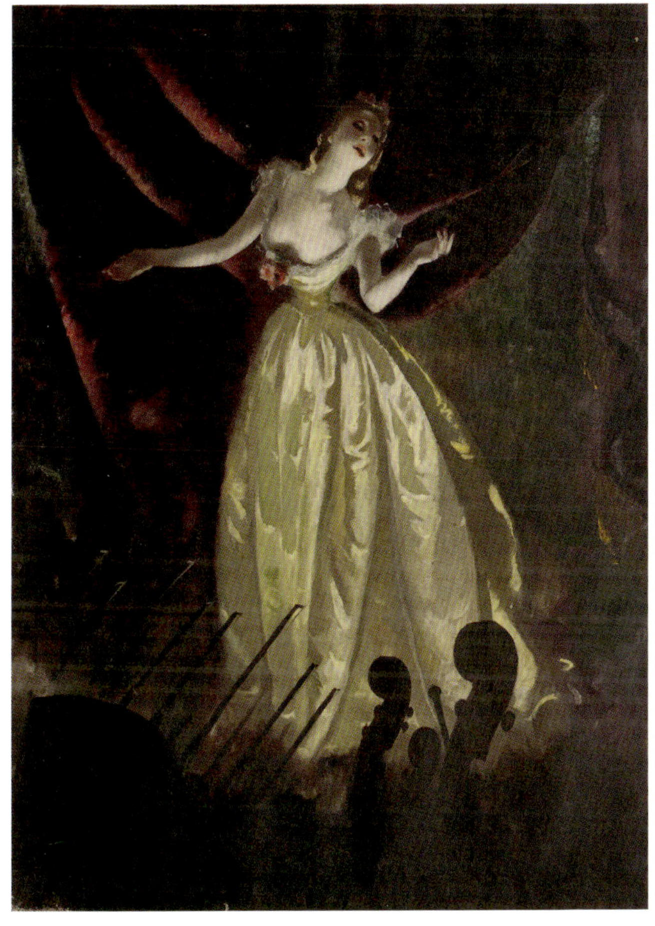

Fig.3.82
Doris Zinkeisen, *Singer on Stage*, *circa* 1950, oil on canvas.

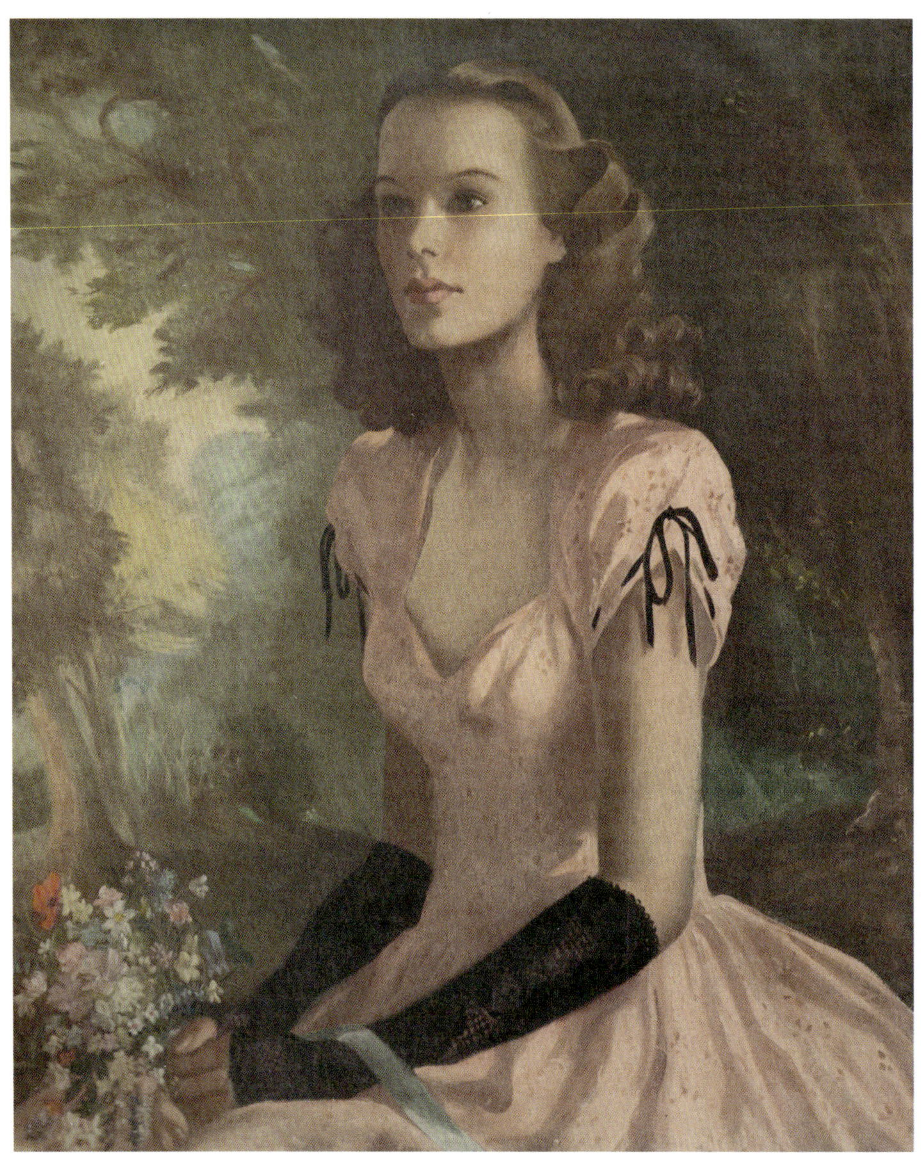

Fig.3.83
Anna Zinkeisen, *Sally Ann Howes*, 1948, oil on canvas. The actress Sally Ann Howes would later famously play the role of Truly Scrumptious in the film *Chitty Chitty Bang Bang* (1968). See also Fig.1.71.

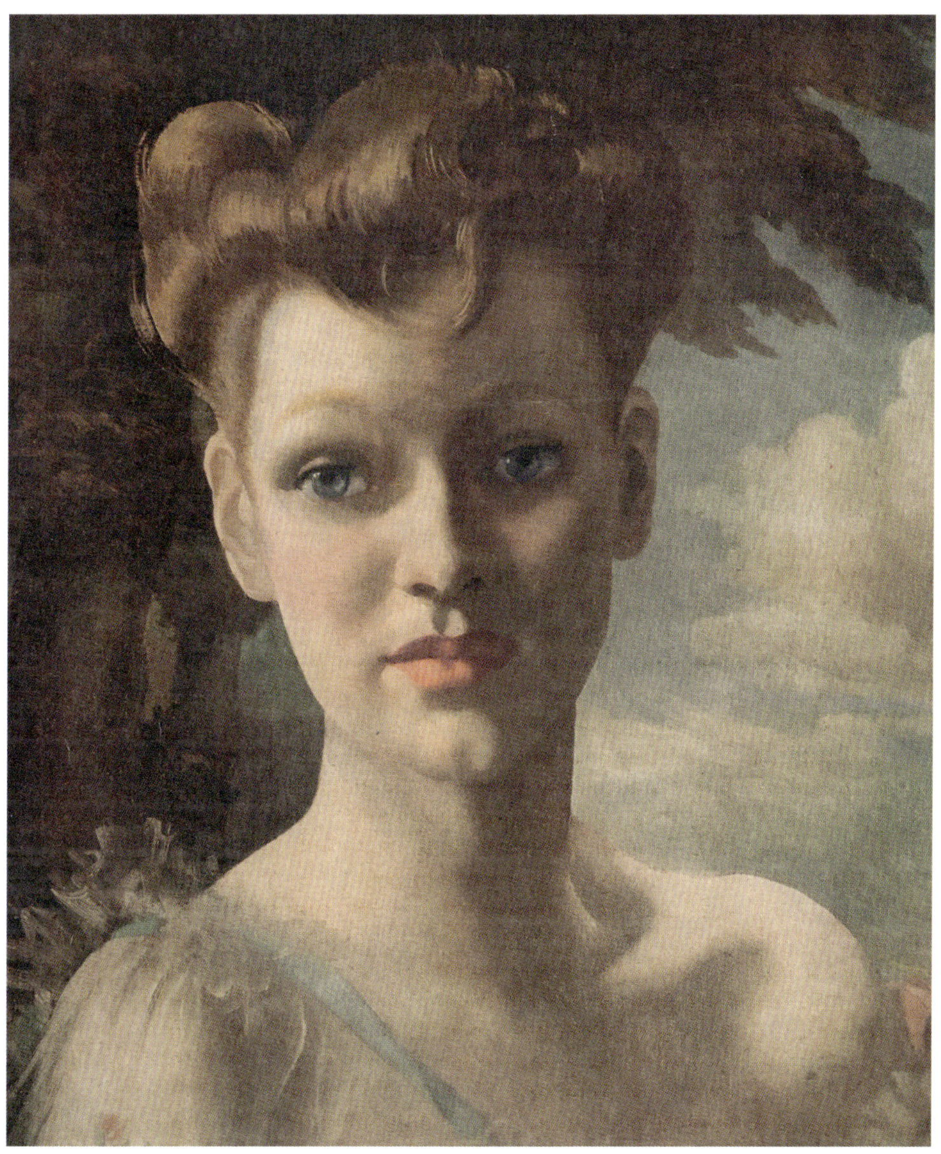

Fig.3.84
Anna Zinkeisen, *Rosamund John*, late 1940s, oil on canvas.
Rosamund John was a popular stage and screen actress, especially during the 1940s. She later married the Labour MP John Silkin (1923-1987).

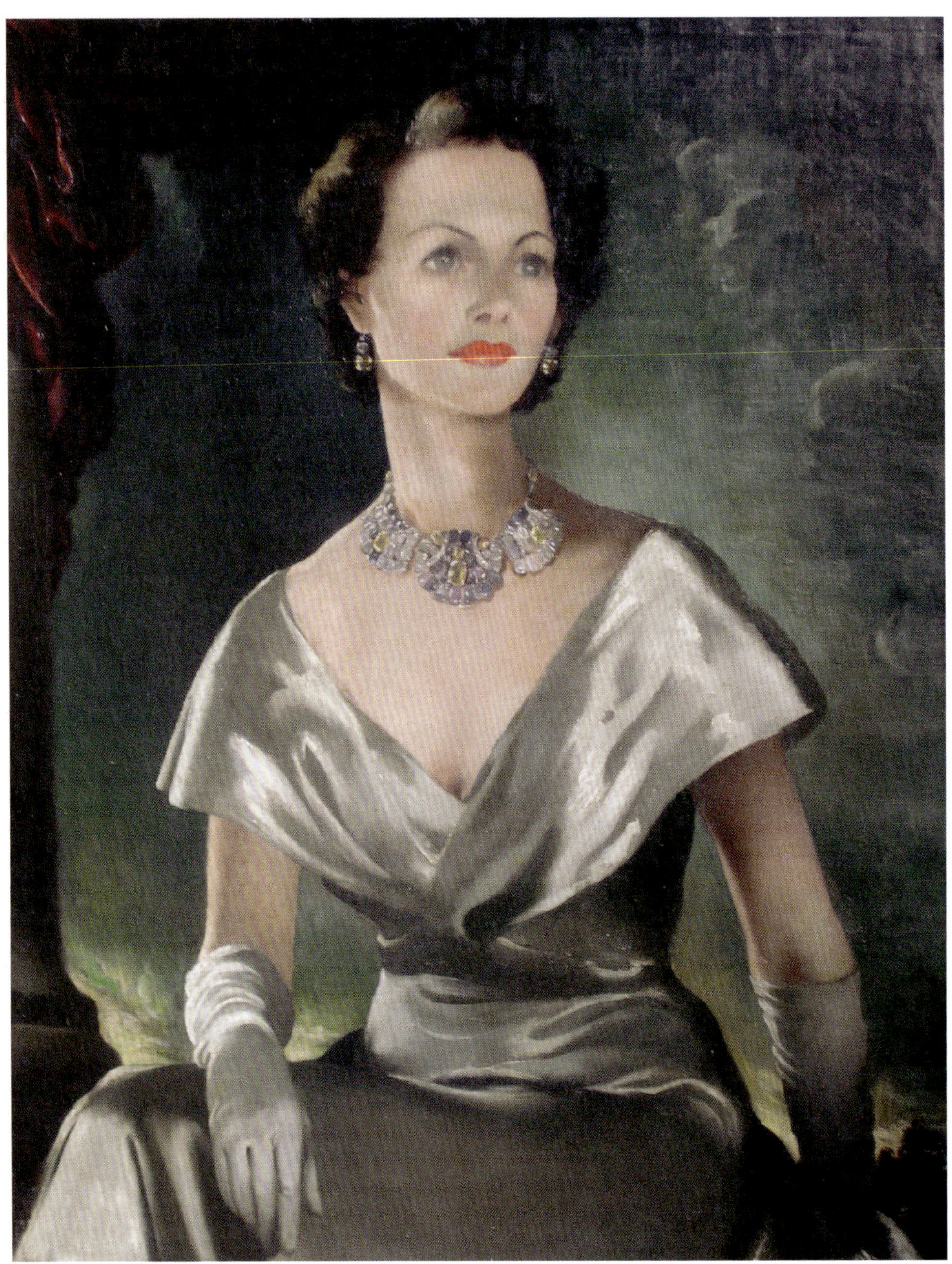

Fig.3.85
Anna Zinkeisen, *Elizabeth Allan*, *circa* 1950, oil on canvas.
Elizabeth Allan acted in Hollywood films during the 1930s. She was noted for her chic sense of dress and in 1952 was voted British television's top female personality. See also Fig.1.72 and Fig.1.73.

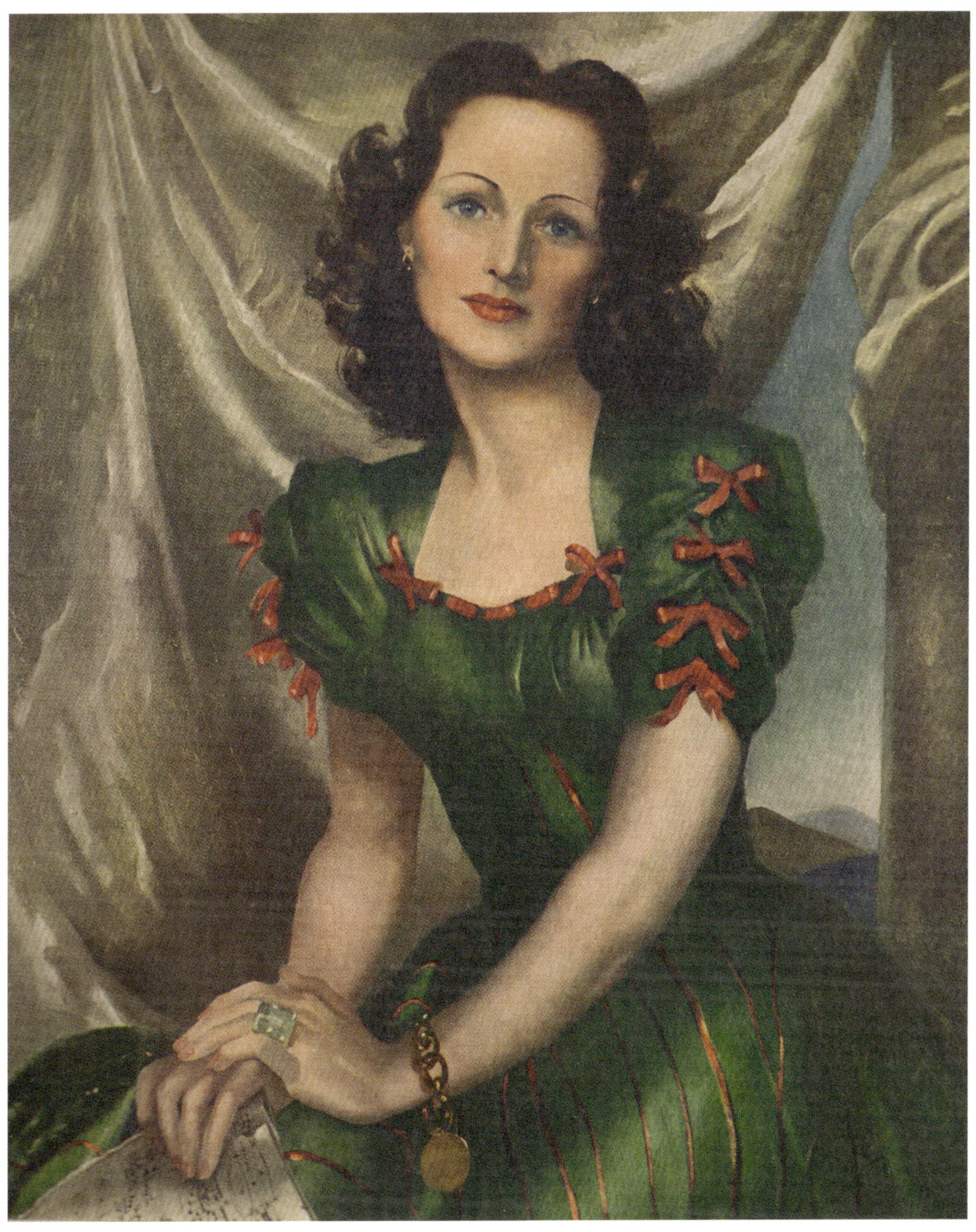

Fig.3.86
Anna Zinkeisen, *Eileen Joyce, circa* 1950, oil on canvas. When performing the pianist Eileen Joyce always wore elaborate dresses, which became part of her trademark. Eileen Joyce is perhaps best remembered today for her soundtrack to the film *Brief Encounter* (1945), directed by David Lean and written and produced by Noël Coward, where she plays the 2nd Piano Concerto by Sergei Rachmaninov (1873-1943). See also Fig.1.74.

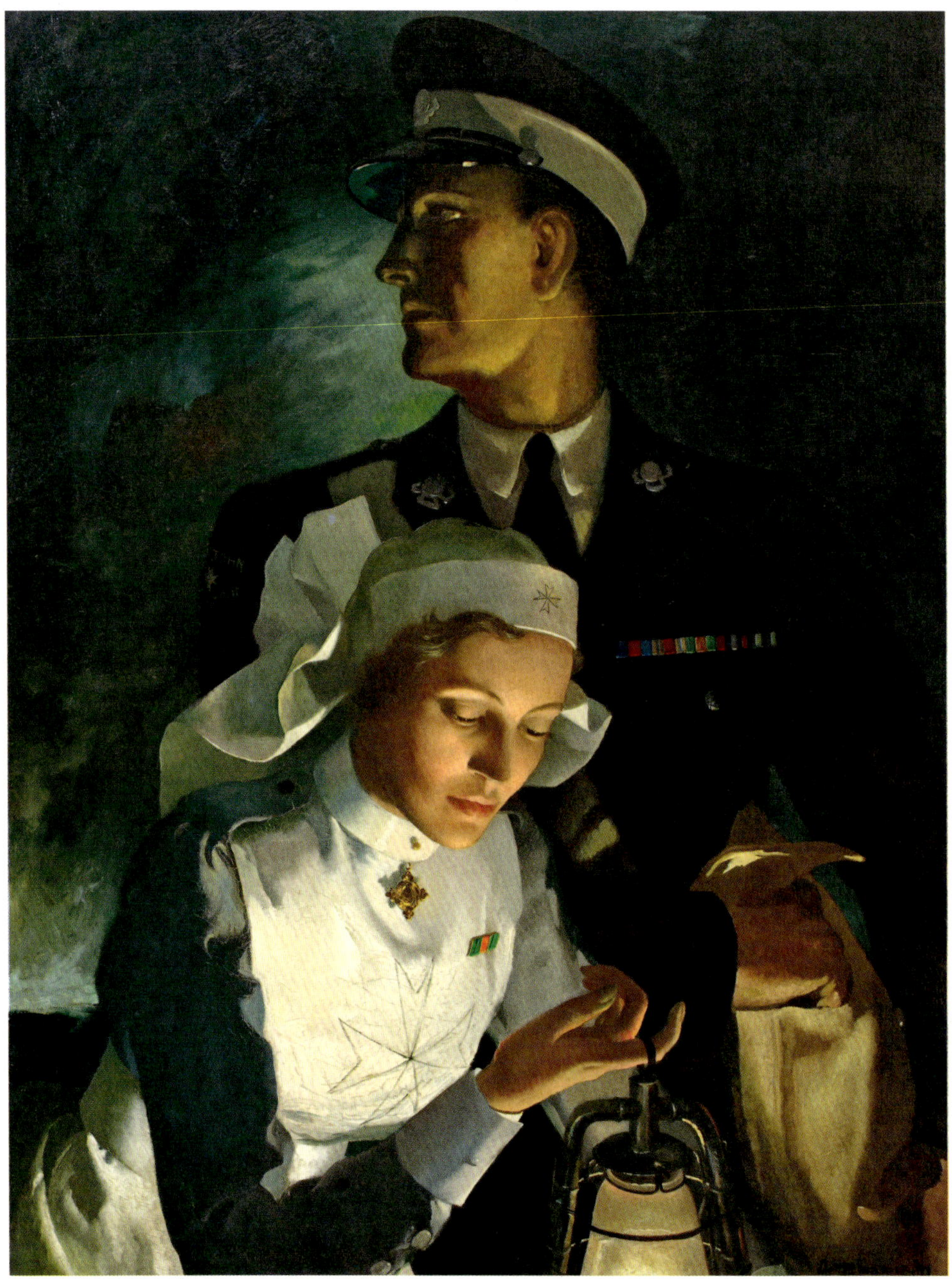

Fig.3.87
Anna Zinkeisen, *Recruitment Poster Design for the St John Ambulance*, 1952, oil on canvas.
This is one of two designs by Anna, which were used for recruitment posters and demonstrates her continued involvement with the organisation after the Second World War. The woman in this particular painting is actually Anna's daughter, Julia Heseltine, who frequently modelled for her mother.

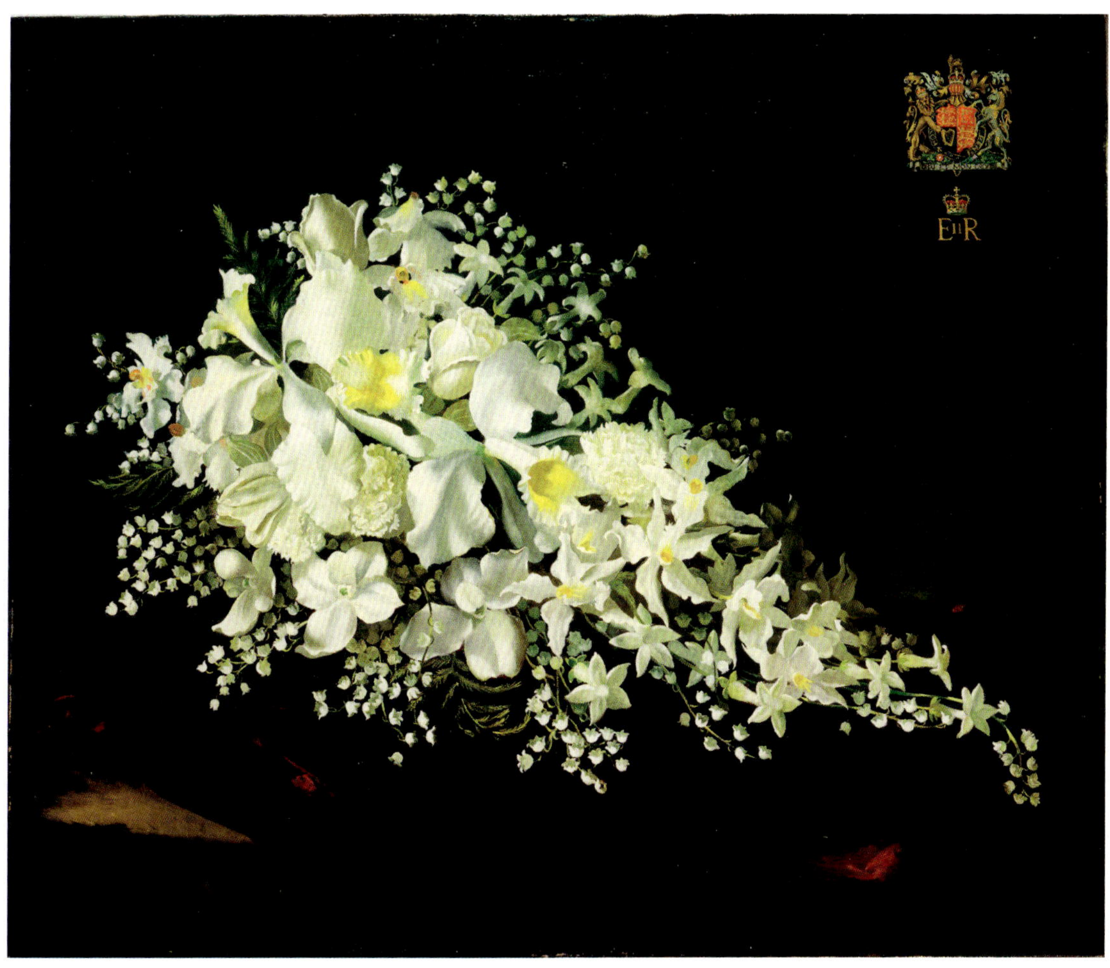

Fig.3.88
Anna Zinkeisen, *The Coronation Bouquet*, 1953, oil on canvas.
The bouquet carried by Queen Elizabeth II on Her Coronation included flowers, such as orchids, lilies of the valley, stephanotis, and carnations, all in white, which were carefully selected to represent the different parts of the United Kingdom. See also Fig.1.68.

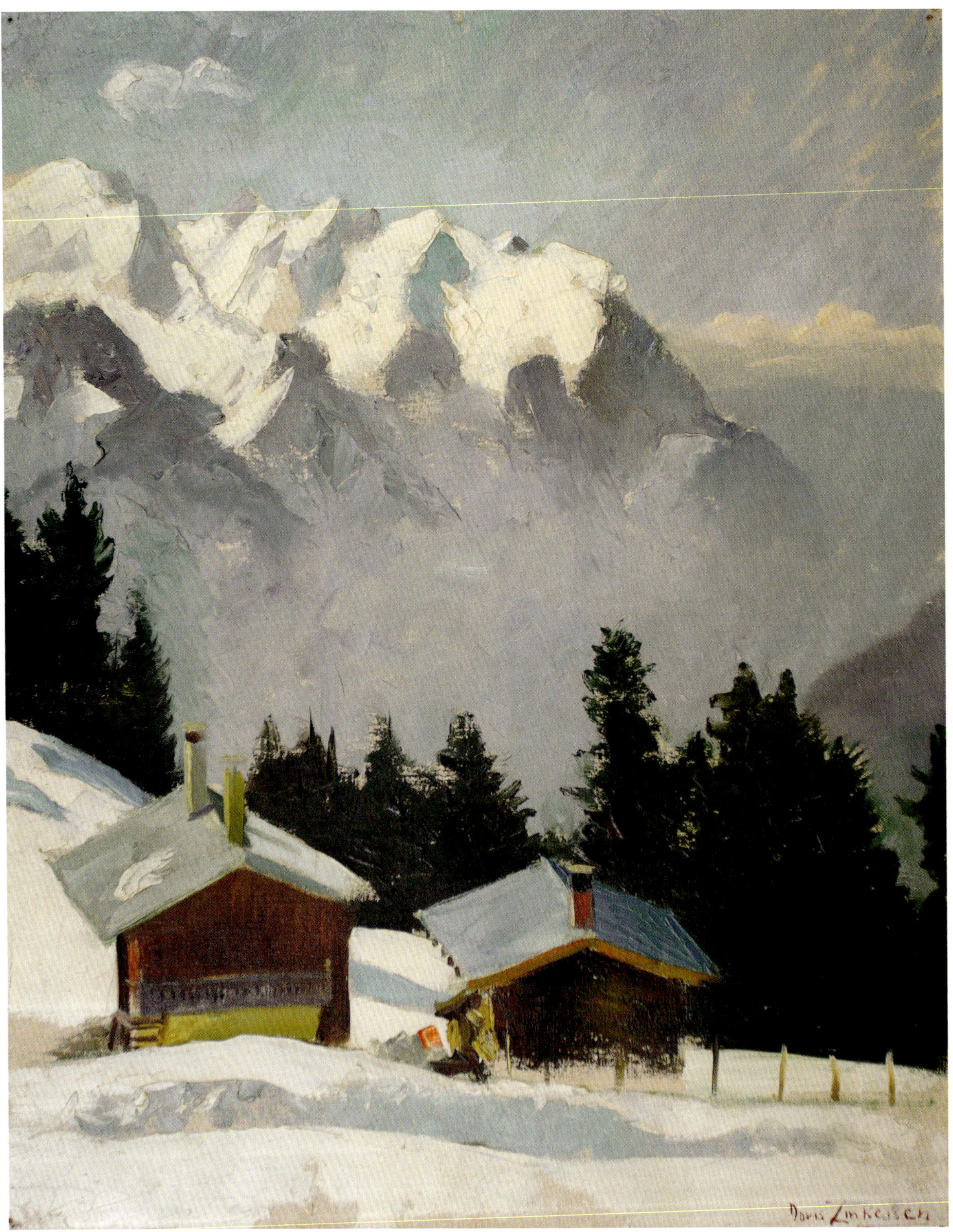
Doris Zinkeisen

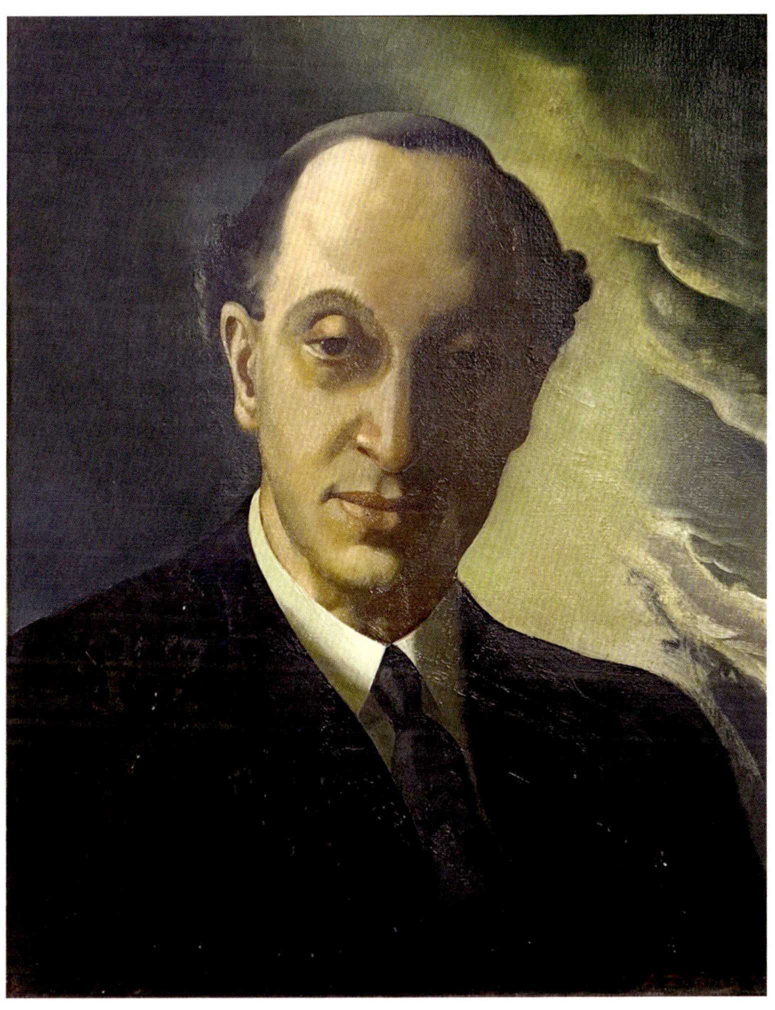

Fig.3.89
Doris Zinkeisen, *Chalets in the Swiss Alps*, *circa* late 1950s, oil on canvas.

Fig.3.90
Anna Zinkeisen, *George Prins*, 1950s, oil on canvas. Exhibited at the Royal Society of Portrait Painters. Throughout her career Anna painted leading business figures. George Prins (1889-1973) was a prominent diamond merchant, at one point a broker for De Beers, and an art collector.

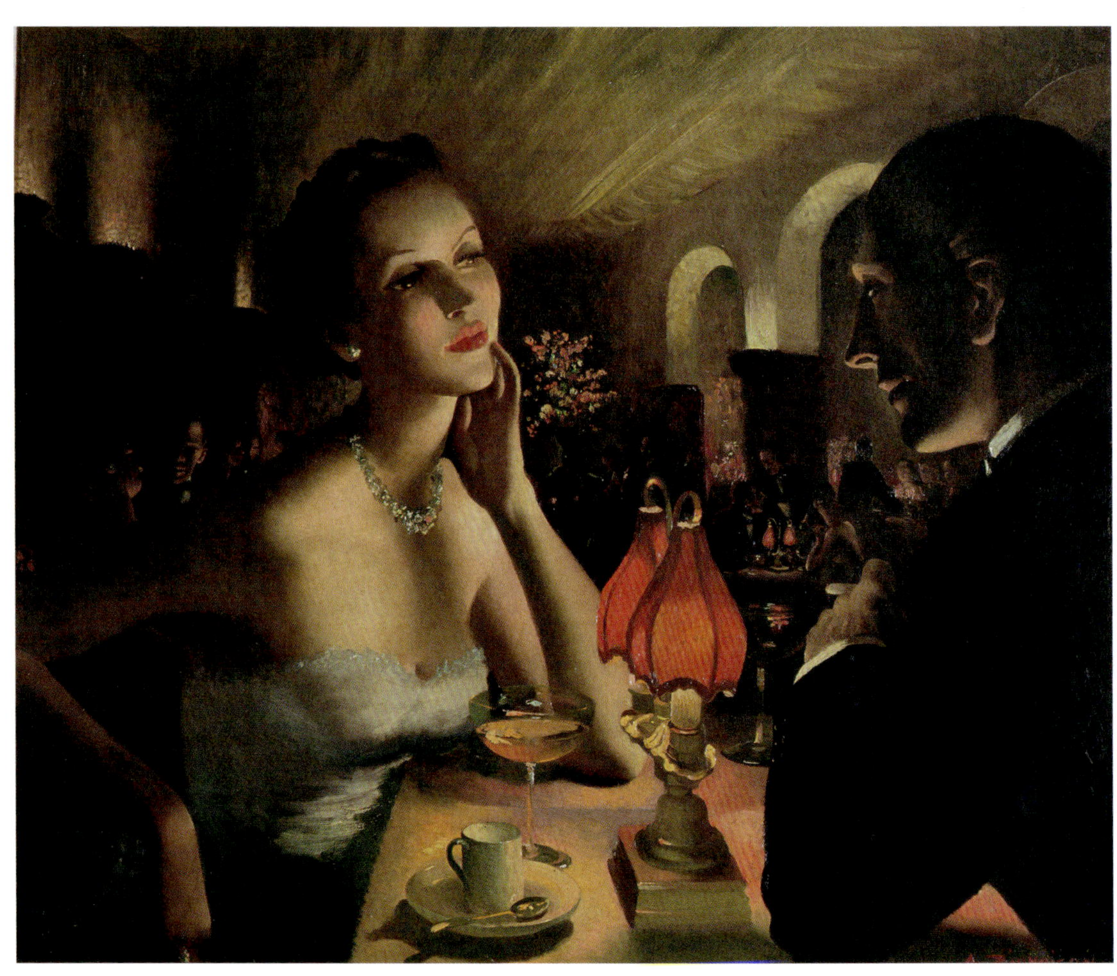

Fig.3.91
Doris Zinkeisen, *An Intimate Dinner,* 1950s, oil on canvas.

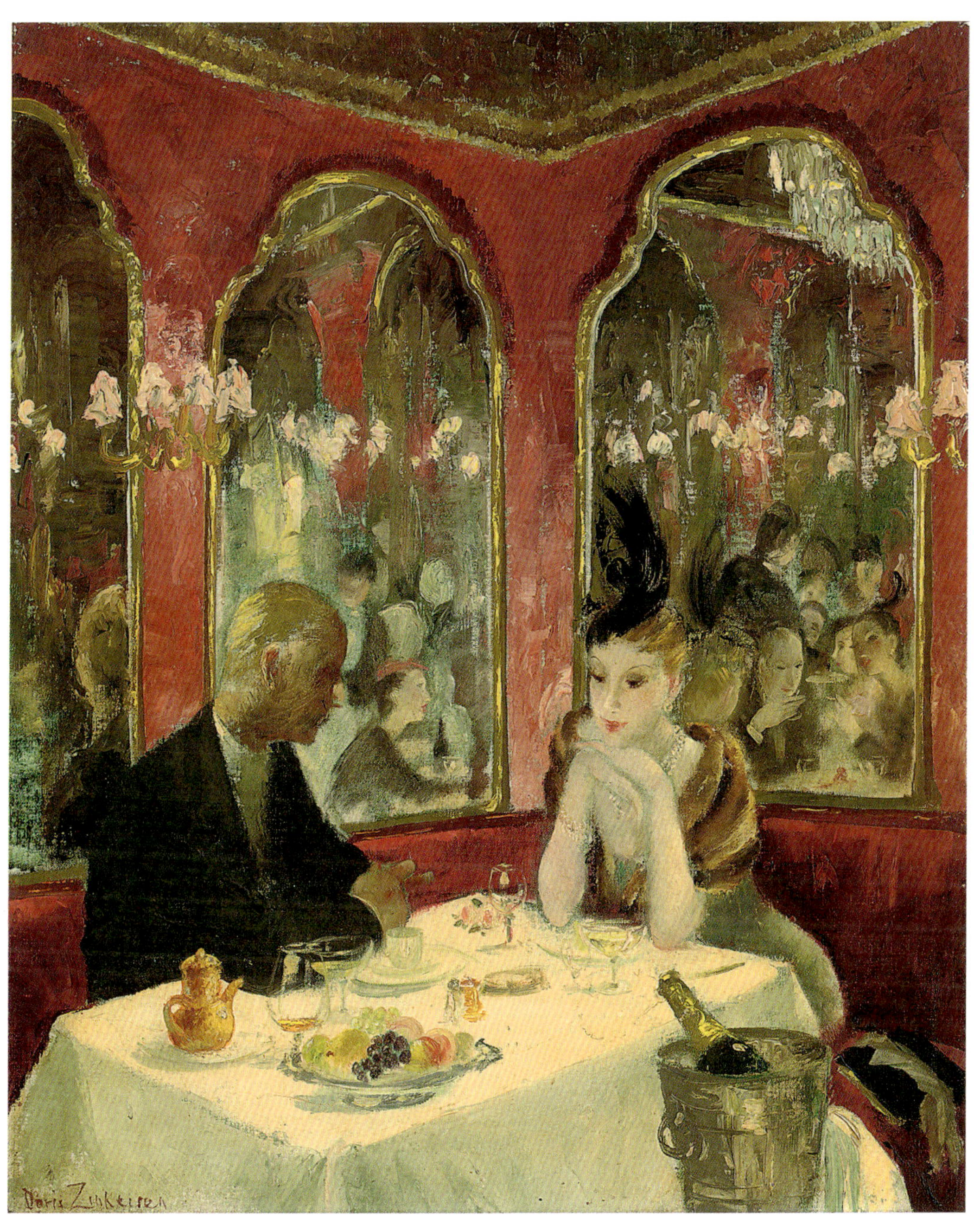

Fig.3.92

Doris Zinkeisen, *Corner of the Café Royal*, 1950s, oil on canvas.

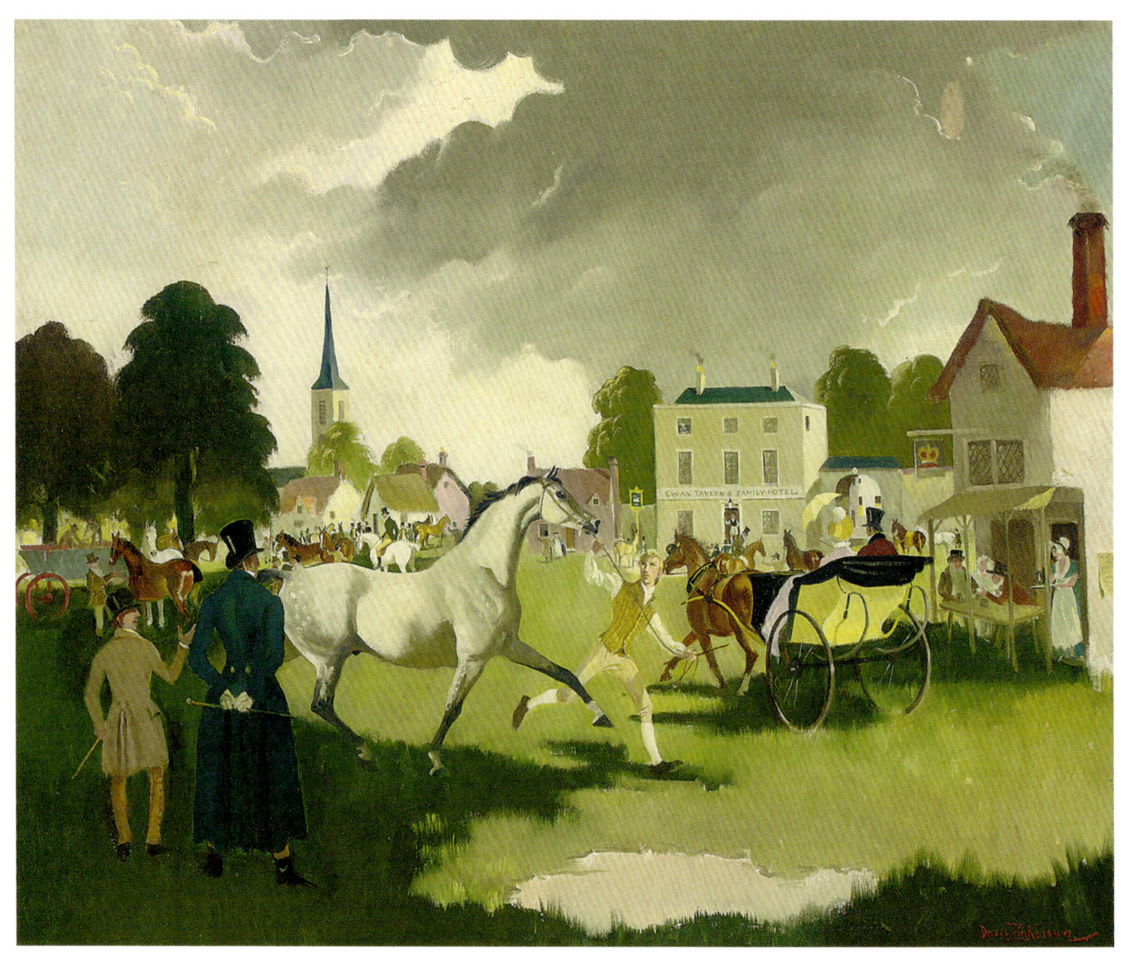

Fig.3.93
Doris Zinkeisen, *The Horse Fair*, late 1960s/early 1970s, oil on canvas.

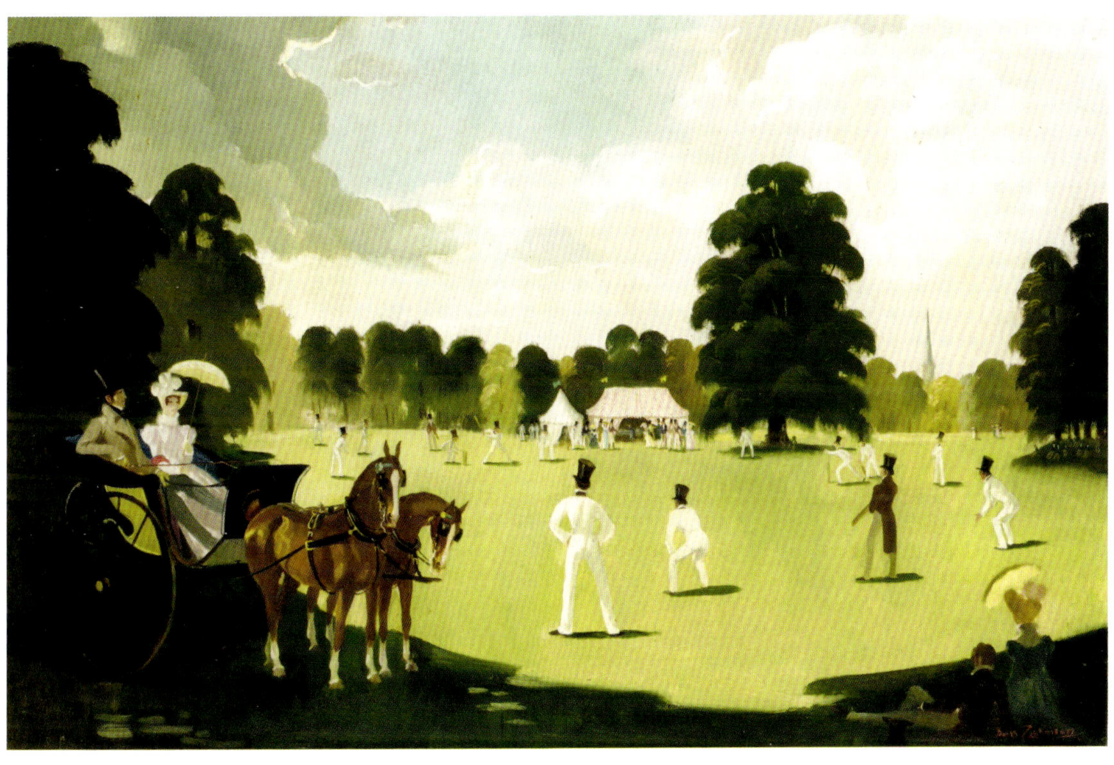

Fig.3.94
Doris Zinkeisen, *The Village Cricket Match*, early 1970s, oil on canvas.

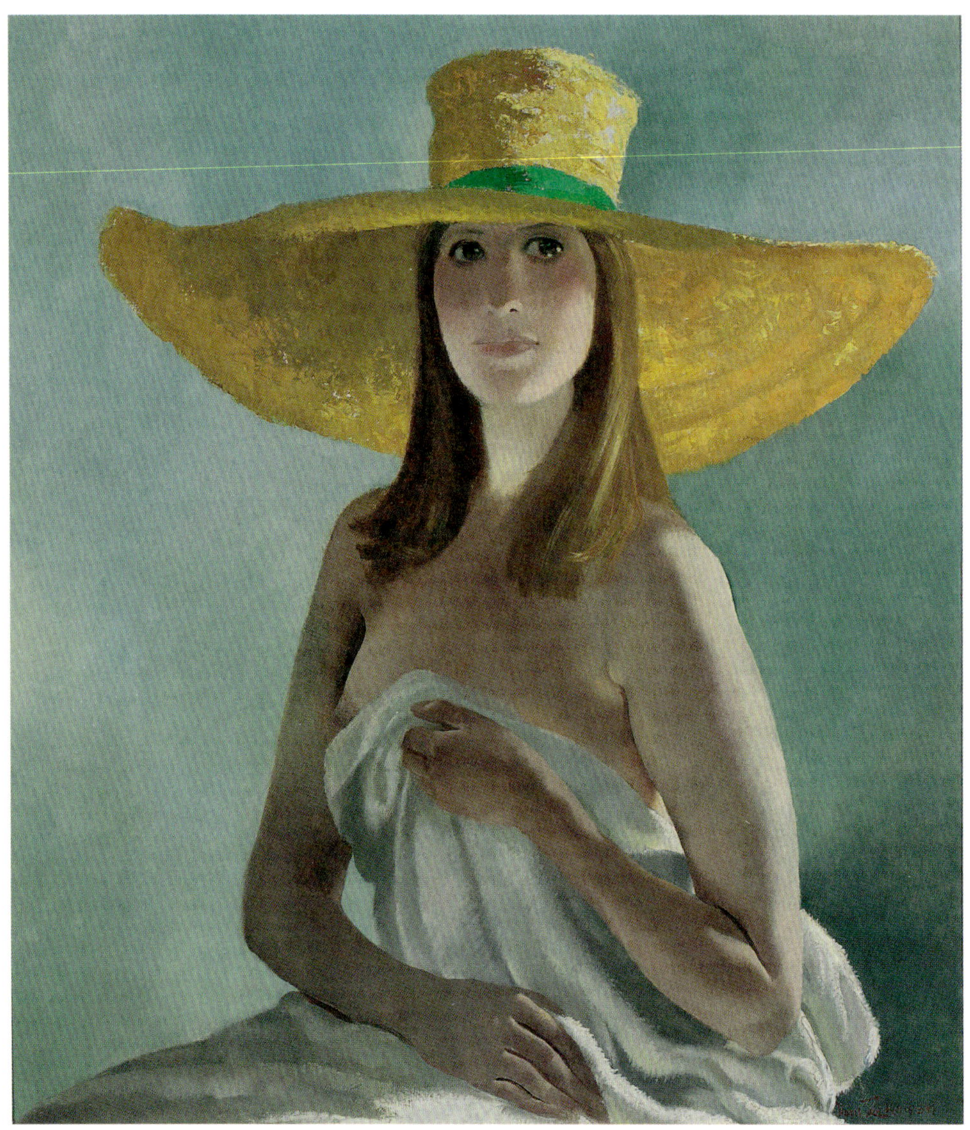

Fig.3.95
Doris Zinkeisen, *The Yellow Hat*,
circa 1960, oil on canvas.
The model is the artist's niece, Julia Heseltine, who in her own self-portraits plays down her glamour, which tells us a great deal about how the Zinkeisen sisters approached their subjects. See also Fig.2.5.

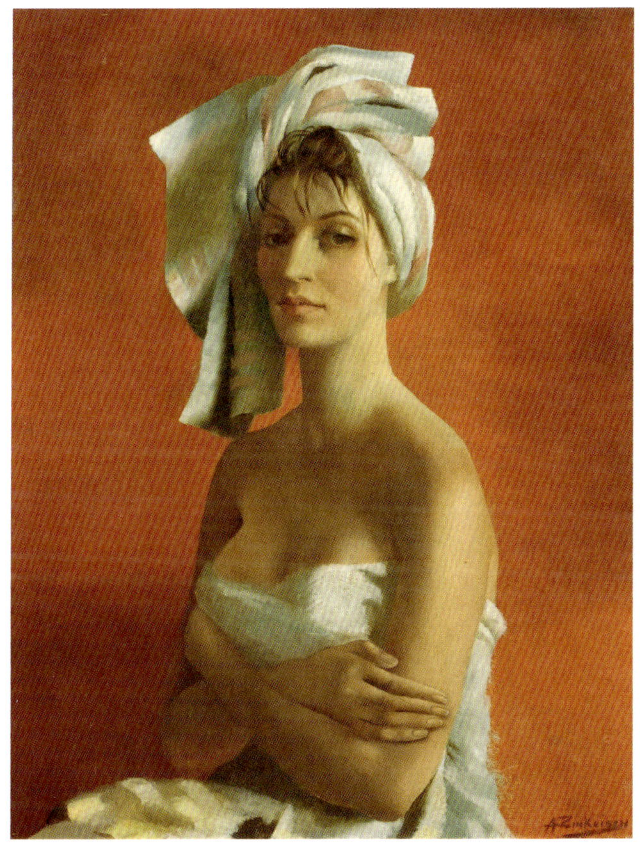

Fig.3.96
Anna Zinkeisen, *Julia, circa* 1960, oil on canvas.
This painting and the preceding one are voluptuous, but because they are in fact portraits of a daughter/niece by women artists, to a certain extent they possibly confound notions of the voyeuristic 'male gaze'. This painting celebrates beauty and the freedom to paint whatever one wants, regardless of gender, remembering the prudery surrounding nudity and life classes that persisted in the early twentieth century in relation to the training of women artists.

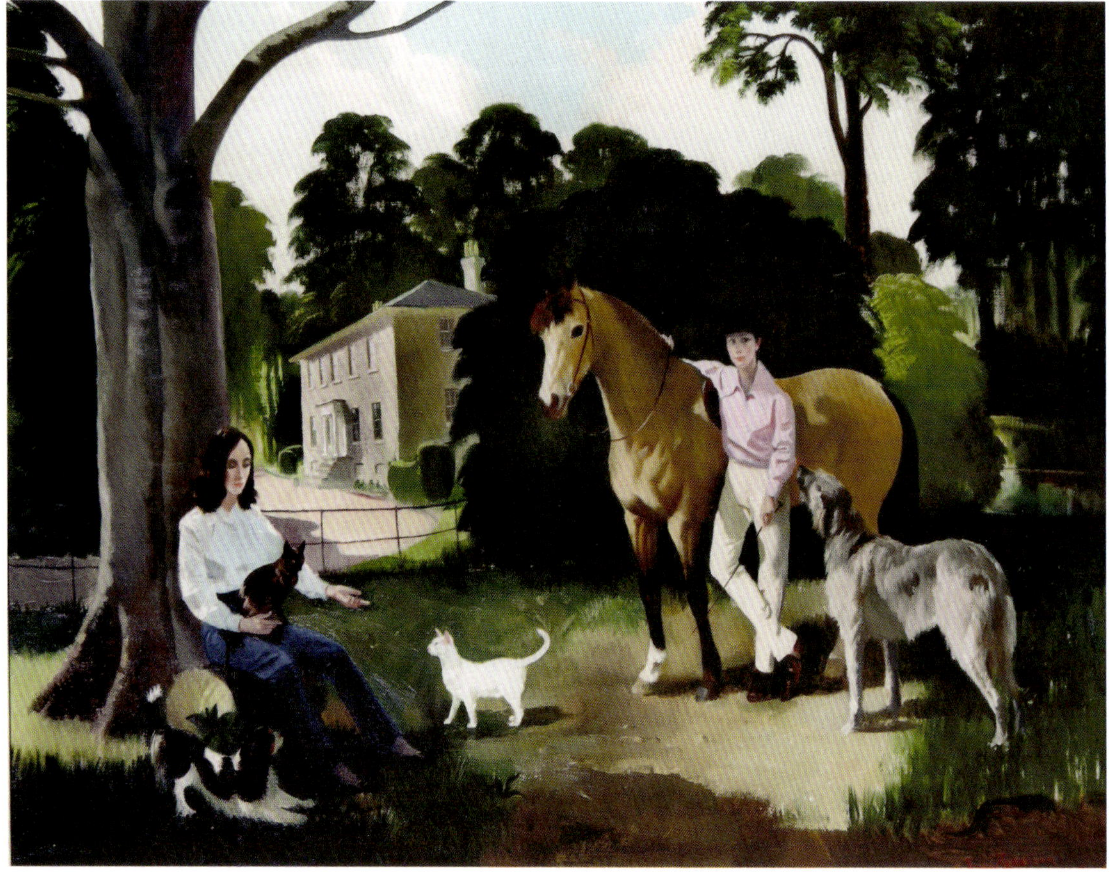

Fig.3.97

Doris Zinkeisen, *The Artist's Daughters at The White House in Badingham, Suffolk, with their Pets*, *circa* 1970, oil on canvas.

Anne Grahame Johnstone sits with Bruno the Burmese cat on her lap coaxing Ming the white cat and with Comus the Spaniel at her feet; whilst Janet stands with the dun mare Victoria and Fionn the Irish Wolfhound. In this idyllic painting Doris paints a group portrait, which projects how she saw life in rural Suffolk and how she wanted it to be seen.

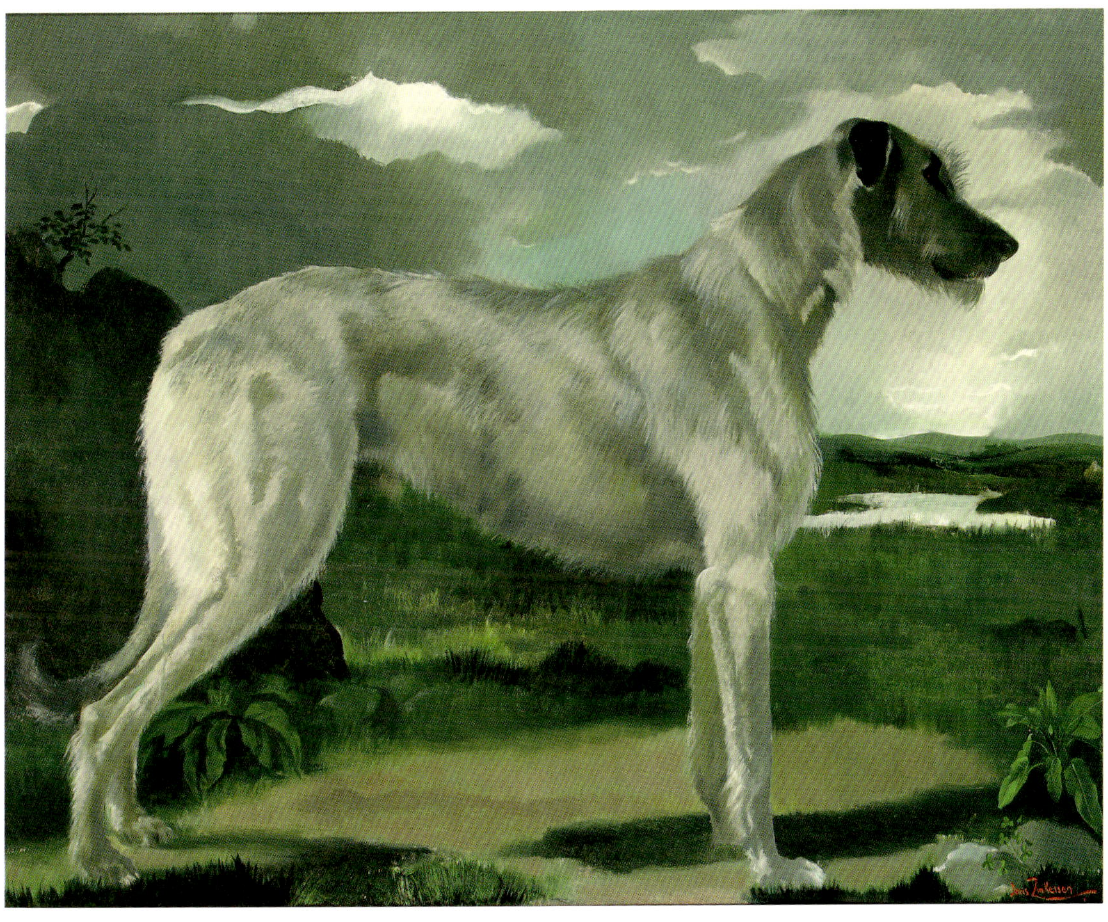

Fig.3.98
Doris Zinkeisen, *The Irish Wolfhound*, early 1970s, oil on canvas.
The sitter is likely to be the artist's pet Irish Wolfhound named Fionn. Doris was a gifted and accurate painter of animals. There is an excellent portrait of the racehorse Mill Reef from 1973 in the collection of the National Horseracing Museum in Newmarket, Suffolk.

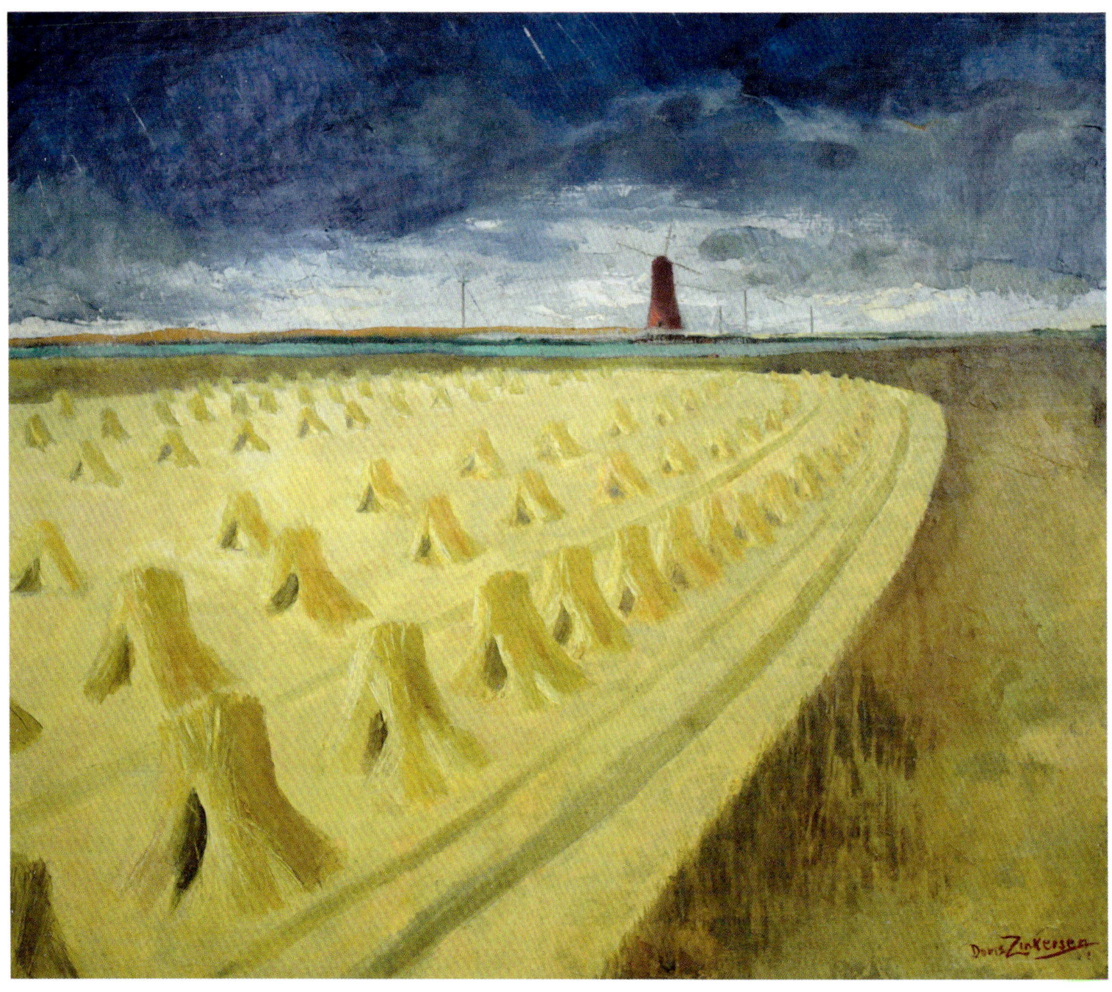

Fig.3.99

Doris Zinkeisen, *Rain on Sheaves and Stooks*, late 1960s, oil on canvas.

Here Doris chooses to paint a field somewhere in Norfolk or Suffolk with sheaves of a cereal crop stacked together into stooks, probably intended for thatching straw, as this was an antiquated harvesting technique at the time the painting was created. The yellow and blue colours used, together with the slanting rain make for a surprisingly expressive composition.

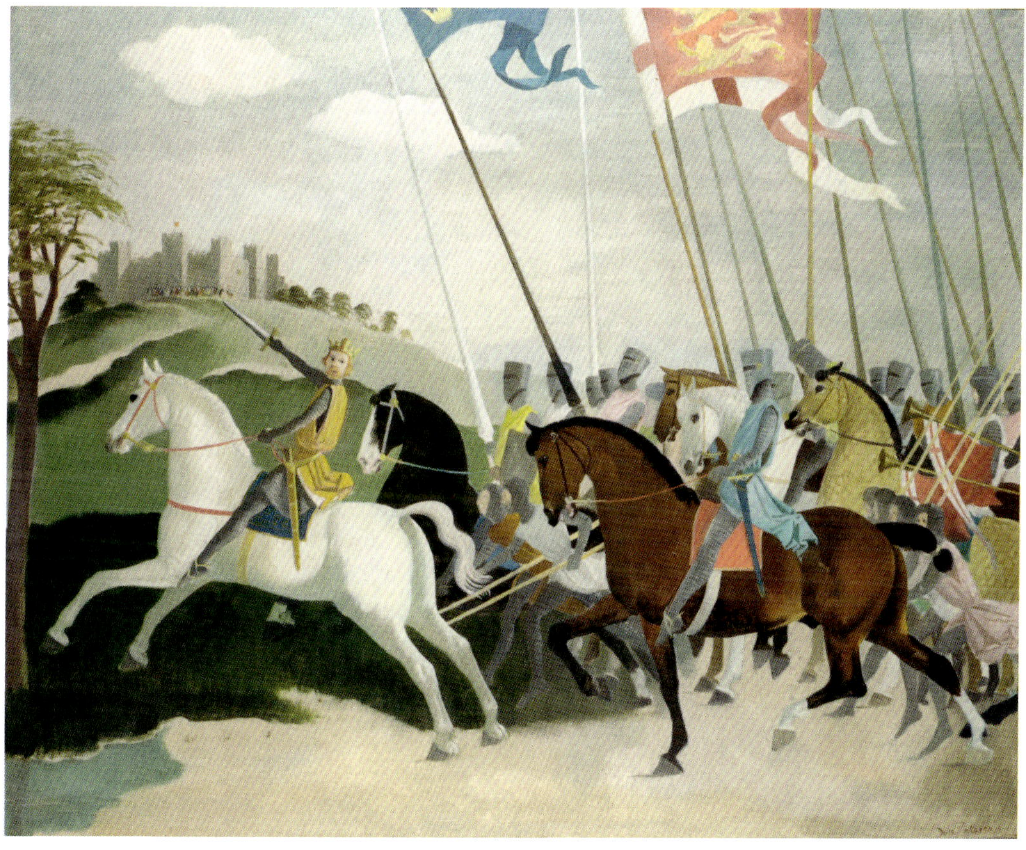

Fig.3.100
Doris Zinkeisen, *The Siege of Framlingham Castle*, late 1960s, oil on canvas.
This painting hung for many years in Doris's dining room at The White House in Badingham. After Doris moved to Suffolk in the mid-1960s she sometimes found inspiration in the history of her adopted county. Framlingham Castle was besieged by King John in 1216, because Roger Bigod, who held the Castle, opposed the King and was involved in the Magna Carta. There is also a superb painting of *The Wolf Guarding the Head of St Edmund* from around 1970 in the St Edmundsbury Borough Council Collection, which draws upon the folklore surrounding Edmund's martyrdom.

Suggestions for Further Reading & Websites

Below is a short list of works covering themes related to this monograph and is intended as a guide, rather than an exhaustive bibliography. A brief directory of websites is also provided for those searching for additional information online. These usually allow their collections and archives to be searched and explored, whilst those of auction houses show both sold and upcoming lots.

Books and Articles:

Celinscak, Mark, *Distance from the Belsen Heap: Allied Forces and the Liberation of a Nazi Concentration Camp*, Toronto, 2015.

Dwyer, Britta C., "Negotiating 'new' venues in art: Doris and Anna Zinkeisen in modernizing London", in: Karen E. Brown (ed.), *Women's Contributions to Visual Culture, 1918-1939*, Aldershot, 2008, pp.117-138.

Finamore, Daniel & Ghislaine Wood (eds), *Ocean Liners: Glamour, Speed and Style*, London, 2017.

Gardiner, Juliet, *The Thirties: An Intimate History*, London, 2011 (First pub. 2010).

Kelleway, Elisabeth, Thomas Spillane, Terry Haydn, "Never again? Helping Year 9 think about what happened after the Holocaust and learning from genocides", in: *Teaching History*, December 2013, pp.38-44.

Kelleway, Philip, *Highly Desirable: The Zinkeisen Sisters & Their Legacy*, Leiston, 2008 (2nd edition, 2016).

Kelleway, Philip, *Julia Heseltine's Dreamscapes*, Leiston, 2009.

Kelleway, Philip, *The Johnstone Twins: An Appreciation of Janet Johnstone (1928-1979) & Anne Grahame Johnstone (1928-1998)*, Wellington, 2013.

Kelleway, Philip, "The Zinkeisen Sisters and Celebrity Culture", in: *Journal of the Scottish Society for Art History: Scotland's Women Artists (1885-1965)*, Volume 21, 2016-2017, pp.27-32.

Low, Rachel, *The History of the British Film 1929-1939: Film Making in 1930s Britain*, London & New York, 1997.

Massey, Anne, "A feminine touch: gender, design and the ocean liner", in: *Journal for Maritime Research*, Vol.17, Issue 2, 2015, pp.169-181.

McGinley, Judi, "The Zinkeisen Sisters: Behind the Glitz and the Glamour!", Posted Monday 22nd January 2018, Museum of the Order of St John Blog, www.museumstjohn.org.uk (accessed 4th July 2018).

Minns, Raynes, "A Brush with War: Official Women War Artists 1939-1946", in: *Everyone's War: The Journal of The Second World War Experience Centre*, No.18, Winter 2008, pp.37-47.

Palmer, Kathleen, *Women War Artists*, London, 2011.

Potter, Neil & Jack Frost, *The Mary: The Inevitable Ship*, London, 1963 (First pub. 1961).

Reid, Betty & Anthony, "Janet and Anne Grahame Johnstone: Illustrators of over 200 children's books", in: *Book and Magazine Collector*, No.204, March 2001, pp.48-63.

Richardson, Peter, "The Art of the Johnstone Twins", in: *Words and Pictures: Online Magazine of SCBWI* [Society of Children's Book Writers and Illustrators], Posted 30th October 2015: http://www.wordsandpics.org/2015/10/the-art-of-johnstone-twins.html (accessed 13th December 2017).

Rideal, Liz (ed.), *Mirror Mirror: Self-portraits by Women Artists*, London, 2001.

Steele, James, *Queen Mary*, London, 2005 (First pub. 1995).

Strang, Alice (ed.), *A New Era: Scottish Modern Art 1900-1950*, Edinburgh, 2017.

Strang, Alice (ed.), *Modern Scottish Women: Painters and Sculptors 1885-1965*, Edinburgh, 2015.

Walpole, Josephine, *Anna: A Memorial Tribute to Anna Zinkeisen*, London, 1978.

Whittet, G.S., "Art in Medicine: The Work of Anna Zinkeisen", in: *The Studio*, 147, 1954, pp.114-115.

Willis, Pamela, "The Theatre of War: Anna and Doris Zinkeisen", in: *Blue Pages: Newsletter of the Society of British Theatre Designers*, Vol.4, 2010, pp.8-9.

Wilson, Douglas, *This Present Age*, Corporate publisher: United Steel Companies Limited, Sheffield, 1946.

Wilson, Douglas, *Trade Winds*, United Steel Companies Limited, Sheffield, 1948.

Zinkeisen, Anna, "Anna Zinkeisen asks for something to look at on the walls of our hospitals", in: *The Studio*, 133, 1947, p.77.

Zinkeisen, Anna, "An Artist looks at Hospital Walls: Anna Zinkeisen ROI, RDI, makes some suggestions born of her practised eye for colour and form", in: *Nursing Mirror*, May 12th 1950, p.1 & continued on p.4.

Zinkeisen, Doris, *Designing for the Stage*, London, 1938 (Reprinted 1945 & 1948)

Websites:

www.artuk.org [Online home for public art collections in the UK].

www.bada.org [The British Antique Dealers' Association].

www.bfi.org.uk [British Film Institute].

www.bonhams.com [Auction House].

www.chisholm-poster.com [Chisholm Larsson Gallery of Vintage Posters].

www.christies.com [Auction House].

www.chronicle250.com [The Royal Academy Summer Exhibition: A Chronicle, 1769-2018: open access and peer-reviewed digital publication produced by the Paul Mellon Centre for Studies in British Art].

www.imdb.com [Internet Movie Database].

www.iwm.org.uk [Imperial War Museum].

www.kstainerhutchins.com [Conservation & Restoration of Fine Paintings].

www.lapada.org [The Association of Art and Antique Dealers].

www.museumstjohn.org.uk [The Museum of the Order of St John: St John Ambulance].

www.npg.org.uk [National Portrait Gallery, London].

www.redcross.org.uk [British Red Cross Museum & Archive].

www.sothebys.com [Auction House].

Appendices

Appendix 1—
Doris Zinkeisen:
Chronological Filmography

As Costume Designer:

Nell Gwyn (1926: Silent Film);
A Night Like This (1932);
Leap Year (1932);
Thark (1932);
The Love Contract (1932);
Good Night, Vienna (1932) - entitled *Magic Night* in the USA;
Bitter Sweet (1933);
The Little Damozel (1933);
The King's Cup (1933);
Nell Gwyn (1934);
The Queen's Affair (1934) - entitled *Runaway Queen* in the USA;
Mimi (1935);
Peg of Old Drury (1935);
Show Boat (1936) - entitled *Edna Ferber's Show Boat* in the USA;
Victoria the Great (1937);
Sixty Glorious Years (1938) - entitled *Queen of Destiny* in the USA;
Romance in Candlelight (1955: TV Film);
Dick Whittington (1957: TV Film).

As Writer & Costume Designer:

The Blue Danube: A Rhapsody (1932).

As Set Decorator & Costume Designer:

Carnival (1931) - entitled *Venetian Nights* in the USA.

Appendix 2—
A Chronological List of Plays, Revues, Ballets and Musicals for which Doris Zinkeisen produced Costume and/or Stage Designs

Body and Soul. By Arnold Bennett at the Regent from 11/09/1922-07/10/1922 for 32 performances. Produced by Nigel Playfair (associate stage manager James Whale). First performed at the Liverpool Playhouse in February 1922.

The Insect Play. By the Čapek brothers at the Regent during the 1922-1923 season, running for six weeks. Produced by Nigel Playfair. Cast included John Gielgud and Elsa Lanchester.

Father Noah (Mystery of the Ark). By Geoffrey Whitworth at the Savoy on the 12/06/1923 for one matinee performance of this one-act play as a curtain raiser for *The Man Who Ate the Popomack* by W.J. Turner in aid of the Library Fund of the British Drama League. Produced by James Whale.

Robert E. Lee. By John Drinkwater at the Regent from 20/06/1923-22/09/1923 for 109 performances. Produced by Nigel Playfair and John Drinkwater. Cast included John Gielgud.

The Way of the World. By William Congreve at the Lyric, Hammersmith from 07/02/1924-28/06/1924 for 158 performances. Produced by Nigel Playfair. Also performed at the Prince's Theatre, Bristol during the 1924-1925 season. Cast included Elsa Lanchester and Nigel Playfair.

Yoicks! A revue by J. Hastings Turner at the Kingsway from 11/06/1924-14/02/1925 for 266 performances.

On With the Dance. A revue by Noël Coward and Philip Braham at the London Pavilion from 30/04/1925-14/11/1925 for 229 performances. Produced by Charles B. Cochran.

Still Dancing. A revue by Arthur Wimperis, Ronald Jeans, Philip Braham, Noble Sissle, Eubie Blake, Ivor Novello, Mark Anthony, Irving Berlin, Vivian Eillis, and Isham Jones at the London Pavilion from 19/11/1925-27/02/1926 for 114 performances. Produced by Charles B. Cochran.

Cochran's Revue. By Ronald Jeans, Donovan Parsons, Pat Thayer, Noble Sissle, and Eubie Blake at the London Pavilion from 29/04/1926-04/09/1926 for 148 performances. Produced by Charles B. Cochran. Other designers include André Derain and Oliver Messel.

Merry-Go-Round. A Cochran Cabaret held at the Trocadero during 1926.

Champagne Time. A Cochran Cabaret held at the Trocadero during 1927. Edythe Baker present in the audience.

One Dam Thing After Another. A revue by Ronald Jeans, Lorenz Hart, Richard Rodgers at the London Pavilion from 20/05/1927-10/12/1927 for 236 performances. Produced by Charles B. Cochran. Cast includes Edythe Baker.

Peggy-Ann. A musical by Herbert Fields, Richard Rodgers, and Lorenz Hart at Daly's from 27/07/1927-19/11/1927 for 134 performances.

This Year of Grace! A revue by Noël Coward at the London Pavilion from 22/03/1928-22/12/1928 for 315 performances. Produced by Charles B. Cochran. Amongst others, Oliver Messel also provides designs. This revue was also performed at the Selwyn Theatre on Broadway from 07/11/1928-23/03/1929 for a total of 157 performances. The cast in England included Tilly Losch and Marjorie Robertson (later famous as Anna Neagle).

Dear Love. A musical by Peter Dion

Titheradge, Lauri Wylie, Herbert Clayton, Haydn Wood, Joseph Tunbridge, and Jack Waller at the Palace Theatre from 14/11/1929-08/03/1930 for 132 performances. Charles B. Cochran is the managing director.

The Sleeping Beauty. A pantomime by J. Hickory Wood, F.V. Maxwell Stewart, Julian Wylie, E.W. Eyre, R.P. Weston, Bert Lee, and Clifford Harris at Drury Lane from 24/12/1929-01/03/1930 for 97 performances. Costumes also designed by Anna Zinkeisen and Dolly Tree.

Cochran's 1930 Revue. By Beverley Nichols and Vivian Ellis at the London Pavilion from 27/03/1930-25/10/1930 for 245 performances. Directed by Charles B. Cochran. Rex Whistler and Oliver Messel also provide designs.

Oh, Daddy! A farce by Austin Melford at the Prince's Theatre from 27/11/1930-31/01/1931 and at Daly's from 02/02/1931-21/03/1931 for a total of 132 performances.

Ever Green. A musical show by Benn Levy, Lorenz Hart, and Richard Rodgers at the Adelphi from 03/12/1930-11/07/1931 for 254 performances. Produced by Charles B. Cochran. Amongst others, Rex Whistler also provides stage designs.

Cochran's 1931 Revue. By Noël Coward at the London Pavilion from 19/03/1931-11/04/1931 for 27 performances. Directed by Charles B. Cochran. Amongst others Oliver Messel and Rex Whistler also provide designs.

Waltzes From Vienna. By Johann Strauss, father and son, arranged by G.H. Clutsam, Herbert Griffiths, E.W. Korngold, and Julius Bittner, together with extra lyrics and storytelling by Hassard Short, Caswell Garth, and Desmond Carter at the Alhambra from 17/08/1931-06/08/1932 for 607 performances. Also performed at the Prince's Theatre in Bristol during the 1932-1933 season. A renamed production of this entitled *The Great Waltz* was performed at the Center Theatre on Broadway from 22/09/1934-08/06/1935 for a total of 298 performances.

Vile Bodies. By H. Dennis Bradley, after Evelyn Waugh, at Vaudeville from 15/04/1932-11/06/1932 for 66 performances.

Wild Violets. A musical by Hassard Short, Desmond Carter, Reginald Purdell, and Robert Stolz at Drury Lane 31/10/1932-08/07/1933 for 290 performances.

Nymph Errant. A musical by Romney Brent and Cole Porter at the Adelphi from 06/10/1933-17/02/1934 for 154 performances. Produced by Charles B. Cochran. Cast included Gertrude Lawrence.

Sporting Love. A musical by Stanley Lupino, Arthur Rigby, Arty Ash, Desmond Carter, and Frank Eyton at the Gaiety from 31/03/1934-26/01/1935 for 302 performances.

Streamline. A revue by A.P. Herbert, Ronald Jeans, and Vivian Ellis at the Palace Theatre from 28/09/1934-02/03/1935 for 178 performances. Produced by Charles B. Cochran. Rex Whistler and Cecil Beaton also provide designs. Cast includes Tilly Losch.

Cinderella. A pantomime by Dan Leno, Julian Wylie, R.P. Weston, Bert Lee, Clifford Harris, Valentine Wylie, Lauri Wylie, James Tate, and Guy Jones at Drury Lane from 24/12/1934-02/03/1935 for 117 performances.

Stop Press. A revue by Clifford Whitley, Irving Berlin, Moss Hart, Greatrex Newman, Arthur Schwartz, Howard Dietz, Noel Gay, and Jonny Green at the Adelphi from 21/02/1935-06/07/1935 for 148 performances.

At the Silver Swan. A musical by Guy Bolton, Clifford Grey, Edmond Samuels, and Percival Mackey at the Palace Theatre from 19/02/1936-04/04/1936 for 53 performances. Managing director is Charles B. Cochran.

This'll Make You Whistle. A musical by Guy Bolton, Fred Thompson, Maurice Sigler, Al Goodhart, and Al Hoffman at the Palace Theatre from 15/09/1936-30/01/1937 and at Daly's from 01/02/1937-27/02/1937 for a total of 190 performances. Produced by Jack Buchanan; managing director Charles B. Cochran.

Mother Goose. Pantomime by J. Hickory Wood, Dan Leno, James Tate, and E.W. Eyre at the London Hippodrome from 23/12/1936-13/02/1937 for 79 performances. Cast includes Chili Bouchier.

The Taming of the Shrew. By William Shakespeare at the New Theatre from 23/03/1937-01/05/1937 for 49 performances.

Happy Returns. A musical show at the Adelphi from 19/05/1938-06/08/1938 for 78 performances. Produced by Charles B. Cochran and Edward Dowling.

Bobby Get Your Gun. A musical by Guy Bolton, Fred Thompson, Bert Lee, Clifford Grey, Desmond Carter, Jack Waller, and Joseph Tunbridge at the Adelphi from 07/10/1938-31/12/1938 for 92 performances.

Sleeping Beauty. Pantomime starring Evelyn Laye performed in Birmingham in 1938.

Under Your Hat. A musical by Archie Menzies, Arthur Macrae, Jack Hulbert, and Vivian Ellis at the Palace Theatre from 24/11/1938-02/09/1939 and 31/10/1939-13/04/1940 for 514 performances. Managing director Charles B. Cochran.

Black and Blue. A revue by Diana Morgan, Robert Macdermot, Peter Dion Titheradge, Desmond Carter, Bert Lee, Clifford Grey, and Kenneth Leslie Smith at the London Hippodrome from 08/03/1939-02/09/1939 for 305 performances.

Lights Up! A Cochran production of early 1940 performed at the Manchester Opera

House and in Glasgow and Edinburgh with settings by Doris Zinkeisen.

Cinderella. Pantomime with Jack Buchanan performed in 1940/1941.

International Ballet productions: Between 1941 and 1950 the International Ballet staged many ballets with costumes and/or decor by Doris Zinkeisen. Because the International Ballet was a touring company the venues of each and every performance are not provided here, but the company reached an audience counted in millions during its lifetime. Ballets Doris designed for include *Planetomania*, *Giselle*, *Sleeping Princess*, *Twelfth Night*, *Aurora's Wedding*, and *Masque of Comus*. Other designers working for the International Ballet include Honoria Plesch and Rex Whistler amongst others.

Full Swing. A musical by George Posford and Arthur Macrae performed at the Palace Theatre during the 1941-1942 season.

Richard III. By William Shakespeare performed at the New Theatre during the 1944-1945 season. Cast included Laurence Olivier, Ralph Richardson, and Sybil Thorndike.

The Quaker Girl. A musical by Lionel Monckton and James Tanner performed at the Hippodrome in Bristol during the 1944-1945 season.

Arms and the Man. By George Bernard Shaw performed at the New Theatre during the 1944-1945 season. Cast included Sybil Thorndike, Ralph Richardson, and Laurence Olivier. Transferred to the New Theatre in London for the 1945-1946 season.

The House on the Bridge. By Edward Percy performed at the Hippodrome in Bristol during the 1944-1945 season.

Big Ben. Book and lyrics by A.P. Herbert with music by Vivian Ellis and produced by Charles B. Cochran. After a provincial tour performed from 17th July 1946 at the Adelphi.

Richard III. By William Shakespeare performed at the New Theatre in London during the 1948-1949 season. Cast included Peter Cushing, Vivien Leigh, and Laurence Olivier.

Arms and the Man. By George Bernard Shaw performed at the Bristol Old Vic during the 1948-1949 season.

Lilac Time. A musical by A.M. Miller and Heinz Reichert. English adaption and lyrics by Adrian Ross using music by Franz Schubert. Performed at His Majesty's Theatre from February 1949 for a six week limited run and recreated later at the King's Theatre in Glasgow on 05/11/1951.

Dear Miss Phoebe. A musical adaption of James Barrie's *Quality Street*. Lyrics by Christopher Hassall with music by Harry Parr Davies. Performed at the New Theatre in Oxford from the end of September 1950, transferring to Theatre Royal in Birmingham for August 1950, and at the

Streatham Hill Theatre by the end of September 1951.

Pagan in the Parlour. By Franklin Lacey performed at the Theatre Royal in Bath, Wimbledon Theatre, and the Lyceum Theatre, Newport, South Wales during the 1952-1953 season. Directed by James Whale. Cast included Catharine Lacey, Hermione Baddeley, and Joss Ackland.

After the Ball. Musical by Noël Coward performed at the Hippodrome in Bristol during the 1953-1954 season, before transferring to London.

The Little Glass Clock. By Hugh Mills performed at the Hippodrome in Bristol during the 1954-1955 season.

Index

Abrahall, Clare Hoskyns 51
Allan, Elizabeth 50, 51, 160
Andy Pandy 66
Ardizzone, Edward 62
Art Deco 15, 57
Austin, Frederic 52
Badingham (Suffolk) 17, 172
Baker, Edythe 45, 46, 82, 83
Baker, George Fisher 102
Beeton, Stanley 84
Bell, Vanessa 43
Bennett, Arnold 52
Bennett, Bethina Alice 35
Bill and Ben the Flower Pot Men 66
Bouchier, Chili (aka Dorothy) 103
Bradley, Helen 54
Bratza, Milan Yovanovitch 45, 103
Brook, Faith 47
Brown, Sir John Arnesby 31
Buchanan, Jack 36
Burgh (Suffolk) 17, 62
Butterworth, Nick 62
Buxton, Irwin 89
Byam Shaw School of Art 62
Cameron, Sir David Young 31
Charles, Clara Bolton (mother of Doris & Anna) 19, 20, 30
Childe, Doria 98
Christchurch Mansion (Ipswich) 55, 61
Christie, Dame Agatha 15
Clark, Alan 64
Clausen, Sir George 25
Cliff, Clarice 31
Cochran, Sir Charles Blake 39, 48
Congreve, William 52
Constable, John 57
Cooper, Susie 31
Coward, Sir Noël 39, 48, 55, 68, 69, 161
Dangerfield, Roland 101
D'Erlanger, Gérard 46, 47
Devis, Arthur 61
Dufy, Raoul 54
Errington, Vicountess 97
Eustrel, Anthony 38, 39
Exposition des Arts Décoratifs et Industriels Modernes 15
Fisher, Samuel Melton 31
Foyles 36
Gainsborough, Thomas 57
Gay, John 52
Gielgud, Sir John 36

Great Depression 42
Handfield-Jones, Ranald Montagu 35
Harmsworth, Hon. Esmé 97
Harrow School of Art 25
Hato, Ana 86
Helm, Brigitte 36
Heneage, David 94, 95
Hepworth, Dame Barbara 31
Heseltine, Colonel Guy Robert Nelson (Anna's husband) 34
Heseltine, Julia (Anna's daughter) 9, 19, 62, 170, 171
Heyer, Georgette 17
Hope, Lady Doria 98
Horowitz, Michael Simon 47
Howes, Bobby 50
Howes, Sally Ann 50, 51, 158
Hughes, Ted 64
ICI 35, 145-149
Imperial Chemical Industries (see ICI)
Inglesby, Mona 39, 48
International Ballet touring company 39
Jeans, Ursula 45
John, Rosamund 51, 159
Johnstone, Anne Grahame (Doris's daughter) 34, 61, 62, 64, 172
Johnstone, Captain Edward Grahame (Doris's husband) 34, 47
Johnstone, Captain Edward Murray Grahame (Doris's son) 35
Johnstone, Janet (Doris's daughter) 35, 61, 62, 64, 172
Joyce, Eileen 50, 51, 161
Karloff, Boris 46
Kauffmann, Angelica 31
Kennedy, Consuela 121
'Kitchen Sink' School 55, 69
Knight, Dame Laura 31, 43
Lanchester, Elsa 36, 45, 46, 81
Lean, David 161
Lempicka, Tamara de 57
LNER 35, 111, 112
London and North Eastern Railway (see LNER)
Looms Cottage (Burgh) 8, 62
Lugosi, Bela 50, 51
McIndoe, Sir Archibald 133
Massine, Léonide 47, 48
Maurier, Dame Daphne du 17
Mayhew, James 62
Milland, Ray 47, 48
Mitford, Nancy 58
Moiseiwitsch, Benno 51
Moser, Mary 31
Mountbatten, Countess Edwina 24, 25
Mountbatten, Admiral Louis, Earl of Burma 24, 25
Neagle, Dame Anna 36, 37, 45, 46
O'Keeffe, Georgia 53
Olivier, Baron Laurence 36
Orpen, Sir William 25, 102
Ould, Hermon 33
Oxenbury, Helen 62
Paris Salon 15
Parker, Geoffrey 47
Parsons Gallery 36
Peel, Eileen 99
Playfair, Sir Nigel 36, 39, 52

Plowright, Joan 64
Porritt, Arthur Espie 35
Powell, Anthony 58
Preston, Eric 96
Prins, George 165
Queen Mary (see *R.M.S. Queen Mary*)
Rachmaninov, Sergei 161
Ribbentrop, Joachim von 21
Richardson, Sir Ralph 36
Royal Academy 15, 25, 31, 64
R.M.S. Queen Mary 43, 44
Royal Society of Portrait Painters 69, 165
Russell-Cotes Museum (Bournemouth) 43, 44
St Botolph's Church (Burgh) 17
St George, Vivien 102
St George, Evelyn 102
St Hill, Ralph Woodford 92
St John Ambulance Brigade 23-25, 128-131, 134, 162
St John the Baptist's Church (Badingham) 18
St Martin's School of Art 64
Salisbury, Frank O. 31
Savoy Hotel 39
Sims, Charles 25, 31
Smith, Dodie 68
Society of Women Artists 32-33
Spike (see Ray Milland) 47-48
Stokes, Adrian 31
Symmington, Philip 100
Taylor, Harold 117
Tempest, Margaret 62
Thorndike, Dame Sybil 36
United Steel Companies 35, 141-144, 150-152
V.A.D. (Voluntary Aid Detachment) 23
Wadsworth, Edward 43
Watney, Sanders 120
Waugh, Evelyn 58
Weaver, Edith 88
Whale, James 45, 47
White House (Badingham) 17, 172
Whittet, G.S. 55
Wilcox, Herbert 41
Zinkeisen, Anna
- accusations of being a fifth columnist 20
- advertisements 35, 108-115, 141-152
- as an arbiter of fashion in Britain 15
- as mother 34, 35
- birth in Scotland 19
- book illustrations 35, 51
- confusion over date of birth 19
- *Coronation Bouquet* 48, 49, 163
- cremation 17
- dating of paintings 56
- early life 19
- education & training 25
- family origins 19-20
- flappers 28
- flower paintings 48, 49, 53
- fundraising for St John Ambulance Brigade 25
- hunting/riding 44
- lifestyle 44
- London homes 21, 52
- Looms Cottage (Burgh) 8, 62
- make-up/appearance 33, 44
- marriage 34
- medical illustrations 25, 35, 36, 126-127, 132

misogyny (dealing with) 31-33, 58
murals (see also *R.M.S. Queen Mary*) 43, 44
Nursing Mirror (article by Anna for) 53
parents (see Clara Bolton Charles & Victor William Zinkeisen)
portraiture 44, 53
press coverage 25, 31, 44, 45
prints of Anna's work 57
Scottish origins 19
signature 56
style of painting 53
surrealism 54, 141-149
V.A.D. auxiliary nurse 23
Woodburn (Kilcreggan) 19
Zinkeisen, Doris
advertisements 35, 108-115, 141-152
aeroplane crash 36
as an arbiter of fashion in Britain 15, 41
as mother 34, 35
Belsen 25, 138-140
birth in Scotland 18
Clynder House (Roseneath) 18
confusion over date of birth 18
costume design 36-41, 56-57
dating of paintings 56
difficulties of designing for black & white films 41
Designing for the Stage 39
early life 19
engagement to James Whale 45, 47
family origins 19-20
figure & dress 44
film industry (involvement in) 36, 41, 42
flappers 28
fundraising for St John Ambulance Brigade 24-25
funeral 17
grooming film stars 41
impact of costume designs on British textile industry 41-42
interior decorator of Nigel Playfair's home 36
loans dresses to Lady Louis Mountbatten 25
London homes 21, 52, 69
make-up 33, 41
marriage 34
misogyny (dealing with) 31-33, 58
murals for *R.M.S. Queen Mary* 43
parents (see Clara Bolton Charles & Victor William Zinkeisen)
portraiture 44, 53
press coverage 25, 31, 44, 45
prints of Doris's work 57
restoration of Christchurch Mansion triple portrait 61
riding accident 41
Savoy (organises Cochran's parties) 39
Scottish origins 19
signature 56
style of painting 53
surrealism 54, 141-149
theatre design work 36
The Blue Danube: A Rhapsody 41
trip to Prague 36
V.A.D. auxiliary nurse 23
White House (Badingham) 17, 172
world tour 35
Zinkeisen, Ian Victor (brother of Doris & Anna)
birth at Woodburn (Kilcreggan) 19

changes his surname to Charles 20
Scottish identity 19
Zinkeisen, Ivan (see Ian Victor Zinkeisen)
Zinkeisen, Jack (see Ian Victor Zinkeisen)
Zinkeisen, Professor Johann Wilhelm (great-grandfather of Doris & Anna) 20
Zinkeisen, Victor William (father of Doris & Anna) 20, 30
Zinkeisen, Zog (see Ian Victor Zinkeisen)

Author Biographies

Philip Kelleway

Philip Kelleway is an art historian. Since completing his doctorate Kelleway has written peer-reviewed journal articles and books on topics including eighteenth-century porcelain, illustration, and landscape painting. More recently he was the editor of *Dutch and Flemish Flower Pieces: Paintings, Drawings and Prints up to the Nineteenth Century* (2020) by Sam Segal and Klara Alen. Kelleway is an authority on the work of the Zinkeisen sisters and has previously published his findings on them including *Highly Desirable: The Zinkeisen Sisters & Their Legacy* (2nd edition, 2016).

Emma Roodhouse

Emma Roodhouse is an art curator and works for Colchester and Ipswich Museums and freelance on research projects at the East Anglian Traditional Art Centre. She has curated exhibitions on a wide range of themes including Rodin's sculpture, hairstyles in art, and Ed Sheeran. More recently Roodhouse received funding from the Paul Mellon Centre for Studies in British Art to research Constable's early years in Suffolk in preparation for the 200th anniversary marking the creation of his famous landscape *The Haywain* (1821).

Nicola Evans

Nicola Evans is a conservator of paintings at KSH Conservation Limited. She initially trained in fine art at Buckingham New University, City College Brighton and Hove, and Brighton University before gaining a postgraduate Master of Arts degree specialising in the conservation of paintings at the University of Northumbria. She has previously worked as a specialist painter for Damien Hirst at Hirst Science and for the National Maritime Museum in London. Evans is also an accomplished artist.